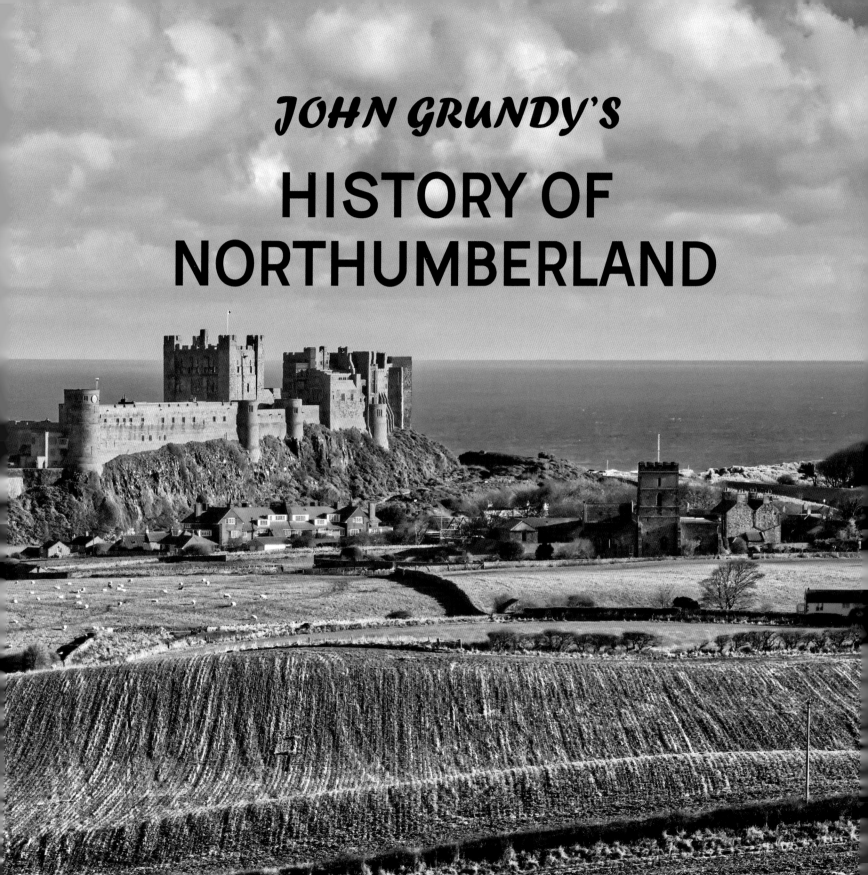

JOHN GRUNDY'S

HISTORY OF NORTHUMBERLAND

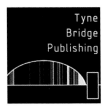

Published by:

City of Newcastle Upon Tyne
Newcastle Libraries
Tyne Bridge Publishing, 2022
Layout: Derek Tree
Cover design: Dave Thompson

CONTENTS

*Dedicated to the extended
Grundy/Coton family who all
love the beauty of the
Northumberland coast*

Collywell Bay

FOREWORD

Though I have lived in the City of Newcastle on Tyne for almost 60 years, I'm not a Geordie, having been brought up in Sheffield arriving in the 1960s as a student at a time when there were just 4,000 or so in the City. In the intervening years I've often noted the contributions of John Grundy in various media, to things Northumbrian in his witty but nonetheless informative style. I gather he also arrived in the region in the 1960s, for the same reason, as a student, but in his case from Cumbria (or was it still Cumberland then?) It is an honour to be invited to write this foreword to his work on the History of Northumberland.

It was never on my bucket list to be a City Councillor, but somehow it happened in 2010, and subsequently I had the honour of being appointed firstly Deputy Lord Mayor in 2018 and Lord Mayor in 2019, a position which owing to the Covid pandemic I held for two years rather than the usual one. In these positions I met John on a number of committees involved with various aspects of the history and historic environment of the City, and found him to be just as down to earth and witty as his broadcasts suggested he was. On one occasion at the Annual General Meeting of the Elders Council, he persuaded me to tell a story about the installation of one of the City's commemorative plaques, to mark the achievement of George Murray, the endocrinologist who introduced the first hormone treatment, for hypothyroidism (called Myxoedema in the 1890s). I regarded it as one of my most significant achievements as a Councillor but had not intended to tell the story even though Murray's Medical School was the very building where the meeting was held. It's now the Sutherland Building of Northumbria University. I'm glad I was persuaded because the story went down well (I think.)

John's feeling for history comes alive in these pages, starting with his account from prehistoric times, in which I confess I was about to reach for my dictionary to determine the meaning of the word 'multivallate' only to find thankfully, John had explained it in the next sentence. That happened a few more times as I read through! John's command of English shines through the stories which he tells with his own inimitable sense of humour. He has a gargantuan knowledge of the buildings of Northumberland which he expertly weaves into its history and their place in it, whether they are the grand castles or the humbler homes of the wider population. He does not neglect the often overlooked role of women, and it is pleasing he notes Sulpicia Lepidina at Vindolanda fort, recipient of the first known example of writing by a woman, a letter from her sister Claudia Severa (in Latin of course) inviting her to her birthday party. The Vindolanda tablets have been acknowledged as one of the greatest treasures of British Archaeology. Housing developers in my ward, Lemington, were persuaded to name Lepidina Close near to the line of Hadrian's Wall, after her.

He takes us from those times to the present, mentioning names we've all heard of and many we haven't. Leaning on his background as a Listed Building field worker, he guides us through the pleasant, but also the deeply unpleasant times of the past 2000 years or so when wars with their dreadful violence and bloodshed have been a sad, and for centuries an almost constant feature. He is however the only architectural commentator I have come across who uses terms such as 'sticky-uppy' and 'sticky-outy' which of course leave us

understanding exactly what he means.

This book is very much John Grundy's History of Northumberland and I recommend it to anyone who appreciates what I hope I can call 'our' beautiful county.

David Cook

Lord Mayor of Newcastle on Tyne, 2019-2021

I.   PREHISTORY

A number of years ago I used to do a bit of tour guiding with groups of retired Americans who were on sort of study holidays at Durham University. My job was to take them to Holy Island and on one occasion we had to cut short our visit because the tide times were a problem. We could have just headed back to base but we would have arrived awfully early and they might have felt short-changed by their day out. I didn't know what to do but our bus driver John Renton, who was a retired Police Officer from Wooler, said that he would take us home by a roundabout route.

We came off the island in the normal way but instead of turning south down the A1 he drove straight ahead on improbably tiny roads towards the empty heart of the county. After a little while he turned left onto even less travelled ways and before long we were driving along the western edge of the Kyloe Hills between Belford and Wooler. We were on a road that may well have been an entirely bus-free zone until that moment, but John knew what he was doing and he stopped the bus on the edge of a ridge and encouraged his passengers to get out, which they did because you don't disobey retired Northumbrian police officers.

We were on a weathered sandstone outcrop, surrounded by bracken and rough grass and the view to the west was tremendous in both senses of the word – it was beautiful and it was huge. The rolling landscape of the River Till was way below us and the strange flatness of Glendale and the Millfield Plain, and, beyond the valley, the great swelling mass of the Cheviots filled the far horizon.

My retired Americans dutifully got out, cameras at the ready, but there was a pause as they all took in the view. A lady turned to me and said, "I have been to the Rockies and I have been to the Himalayas, but I have never seen a view more beautiful than that."

She was, as you will have realised, a woman of taste and discrimination, but not the first to fall under the spell of Northumberland's quiet drama. I can remember the same thing happening to me. I had arrived from Carlisle and places west, convinced that the greater drama and magnificence of my Lake District valleys placed them in top spot, only to find myself being drawn into a fascination with the green rolling hills of Northumberland. So, even as my American friend made her pronouncement, I found myself wondering how many generations of people, visitors and native Northumbrians must have felt the same.

Well, you will be surprised to hear that I now know the answer to that question because I have read it in a learned book – about 400 generations of people have found themselves drawn to these hills.

The first of them arrived about 12,000 years ago, or, to put it another way, the first Northumbrians lived here

Left: Duddo Five Stones circle, erected in the early Bronze Age.

in about 10,000 BC. There was a time before that when nobody would have been able to stand and look at the beauty of our landscape because it was buried under thousands of feet of ice and snow. There may have been people here before that last Ice Age had begun but the cold and the glaciers have wiped away all trace of them – but as the ice retreated and the climate warmed up people came back.

They were Stone Age people, and that period, the first we know about in Northumbrian terms is called the Mesolithic Period or the Middle Stone Age and it lasted for about six thousand years.

I'm going to say that again because it seems to me an entirely extraordinary figure. For about six thousand years Mesolithic hunter-gatherers roamed about Northumberland (as it would become) hunting, of course, and gathering. What they were gathering … well, I'll come back to that in a minute but what they were hunting were wild boar and giant deer with vast antlers, and huge wild cattle or 'auroch'. You can see their extraordinary bones in the Great North Museum in Newcastle and a drift through websites featuring Northumbrian archaeology will quickly bring you to photographs of their hoof prints, which have been discovered, fossilised in a layer of peat from an ancient forest that emerges from time to time beneath the sand dunes at Low Hauxley, south of Amble on the Northumbrian coast.

Our Mesolithic ancestors hunted these creatures using stone tools and for a long time in the study of Stone Age archaeology we assumed that they were all nomads who roamed around the countryside in bands, camping in places like the Tyne Valley, or Allendale or on the Millfield Plain north of Wooler; sometimes they seem to have stayed for a while in rock shelters in or near the hills, where they made and repaired their weapons. In such places vast numbers of tiny flakes of flint have been found, tiny shavings called 'microliths', which were the rubbish left behind as they chipped their arrowheads and spearheads into shape.

A heap of loose chippings is not a lot to go on if you're trying to work out what their lives were like or what they thought of the land of their birth but the impression we had was that they led an entirely hand-to-mouth existence and yet even that small amount of information begged a lot of questions about the sort of lives they were living.

Let's start with the flint. If the only way I could kill (and eat) aurochs was by finding flint and shaping it into tools, I suspect I would soon get pretty hungry. Or dead. I wouldn't know where to start. As far as I know there is no flint in Northumberland; there is a stone called 'chert', which they used as a substitute sometimes, but flint was better but also much harder to find. Some of it was probably picked up on pebble beaches where it had been dumped by the tide and some probably originated as nodules of flint that were carried along by glaciers and left behind when the ice melted; but some of it was imported from North Yorkshire.

How did they find it? How did they get it? How did they learn to make tools out of it? What did they use to fasten it to the wooden handles of their spears and arrows? And who did the hunting? Was it just the chaps like we might expect nowadays and if it was, what did the women do? In some more recent stone-age cultures that we know about – most Native American societies, for example, the men did the hunting and the women did the gathering – searching for edible roots with their digging sticks.

Was it like that in Mesolithic Northumberland? And what did they do in the evening? Did they just sit in temporary shelters batting bits of stone with other bits of stone, feeling cold and chewing on an auroch bone if they'd got lucky? Were they always on the move, randomly zigzagging the landscape at the whim of the prey they were hunting?

Until recently nobody knew the answers to any of those questions, but now we do because archaeologists have got better at finding out.

In Northumberland, in fact in England as a whole, the place to go to start finding out about these things turned out to be Howick on the Northumberland coast, near Craster and just south of Howick Hall.

This was a bit of a surprise to me because one of my favourite books, an eminently respectable textbook published as recently as 1992, had dismissed the possibility of finding such ancient remains on the coast because, as the writer said, '*the contemporary coastline has been largely destroyed by changes in sea level and erosion*'.

And yet just a few years after that was written, in 2002, archaeologist Clive Waddington and his team excavated the site of a Mesolithic house on the coast at Howick. It was the first Mesolithic house that had ever been identified and for a few years the oldest known house in the British Isles. Howick was the first to be found and the first to be accurately dated and that date is remarkable. The Howick house was built about 7800BC and occupied for two to three hundred years.

Until that moment nobody had ever realised that people were living in houses so long ago. The assumption was that Mesolithic people drifted around in bands, living in caves, or in rough and temporary shelters but this one at Howick was a proper house, round and substantial. In fact it was very substantial; it was 6 metres in diameter. The floor was slightly lower than the surrounding ground level and the roof was steeply pointed and made with timbers probably covered with turf or heather. It was shaped like a permanent wigwam and prehistoric people in Northumberland continued to live in very similar houses for the next five or six thousand years.

Now, I have spent time in wigwam-shaped structures. When I was young I was in the Boys' Brigade and we used to go off camping in big, white bell tents like Victorian soldiers in the British Empire. Ten or twelve of us would share each tent and sleep in a ring with our feet towards the pole in the centre and our heads and rucksacks towards the outside. What japes we had. What unusual odours and noises doubled us up into muffled titters throughout the night? Our wigwammy tent was overcrowded but it was companionable and entirely pleasant to be in.

I have also stayed in an actual wigwam. I lived for a while on the west coast of America and shortly after arriving there with my family we were told about a camping experience on an Indian reservation in the desert of Eastern Oregon that involved staying in tepees, so we made a booking and set off after work one Friday evening. We drove through an unknown landscape with just the occasional light flickering among the sagebrush in the distant darkness and arrived late and tired at our destination. At first it felt desolate. The floor was a ring of concrete, the tent bleak and unwelcoming, the landscape outside pitch dark and unsettling ... but then my little son, who had immediately set off exploring, came back with the news that there were piles of firewood lying around outside and within moments there was a roaring fire in the grate in the centre of the tent. It felt glorious, comforting, homely and warm. We loved it and went back many times. During the day we would sit at the door of our Wigwam, gazing over the desert hills, and at night we would huddle around our fire, toasting marshmallows, toes, and the occasional surplus child.

I mention these things because I thought about them the moment I heard about the Howick house and my thought was that it changed everything. You don't build a house to share it with a "band" but because you have a family you want to live with. You build a fire to keep warm and to cook on, of course, but as everybody who has ever gazed into the flames of a real fire knows, it doesn't stop there. Fires make you dream and muse, they make you plan; they bring you together with the people sharing the flames with you.

"So, did you see any aurochs today, pet?"

"We did. They were up on that ridge above the river but we couldn't get close, so tomorrow we're going to try and reach them from the other side. What about you? You'll have been out gathering I shouldn't wonder."

"Oh! I've had a lovely day. I've been down to the beach. Me mam and the kids came too and we came back with a pile of limpets and stuff. I thought we could have them for tea tonight."

It might not have been exactly like that but the display about the Howick house in the Great North Museum does have piles of limpets and whelks and the excavation revealed all sorts of animal and bird bones and hazelnuts too – clear evidence of proper teas and a varied diet. I'm not a great whelk man, personally, but I do like a hazelnut and their presence at Howick turns out to be quite interesting. After the snow retreated at the end of the Ice Age, the first trees to start re-growing

Fossilised trees on Cresswell Beach.

in the wilderness were alder and hazel and archaeologists have discovered that our early settlers would control the growth with fire – partly to create clearings that would attract animals and make them easier to catch and partly because (for some reason that escapes me) fire encourages the production of hazelnuts.

The ground conditions at Howick weren't right for the preservation of ancient wood, but at other sites sharpened digging sticks have been found that would have been used to gather roots and stuff to eat. You might call it salad. The tribal centre near my wigwam in Eastern Oregon had early photographs of almost identical digging sticks being used by women who were not just looking for edible roots but for medicinal plants too. I bet Mrs Howick did the same.

At this sort of distance, it's impossible to say for certain whether the house was occupied the whole year round. It's possible, even likely, that the whole family went off following the auroch and other creatures into the hills in the summer and returned to their nice little house by the seaside when the weather got too harsh to be high up. For thousands of years after those Mesolithic

days, that was what Northumbrian farmers did. They wintered in the valleys and moved up onto the hills in the summer. They were still doing it as late as the 1600s so it is almost certain that they were doing it back then.

But a nomadic lifestyle doesn't mean that it had no pattern to it. Our more recent nomads went back to the same places in the hills each summer. They were called 'shields' or 'shielings'. They were summer pastures and each group had its own places to go, so the hills are littered with names like 'Ridley's Shield' and 'Bellshiel' which were the pastures of the Ridley and the Bell families.

I suspect that the same was happening in Stone Age times as well. We know, and they would have known even better, that animals don't just drift around randomly; some have their own special habitats while others follow regular patterns and migration routes, they turn up in the same places on the same day each year; nowadays we know where and when to go brambling and when the salmon start their run up the rivers. Our Mesolithic chums would have been just the same – making sure that they were in just the right place when the deer passed through and following a regular round of significant places with a house or temporary camps in each of them. Perhaps granny and grandpa stayed and looked after the winter house, or perhaps they all travelled together and came back home again for the winter.

It sounds alright to me. It's what many Native American tribes did until fairly recently and Australian Aborigines as well and they all seemed to like it as a life – in fact I suspect a lot of them would like to return to it or something like it – if only to get away from the necessity of watching endless re-runs of *Friends* and *The Simpsons* on TV.

Those modern Stone Age people suggest something else to me about our Northumbrian ancestors. When their way of life came to an end with the arrival of the European settlers, there was a period of conflict and resistance inevitably, but once that was over it has been extraordinary how adaptable the people have turned out to be. In a couple of generations, native Americans, for example, leapt from the Stone Age to whatever period we're in now – that suggests to me that our distant ancestors could probably have done the same – that they were just as clever and skilled as we are, with just as much potential. I bet they told the same jokes too, dreaded the rain and loved the sunlight as much as we do.

In the few years since the discovery of the house at Howick there have been loads of other Mesolithic settlements identified on the coastal plains. I've already mentioned the hoofprints in the peat at Low Hauxley but on the same beach a whole tangled mass of human footprints has been found, left behind by Mesolithic men, women and children walking over the damp peat. These extraordinary and moving relics have been dated (using pollen analysis) to c.7400 BC. Evidence of activity has also emerged at Boulmer, just south of Low Hauxley so I think it's safe to say that there were people dotted along the whole of that part of the coast.

Further north, settlements have been discovered on Holy Island and at a place called Bradford Kaims, just inland from Bamburgh. There is plenty of evidence that Stone Age people were living on the edge of the marshes beside the river at Alnmouth, and, on the extreme southern edge of the county, a stone axe was found during the excavation of the Roman fort at Newcastle, so it seems pretty likely that all the agreeable and useful places on the coast and at the lower end of rivers were snaffled by early residents – and who can blame them. The beaches were sources of flint pebbles, shellfish and sea birds. The marshes on the fringes of rivers and lowland lakes were rich in fish and water birds; the Low Hauxley hoof prints prove there were wild beasts to hunt; they probably used the reeds to thatch their houses. They were the perfect places to live.

Not all of these settlements have been dated as old as the Howick house but, as I said earlier, the Stone Age went on for a long time. For six thousand years there were hunter-gatherers who gradually got better at doing the things they did and gradually morphed into a new age.

From about 5000 BC we begin to leave the Mesolithic period behind and talk about the Neolithic or New Stone Age instead. They were still the same people, descendants of the original settlers and they still used stone tools – but increasingly sophisticated ones. There's a display of them in The Great North Museum which will strike you in two ways – ~~on the head and on the knee~~ – firstly you will be amazed by the beauty and exquisite elegance with which the stone has been worked and secondly you will be impressed by the distance it has had to travel to get to Northumberland.

Of course there are some which are made of local stone – beautiful pink andesite from The Cheviots, basalt from Jedburgh and Scottish quartz dolerite – but many of them have come from far away, traded on the ancient Stone-Age markets. A lot are from the famous stone axe factories at the Langdale Pikes in the Lake District – but a few have travelled extraordinary distances. One Northumbrian axe head is made of Cornish Greenstone and another comes from Northern Ireland. And if the sources of the stone are varied, so are the sites at which the tools have been found. There are examples from every corner of the county – from the south edge of the county at Blenkinsopp in the valley of the South Tyne to places like Fowberry and Doddington in the far north. Only the higher hills above 300 metres have, so far, failed to throw up any early stone axes.

And it wasn't just axes and arrow heads. As the centuries and even the millennia passed, all sorts of new developments began to emerge. For example, the ongoing digs at Bradford Kaims are taking place at a site that was a lake in Prehistoric times (in fact it is still liable

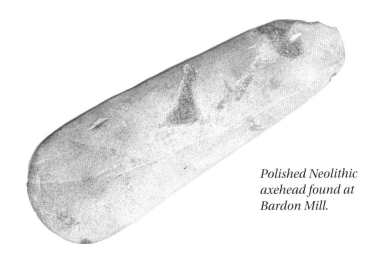

Polished Neolithic axehead found at Bardon Mill.

to flood today in really bad weather) and the excavators are discovering lots of things that show the locals weren't just camping there, scraping a living and using the place as they found it, they were altering it, making changes to improve their lifestyle. Among the finds, there are 'burnt mounds' – piles of stones that have been heated in fire; they are known from several other places in the county as well and they are always associated with trenches or stone cisterns which would have held water and the assumption is that the hot stones were dumped into the cold water in order to boil it. I don't know why. Perhaps they needed hot water to brew some sort of beery stuff; perhaps they were fond of a nice boiled root and auroch stew; or perhaps they liked nothing better (as so many of us do) than a nice long soak in a hot bath. My Native American chums did much the same – they used heated stones to create "sweat lodges", though we might just think of them as saunas.

Near the burnt stones they found a wooden paddle – I think it was the oldest piece of carefully worked wood yet found in Britain and the thought is that it might have been one of a pair to be used like sugar tongs to carry the heated stones from the fire to the water.

Another thing they've found at Bradford Kaims is a timber jetty that has been built out over the margins of the lake, presumably to make fishing easier. The ancestors of the Native Americans at my Oregon wigwam site built timber jetties out over the Columbia River for just the same purpose and though the Northumbrian one is much less sophisticated than the American examples were, well, it is a great deal older and it is undoubtedly a piece of exceedingly ancient civil engineering.

These things might not seem all that impressive to people who have got used to having digital toe-nail clippers and automated hankies and stuff but the point is that in a few short years we have learned a lot more about our Stone Age ancestors than when we had nothing put a few piles of loose flint chippings to go on – and what is emerging now is clear evidence of how skilled they were and the way they could alter their environment in order to make it work better for them.

By about 4000 BC our Neolithic forebears were beginning to leave behind their hunter-gatherer lifestyles; they were turning into farmers and were keeping domesticated pigs, sheep and goats and raising primitive strains of wheat and barley. It didn't happen just like that, of course; there would never have been a day when they stopped being hunters and became farmers instead; the old ways must have hung on for generations while gradually the crops and domesticated animals provided greater and greater proportions of the family's needs – and that, inevitably, led to other changes.

Farmers need a very different landscape from hunters and so they were continually changing the nature of the countryside. Just occasionally, in the woods behind Holystone, for example, you come across fragments of ancient woodland that give an indication of what Northumberland looked like before the tree cover was burnt off. Such places are dark and mysterious, dappled and green, an extraordinary contrast with the wide, open vastness of the bracken and heather-clad uplands that we love today.

The same changes must have occurred on the plains as well, as the trees were replaced by ploughed fields and grassland. It was Stone Age farmers who were largely responsible for that change, as a relatively benign climate allowed them to ply their trade further and further into the hills. By 2000 BC they could grow crops at altitudes as high as 400 metres above sea level, far higher than is possible today.

People lived higher up the hills too. Most of the farms and villages that they built on the plains have been obliterated by later development but on the bare hillsides of the Pennines and the Cheviots, which have never been ploughed, hundreds of hut circles surrounded by complexes of farmyards, paddocks and small fields still exist. They are best revealed by aerial photography, of course, but you can be aware of them at ground level too.

One landowner on the edge of the moors (a Lord, I might add, I move in very exalted company) told me that there were hundreds of prehistoric settlements on his estate …"but, Mr Grundy", he said to me, "I don't think one in ten has been recorded; when I ride across the moors on my horse I can see hundreds more that haven't yet been identified".

I don't personally have many opportunities to ride across moors on my horse but I have seen the buried remains and sensed them constantly when I have been out walking on the hills, skirting bumps and hollows that whisper of age-old lives and giving a frisson of romance to sandwiches munched in the shadow of ancient walls. What auroch bones were gnawed here, I often ask myself, what wild boar sarnies? As ways of life changed, so did the technologies that went with them. By about 3500 BC they had started to make pottery. They were made with local clay – the banks and bed of the River Till to the north of Wooler was a rich source of the most beautiful clay and certainly by 2000 BC the pots that they created were absolutely gorgeous.

They were used as cooking pots and for food storage; they held water and from time to time the cremated bodies of loved ones – but I'll come back to that use in a moment. Their existence is proof, I suppose, that the old nomadic ways of life were coming to an end because pots would surely have been too delicate to carry from place to place, so their existence implies a settled home and a nice thatched IKEA kitchen to keep them in.

By about 2000 BC a new style of pot began to appear. They are commonly described as "beakers" and in some ways they are a bit like me – they are delicately shaped and richly decorated, their walls more slender and finer than cooking pots and they probably wouldn't be strong enough to cope with the every-day stresses of kitchen life. All of that describes me to a T and the beakers share another of my characteristics – apparently they were often filled with alcoholic drink. It's uncanny. Beaker pots didn't originate in Northumberland or anywhere in Britain; they appeared all over Europe

Beaker pot, Corbridge.

before they arrived here and how they got here has long been an enormous source of disagreement. Some archaeologists have believed for ages that they were brought here by a wave of European immigrants; others take it for granted that they were just a new foreign style that became fashionable here, but early in 2018 a pretty definitive report came out into the DNA of bodies associated with beaker burials and they all seem to have their origins in Eastern Europe so the assumption now is that the British Isles experienced a massive invasion of new people with new technology around that time.

What happened to the people who were already here? Your guess is as good as mine and maybe even as good as the experts. As you know, I am a bear of very little brain and I don't know who is right but however the beakers got here they often seem to have been used as drinking vessels. Was it beer they drank? Remember the barley in the new farmers' fields. Beer is made of barley. I bet it was beer.

And then there was metal!

In about 2000 BC or slightly earlier, just when the beakers started to appear, one of the greatest of all changes in human history arrived in Northumberland. The Stone Age ripped off its mask and turned into the Bronze Age, the first metal age of prehistory. Bronze is an alloy, a mixture of 90% copper and 10% tin. Sometimes other metals such as aluminium or manganese are included in the mix and other, non-metallic, elements like arsenic, phosphorus or silica are sometimes added as well, all of which change the character and the strength of the bronze …

… have you ever looked at a rock and said, "Hm! I could heat that up and make something useful out of it? All I'd have to do is find the right rock … oh, and another different rock from a totally different place and possibly some other rocks … then I'll have to work out how to make an incredibly hot fire to melt the rock; that shouldn't prove too difficult."

Do you know I'm going to be quite frank with you

and tell you that I could never have done that. Even living thousands of years after the trick was first performed and knowing, in principle, how it should be done, I wouldn't have a clue, not an earthly and yet the alchemy was first achieved more than 5000 years ago by people who must have seemed like magicians to more ordinary mortals. I can hardly imagine the sort of ore awe they would have been held in, or the level of genius that they must have possessed.

Initially they weren't Northumbrians, though. The technology was first developed in Mesopotamia in about 3000 BC and over the following thousand years spread across Europe until objects made of bronze finally arrived in Northumberland in about 2300 BC. A year or two ago I would have said there didn't seem to be any evidence that any of it was actually made here. I would have assumed that it had all been made in Crete or Cyprus or other places far, far to the east and transported across Europe on ancient but highly developed trade routes. That's what I would have said but a recent event has cast doubts on that position.

In 1935 a Bronze Age burial cairn was excavated in a field at Randalholme near Kirkhaugh on the south Tyne, just over the Cumbrian border, and a tiny gold ornament was unearthed. It has been in Newcastle's Great North Museum and its predecessors ever since. It is a tress ring. Tress rings came in pairs and were used to hold the hair on a man's forehead back from his eyes. They were evidently all the rage about 2300 BC but so far only about 10 of them have been found in Britain and the example from Kirkhaugh was one of the oldest pieces of gold ever discovered in this country.

Meanwhile, as they say in the comics, in 2014 the story took a further twist when the original excavation was revisited by a group that included school children from a primary school in Alston and four small boys, two pairs of brothers, discovered the twin to the original gold ornament. Ten-year old Joseph Bell described the moment. He said, "We were digging carefully in the ground and I saw something shiny. It was gold. Me and Luca started dancing with joy. It was very exciting."

It was very exciting, not just for the boys but for the whole of British archaeology because the finds from this grave turned out to be quite remarkable. No skeleton or organic remains had survived in that acid upland soil but the things that were still there included the following:
- The gold tress ring
- A jet button
- Some broken fragments of a Beaker-style pot
- Some pieces of flint, including 4 beautiful flint arrowheads
- A cushion stone

These things tell an extraordinary story. The gold is probably the first piece of any sort of metal, let alone gold, that anyone would ever have seen in the North East. It must have seemed as extraordinary to meet a man wearing gold jewellery as it would have been to meet someone in a Hawaiian shirt and flip-flops in Victorian England. The locals would have been astounded.

The beaker pot is the oldest ever found in the area as well. The jet bead must have come from far off. The flint arrowheads reveal that the man who died was still a Stone Age hunter or warrior but the cushion stone … well a cushion stone is a class of object that has been found all over Europe and it was a sort of portable anvil for use in metal working and that makes the man who was buried in this grave a very interesting man indeed.

He lived on the very cusp of the Stone Age and the Bronze Age. The thinking is that he was a prospector, part of a small group searching for sources of copper and gold. The grave is on the edge of what later became known as the Alston Ore Field. It turned out to be one of the richest sources of lead and silver in Europe – but there was copper too, associated with the lead and before the earliest metal workers learnt to make bronze they were using copper, which was softer and easier to work with. But how did they know there was metal ore up here? How did they find it so long ago? Put up your hands if you are impressed.

Only two graves of early metalworkers have ever been found in Britain. The other was discovered at Amesbury a few miles from Stonehenge in 2002. That grave dated from about 2300 BC as well and it contained almost identical objects to the ones found at Kirkhaugh.

Enough of the body in the Amesbury grave was left to be studied and analysis of his bones revealed that he had been born in the Alps. We don't know where our man came from but the gold reveals that he must have been a man of immense status, a figure of almost mythical power.

In the 1000-odd years after our metalworker died, stone tools gradually faded out of use and were increasingly replaced with bronze ones. Northumberland is not one of the richest areas in the country for finds of bronze artefacts but even here marvellous things have been discovered – swords, axes and spearheads, brooches and amulets, all sorts of exquisite things.

Some of these objects have emerged from planned excavations but most of the bronze has been found by accident in the course of other activities. In 1835 for example, during the building of the Newcastle and Carlisle Railway, a Bronze Age hoard was found in a cutting near Corbridge. In more recent decades enthusiastic metal detectors have constantly been throwing up new discoveries. I read an account of a Scottish chap on his hols at Haggerston near Berwick in 2006, pursuing his hobby in a field and unearthing:

- 6 gold rings
- 6 copper alloy socketed axe heads
- A number of bronze rings
- A bronze dagger
- An extremely rare ingot of bronze ready to be made into something else.

Once, when I was little, I dug up a Roman coin in my garden in Carlisle. We lived beside the buried remains of a Roman fort so it should not have come as a surprise, but I almost died of excitement and I can easily imagine the thrill of uncovering something like the Haggerston hoard. A discovery like that makes life a bit more exciting for all of us because it suggests that there is always more to be found, that the ground beneath our feet contains undiscovered splendours just waiting to be uncovered. How did such things get there? Were they

deliberately hidden and then forgotten? Did their owners die out and leave the possessions like the tragic detritus you still find in abandoned ghost towns in America or Australia? You can't imagine that a collection on that scale would have been lost accidentally, left on the prehistoric bus by some careless ancient shopper.

In fact, the evidence suggests that lots and lots of these things were buried deliberately, not to hide and protect them, but for spiritual or religious reasons.

Several historic Northumbrian hoards are examples of this. One was found in 1847 during drainage work at Thrunton Farm near Whittingham and another, one of the most important collections, The Wallington Hoard, which contained 26 different objects, was found on the Wallington Estate in 1870, also when a swamp was being drained.

Both of these collections and lots of others seem to have been deliberately buried. The swords and spearheads from Thrunton had been placed point downwards in the peat. Sometimes the tips of the buried spears and swords had clearly been deliberately bent before being buried. This was the case with three magnificent bronze swords that were found buried point down in the peat at Thirlings on the Millfield plain, just north of Wooler.

And peat bogs and marshes weren't the only places the treasures were placed. Bronze objects have also been regularly dredged up from the bottom of rivers and lakes. Several have emerged from the bed of the Tyne at Newcastle, for example, and once again it seems obvious that most of these things weren't lost accidentally but were placed as offerings to the gods in some way. It always seems to have been wet places that were chosen and it's really hard not to think about King Arthur hurling Excalibur into the mere and the mysterious arm clothed in white samite (mystic, wonderful) reaching out of the water to catch it. Is that legend a survival of much more ancient practices? And do we still do it? People still throw coins into the Trevi Fountain in Rome and our own landscapes have lots of holy wells and wishing wells that are often associated with the same process. Even today

Pictured: Gold tress ring found at Kirkhaugh.

the bed of the Holy Well at Holystone is littered with coins. Until recently there was a well called the Pin Well at Earle near Wooler where, each May-day, locals would process out of the town and throw crooked pins into the water. Exactly the same thing happened into the 20th century at Bede's Well in Monckton near Jarrow. It seems that the habit, the compulsion, the superstition to throw precious metal things into water has lasted for thousands of years.

In Northumberland, one of the most extraordinary examples comes from near Carrawburgh Roman Fort on Hadrian's Wall. Just outside the fort is Coventina's Well, a pool on the site of a temple to the water goddess Coventina. When the pool was explored in 1879, 13,487 coins were found there, not to mention inscriptions, pottery, sculptures, incense burners, brooches and the most perfect little statue of a Scottie dog cast in bronze.

In fact it was a custom that predated the Bronze Age by thousands of years. In many places stone axes have been found in similar ritual positions head down in the peat; so it seems that for thousands of years our distant and prehistoric ancestors revered such places, perhaps because they believed them to be the habitations of gods – but interestingly the places they chose were the very places we still revere today.

If we go out for a picnic – I'm talking about the Grundy family here but yours might well be the same – as often as not we seek out water. We dam streams or set up base camp on the shores of lakes; we stroll along the margins of reed-fringed lowland rivers and listen in rapt silence to the ceaseless movement of water. Away from the water's edge there are other natural landscapes that seem to attract us most. We adore ancient trees and if we find ourselves in a woodland glade, we stop to love its peace. If we were animals we would probably mark such places with our own peculiar scents and I am prepared to admit that the desire to do the same can occasionally come over humans as well, though I name no names. Sometimes, when we are not feeling lazy, we love to climb up hills and sit on summits gazing at the beautiful outlines of the blue remembered hills. All of these are things that our Stone Age and Bronze Age ancestors did as well.

You might recall that I started this chapter by claiming that 400 generations of Northumbrians had loved this landscape and you may well have pooh-poohed my claim, wondering how I could possibly know that they already liked the place all of those years ago. Well, the evidence is there, evidence that Prehistoric Northumbrians found special significance in the same beautiful or striking places that we are still drawn to today and the proof is that they have left their beautiful marks in the most beautiful places. Consider their art works for example. Northumberland is richer in Stone-Age (and probably early Bronze-Age) carving than anywhere else in Britain. At least 750 mysterious examples of rock art are known so far and new examples are being discovered all the time so who knows how much is out there, buried still or reused in the walls of later buildings.

No-one knows what these carvings mean but the motifs are remarkably consistent. They are almost always described as "cup and ring markings". All over the Northumberland hills there are rocks covered with them, cups and rings, maze-like swirls and seemingly abstract patterns. People have been suggesting possible meanings for decades. I have read that they might be stylised maps, for example, or diagrams of the stars, astrological almanacs. I have read about these things but have never found them convincing and yet they must have meant something. Occasionally, like everybody else

Pin Well at Earle, near Wooler.

I think I am teetering on the brink of spotting a meaning. Recently I saw an aerial photograph of an ancient henge monument from the north of the county. A henge is a sort of circular temple, Stonehenge is the perfect example, but this one had two rings of concentric circles broken by a complex path that led through the banks to the centre of the monument, to the heart of the mystery. The shape of it looked like the carvings and I wondered, just for a moment I wondered if they were pictures of mystical routes through to the mysterious heart of things. I don't know, though I am prepared to bet that they have some sort of deeply spiritual meaning. But whatever they mean, they are lovely and they are to be found in the most glorious places. Many of them, possibly even most of them, are to be found on the rocks of sandstone ridges that surround the central hills of the county, high-up places, places where land and sky meet and where the views are vast.

The places where they buried their dead are very similar.

The earliest graves that we know about in Northumberland are the ones known as 'long barrows' and they date from the Neolithic period, probably about 4000 BC. Not a lot of them have been identified here as yet, but those that have were placed on prominent hilltops where they could be clearly seen, standing proud on the horizons. The two best known examples, the ones that always get mentioned, are The Devil's Lapful above Kielder and the one on the summit of Bellshiel Law in Redesdale. Their positions speak clearly about how important ancestors were to these people and how important the high places were as well.

In the centuries that followed, as the Stone Age turned into the Bronze Age, the characteristic shape of the graves changed into 'round barrows', (though sometimes they turn out to be egg shaped or even triangular in form). There are lots of these, hundreds of them. Wherever the landscape has been left undisturbed enough for them to survive they can still be seen. In themselves they aren't all that impressive to look at; in fact they look like no more than heaps of stones. One writer says a little bit dismissively that "bulk accounted for more than sophistication" in their design, but he goes

on to say that the "ruinous exteriors can reveal a complex structural history" and this is the thing that makes them so exciting and moving to visit. You stand beside a jumbled pile of stones or a low grassy mound but know that it is a grave; at its heart there is always a central burial; sometimes a body, sometimes a cremation. The remains are placed in a carefully made stone chest (a 'cist') to protect the body from the weight of the cairn. The ashes from cremations will have been placed in a pottery jar and often there might be another jar that will have had food or drink for the journey. These original cairns have often been re-used for other burials, sometimes over several centuries and the ashes of later bodies will have been scattered on the stones or possibly on the fields and rivers round about. Only a fraction of these cairns have so far been excavated, so any stroll across the moors is a walk among the dead, a communion with our distant ancestors.

On the hills they abound. Sometimes they crown the summit of hills, proud and dramatic against the horizon; lots of hills with distinct shapes, hills that stand free and detached from the hills around them have Bronze Age burials on their summits. I'm going to give you a bald list of some that have and if you know them you will recognise their similarities. Hills like Dod Law and Yeavering Bell near Wooler, Thirlmoor in the Coquet Valley and Lordenshaw above Rothbury are all crowned with Bronze Age Cairns.

Other graves are on the sides of hills, almost equally significant in the landscape but often it is the view that you get from them that seems more important than the cairn itself. I once met a man in a graveyard in Cumberland who told me that he often came to sit by the grave of his wife who was buried by the churchyard wall with a glorious view across to the back of Skiddaw. "It's a lovely place to lie", he said. I was young when he told me that and I thought it was odd but I understand it better now and I often think about it when I'm sitting high on a Cheviot hillside by the mound of an ancient grave. There's one in particular that comes to mind, on the side of Wether Hill above the Ingram Valley. It is a sort of egg-shaped cairn and the archaeologists who excavated it realised that it points directly towards the

Cup and ring marked stones at Lordenshaws, near Simonside.

hill called Simonside far away to the south. Now, Simonside is the classic detached hill in Northumberland. It is always recognisable and always striking and from the cairn on Wether hill it is no different. Simonside's flat topped profile is instantly recognisable but if the cairn had been built a few metres lower down or higher up the slope it would not have been visible. It's hard to ignore the feeling that it was built there so that the spirits of the dead or their surviving relatives could see the special mountain in the distance.

Simonside has no ancient settlements on its slopes or summit but it is littered with ancient graves and a pair of splendid bronze swords was found buried there in a ritual way. We know that all over the world aboriginal people have regarded special shaped mountains as sacred and lots of people believe that our ancestors did the same with Simonside … and Yeavering Bell … and Ros castle … and Cheviot itself. They aligned their tombs

and the entrance to their settlements with beautiful places. When they built monuments like stone circles or individual standing stones they were aligned as well, sometime with the rising sun or the noonday sun, but also and often with the beautiful places in the landscape. It seems obvious to me that while they might have given slightly different reasons for admiring such places, the end result was the same – they loved the Northumbrian landscape just like we do today.

The Iron Age

In Northumberland the period from about 800BC until the arrival of the Romans in 79AD is usually called the Iron Age – a title that implies that bronze was being superseded by iron as the metal of choice for the discerning Ancient Briton. As with bronze, it arrived here a lot later than it did elsewhere and as with bronze again, there's not a lot of evidence so far that much of it was actually made here in the North, though given the speed with which archaeologists are discovering new stuff, that information could change by the time you have finished your cornflakes.

In the world at large, iron was (and is) a much commoner element than copper or tin and though it is harder to get out of the rock, requiring much higher temperatures than the others, it produces a finished metal that is stronger and more easily moulded than bronze and more capable of taking a good sharp edge as well. That will be spiffing for making swords, I hear you cry. So true and no doubt warfare was revolutionised by its discovery … but so were chisels and ploughshares, axes and all the other tools and domestic utensils that changed the nature of everyday life and have led eventually to the contents of John Lewis household department. The arrival of iron was yet another of the timeless gifts that our prehistoric ancestors handed down to us.

Now, before writing this chapter I thought I knew a thing or two about the Iron Age. I am a moderately educated man and over the years I've read my *Asterix the Gaul* very carefully so I know all about the men with their splendid moustaches and their splendid warriors' bodies, elaborately tattooed or painted with woad. In my youth I had a bit of a crush on Boadicea, charging into battle with sword blades attached to her chariot wheels, cutting the Roman troops off at the knee before, in typical British style, she finally plucked defeat from the jaws of victory. I knew about druids too, and though I have never been very good at getting up early or keeping white clothes clean, I loved the idea of them, bathed in the light of the early dawn, chanting Welsh poetry to the rising sun. I have always loved Iron-Age art as well – swirling Celtic designs, not in iron but still on bronze or even gold, neither of which rusts like iron, gorgeous filigree patterns on shields and jewellery, on the backs of polished metal mirrors and the helmets of splendid chiefs.

That's what I thought I knew and to be fair, most of it is still all out there. There are endless websites directed at Key Stage Two history projects that still tell the same stories that I was brought up on and the British Museum clearly has myriads of glorious objects which live up to artistic expectations, but some things have changed and some appear to have disappeared altogether. There don't seem to be any Celts these days, at least not in the books that I have been reading. The idea that Iron-Age Britain was invaded by Celtic tribes from afar seems to have been replaced with a picture in which European ideas were gradually transmitted here by a process of trade, cultural exchange and package holidays instead of by conquest. And Boadicea has gone, stripped of her 20th century name and identity, forced now to live with the title of Boudicca.

All of these are hard crosses to bear but if you come to Northumberland there are even worse depredations to follow. I have read everything I can get my hands on and I can't find a single reference to druids or to religion of any sort, I don't know where Iron-Age people buried their dead or what they worshipped. I haven't found any art, Celtic or otherwise, or even any mentions of art, indeed our premier local museum only shows three bits of iron from this period – there's a long bar of rusty metal on loan from the British Museum, a single rusty iron sword and a lump of slag from Witchy Neuk hillfort near Hepple in the Coquet Valley.

It's not a lot, and in the books I've read there's not a lot more about the lives of Iron-Age people or the things that they possessed. The museum has a couple of stone querns for grinding corn to make bread. There have been a few spindles found that show they were weaving cloth. I've seen a photograph of a cart or chariot wheel that was found in 1927 (not in Northumberland to be honest but at Ryton on the south bank of the Tyne). It was too damaged to survive for long after it was found but at least it is evidence that such things existed, even if it seems a long way from Boudicca in full cry.

So, not a lot to convey the power and glory that was supposed to be the Iron Age and yet Northumberland possesses one particular form of Iron-Age construction that pretty much makes up for the lack of all the rest.

I'm talking about hillforts.

For reasons that aren't very clear to me, all over the country Iron-Age people began to build hillforts on top of hills or on the edge of cliffs, surrounded by protective walls and defensive ditches. Across Great Britain and

Ireland about 4000 of them have been identified so far and there may still be more, lurking under later buildings or flattened by subsequent ploughing and awaiting the perfect combination of angled sunlight and an aerial photograph to bring them back into relief. Of these 4000, Northumberland has quite a lot, mainly on the hills that surround the central massif of the Cheviots, but some have been identified on the coast and on relatively flat sites on the coastal plain. For reasons that people have only been able to guess at, there are none in south Northumberland, not even in the upland areas of the North Pennines where you might expect to find them. Some have suggested that a different tribe lived in those areas and had different needs and customs, but who can tell?

The first hillforts were made of wood and archaeologists call them 'palisaded enclosures'. They seem to have been surrounded by a wooden fence and a single ditch – I imagine them looking like the sort of fort that Kit Carson and General Custer built in the Wild West. Most of these were later rebuilt in stone and none of their wood has survived in the damp peaty uplands, but sometimes they were never developed further and the earthworks and the post holes where the wood used to be are still visible, to a remarkable degree in places. The one that people write about most is called High Knowes, just north of Alnham in the southern edge of the Cheviots. It was probably occupied about 500 BC and round about it is a very atmospheric Iron-Age landscape. The OS map is littered with signs for settlements, including, on Castle Hill a mile or so south, a multivallate hillfort built perhaps a couple of centuries later.

That word 'multivallate' requires a spot of explanation. A 'vallum' is a ditch so 'multivallate' means that this hillfort is surrounded by several deep ditches. If there was only one it would be described as 'univallate', if two it would be 'bivallate' but this one is multivallate and still very impressive despite the fact that almost all the stone that made up its inner walls has been robbed away over the centuries and used to build all the field walls and houses and farm buildings round about. It's on an outlying hill with a terrific view over the surrounding valley to the south and back into the main body of the hills to the north. You can see the profile of High Knowes quite clearly and on the hillsides below it there are sundry lumps and bumps, ancient field boundaries and later settlements. It's hard not to come to the conclusion that these upland areas of the county were more densely populated back then than they are today. Between the two forts is the Coppeth Burn, which runs through a narrow point called The Devil's Leap, and just below the later hillfort, where the road passes through a low defile as it drifts off into the high moors, there is a single huge stone, marked on the 6" OS map as The Grey Yade of Coppeth.

It is all very suggestive of ancient times and I love this place. Once, on television, I pretended to be an Iron-Age warrior attacking it – a piece of acting of which I was proud until the TV critic for the *Newcastle Journal* wrote: '*Memo to the producer of 'Grundy Goes': there are people who dress up in unusual clothes and pretend to be other people: they are called actors.*'

Ouch.

Reproduction of an Iron Age roundhouse, Hutton-le-Hole, North Yorks.

I have no regrets though and I still love the wildness and isolation, the deep sense of distant lives led that you experience in places like that and of course our hills are full of them. The Coquet Valley is full of them and there are many clustered around the Ingram Valley. The Millfield plain where this chapter started is surrounded by splendid examples on Dod Law and Ros Castle, Humbledon Hill and most dramatically on Yeavering Bell.

Yeavering Bell is a distinctively shaped hill, on the very edge of the Cheviots, rising directly out of Glendale and the Millfield Plain. It has a twin-peaked summit. one peak of which was crowned with a Bronze-Age or even Neolithic burial cairn. At the foot of the hill there are standing stones and there were long alignments of henge monuments, so this was clearly a place of immense symbolic significance for thousands of years before it received its hillfort in about 400BC.

The fort is 5.5 hectares in area (12.5 acres), which is relatively measly by comparison to the giant hillforts of southern England, but far bigger than any other in Northumberland. It is, or was, surrounded by a massive wall, which has tumbled down and spread nowadays but still gives a clear impression of the strength and power it must have had. Inside the walls there were round houses – at least 130 of them and probably many more in the saddle between the two peaks, an area that has never been properly investigated. Some of the houses were quite huge; the biggest are up to 13 metres or 42 feet across and the thinking is that they might well have had a second storey inside to act as a sleeping platform. Even the smaller buildings were substantial – 8 metres diameter is the average size – so the impression is that the fort must have been quite a substantial town. We know from later Roman sources that this was the territory of a tribe called the Votadini whose land stretched north as far as Edinburgh and so maybe Yeavering Bell was its southern capital.

Like Yeavering Bell, almost all of the hillforts are impressive places, their locations make sure of that, but no two of them are the same. Some are quite tiny, just quarter of an acre in area and if they were lived in at all there can't have been room for more than a single family

or extended family inside them. Some were packed with houses; others show no sign of domestic accommodation at all. They are all sort of vaguely round-ish but the shapes are determined by their sites. Three of my absolute favourites – Middledean above Ingram and the two forts at Old Bewick are built right on the lip of precipices. They needed no defences at the top of their cliff, so their ditches and walls are horseshoe-shaped instead of round. But what they all seem to have in common is a defensible position with good lines of sight, strengthened by relatively formidable man-made walls and ditches. Some of the walls were over a metre thick and up to 6 metres in height ... but …

… but, but, but …

But what were they for? The answer looks obvious and everybody has always assumed that they were built in a period of insecurity, perhaps when the new iron weapons, which were cheaper, more effective and more accessible than the old bronze ones, had given rise to a new society dominated by a warlike warrior class. They have always been seen as sort of proto-castles in which people could remain secure behind their formidable walls and out of which warriors could emerge to biff their neighbours.

But more recently people have begun to question those assumptions because, however well-known these forts are as places to visit, they have rarely been excavated, there are no contemporary written references to them and people have recently begun to realise how little we know about them and what a lot of questions are still unanswered. Here are a few of them:
- Why were there loads of houses in some of them and apparently none in others?
- Being on hilltops, none of them had a natural water supply; how did they cope with that? Even if they had rain-water cisterns (and none have been found) the inhabitants (let's call them the women) would still have had to trudge long distances, often at extremely severe gradients, to get water from the valleys – not to mention the trip back up again!
- Some of them are barely defended at all. Two neighbouring hillforts in the College Valley were apparently impressively walled on the side nearest to

their neighbours but not round the other sides. Were their walls just for prestige and self-image? Were they showing off like people with concrete lions on the gateposts of suburban houses?

- Why do they occur in groups? Some areas like the Ingram valley had hillforts within sight of each other. Were they frightened of the neighbours or were they all worried about attack by warriors from other tribes or distant valleys? Were the defences no more than insurance – like the deadlocks and burglar alarms we protect ourselves with today?

- Were they occupied all year round or just when the animals were brought up to summer pastures? It must have been quite cold on top of the Cheviots in the depths of winter, even if the climate was a little warmer than it is today.

Nobody knows. But until somebody does, I find that I am not bothered. The hill forts and the bare hills around them are such beautiful places that I find myself happy to accept them at face value and with that in mind I have decided to finish this chapter with a brief account of a walk I did in the hills above the Ingram Valley – one of the richest prehistoric landscapes in the British Isles and a place that has been lived in and loved for almost 10,000 years and 400 generations.

The Hillfort Walk

This walk started for me beside the National Park toilets in the Ingram valley about half a mile upstream from the village. There was a time, and not long ago, when such conveniences were rarer than wild boar in rural Northumberland and there aren't any of those, so inevitably decency and respectability depended on the length of the bracken. Not any more. This is a toilet of sumptuous comfort and scrupulous cleanliness so whatever glories the rest of the walk is going to discover, it needs to start by celebrating this monument of upmarket easement.

From the toilet (and the car park beside it) there is a stiff walk up the hill towards Brough Law. Strictly speaking crampons aren't needed, nor do walkers need

to be roped together, but it is quite steep and I was conscious that I was a touch out of shape, or even that my shape had changed from the days when I used to spring up such hills like a mountain goat. New hips, the various troubles that flesh is heir to and a lot of sofas have slowed me down and I set off quite tentatively and might have been slower still were it not for the sheepdog driving me onward and ever upward.

I call her a sheepdog but in fact it was my daughter, who lives in Brighton, returned for a trip up north. Now, one of the advantages of having family living far from home is that when they come back they evince a deep need for the scenes of their youth, so we have to do things and go places. Sometimes it's the coast, sometimes the Roman Wall but for Brighton daughter the first stop is almost always the hills and, quite often, driven by nostalgia for school trips and long ago family picnics beside the river Breamish, the starting point is the Ingram Valley. Several times recently we have walked up the head of the valley, through the exquisite hamlet of Linhope, to the beautiful Linhope Spout

But this time ~~we~~ she decided that we were going to follow the Hillfort Trail which starts, as I have said, beside the toilet, and climbs steeply towards Brough Law.

I call it the Hillfort Trail because they call it the Hillfort Trail and they use that name because there are three hillforts on the route, which is a lot of hillforts to find on one little walk of about 6 miles. Normally you would be pleased with just one hillfort, but the valley of the River Breamish is in fact tremendously rich in prehistoric sites and has been described as "one of the most extraordinary archaeological landscapes in Britain." The archaeology doesn't stop at hillforts; even this relatively short walk takes you past cairns and prehistoric settlements, ancient cultivation terraces and enclosures. On the hills round about, given a bit of practice and an OS Explorer map, you can identify evidence of dozens of other places that were the homes of ancient people.

If, like me, you are not an archaeologist, they are not always obvious to see on the ground but because you know there are so many, every inch of the way feels ancient. A broken wall or a blasted thorn tree seem to have tales to tell, each rough bank and partial enclosure whispers about the past.

About halfway up this first slope there is a dense, modern plantation of conifers. The trees are close-set and dark, tall and thin and in the slightest breeze they sway and rub against each other, making gentle murmuring sounds. It is a very eerie but a very beautiful sound and seems appropriate because beside the trees is the first monument of the walk – a series of cultivation terraces, so worn now as to be barely noticeable, but first constructed in the early Bronze Age, about 1600 BC. Isn't that amazing? The labour must have been immense, especially since there are hundreds of such terraces on the slope all around the valley. You might wonder why it was worth it and the first answer is that they remained usable for hundreds, even thousands of years. 1700 or 1800 years later the terraces were still in use; high on these precipitous hillsides they were producing wheat well into the Roman period. The climate must have been warmer and drier at that time, so every inch of available land was used to produce the crops.

Above the plantation is Brough Law, an Iron Age Hillfort built about 400 BC. Its situation is superb. The views from it are magnificent. To the west, the great

'Grey Yade of Coppeth' near Alnham.

Alnham Hillfort.

swelling shapes of the Cheviot Hills frame the valley. Cheviot itself is straight ahead, Hedgehope off to the north and Cushat Law to the south. There's a smaller, conical hill called Ritto Hill, perfectly placed in the middle distance and in the foreground the hillside falls away in a fearsome and cliff-like scree called the Ingram Glidders.

It was a bi-vallate fort which means that it had two sets of ditches and walls around it. They have fallen down now, and the scene is a richly atmospheric wilderness of fallen stone, but originally the inner wall was at least three metres high with the outer one a little lower. What an extraordinary sight it must have been. The people lived inside, safely protected by the defensive walls and snugly wrapped up against the Cheviot winds.

I think that the landscape west of Brough Law is one of the most beautiful I know, though it's quite hard to say why. When I first arrived in the North East from the Lake District I found it difficult to appreciate these high, wide open spaces which were so different from the wild craggy fells I was used to – but it didn't take long to feel their qualities. The colours are soft – beige and pale; the texture is smooth but wild; the long grasses move constantly in the wind, so the surface feels silky and alive; the skies are vast. G.M. Trevelyan called the hills, "the land of the far horizons". The Hexham poet Wilfrid Gibson said they were places:

> Where time falls
> In solitary places calm and slow,
> Where pipes the curlew and the plover calls
> Beneath an open sky

Curlew and lapwing piped and called around us as we walked and there were skylarks everywhere, hundreds of them. There were flocks of another species as well, small, brown and energetic. I wanted to call then twite but I might have been wrong and perhaps someone out there will put me right. They darted ahead of us all the time, leaping from tussock to tussock. I tried to do the same myself, but it was hard – and I looked ludicrous.

We had a little detour down to the site of a pair of cairns at Turf Knowe, which were excavated a year or two ago. The earliest finds were tiny flints or microliths from the Stone Age and there were Bronze-Age jet beads as well. In one of the stone burial cists they found the bones of a baby who had died of meningitis and was buried about 4000 years ago in this beautiful place.

Our next hillfort was less exposed than Brough Law but just as dramatic. It was poised on the very edge of a cliff over the small but exciting valley of the Middledean burn. Sheep and lambs grazed among the grassy mounds of its walls and ignored us entirely so we left them to it and climbed and climbed up the shoulder of Cochrane Pike. My daughter abandoned her sheep dog role and took on the warm and encouraging tones of a kindly teacher and together we made the top before swooping down again and up to fort number three, which takes over the entire summit of Wether Hill and contains the footing of at least 21 tightly packed round houses.

It seemed to us that these forts must have been villages like South African kraals. There must have been enough insecurity to send their residents up into such inhospitable places, or possibly the lower land was too valuable as farming land so they lived in the places they couldn't plough. These three forts are only a mile or so apart so whether they were occupied by different tribes or merely different family groups; perhaps they needed protection from raiders from other places or perhaps they just wanted to keep the cold at bay.

These are the things we mused about as we sat on the ancient walls and ate our sandwiches - I tell a lie – as I ate my sandwiches and some of hers as well. And then we went down, rather tentatively down an extraordinarily steep cleft called Corbie's Cleugh where alder trees clung at impossible angles to the cliffs beside the stream, and back to the river Breamish where we sat on the bank and drank the last of our coffee and I left my favourite flask on a rock by the river – a minor tragedy at the end of a lovely day.

'Where time falls
In solitary places calm and slow,
Where pipes the curlew and the plover calls
Beneath an open sky'

Blawearie. Bronze Age Cairn. The Cheviots beyond.

2. THE ROMANS

Britain was first invaded by the Romans in 55 and 54BC under Julius Caesar who famously pronounced:

'Veni, vidi, vici'

Which wasn't strictly true. He might have veni-d and vidi-d but he never actually vici-d. He came and saw but no real conquering took place and at the very best this first invasion turned out to be a sort of no-score draw, so Julius returned home leaving some of the tribes of southern Britain as part of the Roman sphere of influence – half-hearted chums of the Empire perhaps, but not a full-scale part of it. After that it was more than 90 years before a permanent invasion took place.

This one happened in 43AD when the Emperor Claudius sent four legions to conquer Britain.

It started quite well for the Romans in the South and South East (it didn't necessarily start well for the people being invaded) but in the end it took them ages to gain proper control, in fact the process of invasion turned out to be so difficult that the Romans didn't arrive in our region for over 30 years which was a long time even by the standards of the British transport system. And when they got here in about 79 AD they didn't stay. Like waves of invaders ever since (tourists for example) Northumberland turned out to be somewhere to pass through on the way to Scotland and so with barely a glance they zoomed straight ahead on their way north.

I say "zoomed" but there were no roads for them to zoom along, so first of all they had to build one.

Nowadays we know all about building new roads; we know it takes forever. Promises to improve the A1 north of Morpeth have failed to make significant progress in about a lifetime. The Romans were faster. By the late 70s they were under the command of a very capable governor of Britain called Agricola, Julius Gnaeus Agricola to give him the full works, and it seems to have taken them no more than a year to build the Northumbrian bit of the road that came north from York and headed up to Edinburgh and places beyond.

Their chosen route took them through Corbridge, where they built a timber fort as a supply base and a bridge over the Tyne. From there the road set off due north. It later became known as Dere Street or, to put it another way, the A68, which follows the Roman route for miles and miles of central Northumberland, as straight as a die (whatever a die is) across the humps and ridges of the Cheviot foothills. At Rochester, about 20 miles north of Corbridge, the modern road veers off towards Carter Bar but Dere Street keeps straight on across the hills until it reaches the Border at Chew Green near the head of the River Coquet. This is thrilling country today – wild, empty and splendid. You can visit it by following the Coquet upstream from Rothbury or by crossing the military ranges at Otterburn if the red flag isn't flying. Nowhere gives a clearer sense of the wild landscape

Left: John stands guard at Hadrian's Wall, near Cawfields.

though which Agricola's men built their road, or indeed how they did it. In the wildest area of all, north of Rochester, the OS map reveals that to house the men responsible for building the road and presumably to keep them safe from any revolting Northumbrians they might encounter, they constructed a whole host of temporary camps. There are seven in the first few miles alone, and at Chew Green on the Border there is an exciting and confusing mass of earthworks, forts on forts in a vast and isolated green landscape.

This road and its associated camps and forts often get taken for granted but I think it is a most remarkable thing to have achieved in that place and in that short time scale. Books suggest that our Northumberland was entirely new country to the invaders but that can't have been true; they must have known where they were going and what they were expecting to find at the other end.

They must have researched the obstacles they might find on the way, so scouts and map makers and engineers must already have travelled extensively in the "unknown" country to work out a plan and a route. The temporary camps reveal how they set about the work, leapfrogging along the road, gangs of soldiers building one section before moving on to the next bit up the line.

Like most Roman roads, Dere Street is as straight as it can possibly be and that tells you a lot about their systematic attitude to stuff in general, but also about their attitude to any locals who lived in the road's path. The Romans arriving in Northumberland didn't come to an empty land – they came to a landscape largely cleared of ancient forest by native Northumbrians who had been here for thousands of years. The countryside (especially the lowlands) was dotted with groups of small farms and divided up into fields with earth or stone boundaries and probably hedges. Some of those farms must have been in the path chosen for the road and you might want to ask whether that bothered the invaders and make them think about their plans …

… Nowadays, if we are thinking of laying down a by-pass or a high-speed rail track, for example, we know there will be collateral damage. We know that newly built estates and historic farmsteads will fall victim to our chosen route; it is inevitable, perhaps, but it doesn't happen without a struggle; planning inquiries are held and court cases, important obstructions (like Stonehenge for example) bring about compromises (and bends) in the route, restitution is made to those displaced and even with all of those legal protections the process almost always leaves a legacy of bitterness.

Do you think the Romans took that much care over the lives and the property, the history and the heritage of those they brushed aside on their breakneck advance? I don't think so. Do you think the Romans managed the whole thing without irritating the hell out of the locals? I doubt it. Do you think they cared?

Nah!

I'll give you a few bits of evidence to support that rather negative view.

It's now accepted that the original and proper name for the fort at Corbridge was 'Coria', which is a native British word meaning 'assembly' or 'gathering place' and there's archaeological evidence that there was already a settlement on the site when the Romans arrived. The same appears to be true of Bremenium, one of the main forts that they built to protect Dere Street north through the Cheviots. Recent excavations of the fort have revealed that it rests on top of a pre-existing native enclosure. Of course there's no proof that either of these places were actually in use at the time that the Romans arrived, any more than there you can say for certain that the plough marks that have been found under every single part of Hadrian's Wall are proof that they built it willy-nilly through other people's property … but you would have to be a bit of a sentimental old plank not to suspect that the Romans chose these places for one or more of the following reasons:
- Because it was there and they could.
- Because they recognised that it was in just the right place and they wanted it.
- To show the locals who was boss.

About the same time that Agricola's men were building the A68, they built a second road that went west from Corbridge to join up with another main north-south road that led into Scotland through Carlisle. As with Dere Street, they protected this east-west road with a line of forts and one of them turned out to be among the most interesting places in the whole of Roman Northumberland … and beyond.

It's called Vindolanda.

A few years ago I happened to stay in an Ibis Hotel in France. Beside the check-in desk was a poster bearing a list of ten things that had happened in the world in the year that the Ibis chain was founded, which I think was 1973. Imagine my surprise when I discovered that one of the ten on the list was something that had happened at Vindolanda … go on, have a guess …

Well, it was in 1973, and at Vindolanda, that the world discovered that Roman soldiers wore subligariorum (you might want to call them underpants).

What happened was this. Vindolanda was first built out of timber in about 79 AD and over the next few years, until 105 AD when it was abandoned for a couple of decades, it was rebuilt and enlarged in timber five times. Each time a new garrison marched (or rode) in, the remains of the previous fort were pulled down and buried under layers of peaty soil that formed the base of a new building.

From this subsoil extraordinary amounts of traditional archaeology stuff has emerged, including so far (at the present rate there is still at least a hundred years of excavation to do!) 500 metric tons of pottery and countless coins and metal bits and pieces.

Such finds would have seemed remarkable in most normal digs but at Vindolanda the soil was so peaty and so lacking in oxygen that it turned out to be an unbelievably perfect medium in which to store things that normally rot when they are buried. So excavations of these earlier layers have thrown up astonishing things in vast numbers. Thousands of shoes have been found, for example, including baby boots, children's and teenagers' shoes, ladies and gents' shoes, bath clogs, indoor and outdoor shoes and one shoe that the Vindolanda website assures me is the spitting image of an Adidas Predator Boot, circa 2017!

It is an excavation that keeps on giving. I am actually writing this in the summer of 2017 and I find I am getting all nervy as I go on. Barely a week goes by without some extraordinary new discovery being made. This September for example, they announced that they had been excavating under the concrete floor of a later fort and 3.5 metres down they came across the buried remains of 8 rooms containing almost ludicrous amounts of stuff, including the only Roman boxing gloves ever discovered and two … not just one you will have noticed … they discovered two complete and brilliantly preserved Cavalry swords in separate rooms not more than a couple of yards apart. These were amazing finds because complete swords are very rare; they were expensive and important possessions and soldiers certainly didn't leave them behind casually; something dramatic must have happened that led to them being abandoned but I'll come back to that point a little later because in this case there was another extraordinary element to the discovery. One of the swords was still in its well-preserved wooden scabbard and still had its wooden hilt and pommel!

You gasp, of course, and you are right to do so because wood is particularly susceptible to decay when it is buried, so wooden artefacts are among the rarest things to find in archaeological digs but because of the oxygen-free (anaerobic) conditions at Vindolanda, lots and lots of wooden things have survived, including, in the room next door to the cavalry swords, two perfectly preserved wooden toy swords, which looked as if they had been accidentally misplaced a couple of days earlier and had been intended for the museum gift shop.

But these were far from being the first wooden finds at Vindolanda. In 2014 a wooden toilet seat was dug up in an equally perfect state of preservation. You could have sat on it. Its discovery caused a major stir (the archaeologists were flushed with success) because it was, and remains, the only wooden toilet seat that has ever been found in the Roman Empire. There are lots and lots of stone ones, including many in this area; indeed the openings to the bell chamber in the Anglo-

From top: Shoes, unique wooden toilet seat and boxing gloves found at Vindolanda.

Vindolanda with the Bathhouse in the foreground.

Saxon church of St Andrew at Bywell in the Tyne Valley are made from re-used Roman stone toilet seats, presumably brought from the fort at Corbridge, just three or four miles further up the valley. But a wooden seat is a different matter …

Now you can accuse me a of having a puerile interest in such matters, given my apparent obsession with underpants and toilet seats you may well be right, I was ever a childish man, but such things matter. They must have mattered even more 2000 years ago to people having to cope with Northumbrian weather. I know they would have mattered to me; given a choice between underpants or no underpants while marching into the heart of the Cheviots, I know I would have opted for underpants; and offered a stone lav or a wooden one to use on a winter's morning, well, suffice to say that I would have crossed my legs and waited patiently in the queue until the wooden seat became available.

So the peaty soils of Vindolanda have yielded up all sorts of unexpected treasures but all of them, even the toilet seat, pale into insignificance by comparison to the astonishing Vindolanda Tablets.

So far (and after more than 40 years they keep on coming) hundreds and hundreds of postcard-sized wooden writing tablets, often bound in pairs and no more than 2mm thick, have been found. Some have handwriting that is still clearly visible (though obviously only readable by very clever people); others have had their contents recovered under infra-red photography. When they first began to emerge they were unique, and though more recently other examples have emerged in the city of London and in Roman excavations at Carlisle, they remain among the most impressive things ever dug out of the soil of Britain.

The thing that makes them different from all the similar items found elsewhere is the range of writers and the variety of subject matter … including, of course, the old subligariorum. This "underpants" letter seems to have been written by a family member back at home to a soldier in the fort. The writer says: "I have sent you … pairs of socks from Sattua, two pairs of sandals and two pairs of underpants. Greetings to … Tetricus and all your messmates with whom I pray you live in the utmost

The church of St Andrew, at Bywell, showing where stone toilet seats were re-used as bell openings.

good fortune"

I've written letters like that; we all have.

And it wasn't just underpants. They wore vests as well. Were they men or mice? The vests (you are probably more familiar with them in their Latin form of 'paenulae') come as part of a list of the possessions of Flavius Cerialis, the camp commander in about the year 100AD; he had white blankets too and assorted tunics, including special formal ones for dinner parties.

Another letter gives an indication of what he might have eaten at one of his dinners because it includes a list of tasty morsels such as might have titillated a soldier's tastebuds. I personally share the enthusiasm for porky scratching and I'm not even averse to gruel but I am a bit more dubious about pigs' trotters because I remember my father cooking them when I was very young and the memory has left me wounded. Not so Cerialis, who wrote about these things to his chum Aelius Brocchus, the commander of one of the neighbouring forts. You might be surprised to learn that Flavius and Aelius weren't alone out here on the wild frontier, they both had wives and children living with them and by far the most famous of the letters to have been found so far was written by Claudia Severus, who was the wife of Aelius Brocchus, to her friend Lepidina who lived at Vindolanda and was the wife of Flavius Cerialis. Part of Claudia's letter seems to have been written for her by a scribe but parts of it are in her own handwriting which makes the letter the earliest known example of writing in Latin by a woman. That makes it an important historical document of course – but the letter has a warmth and simple beauty which makes it extraordinary in other ways too. This is how it goes:

Claudia Severus to her Lepidina greetings on 11th
September, the day of the celebration of my birthday, I give
you a warm invitation to make sure that you come to us to
make the day more enjoyable for me by your arrival if you
are present. Give my greetings to your Cerialis. My Aelius
and my little son send him their greetings. I shall expect you
sister. Farewell sister, my dearest soul.

To Sulpicia Lepidina, wife of Cerialis, from Severa

So far more than 200 named individuals have been identified in the Vindolanda letters. Cerialis, as you might expect from a commanding officer, is the commonest name; he features in more than 80 letters; but they weren't all from officers and their families, they were written by all sorts of people. A soldier writes asking for leave; another has received a gift of 50 oysters from a friend and sends half of them on to someone else. There are official letters about supplies. One of the outlying bases is short of beer. There are letters written by slaves and travelling salesmen, requests for help in making contact with important officials – what is gradually emerging from these letters, as new examples keep on being discovered, is a minutely detailed record of life in the fort and on the frontier.

And do you know what's extraordinary about it all? The really remarkable thing is how un-extraordinary it was, how normal, how day-to-day. When the letters were written, between about 90 AD and 105 AD most of the Roman army had moved on north into wild, unknown and unconquered country leaving just a couple of roads,

a few temporary camps and a few hundred soldiers in what we now call Northumberland, surrounded by hairy Britons. You might have expected them to be scared, huddled in their camps for safety, gazing worriedly into the darkness …

… but no, they were organising birthday parties, going hunting, planning holidays, buying new shoes for the bairns and sitting on nice cosy wooden toilet seats before making themselves comfy by pulling up their brand new subligariorums.

Meanwhile, in a country further north, the rest of the Roman army was conquering the Scots … or not.

The invasion of Scotland had started well. They had roared up their nice new road through Northumberland in 79 AD, you will recall, and within a year or so were north of the River Tay. There was opposition of course, you know what the Scots are like, but it didn't seem to be anything the Roman Army couldn't handle and in 83 AD, in a battle at a place called Mons Graupius, they appeared to have destroyed the Caledonian forces.

After this battle they must have thought it would be easy-peasy to complete the conquest of Britain but for a whole heap of reasons it never happened – initially, or even mainly, it didn't happen because the Scots couldn't be drawn into battle again and the Romans weren't used to the sort of guerrilla warfare that they adopted instead. There were no towns to attack or farmsteads to burn, just shifting bands of Scotsmen, high on Irn Bru, appearing out of the mist, so by shortly after 100 AD the Romans had more or less given up and retreated back to the Tyne-Solway Gap. which they had left behind more than 20 years earlier and where they now stayed until the arrival of the Emperor Hadrian.

Hadrian arrived in Northumberland in July 122 AD, right in the middle of the school hols, a time when we locals know that the weather can be extremely uncertain. I don't know what it was like that year, but one of his biographers, the poet Florus, thought he was taking a bit of a risk coming north at such a time. He wrote, rather wittily I believe: '*Nolo ego Caesar esse*

Ambulare per Britannos'

… which I am told means "I'm glad I'm not Caesar, having to travel among the Britons" and he then goes on to make some disparaging remarks about the 'Scythian winters' to be experienced in these parts. So, why did he come and had he packed enough subligariorums?

He came because of what happened after his predecessor, the Emperor Trajan, died in 117 AD.

Trajan had been one of the good-egg Emperors, popular at home and successful abroad. He was a great believer in expanding the Empire and over his reign he had pushed the boundaries further out in Germany and Judaea and Mesopotamia and south into the deserts of North Africa, but when he died it seems that lots of the newly conquered districts saw an opportunity to regain their freedom. There was an uprising on the Danube frontier; in Judaea the Jews revolted as well and there were difficulties in Mesopotamia too and finally, by about 119 AD there seems to have been a major revolt in our region which made it look as if the Romans might not only lose Scotland but the whole northern half of Britain, so …

… enter Hadrian (pictured), who was spending the first few years of his reign touring the outer edges of his Empire to check for himself how things were going and what he found inevitably troubled him. He came to the conclusion that the Empire had got too big, despite its many boots, and he decided that a bit of consolidation was needed. He made the decision to abandon some of Trajan's conquests in Germany, Mesopotamia and North Africa – and the Northern half of Britain turned out to be no different. Scotland (and most of Northumberland) had been a step too far. It needed to be abandoned and so in our neck of the woods he set about creating a new northern frontier for the Empire.

In some of the other places where Hadrian had decided to reduce the size of the Empire he had merely redrawn the map to indicate the new boundary; at others, in Northern Germany for example, he had built an actual barrier, a ditch with an embankment and a fence on top but for some reason his plan for our border turned out to be very different indeed.

It was certainly much more substantial than a mere fence. Hadrian decided that our boundary was going to be a structure on an altogether different scale. It was to be a stone wall, 78 miles long, from the north bank of the River Tyne at Newcastle (or where Newcastle would later be) to Bowness on the Solway; it would be 15 to 20 feet high, with a milecastle every Roman mile and a couple of turrets between every pair of milecastles. Protecting the north side of the wall there was to be a ditch, about 12 feet deep. In the first plan there were no forts added to the wall; the main garrison would be stationed at forts like Vindolanda a few miles further south, but the decision was soon taken to build forts into the line of the wall itself. There were 14 of them altogether (8 in Northumberland) and each one was designed to hold about 1000 men. Almost immediately after the construction started there was a decision to extend the wall 7 miles further east, to Wallsend where, as the town's name suggests, the wall now ends.

And I'll tell you another thing – in places at least, possibly for the whole of its length, the wall was covered by a layer of pale whitish-coloured plaster. Can you imagine that – 78 miles long, 15-20 feet high and white –a vast white streak across the prehistoric North? Humphrey Welfare of English Heritage wrote once that it must have looked as extraordinary in this landscape as a motorway would have looked in 19th century Africa. It was by far the largest structure in Europe or anywhere in the Roman Empire when it was built and in lots of places it is easy to tell that the quality of the workmanship was astonishingly high … so, why was it built at all? And why was it built so big and beautiful?

Hm! That is a question …

Knowing that I was about to write this chapter and conscious of the gaps in my knowledge, I started

Bathhouse at Chesters Roman Fort.

immersing myself a bit in the Roman world recently, peering at altars in museums and walking along Hadrian's Wall and so on and what a pleasure it has been. Whatever else they did, the Romans certainly seem to have had an eye for landscape and a sense of the future tourism potential of their work. Even now, when comparatively little of it is still standing and so much of the stone has been pinched in the intervening centuries to build houses and farms, churches, field walls and castles that it is quite difficult to imagine the full impact it must have had when it was complete, it is still an extraordinary sight, especially given the astonishing romance of the glorious and wild landscape it rolls across.

I went to Chesters Fort, for example, which isn't one of the great set pieces of the wall; it lacks the wild splendour of Housesteads and the cliffs above Crag Lough, but it is extremely beautiful in a gentler sort of way, surrounded by rich pasture and the swelling green hills above the North Tyne. I went on a lovely clement day in early April and the fields around the fort were awash with lambs, there were celandines aplenty and the lady in the tea room was cooking bacon in a frying pan. What more could any man ask?

Stones.

Well there were stones, even more stones than celandines and lambs combined, and they had beauty too. They were worn and weathered by Roman feet and the patina of age. In the pure northern air they were covered with lichen and mosses in soft greys and greens and they told extraordinary stories – about horses and bath houses, the wealth and status of commanding officers, what phalluses represent, about gods and love and loss, about what it was like to be an exile in a land far from home. The stones addressed all of these things and many more that I will (or might) come back to later on, but the one thing they never really answered is what they were doing there in the first place. I was surprised to see, among Historic England's many splendid information panels, one that bore the question, "What Was Hadrian's Wall For?" to which the answer turned out to be, "No one really knows".

The museum at Chesters Fort holds many fascinating artifacts.

I was surprised. I was surprised because I had been assured by that notable Tyneside poet Ridyard Cuddling that he at least knew …

The Truth Aboot the Waal

It was the Emperor Hadrian who started it all
When he ordered the peasants to build him his waal
Just what it was there for there was neebody sure
And the reasons he gave were a trifle obscure.
This waal, said the Emperor rubbing his chin,
Is to stop all them Scots and them Picts getting in
A'm used to the Geordies, a knaa aal theor tricks
But I just cannot stomach them Scots and them Picts.

I think Ridyard got some things right here and some things wrong. He was wrong about the peasants who didn't build the wall at all because it was built by the Roman soldiers themselves; they had all the skills within their ranks to do any of the jobs needed – there were architects, engineers and surveyors; there were stone masons, builders and brickies and so they kept the whole job in-house and as a result they were probably able to keep the costs under control. They were there anyway and already being paid so the increased costs were minimal. They found the building materials wherever they were. They opened sandstone quarries as near the route as possible to provide the facing stone and burned limestone to make the mortar; they apparently decimated the surviving woodland of the area to provide timber.

On the other hand Mr Cuddling was of course ~~reet~~ right about the Emperor Hadrian who was indeed responsible for starting it all but, to return to that mysterious notice board at Chesters Fort it's not at all clear why he did or what he was trying to achieve with it.

This is what the board says: '*What was Hadrian's Wall For? The Frontier's exact purpose is debateable. The imposing defences forced travellers to cross into and out of the Empire through guarded gateways. The wall fortifications were strong enough to deter a small force but difficult to defend against a large-scale determined attack. The wall might have been a base from which to patrol and attack when necessary since Roman armies preferred to confront their enemies in battle.*'

So what is that saying? The wall was a guarded customs post. It was a defence against attack (but not a

Relief showing three water nymphs. Probably excavated at Carrawburgh Fort in 1876.

very good one) and it was a base from which to launch attacks on enemies. Hmm! That doesn't seem enough to me. Specifically it doesn't explain why it was so big and so posh. There must be other explanations for that.

One suggestion lies in the character and the history of Hadrian himself who is known to have liked buildings and architecture because he built stuff all over the place. He left beautiful buildings in Athens (a place he loved), and in Rome he rebuilt the astonishing Pantheon that still stands today, so it may well have appealed to him to create an architectural legacy that he could be proud of. The bridge he built between present day Gateshead and Newcastle was called Pons Aelius. Aelius was his family name so he must have been sufficiently proud of the bridge to give it his name. I have heard it said that the only other building in the Empire that bore his family name was another Pons Aelius over the Tiber in Rome; it was the bridge leading to his own vast and imposing mausoleum. All of this suggests a level of pride in his achievements in defining the limits of empire and a desire to celebrate them with a fitting monument.

And the wall was a fitting monument!

I suggested a moment ago that the quality of the building was evidence that it was more than a mere defence, that it was a prestige monument instead, and all sorts of things point to this. The Museum at Chesters (a little Victorian masterpiece, incidentally, gloriously overcharged with a wonderful jumble of splendid things) is packed with beautiful inscriptions, richly carved arches from doorways, sculpture that had formerly enriched the gateways of forts. Inside the fort, enough survives of the Commanding Officer's house to show that it was rich and elegant. At its heart was an open-air atrium or cloister with colonnades surrounding a pool and fountain. The Regimental Headquarters building was even grander. It too had a courtyard and a rich loggia in front of the company offices. Even the barrack blocks for the ordinary soldiers (and their horses with which they shared distinctly cosy and even intimate accommodation) had colonnades in front and the fort's Bath House was clearly beautifully built.

Such quality is visible throughout the wall, not just in the posh bits of forts. Milecastle 37, immediately west of Housesteads Fort has part of its north-facing gateway still standing; some of the arch stones are still in place and others are lying round about; they have been cut to perfection – smooth blocks of perfect sandstone ashlar. At Benwell Fort in the west-end of Newcastle, parts of the gateway that protected the crossing over the vallum show exactly the same level of stone-mason's care and skill. You don't take this much care over mere defensive walls and guard posts. This was a prestige project, a statement …

… but what else was it? What job was it actually meant to do?

Well, as I, Historic England and good old Ridyard have already said, "Just what it was there for there was neebody sure". It could of course have been a sort of castle or very long town wall designed "to stop all them Scots and them Picts getting in" as the man said and to be honest the defences were formidable enough to suggest that they wanted to use it in this way. They used natural barriers (like the fantastic cliffs in the central section) whenever they could and the ditch in front of it must have acted as a deterrent. There has even been evidence uncovered at Byker in the east end of Newcastle that the ditch was enhanced by sharpened stakes pointing towards the north. That is quite a castle-y thing to do, a not-so-subtle indication to the baddies that they weren't welcome.

There's another thing. In the Historic England guide book to the wall there's a picture of a bowl called The Rudge Cup, which seems to have been a sort of souvenir of the wall; it is marked with the names of all the forts and it shows the wall with battlements on top … hm … … battlements and a wall wide enough to walk along … it does make it look like a sort of castle-y thing so it is quite a seductive argument that the wall was built mainly to keep the Scots out. However there are a number of things that cast doubt on it.

First of all the Romans didn't like hiding behind walls when there was an enemy to confront. In another book I wrote that "for the Romans, used to being tough eggs and having an army which over the centuries had duffed up any opposition, forts weren't intended to be places where you could defend yourself against attack.

They were barracks for soldiers to live in and they were launching pads with gates on all four sides through which well-trained troops could pour out and bop any intruders." (J. Grundy: Another Book).

Their forts were evidence of this; they weren't hidden away modestly behind the wall; They jutted out boldly into enemy territory; each one of them had four gates, three of which were north of the wall so that the soldiers could charge out on duffing duty with maximum efficiency.

Secondly there is the question of the vallum. The vallum is the name given to another ditch, which, at some unknown point after the construction of the wall, was built from end to end of the line, a short distance to the south. It was a formidable barrier, ten feet deep and twenty feet wide with high berms on both sides. Berms are not Inspector-Clouseau-like bombs, as you might think, but banks made from the up-cast contents of the ditch. They were ten-feet high and lined in dressed stone – no mean barrier then – and what they suggest is that the Romans needed to be as concerned about who was behind them on the south side as they were about the Scots to the north.

Increasingly the whole structure is looking more and more like the Berlin Wall, a militarised zone through which all movement, north and south could be controlled. Between the vallum and the all they added a road; sometimes it was built in the gap between the two structures and sometimes it seems to have been along the north berm of the vallum. It was clearly a military road, a way for soldiers to move rapidly and unrestricted along the line of the wall.

And then there are the gateways. Nations love gateways. As I'm writing this in the Summer of 2017 President Trump is rattling on about his Mexican wall with its 'big beautiful gates' and the debate about Brexit is still raging in Britain, fuelled by a desire to control who is allowed through the gates – and Hadrian's Wall seems very similar. It was awash with gateways. There were four at each fort and every milecastle had a gateway to the North, towards the land beyond the Empire, but what were they for? Were they to let outsiders in or to let soldiers out, or both? Quite often people have assumed

that the milecastles were sort of customs or control posts to let people through the wall – a way to allow legitimate access but to control illegal immigration. The problem with this is that there are no roads which lead to or from the gateways on the north side and on the south there is no way across the vallum except at the forts, so that any traveller who came in through the milecastles would have nowhere to go. They would be trapped in the militarised zone. So nope! The milecastles don't look like customs posts to me, they look more like bopping zones, launching pads for soldiers to leap out and deal with any minor problems to the north.

It might seem a bit nitpicking to ask these questions, whether the wall was to keep people out or to control the people coming in, but I don't think it is. I think it would have mattered at the time. I think it would have made a really big difference to the local people, especially in those early days. The wall hadn't been built on the site of an existing boundary, it was dumped willy-nilly on land that belonged to the people who already lived there so it blocked all of the little paths that they would have used from time immemorial – the way they would have gone to call on granny and grandpa or to see that bloke on the Tyne who made nice chariot wheels. It ran right through the middle of Brigantes' tribal territory so families and chums and work mates must have been cut off from each other; they must have been sore as gumboils that their old routes and paths had been taken away and it would have mattered like mad whether they could get through a gate or not.

Let's imagine, for example, that your family had always lived a mile or so from a holy site or a really great fishing spot on a stream and suddenly there's a 20 foot high wall blocking the path and the only way to get there was to walk several miles along to a fort and miles back on the other side. The situation might even have been worse. Perhaps the only ways through were at the main roads near Corbridge and Carlisle. It sounds extreme but it could have happened. That's what the border between East and West Germany was like before the fall of their particular wall. That's what borders do and the Roman Wall was one of the borderiest borders ever built. It was built by and for the Romans and I think it's safe to say that they didn't give a second thought to what the locals felt about it.

The trouble is that the Romans were invaders, empire builders, and you don't get very far in that role by being nice to the locals. There is no shortage of other examples: Portuguese and Dutch colonial invaders in Asia, American settlers moving west through the lands of Native Americans, the Spanish in South America, the British in India and Africa, almost everywhere in fact, the Nazis in 20th century Europe – we have realised now that all of these and many others were cruel and brutal in their treatment of the conquered people – that you don't get an Empire without arrogance and violence.

However much the colonial nations have tried to dress it up as 'destiny' and 'bringing civilisation to primitive people', the bottom line has always been that the conquerors took what they wanted and the conquered people resented it. In Roman Britain, even at the time, there were people who recognised that this was what was happening. The Roman historian, Tacitus, who was the nephew of the general Agricola who led the invasion of Scotland puts these words into the mouth of Calgacus, the leader of the Picts at the Battle of Mons Graupius: '*These plunderers of the world, after exhausting the land by their devastations, are … stimulated by avarice … to ravage, to slaughter, to usurp under false titles, they call.*'

The speech as a whole is extraordinary, one of the greatest speeches about liberty ever recorded and while it could easily, and probably did, record the actual feelings of the Britons, most people think that it also represented the feelings of Tacitus himself, who believed in the values of the old Roman Republic and disapproved of its colonial expansion.

So there was bitter opposition to the Roman occupation and Northumberland can't have been any different. The locals must have hated and resented the invaders and the Romans must have feared and despised the locals. That's what happens whenever there are empires and there is plenty of evidence for it here.

The only explanation that the Roman ever gave for the wall was that Hadrian had built it '*to separate the Romans from the Barbarians*'. 'Barbarians' is an ugly word, unpleasant and dismissive but if you look carefully at Roman Northumberland there's plenty to show that 'barbarians' was the way that they thought of the natives.

Among all the quite jolly correspondence found on the wonderful Vindolanda writing tablets only one letter has been found so far that mentions the locals. It says nothing about their cooking or their social habits or clothes or anything – it talks about how they fight. They don't wear armour, we're told, but they do have lots and lots of cavalry. The cavalry don't carry swords; they use javelins but don't mount up to throw them. It's rather a confusing picture if I'm being honest but what it does show is that in this frontier zone at least, at this time the Romans were still surrounded by a well-armed local population and I think it's possible to deduce that they didn't like it.

This letter also introduces a new word to describe the Britons which hasn't been spotted anywhere else so far. They are described as "Brittunculi" which apparently translates as "nasty little Britons". The nasty little Britons, the letter says, don't mount in order to throw javelins. There's dark feeling in that phrase. The writer might be sneering at the Britons or patronising them, but it's clear that he's seen them fight and didn't like the way they did it.

Those two iron swords excavated in 2017 are further evidence of stuff going wrong. Possessions as valuable and useful as those don't get left lying around because somebody forgot to pack them. They get abandoned because their owners are in a panic, or desperate, or dead. The toy swords suggest the same story, a scene of flight and chaos. This is all evidence that in those early years of the Roman occupation of the North there was still conflict with the locals. Among the debris dug out of the Vindolanda trenches is a native skull that seems to have been stuck up on a parapet as a trophy and in Hexham Abbey there is a remarkable tombstone to a Roman cavalryman called Flavinus, which reinforces the impression that relations between the conquerors and the conquered weren't all that you would want them to be.

It is a huge stone, over 9 feet tall and immensely heavy. The assumption has always been that it was

Tombstone of Roman cavalryman Flavinus, at Hexham Abbey.

I have a deep and vested interest in him, not because gentlemen prefer blondes, but because the Petriana regiment was later stationed at Stanwix on the northern edge of Carlisle. My junior school was on the site of their fort and my house was next door and once, while digging a den in my back garden, I found a Roman coin and the corner of a Roman turret which has since been excavated more scientifically than my childish butchery permitted and is still exposed to view.

Flavinus seems to have died in Northumberland however, before his regiment went to Carlisle in 98AD. On his tombstone he is depicted on a horse that has reared up on its hind legs. He, Flavinus I mean, not the horse, is wearing a helmet with a high crest and a plume and he has a torque around his neck. These things reveal that he was of high status and he is carrying the standard of his troop, which bears the symbol of the sun god in a circle. It is a fantastic image made all the more remarkable because beneath the flailing hooves of the horse crouches a naked barbarian, holding a sword and cowering under a shield.

It's not unique this image – I have seen at least one other like it from Colchester and I think there are others, but this is the largest and the most impressive. Some people describe it as a standard image for a cavalryman's tomb and suggest that we shouldn't read too much into the apparent brutality of it – but that seems like rubbish to me. If you represent yourself as somebody who crushes naked barbarians beneath your hooves it's because you don't think much of barbarians and think it's OK to crush them beneath your hooves.

So, there's Hadrian's Wall, "separating the Romans from the Barbarians" to the north, but what was it like in the land that had been left to the barbarians? What impact did the Romans have in the rest of Northumberland, to the north of the wall?

Well, lots of other writers have said that there is no evidence of conflict with the northern neighbours and the rest of the county is often described as 'a buffer state' between the barbarians proper and those settled within

brought from the Roman settlement at Corbridge to become part of the church being built by St Wilfrid in Anglo-Saxon times though why they would lug something so vast is anybody's guess. It commemorates Flavinus, a 25-year old who had been in the army for seven years when he died and served in the cavalry regiment known as the Ala Petriana. 'Flavinus' seems to have been a nickname meaning 'blonde' or 'blondie' and the empire, but I don't know.

It's difficult to say for certain, but it just seems to me that there is quite a lot of evidence to suggest that the immediate effect of the wall wasn't very good on the rest of our county. Recently (in 2017) there has been a series of excavations of Iron Age sites at housing developments on the northern edge of Newcastle and also in advance of open-cast mining at Blagdon and other places in the SE corner of the county, and a whole mass of native farms (at least 50 so far) have been uncovered, which seem to have existed for several hundred years before being abandoned in the early 2nd century, round about the time that Hadrian's Wall was built. Nobody knows why this happened but perhaps the owners of these houses found that the wall had cut them off from their traditional markets and contacts and they had to move to make a living. Perhaps they had all been watching *A Place in the Sun* and were seduced by the greater possibilities further south, on the other side of the wall. Or perhaps the Romans cleared them out of the way to create a sort of 'no-man's land' near the wall or because they needed the land to provide pasture for the thousands and thousands of horses that the cavalry possessed. Nobody really knows but the implication is that the wall disrupted local life and broke up established communities in these areas.

Elsewhere in the country north of the wall, Northumberland seems to have remained a relatively Roman-free zone. A couple of extra roads were built – one (the Devil's Causeway) went from Corbridge towards Berwick, and a third recently discovered road joins the other two roads together across the southern foothills of the Cheviots. So the Romans definitely had a presence and of course, the main road to Scotland still existed and for the next 200 years it continued to be protected by two very substantial stone forts – one at Risingham near West Woodburn, defending the crossing over the River Rede, and the other at Bremenium (High Rochester) on the fringe of the high moors.

Both of these forts date from the original foray into Scotland, long before the wall had been built, and they were both large and well manned. Each one had a combined infantry and cavalry regiment of about 250

Challenger tank training at Otterburn.

cavalry and 750 foot soldiers. That is a whole heap of soldiers in sparsely populated hill country and they were two of only five forts in the whole of Britain to have this impressive combination, which suggests to me that they needed a lot of chaps to stay safe in such isolated and difficult country. Their role, of course, was to protect travellers on the road north but they had another job too. An inscription reveals that they were known as the 'exploratores Bremenienses' or 'the Bremenium Scouts'. They were there to watch out for invaders, to snuff out any hints of rebellion and to keep an eye on the old brutunculi. It seems to have been a job that needed to be taken very seriously.

You can tell this because they surrounded both forts with multiple circles of deep ditches to strengthen the defences provided by their stone walls and at High Rochester (or Bremenium), as you turn off the A68 onto the small road that leads up to the fort, you pass the Old Schoolhouse, a cottage that has a porch constructed out of a fascinating but rather bizarre mixture of carved Roman fragments. Among the bits of friezes and cornices there are a number of stone balls or 'ballistae', stone projectiles that were made to fire from giant catapults, which presumably stood on the 'ballistaria', the four stone platforms that strengthened the defences on all four sides of the fort. These are quite rare things to find in Roman forts apparently, and their presence here, along with the ditches, suggests at the very least, that they had an above average threat of security issues.

The fort at High Rochester is one of the most atmospheric of all of the Roman remains in the county. It has bumps and ditches, some visible fragments of stone and one splendidly preserved gateway on the west side and you will feel like one of the early antiquarian explorers of the site as you wander round making sense of the whole thing. You will also be alone, which will double the pleasure of your exploration and as you stand by the west gate looking down on the modern army barracks at Otterburn and the wild emptiness of the Otterburn ranges beyond, you will be struck by an extraordinary sense of continuity – military manoeuvres way back then and still going on today. I can't resist telling you a story to illustrate this point.

I was walking once along the edges of the firing ranges, near the River Coquet and I passed a sign that read …

UNCLEARED MILITARY TARGET AREA
DO NOT LEAVE THE PATH
DO NOT PICK ANYTHING UP OR IT MAY EXPLODE
AND KILL YOU

A moment or two later a riderless horse with a nasty look in its eye appeared on the hillside above me. It saw me and started to gallop towards me and I was left with an uncomfortable choice – risk being blown to bits or wait to be kicked to death. I was more frightened of the horse than the abandoned military hardware so I fled and jumped over a drystone wall.

It must have been like that 2000 years ago. As if normal life wasn't hard enough, for both sides there would always have been the risk of bumping into the enemy, finding yourself in difficult and potentially dangerous situations. The Romans were clearly aware of this.

But … I have a but and as you all know, it is a big

but, and I have to admit that there is another side to the picture. All around the two forts in Redesdale there are lots of native settlements. They are only visible in aerial photographs but there are quite a lot of little groups of two or three roundhouses surrounded by extensive stretches of cord-rig fields, characteristic iron-age fields with narrow strips of ridge and furrow. The assumption is that these farmers were willing to stay where they were and grow corn for the forts. So perhaps it wasn't all fear and loathing; perhaps a lot of the time there was normal life and acceptance.

However, the Roman authorities would not have spent the money and effort to maintain a garrison of 2000 soldiers in the middle of the hills if everything was hunky and dory. They must have been constantly expecting and waiting for it all to go wrong and quite regularly it did. At times the security issues won for a while before life got back to normal, but eventually they won altogether. In 197AD the two forts were attacked and destroyed, only to be rebuilt a decade or so later and then in 311AD they were destroyed again by the Picts, abandoned and never re-occupied and as far as I know this means that for the last hundred years of the Roman occupation of Northumberland there were no permanent forts north of the wall. There may have been scouts, or forays, spy missions or punitive attacks on restless natives, but in the main the rest of Northumberland seems to have been relatively free of Romans.

Meanwhile … back at the wall

When the wall was first built and for some time afterwards, the problem must have been that there were 'barbarians' living alongside the Romans on the south side as well as the north side and presumably they too were sore as gumboils to be cut off from their chums and relatives and business contacts further north. There must have been angry locals to the north and equally angry ones to the south and that seems to me to be enough of an explanation for why the vallum was added to the defences, creating a sort of sanitized locals-free zone that could be securely held by the Roman army.

The atmosphere must have been very uncomfortable for a while, but over time the situation clearly began to change.

The locals south of the wall began to change their attitudes to the Romans and you can see how that would happen. Surrounded by soldiers you could sell things to or fall in love and start a relationship with; offered jobs by the invaders and the chance of a decent wage if you joined their army; seduced by baths, oysters, imported wine and the trappings of a 'civilised' Roman lifestyle, the locals on the south side of the wall became relatively Romanized. Ancient Northumbrians had never lived in towns or villages but after the wall was built settlements sprang up around the 'safe', southern side of each of the forts. These settlements weren't insubstantial little fly-by-night temporary camps; after all the Romans army stayed on the wall for almost 300 years, so the towns had all the time in the world to become real places.

One of the Historic England panels at Chesters Fort has a drawing of the town (the 'vicus' if we're being posh) that developed there and it was substantial. I'm not sure how accurate the drawing on the panel is meant to be but I assume it's backed up by excavations or geophysical surveys and things and what it shows is about 150 houses, stretched along 9 streets or little lanes and covering an area almost as large as the fort itself. The similar vicus at Housesteads is estimated to have had a population of about 2000 and if you add to that the 1000 soldiers in the fort there was plenty of scope for a good party on a Saturday night. They were proper little towns, in fact, which probably contained all those essential adjuncts to military life – pubs, pie shops, brothels and homes for soldiers and their families.

That's a statement that needs a little bit of explanation because Roman soldiers weren't allowed to marry until their active service came to an end but evidently (and inevitably) many of them started informal families with local girls and many went on to marry and settle in the area once they had retired from active service. This is quite interesting actually, because for the most part the soldiers who manned the frontier weren't Romans. The wall itself, the roads and the forts might have been built by actual Roman legionaries but

they were manned by auxiliary troops drawn from all over the Empire. Eventually some of these would have been from Britain itself but there were Tungrians from Belgium and Holland, Germans and Gauls, Pannorians from Hungary, Thracians from Bulgaria. A Cohort of Lingones came from central France and the fort at Risingham, north of the wall, was also full of Frenchmen at one period – the 1st Cohort of Vangiones who were a cavalry unit 1000 strong …

'*Cohors Primae Vangionum Millaria Equitata*'

… as it says on an inscription. There were Dalmatians from Croatia and Asturians from central Spain. South Shields was manned by boatmen from the River Tigris in modern-day Iraq and there was a cohort of Syrian archers, Hamians, from the city of Hama in northern Syria. The Great North Museum has the gravestone of one of these Hamian archers who died at Housesteads. He is depicted wearing a picturesquely pointed Phrygian cap and bearing a distinctively Middle-Eastern bow.

All of these people from the far-flung corners of the empire, all of these different races, many of them from desert lands and soft Mediterranean climes: I can't help being tickled pink that for three hundred years at least, Northumberland was an entirely multicultural society; on the other hand, I can't help wondering how they bore it up here on our northern hills? Many of the cohorts were here for decades or even centuries. What must have it been like for them to spend their whole working life in this wild, cold and isolated spot?

In 1938 W.H. Auden imagined an Auxiliary soldier from Tungria, missing his girlfriend, cold and miserable on the moors …

Over the heather the wet wind blows
I've lice in my tunic and a cold in my nose
The rain comes pattering out of the sky
I'm a Roman Wall soldier and I don't know why.

It's bad enough for us nowadays. I once took a party of Germans (modern-day Tungrians) for a walk along the wall near Housesteads and it suddenly started to snow. It wasn't exactly a snow 'fall' because soon we were being struck by bitter blasts of horizontal snow … did I mention that this was in mid-June? My German visitors were either very tough or they were rather silly because they expressed delight with the experience.

Their ancestors may well have had the same response because they created an extraordinary world up here. They brought their beliefs with them and built temples to Gods who had started off in far-off Persia or the sands of Egypt. They enriched their towns and their fortresses with beautiful inscriptions and sculpture that may have been a touch rougher up here on the wild frontier than it would have been in Rome itself, but was nevertheless a hell of a lot better than I could have done.

Some of the inscriptions are dedications to the many gods of the Roman Pantheon, many are in honour of Emperors and the great and good, often the army itself is commemorated, the pride in its achievements recorded as armies have done ever since; but many of them are more personal, memories of those who stayed, found wives, bore children, lived and eventually died on this distant edge of the world Some of the most beautiful things to have survived from Roman times are the tender memories of love that they left behind them….

… to Aurelia Lapula, most dedicated of mothers. Dionysius Fortunatus her son placed her within the gentle earth …

… Aemilianus, 10 years old; Satirus Honoratus, 5 years 8 months …

… to the sweet daughter of Blescius Diovicus who lived for one year and 21 days …

… to the sacred spirits of the departed and to Aurelia Quantilla who lived for 13 years, 4 months and 22 days, Aurelius Quantinus placed this for his daughter.

Lovely things … our Roman past is full of lovely things, all of which deserve more time than I have got to talk about them, but I just want to give specific mention to one object from those far off days that was eventually rescued from the soil in which it was buried – deliberately or accidentally, nobody knows. It's called The Corbridge Lanx.

In February 1735, Isabel Cutter, the 9 year old daughter of a Corbridge blacksmith (or cobbler – it depends who you read) went out to collect some firewood from the banks of the Tyne and she noticed something shiny peeking out of the soil a couple of hundred yards upstream from the bridge. She pulled it out and took it home to her dad and it turned out to be The Corbridge Lanx.

A lanx is a dish, a serving or display dish such as would have been used at a banquet and this one is of superlative quality. It is richly decorated with scenes that relate to the story of the God Apollo and it has the reputation of being the finest piece of Roman silver yet found in Britain. In subsequent years five other pieces of silver in various forms were discovered in roughly the same place but all of them have since disappeared. Only the lanx remains.

Since Isabel took it home it has had an interesting history. Her dad sold it to a Newcastle goldsmith called Isaac Cookson for £33.6s – a relatively vast amount of money for an ordinary person in those days. One hopes that Isabel was at least bought some sweeties in recompense for her sharp eyesight.

It was of such obvious high quality that it immediately got noticed by the world at large and specifically it got noticed by the agents of the Duke of Somerset who was, for complicated historical reasons, the owner of the estates of the Percy family and Lord of the Manor of Corbridge. The Duke claimed that as Lord of the Manor, anything found on his property belonged to him and he tried to insist that Isaac Cookson hand the lanx over to him. Cookson refused and there was a court case which inevitably the Duke won. I say 'inevitably' because the Duke was very rich and I am an old leftie with a cynical attitude.

His victory set a precedent that is still significant today because for the first time in English Law it established the notion of treasure trove. Isaac Cookson got his money back, which was nice. Isabel's dad was fined 6d for failing to report the find to the lord of the manor and the Lanx remained in the property of the Percy family until 1993 when it was sold by the 11th Duke of Northumberland to the British Museum. He was paid £1,858,000 for it which I make a rough profit of about 6000% over the original price. I think I'm going to come back as a Lord of the Manor in my next life.

The Corbridge Lanx, one of the finest pieces of Roman silver found in Britain.

So there you are. Someone in Roman Northumberland could afford a silver tray worth £1,858,000 – even if he did lose it.

I was being a bit savage about the Romans earlier in this chapter, banging on about the cruelty inherent in creating an empire and I don't want to forget that. It irritates me that the native population has been left invisible in the whole story and it infuriates me that the Romans still get such a good press, as if they were goodies when they clearly weren't. They were the baddies, ruthlessly imposing their rule on a people who didn't want them, stripping the country of its wealth (tribute, silver, lead, copper, whatever else they could rip out of the land) and sending it back into the coffers of Rome and there is lots of evidence that they were continuously resented by the native population. They successfully persuaded some of the people, some of the time that they were a good thing, but it couldn't last. There were rebellions constantly and plenty of failures.

After Hadrian died in 138AD his successor, Septimus Severus, abandoned the wall and tried once again to capture Scotland. Twenty years later that adventure failed and the troops were back in Northumberland again. In the 180s there was a major revolt by the northern tribes and it took four years to get control of the situation. Later in the same decade it was the army itself that rebelled and elected its own replacement emperor. It took more than 10 years to settle that little disagreement.

In 211AD - there was another revolt.

And in 297AD – yet another massive war as the Picts invaded from the North – it took at least nine years to bring that one under control only for there to be another Pictish attack in 342AD … and in 367AD … not to mention 382AD … and between about 407 and 410 AD when it all finally unravelled, the army left and Roman Britain gradually drifted away until it was just a memory with barely a trace left behind.

There have been programmes, perhaps even whole television series with titles like "What the Romans did for us" and in some ways I think it is rather a paltry legacy. I have read that they gave us carrots and peas, possibly even apples and pears, all of which are desirable things. I came across a suggestion that they were responsible for nettles with which they used to flog themselves as a way of keeping warm, definitely a thing I wouldn't do myself. Their roads survived for a long time and in some cases (the A68) are with us still. But there doesn't seem to be much else. Any Latin words in our language were re-introduced hundreds of years after they left. Their extraordinary building skills were lost for centuries, town life faded away until it was re-invented by new invaders hundreds of years later. It all seems so little and yet what would our northern county be like if they hadn't come?

Poorer is the answer. Less interesting. Hadrian's Wall is rightly a World Heritage Site, extraordinary in its wild and wonderful landscape but immeasurably enhanced and lifted to sublime levels by the romance of history. Sycamore Gap would always be a beautiful place but the wall that frames the iconic tree gives it an almost mystical power; Housesteads, as a piece of landscape, is a wild moorland like hundreds of others in the county, but the fort make it irresistibly moving. Our Iron-Age ancestors would never have agreed with this, but we are lucky that the Romans chose to make Northumberland the northern edge of their empire.

AFTER THE ROMANS

Nowadays everybody knows what happens when Empires collapse or when countries that have been ruled by rigid leaders break up. We've seen it so many times. We saw it in the wake of the British Empire in India and in vast areas of sub-Saharan Africa. There was chaos, violence, death on a huge scale. We saw the same after the Russian Revolution, or the French Revolution or almost any revolution you like to think about; we have seen it in the former Belgian Congo, the USSR, all over the Middle East, Libya, Somalia, the Balkans, Vietnam and the rest of French Indo-China, whenever you open a history book or turn on the news it seems that even more countries … countries that had seemed up to that moment to be more or less working normally … descend into violence as soon as their hated, or terrifying, leaders die or begin to show signs of weakness.

The sequence is always more or less the same. There's always a brief period of euphoria and optimism. People wave their arms in the air and talk about 'freedom'. A sort of government emerges that tries to keep things going and hold on to the best bits of the life that had gone before – but it never lasts. Suddenly there are 'warlords' everywhere, carving out savage little fiefdoms for themselves, fighting bitter little battles with the warlords next door or with the vestiges of the defeated government, or with the people they don't like. Places that had looked like unified countries suddenly turn out to be just a collection of tribes – ethnic tribes, religious tribes, geographical tribes.

Gosh! I've just read those two paragraphs over again and they sound terribly cynical – perhaps it's something I've eaten – but I think they are a pretty fair description of what goes on and I bet they would have been a fair description of what happened to Britain in general and Northumberland in particular when the Roman Empire fell apart in the early 400s.

Not that the collapse would have come as that much of a surprise to anybody who had been watching things go sour over the previous few decades. There seems to have been plenty of warning signs that the Romans were in trouble. The money to pay the troops stopped arriving for a start and as a result there were revolts and mutinies. Savage punishments were introduced to stop soldiers deserting or avoiding conscription. The barbarians beyond the frontiers began to get bolder and attacks by the Picts and the Scots and raids by Germanic tribes from the other side of the North Sea became more frequent and harder to repel.

The whole situation came to a head in the early 400s AD when the army was withdrawn to shore up the defences of Rome itself. The Britons appealed to the Emperor Honorius for help but he offered no comfort at all and in a jiffy the country broke into pieces and little British warlords carved out lots of little British kingdoms. The one that included Northumberland was called Brynaich and it covered part of the lands of the Votadini tribe, south of the Tweed and north of the wall, but to be honest I know nothing about it; as far as I can see nobody knows anything about it.

There are rumours and stories that there might have been some survivors of the old regime, perhaps surviving elements of the Roman army who tried to hold back the drift into chaos. For a thousand years stories have been told about King Arthur, for example, and over recent centuries there have been some historians who have seen those legends as partial memories of real events with the King as a sort of upmarket warlord fighting against the barbarians who were threatening to destroy the old Roman civilisation.

It would be lovely to believe that Arthur and his chaps did exist and were really here, heroically holding back the darkness for a few decades. The North is one of many parts of the country that is eager to claim the story for its own and it's as good a place as any; there would have been a clear logic in trying to hold on to the line of the wall and keep the Picts at bay and there are plenty of specific sites in our area that are associated with the Arthurian legends. Lancelot is said to have seduced Arthur's queen, Guinevere, at Bamburgh Castle for example, and Arthur's first battle is recorded as being on the River Glen; there are only two rivers called Glen in England, one is in Lincolnshire, a county with no other Arthurian connections, the other runs past Wooler into the Tweed across a landscape rich (as I'll be pointing out a little later) in ancient British and Anglo-Saxon significance. At the other end of his career, Arthur is supposed to have died in the last great battle of Camlann at the Roman wall fort of Camboglana just across the county boundary in Cumberland and to complete the story, his body… you'll be surprised to hear this and I want to warn you that there are elements of this story that could possible come under the heading of 'fake news'… his body was apparently spotted by a Northumbrian shepherd in the 19th century.

What happened was this. The shepherd had dropped his sarnies or something down a hole at Sewingshields, which is an intensely beautiful and dramatic crag just to the east of Housesteads on Hadrian's Wall, and when he climbed down to retrieve them he was surprised and possibly pleased to come across the King and Guinevere, accompanied by all of their knights, sleeping in frozen splendour at a round table in a great cavern below the crag. This is not something you come across every day and the shepherd was understandably excited, and there was more, because Arthur's splendid sword, Excalibur, lay on the table before him. The shepherd couldn't resist drawing the sword from its scabbard but suddenly Arthur began to wake and utter dark and dire warnings. As you can imagine the shepherd fled and the assumption is that the King is down there yet, waiting for the blast from the great bugle that will rouse him from his centuries of rest to emerge and rescue his country (or possibly just Newcastle United) in its hour of greatest need.

Myths and legends like these were not written down until hundreds of years later and, while there might be underlying truths beneath the stories they tell, what we actually know about the kingdom of Brynaich is virtually nothing. It seems probable that for ordinary people life went on much as it had done before except when the neighbouring warlords were on the rampage. The Roman fort at Vindolanda continued to be occupied, for example – in the beginning, at least, people continued to live in its surviving stone buildings before they fell down and were gradually replaced with wooden houses.

The Christian religion, which had been one among many available faiths in later Roman times and had finally become the official Roman religion in the 370s, continued to be followed after the Romans left. There was a church inside the walls at Housesteads and at least two others at Vindolanda. Vindolanda even has a gravestone to a man called Brigomaglos which was inscribed with a clearly Christian symbol, and in 2017 (I think) fragments of a 5th or early 6th century chalice, which is a scrawled mass of Christian symbols, were excavated. It has roughly scratched doves, for example, and angels; crosses, fishes, butterflies (symbolising eternal life), palm fronds and symbols of Christ are randomly carved all over it. These are all suggestions that things went on in the old ways to some extent, though there are also suggestions that life got less secure than it had been and that some of the hillforts in the Cheviots were re-occupied, presumably for added protection.

Among the few pieces of hard evidence is a post-Roman knife that was discovered at Brough Law above the Ingram Valley – but that's about it. In fact there isn't much more for the country as a whole. Records just stop. For a couple of hundred years after the Romans went there are virtually no written records at all, there are no carvings or statues, no inscriptions, nothing to give us a clue as to what was going on. In Northumberland, so far as current archaeology can show, there aren't any settlements that can be certainly dated to those years immediately after the Romans left and, except at Vindolanda, there are no cemeteries where we can assess what people believed or what they possessed.

So we know nothing and that's why this period is called "The Dark Ages". How could it happen? How could it all disappear so completely? What was going on?

Invasion!

All over Europe this was a time of migration and invasion, in particular by the Saxons from North Germany and the Angles from Germany, Denmark and the Netherlands who expanded out of their original homelands in vast numbers. By the time the Emperor Honorius died in 423 AD, most of Gaul and Spain had been lost to northern invaders and it seems obvious to me that if it hadn't already happened to Britain, the takeover was well on its way.

The Saxons were coming …

North Gate of Housesteads Roman fort, looking east towards Sewingshields.

3. ANGLO-SAXONS

Actually, the Saxons had been coming for quite a long time, even before the Romans left. Some of them had been invited in as mercenaries by the Romans, who were having trouble finding enough recruits for the army, and for much of the 4th century others had started taking a more direct approach, to the extent that the Romans had needed to build a line of defensive forts along the east coast to keep the attacks under control, but before, during and after the Roman withdrawal, the Saxon invasion clearly became an unstoppable force ... a force that probably didn't seem like a good thing at the time but which turned out to be one of the greatest things that ever happened in the North East.

This is because under the control of the Anglo-Saxons, Northumberland became a force to be reckoned with. Instead of being an insignificant area a long way from London as we are now, the last match on Match of the Day and the place where weather presenters place the randomly unwanted rain stickers on the weather map, under the Saxons we became a hugely impressive place, brilliant at art, influential in the courts of kings throughout England and throughout Europe too. For Northumberland, in the reasonably long term, the arrival of the Saxons turned out to be a JOLLY GOOD THING.

The ones who came and settled in Northumberland seem to have been mainly Angles from the Netherlands and southern Scandinavia. So far there's not much evidence from our neck of the woods of exactly who they were, but the invasion force wasn't just a few mercenaries or boatloads of raiders. There were whole families settling here, women and children as well as warriors, and like anybody else emigrating to a new country, you have to assume that they came because they liked it. They would have heard enthusiastic reports from the soldiers who had already been. There were probably notices on the mead hall walls advertising cheap pre-Christmas shopping weekends in Pons Aelius so they came to live in Northumberland because it was beautiful, fertile and available and they brought their language with them, their customs and their possessions and it's clear that like many newcomers and new civilisations they were packed with drive and energy and within a relatively short period of time they took the place over.

By 541 AD the old British Kingdom of Brynaich had a new name and a new set of rulers. In the language of the invaders it was now called Bernicia and its King was an Anglo-Saxon chief called Ida the Flamebearer. Those of you who had a great aunt or even a granny called Ida might find yourself puzzled by the nickname 'Flamebearer' since your Ida was probably known as Ida the Knitter, or Ida the Sconemaker but you are going to have to get used to the oddness of Anglo-Saxon names.

Most of all it's difficult to tell them apart. Northumberland had a king called Oswald, for example, but there was another called Oswin and one called Oswui. There was an Osric, an Oswulf, an Osred and even an Osred the Second, but the Ozzies pale into insignificance by comparison to the various Aethels and friths and berts.

Aethelfrith, for example, was one of the great kings. He was grandson to Ida actually and we'll come back to him eventually, but after him there was an Aldfrith, and Egcfrith, an Eadbhert, an Aethelwold, an Aelfwold and an Aethelbert. Aethaelred, rather confusingly reigned twice with a gap of ten years in the middle and to make matters even worse, Aethelbert, despite having a 'bert' at the end of the name, was a woman (unless she was two people called Ethel and Bert). She was wife to King Edwin, whose name may have been quite ordinary but whose grandfather was called Yffi ("What's he like?" his neighbours might have asked. "Oh! He's a bit Yffi").

The important thing to remember for the time being though is that these were all Anglo-Saxons and they all ruled the Kingdom of Northumbria.

But Ida the ~~Sconemaker~~ Flamebearer was the first and he ruled from Bamburgh and whatever the stages were by which he conquered his British predecessors or persuaded them to accept him, his takeover was complete. From that moment on, the Britons seem to virtually disappear from the Northumbrian scene.

Take language for example. We speak English. All of us speak English. Even the Geordies speak English (of a sort). English is, of course the language of the English, the Anglo-Saxons. It started as Old English, turned inexorably into Middle English and finally, from about Tudor times onward became the language we speak today, but the extraordinary thing is that if you read the learned vols you will discover that it includes virtually no words at all that would have been spoken by the people who lived here before the Saxons arrived.

I exaggerate a touch. I usually do and in fact there are a few words from the Ancient Britons that are still part of our language today. I think there are about ten. Literally, I think there are only about ten Ancient British words, of which I can remember the following brief list:-

Ass, Basket, Bannock, Brock, Crag, Flannel and Gob.

It's not a lot is it? It would make a good name for a firm of solicitors, but you couldn't write a lot of poetry using only those words, they would even make a rubbish shopping list – but that's all there are – about 10 words from the Britons and all the rest, the other thousands and thousands of words in the English language came from the Anglo-Saxons.

The same is true of places. I have already pointed out that people had been living in Northumberland since the end of the last Ice Age. Over thousands of years they had turned from being hunter-gatherers into farmers and miners and craftsmen and so on; after that, for 350 years or so, they had been under the control of the Romans and for all of that time the places where they lived must have had names...

"What's the name of the place where you caught that last auroch, pet?"

"We found it over by *$£&*@#**"

...but hardly any of those names have survived because the Anglo-Saxon newcomers replaced them with new ones of their own. Think of a Northumbrian place name and I can pretty well guarantee that it will be an Anglo-Saxon name. Go on, think of a few...

Erm … Rothbury, Gosforth, Ovingham, Norham, Wallington, Ovington, Rothley, Newburn, Berwick, Blakelaw, Elsdon … how am I doing?

You're doing very nicely indeed; that is an excellent and informative list. I think you might have been doing a bit of research on your own.

As if I would.

Whatever.

The giveaways are the name endings. Ovingham is a fine example. 'Ham' is the Anglo-Saxon word for a farm or a settlement, or a home. We still use the same word today in modern English. When we talk about a hamlet we mean a little ham or settlement, and Geordies, if they are being traditional, will still say that they are 'gannin yhem' instead of 'going home'. 'Yhem' is a dialect survival from Old English, sort of halfway between 'ham' and 'home'.

The 'ing' sound in the middle of Ovingham is Anglo-Saxon too. It meant 'people' or 'folk', while the 'Ov' bit is

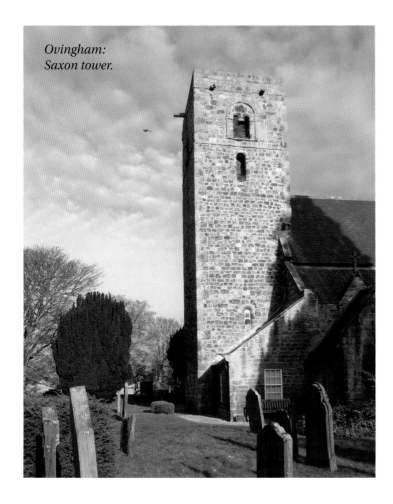

Ovingham: Saxon tower.

probably a version of somebody's name, possibly a chap called Offa so the whole name of Ovingham means the farm (or home or settlement) of Offa's people.

England has lots of 'ingham' names; Birmingham and Nottingham spring to mind; but Northumberland is absolutely littered with them and they have a rather odd little regional peculiarity. Almost all of them share a strange Northumbrian distinction of being pronounced with a 'j' sound instead of a hard 'g'. Ovingham is like this, it is pronounced as if it was spelt Ovinjum and so are Whittingham and Bellingham; Ellingham, Edlingham and Eglingham are the same. Only Chillingham is different; I think Chillingham is the only 'ingham' place in the county that is pronounced with a hard 'g', making it sound like similar places elsewhere in the country.

I don't know why this should have happened. Perhaps Northumberland was settled by Saxons with a distinct dialect or accent of their own. I suppose that's possible, but what I do know is that I was once mocked unmercifully by a presenter on Radio Two when I inadvertently pronounced Billingham in County Durham as 'Billinjum' as if it was in Northumberland … just a little bit of evidence that our county is different from anywhere else.

Northumberland also has lots of 'tons' at the end of Anglo-Saxon place names (tons of tons, I might have said) and it doesn't take a great leap of imagination to see that 'ton' is the origin of 'town' so Choppington or Cramlington and Bedlington are all towns started by the old ings or people of Bed or Cram or Chop whoever they might have been.

I'm not going to go on about this ad infinitum. You can look up your child's Key Stage Two history project to find out about this sort of stuff, but it is enough to say that virtually every place name in the county reveals the Anglo-Saxon origins of the place and of the powerful settlers who named it …

–   If the name ends with an 'ee' sound (like Rothley for example) it refers to a clearing.

–   The 'law' in Blakelaw was a hill.

–   'Don' (as in Elsdon) was the same word as 'dene' and meant valley.

–   Bamburgh's 'burgh was originally the Saxon word 'burh' and was applied to a town.

–   'Wick' was a farm etc. etc. etc.

Every one of them is Anglo-Saxon and that does beg a question. How did the Saxons come to completely obliterate the language and the history of the people who came before them? It isn't really normal for invaders to wipe the racial slate clean in this way. It wasn't even normal then. When the Germanic tribes swept down through France and Spain and Italy they didn't wipe away the language of the defeated French and Italian people who still speak the Latin language of the Romans with barely a trace of the invaders' tongue left behind. The English who invaded India created virtually no English place names, and even the European settlers in North America, who did a pretty efficient job of wiping out the native populations, still use tens of thousands of Native American place names – but the Anglo-Saxons who settled in Northumberland (and the rest of England) didn't do that. Why and how did the British populations disappear so completely? What did the Saxons do to them?

Well, the traditional picture is that they came, saw and slaughtered, massacring the native British population and driving them west towards Wales and the western half of the country. The Venerable Bede, writing a couple of hundred years later gave a ghastly and apocalyptic account of burned down buildings with the bodies of the dead lying in heaps, the survivors fleeing west and north into the wilderness or being sold into slavery. It's a picture that seems to fit pretty comfortably with the existence of the Scots who continued to speak Gaelic and by the Welsh, many of whom still speak the language of pre-Anglo-Saxon Britain, and even by the Cornish who remain so determinedly independent even today.

But it isn't a picture that quite works in other ways because there are some British place names that have survived; there might not be many but there are some. For example, virtually all our local rivers still have their British name. 'Tyne' is a British word. It's supposed to have meant 'river' in Ancient British so when the newcomers came along and asked the locals what it was called, the puzzled reply was probably, "well, we call it the river" so the invaders, the Romans and later the Saxons, did the same; they called it the River Tyne, or to put it another way, the River River.

Aln is another British river name which survived the Saxon takeover and so are the Blyth and the Allen, the Derwent and the Breamish. Kielder seems to have been British for 'violent stream'. But it isn't only river names that have survived. The villages of Cambo and Cambois are both corruptions of Ancient British names. So, you can see that there are quite a lot of surviving British place names and in some areas whole groups of them

continued to be used.

One such group is just beyond the village of Birtley in North Tynedale, which is a glorious area of wild country, remote and little visited, mainly because the roads are difficult and frequently gated. I went there recently and my trip turned out to be a 10-gate trip, many of the gates were heavy and cumbersome, requiring much lifting and manoeuvring – thank goodness I had brought my wife with me. How would I have managed otherwise?

The gates take you into a magical piece of the county. It seems almost empty apart from the sheep, but this little area is one of the places in Northumberland that is still filled with names dating from pre-Roman times, left behind in ghostly form, barely recognisable in their modern English forms. For example, the suffix "caer" meant a fort or enclosure in Celtic languages (remember Caernarvon or Caelaverock Castle near Dumfries). Well, this little area just off the A68 is covered with places that still hold a memory of that 'caer'. Camogon, Carry House, Catreen, Carrycoats are all "caer" names. Even a name as modern sounding as Garret Holt (according to the writer Godfrey Watson) comes from the Celtic Caer yt holt meaning the castle on the hill. Godfrey Watson's book on Northumbrian place names is called *Goodwife Hot*, which is the name of a hill in the same little area and one of Northumberland's more mysterious place names – but it too refers to a "holt" or hill and all of these names are British survivals, mainly associated with ancient hilltop settlements.

However, the interesting thing is that even in this unusual area, interspersed with all these ancient survivals there are plenty of Saxon names as well. Birtley is a Saxon name; the suffix 'ley' tells us that the village was created in a clearing. Another example is a farm called Buteland, a bit north of Birtley, high up on a ridge overlooking the valley of the River Rede. Buteland is surrounded by all the places with British names but it is a Saxon settlement. Its name means Botha's Land. There are plenty of other possible examples and put together they all suggest that in that area of Northumberland at least, and probably everywhere else as well if you look carefully enough, the Britons continued to live cheek, as they say, by jowl with the invading Saxons.

Apart from place names there is other evidence that suggests quite powerfully that Bede's racial cataclysm theory might have been a bit of an overstatement. Recently there has been a big movement to look at what our DNA can tell us about the past. The book I read that explores this evidence is called *Blood of the Isles* by Brian Sykes and one thing that emerges from it is that the vast majority of us, wherever we come from in the British Isles, have clear traces of our British origins in our DNA; Scots have it, Welsh people have it … but so do we who live in Northumberland, which suggests that the total destruction or dispersal of the previous population never happened and some at least, or many, or all of the Ancient Britons stayed and lived alongside and probably intermarried with the newcomers until eventually there were no Britons or Saxons at all … just English people.

However, I do recognise that none of this evidence explains what happened after the Saxons arrived or why their language became so utterly dominant … but they did come and they did take over and Ida (the Knitter) was the first Anglo-Saxon ruler of this little Anglo-Saxon land called Bernicia. A little further south, south of the River Tees and including most of the land that is now Yorkshire, was a second Anglo-Saxon kingdom called Deira, whose ruling dynasty had been established by the old Yffi one.

The descendants of these two kings, Ida and Yffi, were going to rule the North East for hundreds of years.

In many ways Anglo-Saxon rulers were pretty much what you might have expected, especially in the early days. They were rough, tough and dangerous to know – constantly fighting against the people next door, taking over neighbouring countries, desperately trying to hold onto their power in domestic conflicts, as members of their own family jostled for position. There are stories of exile and murder, attempted murder, duplicity and betrayal. Men who had failed to get the top job at home joined the King's enemies in other countries and fought against him. They were just as likely to murder their own brothers as rivals from other dynasties.

Aethelfrith, Ida's grandson, was an excellent example. He became King of Bernicia in 593 AD, almost certainly by pushing aside the family of King Hussa, who ruled before him and may well have been his brother or half brother. He set about expanding the boundaries of his new kingdom on an extraordinary and ambitious scale. The country he had taken over was still small and based largely on the coastal strip of Northumberland round its capital at Bamburgh.

Aethelfrith's new kingdom in 593, with its centre at Bamburgh, probably included the Tyne Valley and the whole of what is now County Durham, but inland and to the north was the British kingdom of Gododdin and it was the people of Gododdin that Aethelfrith seems to have tackled first. He niggled and needled them, pushing back from the coast into their territory until, in about 600 AD, they retaliated by sending a force of 300 warriors against him and the two sides fought a decisive battle at a place called Catreath (possibly Catterick in north Yorkshire) (or possibly not), which was recorded in a remarkable poem known as the Y Gododdin:

Men went to Catraeth at morn
Their high spirits shortened their life span
Red their swords
Let the blades remain uncleansed

The Gododdin army was utterly destroyed; only one warrior survived and the point of the poem is to commemorate each fallen warrior in glorious and heroic terms. Each man got a verse to himself: one of them was a warrior who was…

In might a man, a youth in years
Of bristling valour
Quicker to a field of blood than to a wedding
Quicker to the raven's feast than to a burial

Once Gododdin had become part of Bernicia, other British kingdoms further west and north became alarmed at the threat that Aethelfrith posed. The kingdom of Dal Riada included parts of Antrim in Northern Ireland as well as much of western Scotland from Strathclyde, right up north into Argyll. Its king, Aedan mac Gabrian, challenged Aethelfrith but was defeated in AD 603 so that the Angles of Bernicia had control over huge areas of Scotland. The Kingdom of Rheged, based on Carlisle, also became part of his conquests and in a pretty short period of time the whole of the west coast down as far as the Wirral.

These were all British kingdoms but then, in about 604, Aethelfrith went one step further and took over his next-door neighbour's country as well – he took control of the Anglo-Saxon Kingdom of Deira.

Deira, of course, already had a ruling dynasty of its own; it was ruled by Edwin who was not just any old king – he was also Aethelfrith's brother-in-law. Aethelfrith was married to Acha, Edwin's sister; they had eight children together but a little blood-tie like that wasn't allowed to get in the way of ambition among the kings of Anglo-Saxon England, so Edwin had to go and he was forced to flee into exile leaving Aethelfrith as the king of the combined Bernicia and Deira, a brand new kingdom, the kingdom of Northumbria, which was now extended far beyond the boundaries of our present county. It stretched south as far as the Humber and north right up to Edinburgh and the Firth of Forth. It had control over much of Scotland and at its greatest extent incorporated practically the whole of what is now Northern England.

Sometimes it was ruled by the descendants of Ida (the Flamethrower), men who came from Bernicia, from the modern county of Northumberland; at other times the power swung to the South and it was the rather more Yffi royal family of Deira which assumed control.

But initially it was Aethelfrith who held the power once he had driven Edwin into exile. He remained in control while Edwin drifted around for a while, first of all to Wales and then to Mercia in the West Midlands before finally settling as the guest of King Raedwald, the king of the East Anglians, who is famous these days as being the man whose grave contained the extraordinary Sutton Hoo treasure.

Aethelfrith wasn't satisfied by having driven Edwin out though; as all families know very well, an exiled brother-in-law is still a potential threat, so while Edwin was in the East Anglian court, Aethelfrith tried to have him killed. He promised Raedwald a reward if Edwin was poisoned, but Raedwald seemed to have had a bit of a conscience – she was called his wife actually – and she persuaded her husband that it would be just a touch dishonourable to murder his guest, so instead of murdering Edwin, Raewald attacked Aethelfrith. He seems to have caught him unprepared and, in a battle by the River Idle on the south side of the Humber, Aethelfrith was killed and the Kingdom of Northumbria passed into Edwin's hands.

Inevitably with power now in Uncle Edwin's hands, Aethelfrith's children weren't safe, so it was their turn to flee into exile. I'm not sure how many of them had survived but at least three of them went north into Dal Riada, one of those bits of Scotland that their father had conquered. The three that I know about were Oswald, who was 11 at the time, his younger brother Oswui and their sister Ebba. I say 'their sister', but she was more likely to have been their half sister because Aethelfrith, like all the kings of Anglo-Saxon England it seems, had more than one wife! I'm not talking about serial wives, one after the other; Anglo-Saxon rulers seem to have been polygamous and Aethelfrith was no different. I've already mentioned Acha, Edwin's sister; she was wife (b); wife (a) was called Bebba (Bamburgh is evidently named after her). Anyway, the three siblings and apparently both the mothers went off to Scotland where they lived for the next 18 years, sometimes in Antrim in Northern Ireland and partly on the Scottish island of Iona … of which more later.

Meanwhile Edwin ruled Northumbria and the word is that he made a pretty good shot at it. Instead of hiding himself away in a palace, remote from his subjects, he processed around his kingdom in a splendid fashion, moving from one royal centre to another, making sure that his subjects knew who he was. Sometimes he would stay for a while in York, sometimes at the great Royal fortress of Bamburgh and sometime at the Royal palace of Ad Gefrin, in Glendale, near Yeavering on the northern edge of the Cheviots.

The site of the Saxon palace at Yeavering is a lovely place. It lies in the valley of the River Glen, on a minor road that goes north-west from Wooler towards the Scottish border. It is a place of deep archaeological significance because the hills around about are crowned

with ancient hillforts and Bronze Age burial cairns. Yeavering Bell, the greatest of the Cheviot hill forts towers above it. In the valley itself, alignments of Prehistoric standing stones have been identified and at least three curious henge monuments made of spirals of banks and ditches but in about 600AD, or to put it another way, when either Aethelfrith or Edwin was king, it became a Royal palace for the Kings of Northumbria,

There's nothing visible on the ground at Gefrin nowadays. For hundreds of years the name was known only from the writings of the Venerable Bede, but nobody knew where it was or even if it had really existed. It was re-discovered by aerial photography in 1949 and since then there have been two or three extensive excavations that have revealed that it was a quite extraordinary place with a wide range of odd and remarkable timber structures dotted about over a wide area on the north bank of the river.

There was a great enclosure surrounded by a bank, a ditch and a palisade. It seems to have been a re-used survival of the Prehistoric landscape and nobody knows what it was for, though there have been suggestions.

In those day taxes were paid in form of livestock, so one idea is that it was a sort of holding pen for the cattle brought in as taxation for the king; another suggestion has been to do with mass gatherings or rituals. Nobody knows, but the existence of vast numbers of horse bones including complete skeletons that have been found around the gate into the enclosure makes it seem even more mysterious – so you can probably allow your imagination to roam free.

South of the enclosure there was a sort of timber grandstand – originally six tiers of curved benches like a segment of a circle but later doubled in size until it was evidently big enough to seat about 350 people. That was clearly and obviously a meeting place, an open-air parliament or council of some kind, though I suppose it could have doubled as a sort of theatre or concert venue (I believe the Rolling Stones were touring in those days). There was a temple, a pagan temple which was later converted into a Christian church. There were all sorts of halls and smaller houses, a kitchen and various other ancillary buildings like a weaving shed and other workshops – and there was a Great Hall.

It was a very great Great Hall, 85 feet or 26 metres long and splendid. I live in a reasonably substantial terrace house in Newcastle and I have just roughly paced out 26 metres from my front gate, through the garden and the porch, along the hall into the breakfast room and kitchen until I was stopped dead at the washing machine with still 2 metres to go. So you could imagine that the Great Hall was a big room and considerably wider than my house too with a central nave and aisles down the sides. You could hold a very impressive party in a room like that and I am sure that would have happened.

Feasting would have taken place with the king on his dais gazing down over the ranks of his thanes and royal officials. I imagine his standard bearer would have been there and the couriers who carried messages to other parts of the country. There would be reeves who controlled local estates and possibly ambassadors from other kings elsewhere in Britain. Knowing the clergy as I do, I imagine the chief priest would have sneaked in for a crafty pint, but there they would all be, chomping on cow bones and knocking back the mead in copious drafts. There would have been a fire flickering and filling the rafters with smoke as minstrels and poets sang and told tales of the great deeds of heroes and ancient times. I imagine an ancient bard reciting the story of *Beowulf* …

Beowulf takes place in southern Scandinavia. Hrothgar, king of the Danes, has built a great hall called Heorot which is troubled … that is not a strong enough word … it is terrorised by a monster called Grendel, which bursts down the doors of the hall when the thanes are all sleeping off their mead and drags his victims off into the howling darkness to devour them. This was clearly a bad thing; it would be a nasty end to any party, but fortunately Beowulf, a young hero of the neighbouring Geats, saves the day. He feigns sleep and lies in wait for the monster, which duly arrives and reaches out for his prey, but Beowulf seizes Grendel's arm and in the fight that follows, wrenches it off at the shoulder. The monster rushes off howling and dying into the surrounding fens. You would think that this might be the end but no, Grendel's mother (because even monsters have mothers) is understandably miffed and seeks revenge until Beowulf dispatches her too and Heorot, the great hall is made safe against the forces of darkness that surround it.

Such stories would have had a resonance in a hall like the one at Ad Gefrin because there was a literal darkness and dangerous fens outside and they were living in unsettling and politically unstable times. Edwin's Hall was burnt down twice by his enemies and once, during a feast, an assassin burst into the hall like Grendel and launched himself at the king, who was only saved by the bravery of his personal guards.

Despite the dangers, the country Edwin ruled had a reputation for being stable and well ordered, relatively free, I believe, of man-eating monsters. The Venerable Bede gave a nice bit of evidence that this was the case. Apparently on the king's orders they hung up brass bowls beside wells and springs so that travellers could always get a drink if they needed one – and do you know what? Nobody pinched them! You gasp. It's like when people stare in amazement if they discover a community where the telephone boxes still work or the public toilets are fit for human use. It's one of those short-hand signs that there's still a bit of civilisation and decency to be found.

Bede had another example. He said that in those days a woman could carry her child from one side of the country to another without fear of harm. Those were both lovely examples, of course, but from Bede's point of view the best thing of all about Edwin is that he became a Christian and introduced the religion to Northumbria. It happened like this:

Edwin's wife, Aethelbert (or Ethel and Bert as she has become in my mind) was already a Christian when they married. She was the daughter of the King of Kent, a kingdom that had already been converted to Christianity by missionaries from Rome led by St Augustine and sent by Pope Gregory the Great. You may well have heard the story of how Gregory was in a slave market in Rome when he came across some blonde-haired and blue-eyed children from northern England waiting to be sold. He asked who they were and was told that they were Angles from Britain.

"Angels not Angles" he is reputed to have quipped wittily (of course he said it in Latin so it is usually quoted as being "Non Angli sed Angeli" but the words actually given to him by Bede, who was the source of the story, were quite specifically pro-English and quite possibly the first (and only) time an Italian has said anything really nice about anybody from the North of England. He said, "… they have the faces of angels and such should be the co-heirs of the angels in heaven" and he sent his missionaries to Kent to start the conversion of Britain.

So, when Edwin married Aethelbert he was a pagan and she was a Christian but she made it a condition of the marriage that she would have the freedom to follow the religion of her conscience and she arrived in York with her own priest, an Italian bishop called Paulinus who had been part of St Augustine's group of missionaries. Between them they must have been pretty persuasive because before long Edwin and all his court had been converted, including, incidentally, the chief priest of the pagan religion that had held sway until that moment; the priest marked his conversion in a very dramatic way; he denounced his gods, grabbed a weapon, got on a horse, rode into his temple, destroyed all the existing idols and burnt the place down! Extreme you might think; but he wasn't alone. Edwin built a wooden church in York and on Easter day AD627 the King, with all of his thanes and things, were baptised into the new religion.

Whether they were all convinced followers or merely saw it as a sensible action to follow their king, well … you'd have to go and ask them, but it was the start of Christianity in the North and it didn't end there. Paulinus went on to convert people all over Northumbria including our bit. Legend suggests that he had a 36-day baptism-fest at Ad Gefrin where hundreds, or possibly thousands, or at least some people were baptized in the River Glen, which runs along the northern edge of the palace complex.

With all of these nice things going on, I'm sure you can understand why Bede felt that Edwin's reign and the reigns of the other early kings of Northumbria were a sort of Golden Age of peace and prosperity.

Well … yes! Up to a point. There may well have been prosperity of a sort but peace was in shorter supply. The problem was that there was always some aggressive whippersnapper nipping at the heels of a successful leader. Like young guns in Hollywood Westerns, desperate to replace John Wayne at the top of the gunslinger's ladder, Anglo-Saxon England was full of ambitious rulers trying to expand their kingdoms.

Edwin was ultimately destroyed by two of them. Penda, king of Mercia, the Anglo-Saxon kingdom in the Midlands was one; his chum (his pardner, John Wayne would have said) his co-aggressor Cadwallon, the British king of Gwynedd in Wales, was the other. They were nothing if not persistent. They attacked Northumbria at least twice, each time burning down Edwin's Great Hall at Gefrin, and they eventually won. They brought Edwin's pretty successful reign to an end at the Battle of Hatfield in 633AD when Edwin was killed and Cadwallon

The replica of the wooden cross Oswald erected at Heavenfield.

took over the throne of Northumbria.

This was a bad moment for Edwin of course but rather a good moment in the history of our county of Northumberland because it was the cue for the Royal dynasty of Bernicia to make a comeback. Aethelfrith's son, Oswald, now 29 years old, re-emerged out of exile, leading a borrowed Scottish army. He challenged Cadwallon and Penda to a shootout at the OK Corral, or Heavenfield, to put it more accurately.

The Battle of Heavenfield in 634AD was one of the defining moments in the History of Northumberland. It was also one of the great set pieces of early Anglo-Saxon political and religious theatre, but you need a bit of background to see what makes it stand out among all the myriad other nasty little battles that kings insisted on in those days.

First of all it happened in a wonderful place. Heavenfield is on the Roman Wall, high above the crossing over the North Tyne at Chollerford. A church dedicated to Oswald marks the highest point of the battlefield and the view from it is glorious, wide and wild, isolated, with tremendous views west along the line of the Wall and north into the hilly heart of the county. When the battle was fought the wall itself must still have stood to its full 20 feet and the vallum dropped to its full depth of 12 feet, together forming an impressive and impenetrable backdrop to the fighting.

Secondly it had a great name. The place where it happened was actually called Hefenfelth in those days, which is translated as 'Heavenfield' nowadays and that makes it sound more like a religious experience than a battle. You see Oswald was a Christian; he had been converted when he was living at a monastery founded by the Great Irish monk St Columba on the island of Iona off the Scottish coast; the army that faced him was largely a pagan army. Actually Cadwallon himself was a Christian but Penda was aggressively pagan and Oswald

SAINT OSWALD

used that fact to his advantage. He presented the battle as a fight for the soul of Northumbria rather than just the crown. Bede describes how the night before the battle he prayed and had a vision of St Columba who told him not to hang about because victory was certain; God was on their side. To reinforce the message, Oswald erected a high wooden cross (a replica stands there still) and told his men the whole story, promising them conversion if they won the battle – and of course they did. The forces of Penda and Cadwallon were scattered and Oswald took control of the country that had belonged to his father.

He ruled from Bamburgh.

Nowadays Bamburgh Castle is one of the most dramatic and glorious settings in Northumberland. I think it has been statistically proven to cause more people to gasp and say "Ooooo!" when they first see it than any other building. The reason for its drama is, of course, the rock it stands on, a proud and glorious outcrop that had attracted people from Prehistoric times onward. The Romans had at least a signal station there and the British kingdom of Brynaich made it their capital before the Anglo-Saxons took over and turned it into their fortress/palace in the 6th century and for several centuries it became the home and the capital of a great sequence of Saxon kings who presided over what is often described as The Golden Age of Northumbria.

Since those days it has seen continuous development and use. It became a major castle in Norman times and was altered and added to throughout the Middle Ages. It had an extraordinary period of charitable use in the 1700s under the control of the trust set up by Nathaniel Crewe, the Bishop of Durham and in late Victorian times it became a home of Lord Armstrong, the builder of Cragside whose family own it still. All of these stages in its history are likely to be

Pictured: A very Victorian St Oswald as 'soldier' saint in Rothbury Church.

enough to ensure that the building will reappear from time to time later in this book, but such a history, such a wealth of past, such long continuous use means that the castle we know today is rich in buried secrets that are still and continuously being uncovered.

For several decades now, the Bamburgh Research Project has been exploring the Anglo-Saxon history of the site, which seemed to have completely disappeared, and what is beginning to emerge is a great and complex place. Some of what is emerging is typical of the palace it was – a gatehouse and a church, great timber halls like the one at Ad Gefrin have been identified; but there were also more humble building like workshops, probably workshops for metalworker since lots of elaborate metal objects keep emerging from the soil. There have been bronze belt buckles and mysterious bronze beasts. There has been an elaborate, possibly uniquely elaborate, sword and hoards of coins.

The scene that is emerging is that the settlement was more than a palace but a town as well and recently, from 2016 onwards they have been excavating a great Saxon cemetery in the dunes just outside the later walls of the castle and found hundreds of bodies – evidence of the scale of the population. Detailed analysis of the bones has revealed that some of the graves contained locals, born and bred in Northumberland, but many came from elsewhere – from all over the British Isles, Northern Europe, the Mediterranean and even North Africa. It's becoming clear that this extraordinary place was not just the small local capital of a minor provincial leader but the centre of an international network of trade and communication and the reason for that, the thing that gave Anglo-Saxon Northumberland its extraordinary reach and power wasn't politics and war … it was religion.

––––––––––––––

You will recall that a form of Christianity existed in Roman times and that Edwin and Paulinus had already re-introduced the religion into Northumbria eight or nine years previously; well, after the Battle of Heavenfield and when he became King, Oswald was to do it all over again except that his version of the religion was different from the Roman version that had been brought by Paulinus and Edwin. Oswald had learnt his Christianity on Iona, at the monastery that had been founded by St Columba.

I'm not sure that there were massive differences between what the Roman church believed and the Irish church. The obvious differences seem like rather superficial things. They calculated the date of Easter differently, for example, and they had a different style of tonsure. The Roman priests shaved that circular bit on the top of their head that we still know so well today but the Irish monks shaved the whole front of their heads to about half way back, as if they had massive foreheads, sort of like an exaggerated Shakespeare haircut.

These were small enough differences (though you've just got to think about punks and heavy-metal fans to realise that people can get pretty worked up about haircuts) but the really big difference was political; it was to do with the way the church was organised. The Roman church was (and still is) centrally organised with a hierarchy of priests from parish priests to bishops to the Pope. Just like today the religious landscape was divided up into parishes and the rules about what you had to believe were passed down the chain of command from top to bottom.

The Irish church wasn't like that.

The Irish church had totally independent monasteries which could be founded by anybody who had the urge, the influence and the money. Usually the money and the land came from a King or a member of the ruling family because they were the only people with enough spare cash to make it happen. Each monastery was ruled by its Abbott or Abbess who tended to be members of the ruling families too.

In these monasteries the monks and nuns lived the lives you would expect (and hope for) – lots of worship, prayer and quiet contemplation, they lived very simple, holy, pared-down lives, without treats or material comforts; the Irish church encouraged a very ascetic sort of life but, perhaps because the monasteries were often in remote places and they thought it was the right thing to do, they did practical things too; they made their own stuff, their food and clothes, the vestments and chalices and things for the services; they made the books they needed. In the context of what was going to happen in Northumbria it's important to realise that they weren't just self-sufficient, they were skilled craftsmen and highly creative too.

So, when Oswald became king he decided to fund a monastery and sent a request up to Iona for a suitable person who would and help him do it. That's what happened – up to a point. Oswald provided the Island of Lindisfarne or Holy Island as a suitable base for the new venture and Iona sent a monk.

Sadly the first monk they sent was a plank. He was called Corman and he seems to have been a deeply unsympathetic character – the sort of Christian who would never have made sainthood. He was unapproachable and grumpy. He hated the Northumbrians and thought them rude and uncivilised so Oswald booted him out and asked for somebody else and he got Aidan instead. Lovely old Aidan, who turned out to be one of the good-egg monks; if Corman had been made of screechy-scratchy chalk, Aidan was made of finest mature farmhouse cheddar

Aidan did all the things he was supposed to do in order to be good at his job. He founded the monastery on Lindisfarne, about which there will be much more in a minute, and he set about converting the people of Northumberland to Christianity – that's what he was here for of course but he did it well. He reached the people, to misquote the old advertising slogan, that other missionaries didn't reach. Paulinus, you will recall, came a-missionarying in the north but seems to have restricted his activities to converting the people he found in Edwin's royal enclave at Ad Gefrin. 'A posh priest for posh people' might have been his motto, but Aidan was also deeply concerned about the ordinary people. He spent his time, 16 years of it, wandering about the countryside talking to people and preaching to them wherever he went. He always walked so that he could meet people on their own level. He's my favourite

saint actually because he seems curiously modern. When you see pictures of him in stained glass windows or statues, he looks like your typical monk – serene and holy – but he had more to him than that. For a start he must have been tough – all of that walking! He must have had muscles like a body builder and there are other ways he wasn't just your conventional holy man.

The thing is that he wasn't just concerned with people's souls but with their welfare too. He was interested in their souls, of course, and wanted to bring them to his new religion, but he was concerned about bodies as well. He was a charitable man; if somebody gave him a donation he passed it over to help the poor and he wasn't shy about telling his king that he needed to do the same.

On one notable occasion Oswald was celebrating Easter in his great hall when Aidan reminded him of the poor beyond his doors. The king's conscience was stirred but he had no coins to give to the people so he took the silver platter on which the meat had been served, cut it into little pieces and gave those to the poor instead. The story's not entirely simple because it's not quite clear what they would do with them. I've noticed that my local supermarket is reluctant to accept any lumps of silver that I have proffered in payment for my teabags and I imagine it was the same in those days but it was a nice gesture.

On another occasion the king, not Oswald this time but his successor Oswin, gave Aidan a horse, a nice royal horse with splendid royal bits and pieces of horsey accoutrements; Aidan immediately gave the whole lot to a beggar who happened to be outside the door and the king was understandably miffed that his gift had been treated so casually. Aidan wasn't at all fazed though because as well as being a nice cheese he was also a good egg and a tough cookie so he looked the king in the eye and asked him if he genuinely thought the horse was worth as much as a human being. Oswin was mortified and apparently threw himself at Aidan's feet, begging his forgiveness. Characters in stories are always throwing themselves at people's feet and I have always wanted to see it happen. I think it would be a hoot.

When Aidan first came he couldn't speak

Northumbrian. It's a problem visitors have been having in the North East ever since of course (the American travel writer, Paul Theroux, wrote that the accent of people on Holy Island was incomprehensible to him, '… *a mixture of Scottish and Geordie with a kind of Gaelic gargle*', but it was a real problem for Aidan because he was trying to preach to people. One of my cousins had a similar problem when he was a missionary in India. He was in an area where the accent was difficult and there were lots of different ways of pronouncing the same letter. In his case I believe he had difficulty with the letter D and was disconcerted to see how puzzled his congregation looked when

Lindisfarne Church and St Aidan's statue.

he urged them to believe in the Lord. It turned out he was telling them to believe in the donkey and they were surprised. Well with Aidan the problem was overcome by King Oswald. In his early travels the king came with him and acted as his translator. Isn't that nice? No wonder Oswald ended up as a saint as well.

As you all doubtless know, the land that Oswald gave Aidan as a base for his new monastery was the island of Lindisfarne (or Holy Island which is its other name) a few miles up the coast from his royal stronghold at Bamburgh. Lindisfarne used to be a full-blown island. I have a book, published as recently as 1964, which tells me that Holy Island '*can be reached at low tide from Beal following a track marked by tall wooden posts*'. My wife, who spent all her childhood holidays at Bamburgh, recalls that her family used to leave the car on the mainland and transfer to the island in an ancient taxi that had been running across the salty sands for so long that as it splashed through the shallows, water spurted up through holes in the floor and soaked their legs.

Nowadays, of course, there is a road, a causeway that emerges from the sea twice a day allowing anybody to drive across, but the event is still invariably thrilling. The thrill is partly caused by the sky which, I suppose, is technically no bigger than any other sky but looks it

because it mingles with the vastness of the sands and the sea to create a great bowl of light.

Partly the excitement is caused by the closeness of the sea which has either just gone out, allowing you to drive on the salty road through a watery landscape of little pools, mollusc-encrusted stones, seaweed and seabirds, or is about to just come in again providing most drivers with that little niggling worry about how fast the tide can travel.

The answer, of course, is very fast; it races around both sides of the island, approaching the road in a sort of pincer movement that manages to catch out the unwary traveller time after time. The mean spirited among us (among whom I include myself) have been known to park at the end of the causeway as the tide approaches and watch tense-eyed drivers, tempting fate and gripping the wheel, ignoring the imploring faces of their passengers, charging through the encroaching waters as they lap at the edges of the road. I've never actually seen anyone fail to win the race but people do, including (I recall with a sort of dark fatalistic pleasure) a couple of policemen a few years ago who had to make for the safety of the little wooden refuge tower half way across.

But the crossing is also thrilling because these are the sands, the very sands that St Aidan walked across in 635 AD on his way from Iona to found the monastery that was to become one of the holiest places in Britain.

What Aidan built, what form his original monastery took back then in 635AD, is still a bit of a mystery because it lies beneath the soil and beneath a thousand years of later development, and vast amounts of archaeological effort over the years still haven't provided many clues. There are assumptions based on what has been observed elsewhere in other monasteries from those days that suggest that the monks lived in little individual round huts and that the site would have been enclosed within a protective bank. It seems to have been normal, or at least common, for there to be two or more churches rather than just one and The Venerable Bede, writing about half a century later says that the churches here were built in 'the Scottish style', by which he seems to mean that they were made of timber and roofed with some sort of thatch, as against 'the Roman Style' of stone churches that had been used in his own monastery at Jarrow on the River Tyne.

None of these things have been found with any certainty yet and to be honest it isn't even clear exactly where the original monastery was. People used to assume that it lay under the parish church and the ruins of the later mediaeval monastery, which seemed logical because the site has at least one very attractive characteristic – it lies nestled and sheltered from the sea and the worst impact of the easterly winds by a high, rocky, volcanic outcrop called The Heugh (a word that is difficult to pronounce convincingly without sounding as if you have a nasty chest cold). You can imagine the monks living there just like all subsequent occupants of this fairly inhospitable island have chosen to do.

However, there is a problem with that assumption

St Cuthbert's Island at sunset.

because those early Northumbrian Christians don't seem to have been very good at nestling in comfortable places. They regularly seem to have chosen places which exposed them to as much weather as possible. All along the North-East coast they built on headlands – at Beadnell, for example and Tynemouth, Hartlepool and Whitby. All places with 7th century monasteries and all the windiest places you could imagine. At Hartlepool, for example, there's another headland called The Heugh and I was there one winter day when there had been a report that a rare Arctic bird had been sighted, blasted off course by the bitter North winds. The headland was lined with passionate bird watchers who could barely stand up straight in the wind and who, to a man and woman, were very cold but very happy.

Anglo-Saxon monks were rather like ancient twitchers, happily suffering for their beliefs so people have long wondered whether the original monastery at Lindisfarne could have been on top of the Heugh instead of sheltering behind it and recently, in 2017, a series of community excavations have uncovered possible evidence that it might have been.

Cuthbert carrying the head of St Oswald.

They uncovered the foundations and floor of a church on top of the Heugh. It is definitely a church. I don't think anybody doubts that, but the big question is when it was built. It looks rough and very early. Could it be the original church of 635AD or just after? We know that by the end of the 600s much posher churches had been built (at Hexham, Jarrow and Monkwearmouth, for example) and it seems very unlikely that they would have still been building a rough, primitive church on Lindisfarne at a later date so I bet that it is the original church or at least a very early one. From it you can see Bamburgh, the fortress of King Oswald and you can see the Farne Islands, which were to play a huge part in the life of the next great saint associated with Holy Island.

His name was Cuthbert.

Cuthbert was a member of a noble Northumbrian family who became a monk after he saw St Aidan's body being carried up to heaven by bands of angels on the very night of his death in 651AD. That's what the story says and who am I to doubt the veracity of his vision, given that I was a boy who, on Christmas Eve 1951, saw Santa Claus in his sleigh, flying through the sky above Kirby Lonsdale?

After his vision, Cuthbert went first to the Abbey at Melrose, where he got a terrific reputation for effective holiness, before being persuaded by his Abbot to go and help out at Lindisfarne, where he did similar stuff to his hero Aidan. Bede tells how he, too, wandered around the countryside, sometimes on horseback, though mainly on foot, preaching to and converting the ordinary people and pulling them back into the fold when they started backsliding. Sometimes he was specifically sent for when there was felt to be a need and one such occasion gave Bede a chance to tell a terrific story about him.

He had been summoned by the Abbess Ebba, who was sister to two kings, Oswald and Oswui, and had spent those 18 years in exile with them in Scotland. She had gone on to found a monastery at Coldingham, on the coast of what was then part of Northumbria but is now across the border in Berwickshire, and Cuthbert went there to do some teaching.

This is (a translation of) Bede's account of what happened:

'In his customary fashion he went out alone at night to pray while the others were at rest, and after keeping long vigil through the dead of night, he would at last return home at the very hour when they said the office together. One night one of the brothers of the monastery saw him going silently out and secretly followed in his footsteps seeking to discover where he was going and what his purpose was. Leaving the monastery with the spy following, Cuthbert went down to the sea shore beneath the monastery; and going deep into the water until the swelling waves rose up to his neck and arms, he spent the dark of the night watching and singing praises accompanied by the sound of the waves ...'

I would like to point out that it was the North Sea he was doing this in, not, say, the Caribbean or the Indian Ocean or some hot tub on a middle-class patio deck. I assume that what he was doing was deliberately mortifying his flesh, preventing himself from having

naughty thoughts and it would have to be said that he couldn't have come up with a more effective way of doing it. There are few things better at mortifying the flesh than dipping it into the North Sea. I have dipped myself into the North Sea and parts of me were rendered useless and ineffective for some time afterwards.

... when dawn approached he went on to the land and again began to pray, kneeling on the shore. As he did so, there came out from the depth of the sea two four-footed creatures which are commonly called otters. Stretching themselves out in front of him on the sand, they began to warm his feet with their breath and sought to dry him on their fur …

I'm not absolutely certain that that is legal nowadays but it is a lovely thought none the less. Nowadays the go-to Saint for communication with animals is usually St Francis of Assisi but it is nice that our own home-grown product has the same qualities. Those qualities are shown particularly when, a little later in his story, he retired from Lindisfarne to become a hermit on the island of Inner Farne, a few miles off the coast at Bamburgh. The island is an internationally important bird sanctuary nowadays and it must have been just the same then and Cuthbert's story has a couple of birdy incidents which show him in a nice light.

There are the ducks first of all. The Farnes are a major breeding ground for eider ducks and though Cuthbert was prepared to cut himself off pretty firmly from other human beings, he always seems to have had time for the eiders. He even allowed them to nest under his bed and locals have called eider ducks 'Cuddy's ducks' ever since.

And then there were the crows. Living alone he had needed a source of food and, after a difficult failure with his wheat crop, he had planted a little field of barley which the crows, being crows, took to eating. Cuthbert called them together to have a meeting and said (more or less) "Look lads, I don't have a lot of barley and I just wondered if you could see your way to finding your food

Farnes favourites, left, the puffin and eider duck.

by MiE Fielding.

somewhere else." The crows looked at each other and said (in crowish) "That's fine, sir, we'll be off and leave you to your barley", and presumably they went off to the mainland and pinched somebody else's cereal.

Nice stories of course, but do they tell the whole truth? Is there something else to uncover? To his contemporaries the big question about Cuthbert on the Farnes was how he coped with the Devil. It was a bleak and dangerous place and well known as the haunt of evil spirits, but as the Venerable Bede describes in his *Life of Cuthbert*, our saint had no bother at all … *No one before the lord's servant had been able to live alone on this island without trouble, as it was haunted by evil spirits; but when the soldier of Christ entered there … the wicked foe himself … was driven far away …*

Nowadays, of course, we know it's all very well to be able to deal with the Devil but how did he cope with the Arctic Terns? The historical record keeps quiet on that, but no-one who has visited Inner Farne in June can ignore it. I went this year along with all my family and it was an extraordinary and wonderful experience. The surface of the sea around the island was alive with birds. Puffins to the right of us, razorbills to the left; seals rolled in the gentle waves and lounged on the shore. It was like being present at the beginning of the world. But being ashore, while no less extraordinary and no less wonderful, was a different experience because of the arctic terns which dived and pecked in defence of their eggs. Blood was drawn from several Grundy foreheads and at least one Grundy finger – and we were wearing full suits of armour. I exaggerate – but not much and I did think that if Cuthbert was able to cope with the terns (and it must have been the same when he was there) he really must have been a saint.

You will have realised that Cuthbert was quite an odd character to modern eyes and the house that he built for himself on Inner Farne was another example of the difference. It was a sort of compound, or, as Bede puts it … "a structure almost circular in plan, measuring about four of five poles from wall to wall."

A pole, you might recall from the maths books of your youth, was (like a rod or a perch) a length of about sixteen and a half feet; so Cuthbert lived in a compound roughly 70 feet across. From the outside the wall that surrounded it was a bit higher than a man standing upright, ' … *but on the inside* (wrote Bede) *he made it much higher by cutting away the rocky ground, so that he could see nothing but the sky from his dwelling, to protect his holy life against tempting sights or thoughts and raise the whole tenor of his mind above earthly desires*".

To make the story even more extraordinary, the walls of his compound were constructed using supernatural help. Some of the stones that he used '*were so large that it hardly seemed possible that four men could have lifted them, yet with the help of angels he was found to have brought them there from elsewhere and put them on the wall*'.

Cuthbert lived on Inner Farne for two separate periods of his life, punctuated by spells when he was persuaded by the powers-that-be to come back to the mainland and lead the monastery and play an active part in the management and political life of the Northumbrian church, but his last two years were spent on the island. He died there in 687AD and his death was signalled by the smoke from a beacon that would have been visible from our newly discovered church on The Heugh. His body was brought back to Lindisfarne to be buried inside the church, where it lay for eleven years before it was dug back up again.

It always puzzled me that the monks should have done this. It seems an odd thing to do but it turns outs to be susceptible of a ready explanation. Knowing what a good man he had been and aware of the sorts of miraculous events that had happened to him, his colleagues realised that he was a saint and dug him back up so they could re-inter his body in a suitably decorated shrine alongside the altar in the church where pilgrims could come (with their offerings) and pray to him.

Imagine the monks' surprise when they discovered that this body, which had lain in the ground for 11 years, was not a mere skeleton or some ghastly cadaver. Instead (to quote the Venerable Bede yet again) '*when they opened the tomb they found the body whole and intact as if still alive*'. His joints were still flexible and the clothes he'd been buried in were '*not merely unsullied but marvellously bright and fresh as when they were new*'.

To our suspicious modern eyes these things seem awfully odd, but Bede wrote about them just a few years after the events had taken place and, like all proper historians, he had good sources. He interviewed people who had actually been there at the time and there's no reason to suspect that they weren't good men, recalling what they had actually seen or thought they'd seen; but whether it all happened exactly as described, or whether they were all deceived, or cynical, or wishful thinkers, the end result was that the community now had their resident saint, safely installed in his shrine and a hugely significant centre of pilgrimage and veneration over the next couple of centuries.

I don't think we know what the shrine itself actually looked like, but we do know lots about what it contained and the artefacts with which it was associated. We know about these things because lots of them have survived and are now among the treasures at Durham Cathedral where, as we will see, the saints' body finally settled in later centuries. His coffin has survived: it is made of wood carved with inscribed figures of the Apostles and Archangels and it is the oldest substantial piece of decorated woodwork from that period in the whole of Europe; the exquisite gold cross that he wore upon his chest is now unique. There's an ivory comb and a portable altar which are also the only surviving examples of their types and his copy of the *Gospel of St John* is the oldest book in Europe to have survived in its original binding. These are fantastic things and all the more astonishing when you realise how far the materials that went into them had travelled. We used to think of Anglo-Saxon times as "The Dark Ages" but a brief look at Cuthbert's possessions disproves that title straight away.

They lived in a connected world, perhaps not quite like we do now, but pretty damn impressive. His comb is made of ivory from an African elephant. His cross contains lapis lazuli from Afghanistan and garnets from the Indian Ocean, while the most impressive of the treasures takes its inspiration from virtually the whole of the known world.

I'm talking about the *Lindisfarne Gospels*, which now live in London, in the British Library where they are regarded as one of the greatest treasures of British art. Here is a little flavour of what the British Library says about them: '... *the book is a magnificent work of art, its pages adorned with breathtaking illumination and elegant calligraphy.*'

The British Library's little guide to the Gospels goes on to emphasise the Gospels' particular glories. The writer even does something you don't see very often. He uses the word "breathtaking" twice on the same page. That's pretty impressive. Even I, a noted exaggerator, try not to do that, but the British Library is adamant – '*The illuminations*', they say, '*are of breathtaking artistry*' and page after page displays an '*exuberant riot of ornament*'. To a humble little Northerner, this level of praise for a northern product is almost overwhelming. We are used to being ignored or patronised, or even downright savaged for our cultural attempts. Remember the late art critic Brian Sewell responding to an exhibition at the Baltic Art Centre on Tyneside by saying "Gateshead is an awful place. Most of the north is awful. Bomb it and then you'll improve it".

Needless to say the *Lindisfarne Gospels* don't get this treatment because everybody accepts that it is a work of superlative quality and one of the most complex works of art ever created, but amazingly it seems to have been the work of just one man, Bishop Eadfrith, who was the leader of the Lindisfarne Community from 698 to 721AD. If he was entirely responsible, he must have been a man of extraordinary powers and ingenuity because the British Library points out that, as well as writing and decorating the book, he seems to have invented the lead pencil and the light box.

He was a brilliant chemist too and found ways of re-creating all of the colours of the Mediterranean world using things that he could get locally. His green paint came from copper, yellow from arsenic; toasted lead gave him reds and oranges, local plants provided all the blues he needed, crushed shells made white paint and carbon from charred wood made black. There are, apparently 90 different colours used in the book and Eadfrith created all of those using only 6 locally available minerals and plant extracts. He had to make his own pens and brushes too, but the pages of his book (there were 259 of them) were made elsewhere on the monastery. A farm has been excavated with thousands of calf bones buried round about it (I'm talking the bones of young cows incidentally not leg bones) and 150 of those calves would have had to die to create this one book.

The Gospels are not just an example of technical mastery though. In a quite extraordinary way Eadfrith brings together artistic elements from all over the known world, mixes them up and creates something quite new – turns them, in fact, into something that, until then, had never existed – a new and recognisably English form of art. He has included designs, such as classical columns, from Ancient Rome and mingled them with wonderful swirling, abstract Celtic designs from Scotland and Ireland. He has used Norse elements from Scandinavia. There are things from southern Italy – beautiful vine scrolls for example and sometimes his people seem Italian too – splendidly drawn naturalistic figures that look like the great mosaics in Ravenna, but sometimes (as the British Library's book puts it) '*the evangelists are depicted as exotic mystical icons, redolent of the art of the eastern Mediterranean.*'

The decorations of the pages are typical but perfect examples of Anglo-Saxon art, stuffed with interlaced patterns, every inch inhabited by wild beasts and dragons. Some of the pages are pure decoration. They are known as "carpet pages" and they do look rather like oriental carpets or possibly prayer mats, dense and wonderfully symmetrical abstract patterns.

Pages from the Lindisfarne Gospels. Left: Decorated initial page at the beginning of the Gospel according to Saint Matthew. Right: Image of Evangelist Saint John, accompanied by his symbol - an eagle carrying a book.

By the time that Cuthbert died and before the *Lindisfarne Gospels* were created, the Celtic church brought to Northumberland by Oswald and Aidan had long gone. In 664 at the Synod of Whitby, after less than 30 years of existence, the Celtic church was driven out and Northumbria became part of the Roman Catholic Church, but despite this, the strange, rather mystical Celtic influence hung on in places like Lindisfarne. It's quite odd because in some ways it is quite an ordinary place. It can be filled with tourists; people often arrive in vast droves and what they are expecting is a sort of holy Celtic theme park, but the landscape is quite flat and the village nice but often overcrowded. I have played my part in this. I did some tour guiding once and on one occasion the bus I was on was the 56th to arrive on the island that day ….

… and yet there is still something special, an atmosphere that clings to the place. I remember a former vicar of the parish church saying to me, "In a place where a saint has trod, the gap between heaven and earth is narrower." I'm not personally a great believer in heavens but whenever I go there, I can sense what he meant. Perhaps it's the light, perhaps it's the knowledge of what has happened there, but it is very, very easy to forget about the 21st century crowds and recapture a gentler and more spiritual mood … the mood of the Celtic Christianity that gave birth to the Lindisfarne Gospels.

The Lindisfarne Gospels and the relics of St Cuthbert are definitely the high point of the flowering of Anglo-Saxon art and creativity in Northumberland, but they certainly don't stand alone because the county is extraordinarily rich in stuff from that period.

It is mainly churches of course. Apart from Ad Gefrin and Bamburgh and all the tens of thousands of Anglo-Saxon place names and apart from a few pieces of bronze and iron in the museums, belt buckles, strap ends and the like – apart from these the visible remains are all to do with churches and there are lots of them.

Bolam, a few miles north of Belsay, has a beautiful Saxon tower that escaped being blown up in the Second World War when a German bomber heading back home released his remaining bombs, one of which bounced through a window of the nave but failed to explode.

In 1845 the Reverend Goodenough, the vicar of Whittingham near Alnwick, thought that his splendid Saxon tower wasn't – wasn't good enough I mean – so he stuffed it full of dynamite, blew the top off it and was about to finish the job when his villagers stepped in and said, in a remarkably early example of community heritage activism, "enough is enough, Goodenough."

Elsewhere, the Tyne Valley has one of the densest collections of Saxon churches in the country. Corbridge, Ovingham, Heddon-on-the-Wall, Bywell and Warden all have impressive Saxon remains in their walls, in fact at Bywell there are two Saxon churches; St Andrew has a gorgeous Anglo-Saxon tower (with reused Roman toilet seats for its bell openings) while St Peter is bigger and must have been grander – it has Saxon windows high up on the wall of the nave. At Corbridge the arch into the Anglo-Saxon tower is a complete, reused Roman arch. Warden has another Saxon tower and might possibly be on the site of an early church where St John of Beverley used to sneak off from being Bishop of Hexham to catch a bit of private meditation time.

But Hexham was the pick of the bunch. Hexham Abbey was founded and built by St Wilfrid, another of the great founding saints of the Northumbrian church. He was a very different creature from the saints we've been talking about so far. He was posh. He was a member of the aristocracy and his behaviour seemed very different from the sort of Christianity followed by Aidan and Cuthbert. He wore posh clothes (though apparently he always wore rough hairy underwear underneath to keep himself focused on the job) and wherever he went he travelled with a great train of supporters or servants or something behind him.

On one occasion he was down on the south coast and was attacked by a band of pagans but he just happened to have 160 armed followers with him and they drove the attackers off; it's the only way to travel. Wilfrid was closely involved with the various royal families of the time and not always in the most comfortable of ways. King Oswui put him in prison at least twice for example; he encouraged King Egcfrith's first wife to follow her religious instincts and refuse to consummate her marriage for 12 years; the king, as you can imagine, was not best pleased.

But for all his strange foibles he had great qualities too. He was the first Englishman to go on a pilgrimage to Rome, in fact he went several times without benefit of Eurostar or EasyJet. He was the first Englishman to go to the continent as a missionary and he was the man who converted the South Saxons to Christianity. He introduced the Rule of St Benedict to England. He persuaded the Northumbrians to abandon their allegiance to the Irish church and join the Church of Rome itself … and he built a church at Hexham.

It's not a bad list and, to be fair, he must have had a good relationship with at least some members of the royal family because in 671 or 672 AD the site for his church at Hexham was given to him as a present by the Northumbrian Queen, Aethethryth. As far as I know there was nothing already on the land that she gave him and nobody else ever seems to have lived there. She gave it to him so that he could build a monastery.

It was a good site. In fact if you were to take modern-day Hexham away entirely so that you were left just with the landscape that Wilfrid was given, you would realise what a spiffing setting it must have seemed to him and his original builders. The queen had provided them with a broad, flat platform of land, nicely safe and high above the flood plain of the River Tyne. The valley below them was broad and fertile. There were ancient

Roman roads still utterly usable nearby and at Corstopitum (or Corbridge), a couple of easy miles downstream, there was an abandoned Roman town from which they could snaffle ready-cut blocks of stone to build their church.

Wilfrid used the gift well. He went on to build a church that was described as the finest church in Europe north of the Alps and among the things that he put into it was the knee bone of the apostle Andrew, which he'd acquired on one of his many trips to Rome. He displayed the holy relic brilliantly, with a real eye for the dramatic. In a crypt beneath his church, a dark and mysterious space with a small maze of corridors to resemble the Roman Catacombs from which the bone had come, he placed the Apostle's knee bone on an altar lit by flickering lamps in little niches. The stone came from Roman Corbridge so the walls are enriched with odd bits and pieces of Roman friezes and cornices and fragments of inscriptions including one to the Emperor Septimus Severus.

The crypt is an extraordinary and moving space and the only part of the church to have survived, but in the later church above it is a stone seat from those early days. It is known as The Frith Stool (or Fridstoll in early English). Frith Stool meant 'the seat of peace' and there are two famous surviving examples of such thrones, the one here at Hexham and one in Beverley Minster, a church founded by St John of Beverley who had been one of Wilfrid's successors as Bishop of Hexham. The Hexham Frith Stool is a simple carved square stone block with a rounded seat cut into it. There is beautiful elegant interlace decoration on the arms of the chair, as perfect as if it had been drawn by a computer. It is a bishop's throne, but a throne so restrained and dignified that you have to believe in the sincerity of the person who made it … that was Wilfrid, of course, so maybe the hairy underpants worked.

Northumberland is filled with beautiful carved Anglo-Saxon stonework. The richly carved stone crosses are the most obvious. They derived from Ireland originally, but they are among the glories of Northumbria's golden years. Hexham has one of the best – in the North Transept is Acca's Cross, made to celebrate the death of Bishop Acca, who died in 720AD, but there are lots of others; you see them in church after church, except for those that have ended up in the Great North Museum in Newcastle – fragments of ancient carving 13 or 1400 years old.

The one at Warden is one of the simplest and could be the oldest, because, in my opinion (and this is my book after all), it almost certainly dates from sometime in the 600s; but others might be carved with little bits of interlaced stone or strange mythical beasts. Often they have survived just as fragments so there must be hundreds more bits and pieces awaiting discovery, built into later church walls or carried off to be used in field walls and the walls of farmhouses. They must be somewhere.

My favourite fragment is part of a cross in Rothbury church, reused as the base of a 17th century font. One side of it shows a little bit of Christ in majesty though it takes a bit of looking to see it. At the bottom there are a crowd of hands reaching up towards what looks like a pile of apples but isn't. The hands belong to the apostles and the apples are in fact clouds. Above the clouds sits Jesus – well Jesus' knees and feet are all you can see because the upper part of his body is in the museum at Newcastle, but the feet, and the lower part of his garment are beautifully carved; the feet are resting on a cushion in the most realistic and comfortable way and the garment looks like a Roman toga. We used to think of Anglo-Saxon times as 'The Dark Ages' but this fragment of a figure is enough to prove that idea wrong – its carver was a Christian who knew about Rome and knew how to carve the human figure in a proper and convincing way. I have seen carvings from those days in other places where the human figure has defeated the artists' level of skill and the best they could achieve were pictures of ungainly little dolls. Not in Northumberland though. They were very civilised people, the Anglo-Saxons of our county.

For personal reasons I want to end this (rather long) chapter on the Anglo-Saxons by mentioning an unusual little carving in the wall of the Church of St Gregory the Great at Kirknewton, north of Wooler and just a mile or so from the site of the great royal palace of Ad Gefrin at

The Firth Stool in Hexham and (bottom left) The Saxon tower at St Andrew's, Bywell, and (below) a 7th century fragment re-used as base of the font in Rothbury Church.

Left: The Adoration of the Magi at Kirknewton. Probably 7th century as it shares many similarities to the Frank's Casket (right).

Yeavering. The church is most famous for the remarkable stone vaulting over its chancel and south chapel and there is no doubt that I will want to return to talk about that feature when I reach the chapter on the Border Wars of the later Middle Ages, but this little carving is a different kettle of fish.

It is a representation of the Adoration of the Magi and it shows the three wise men approaching the Madonna and Child. This is what I wrote about it when I was involved in writing a second edition to *Niklaus Pevsner's Guide to Northumberland* in The Buildings of England series:

SCULPTURE. Relief of the Adoration of the Magi, the background cut off above the figures. Very rude workmanship; the Virgin, e.g., raises an arm stiff like a pole to greet the Kings. The date is most probably C12.

Oh no its not, Grundy. Not 12th century I mean. Grundy failed to look. I was a plank but I have subsequently read a little booklet by the late Roy Humphrey OBE, a former Chairman of the Glendale Local History Society and he pointed me in a new direction. Mr Humphrey compared the carving to one of the scenes on the Frank's Casket which is an extraordinary box carved out of whalebone in the period round about 700AD. It was made in Northumbria and is now in the British Museum though there is an excellent copy of it in the Great North Museum in Newcastle. The similarities are startling. The composition is the same. The Magi in both are wearing "kilts" or at least kilt-like garments; they are also wearing Phrygian caps. The front one has a bended knee. They are bearing gifts aloft in their left hands while their right hands help to support the arm. The Madonna and Child are seated almost identically and both have haloes that fade into their shoulders ... and so on and so on. The similarities are very startling and Mr Humphreys goes further and compares them to other 8th and 9th century representations of the same scene.

I was convinced. I am convinced. St Gregory the Great was the Pope who made the crack about "Angels not Angles" and who sent St Augustine (and St Paulinus) to convert the English. St Paulinus spent three weeks converting the English at Ad Gefrin just a mile from this church. It's all too much of a coincidence. That carving is not 12th Century but an Anglo-Saxon work of art that has been hiding in plain sight for hundreds of years – I wonder how many more are still hiding a bit more deeply and will re-appear in the years to come.

Mark my words.

Lindisfarne Coves Haven - did the Vikings land here?

4. THE VIKINGS

I don't suppose it's all that surprising but lots of times, when you start looking at a period or a life or a career, the really exciting developments take place at the beginning and once they have burst on the scene thing seem to settle down into a more normal and humdrum pattern. It seems to be difficult, to quote the poet Browning, to recapture that first fine careless rapture and that's what seems to have happened to the Anglo-Saxons in Northumberland.

After that first extraordinary burst of creativity, by the time that Cuthbert had been made a saint and the *Lindisfarne Gospels* had been created, there doesn't seem to be anything really new and thrilling to write about for ages – no new artistic masterpieces, no new great saints. On one side of society the church just went on being churchy while the other half of the Anglo-Saxon Northumbrian world continued in ways that never seemed to change but were in no way humdrum or what we would think of as normal. To put it bluntly, for hundreds of years the ruling families of Northumbria behaved grotesquely and hardly ever seem to have got any better. Here's a little flavour of what they were like, pinched from a Wikipedia article about The Kings of Northumbria:

'The killing of Uhtred by Thurbrand the Bold started a blood feud that lasted for many years. Uhtred's son subsequently avenged his father by killing Thurbrand, but Ealdred in turn was killed by Thurbrand's son, Carl. Ealdred's vengeance had to wait until the 1070s, when, Ealdred's grandson had his soldiers kill most of Carl's sons and grandsons.'

For hundreds of years, if the Friths weren't killing the Aethels then it was the Egcs who were slaughtering the Ossies in a spiralling vortex of blood feuds. Spare a thought for little Osred I who was only 9 when he inherited the crown after the murder of his half-brother. Obviously there was an attempt on his life almost immediately (you wouldn't have expected anything different) but, with the protection of the church, he was able to hang on to his kingdom and his life until he suffered the inevitable slaughter at the age of 19.

I've just made a rough list of the first 25 kings of Northumbria and as far as I can make out (my brain hurts with all of their utterly confusing names) 11 of them were killed in battle and 7 murdered. Many of them had been deposed and exiled in the years before their violent deaths. Two or three of them gave it all up and went off to become monks or hermits (including one who was described as a violent man and a murderer but still ended up in the monastery on Lindisfarne). I think that leaves three who died of natural causes at the end of their reigns.

All of this dark and convoluted slaughter would make (and probably has made) excellent material for

Dark Age dramas on Netflix but I'm afraid I can't be bothered with it so I'm going to cut to the Next Big Thing – the event that was going to open the door to vast changes in English history and even create a few waves in Northumberland.

You'll have guessed what it was? It was the appearance of the Vikings on the international scene.

———

OK, it's the 8th June 793AD. Cuthbert had been lying in his shrine beside the altar of the monastic church on Lindisfarne for almost a hundred years. I'd like to ask you to imagine the scene but it's very difficult to do because, if you recall we didn't really know what it looked like originally, where the church was or what it was like and nobody has any idea at all about what changes had taken place in the century since then, but I think we can take it for granted that it looked pretty splendid.

A lot of monks would have spent time in the intervening years beautifying the place and a whole heap of pilgrims would have knelt before the shrine and left money to glorify it even further. Everybody involved with the monastery would have felt such pride to be associated with a place that had the reputation of being one of the holiest sites in Christendom.

On the other hand, the weather had been really awful recently and you could say (as the *Anglo-Saxon Chronicle* reported some years later) that '*terrible portents had come about over the land of Northumbria and miserably frightened the people*'. Not only that, there were immense flashes of lightning and, even worse and even more unexpected, fiery dragons were seen flying through the air. I think you always know, when you see fiery dragons flying through the air, that something unpleasant is about to happen…

… and of course it did. The Vikings appeared out of the sea and wrought terror. In fact one correspondent wrote that '*never before had such terror appeared in Britain*'. The attackers had left the church of St Cuthbert '*spattered with the blood of the priests of God, despoiled of all its ornaments …*'

That's the story that everybody who has ever been to Lindisfarne or read anything about these matters knows and there's no reason to think it didn't happen. The correspondent I quoted before was Alcuin – one of the greatest scholars and teachers of the age, a Northumbrian who had become a major figure in the court of Charlemagne and he, along with the rest of Europe, heard about the attack straight away. He was shocked to his core and immediately wrote a letter to Higbald, the Bishop of Lindisfarne in which he said:

'Your tragic sufferings daily bring me sorrow, since the pagans have desecrated God's sanctuary, shed the blood of saints around the altar, laid waste the house of our hope and trampled the bodies of the saints like dung in the street.'

He is clearly responding to recent news and there is a tone of personal pain in the letter, a clear and massively sympathetic response to a recent event

I can only cry from my heart before Christ's altar: 'O Lord, spare thy people and do not give the Gentiles thine inheritance …"

You can't doubt a man as reliable as Alcuin and though the other main source for the story of the attack, the *Anglo-Saxon Chronicle*, was only written down more than 100 years later, it was based on contemporary accounts and also seems pretty convincing.

In the same year, (says the Chronicle) the harrowing inroads of heathen men made lamentable havoc in the church of God in Holy-island, by rapine.

So it happened. The Vikings came and … did stuff, but there are still things that seem to suggest that we don't know the whole story… we don't really know what it was that they actually did.

For a start you would think that if they had gone to the trouble of rowing across the North Sea with lightning storms and fiery dragons all over the place, they would at least have tried to make it all worthwhile by making a better job of the pillaging. That particular band seems to have been really rubbish pillagers. They missed the saint (who they clearly failed to '*trample like dung in the street*') and whose body was clearly worth a bob or two; they missed his gold and garnet cross and his rare elephant ivory comb. They missed his fab personal copy of *St John's Gospel* and of course they missed the *Lindisfarne Gospels*, one of the greatest books in the world with a cover absolutely dripping in gold and jewels …

… and there's more. As Julian Richards said in *The Blood of the Vikings*, they don't seem to have been very good at burning and looting either, because nobody has yet found a single sign of any destruction that occurred on Lindisfarne in those days. Julian goes further. He says that evidence – I'm talking about solid, physical, archaeological evidence of Viking destruction – has only ever been found at one British monastery, at Tarbut on the coast of North-East Scotland. On Lindisfarne in particular there is, as yet, no evidence of burning, no smashed or destroyed buildings, no bones bearing signs of violence.

I'm sure you can see what I'm getting at. I'm not doubting that an attack took place; just that the attackers weren't quite so efficiently devastating as the contemporary accounts suggest.

There's another example. The following year the Vikings came back, not to Lindisfarne this time but to attack the monastery at Tynemouth. On this occasion, however, the monks were waiting for them and well armed. I recall an old joke about a vicar beating a choirboy on the head with a bible and shouting 'God is Love' in time with the blows. The Tynemouth monks didn't do that; their blows were deadly serious and made with brandished swords. The Viking leader was killed. The rest of the attackers were forced back to their boats but, as they tried to escape, the boats were driven on to rocks by a storm and destroyed. Any survivors who managed to scramble back to shore were put to death.

After those two raids, I don't really know what happened. It's quite likely that there were other attacks up and down the coasts and it's quite possible that some of the targets were monasteries since the Anglo-Saxon church was in the habit of settling on exposed and vulnerable coastal headlands but nothing is clear or certain. On Lindisfarne, for example, the monks didn't run away and find somewhere safer to live; for at least 50 years monastic life went on as before – but eventually they did leave their island home so perhaps things were getting worse. Sometime after 830 AD they set off from Lindisfarne with their luggage – a few spare pairs of hairy undies and so on and presumably all the treasures that hadn't been nicked by raiders – the jewels and the best books and crosses and what not; they took the body of the saint, of course, in his coffin (they carried that on their backs) and one of their churches.

There were two churches on the island, a later stone one and the original timber church that had been put up by St Aidan 200 years before; they carried that on their backs as well and re-erected it at Norham, about 20 miles inland on the River Tweed and much less exposed to attack than they had been on the coast.

But you see, what happened to them next is all a bit mysterious. They stayed at Norham for a few years and then, by the 870s they went back to Lindisfarne. They returned to their supposedly dangerous island just at the moment that the Viking situation really took a turn for the worse. Isn't that odd?

What happened was this. In about 865 AD the Vikings stepped up a gear and changed from being raiders to becoming invaders and settlers. A great Viking army landed in East Anglia and in no time at all it had taken over a huge area including large parts of southern Northumbria … and yet, it was in the teeth of this new situation that the monks moved back to their exposed coastal home. Odd!

So, leaving the question of what happened to Lindisfarne as a bit of a mystery for the time being, let me turn to the country as a whole and ask what the

Viking age stone, St Andrew's, Bywell.

Vikings actually did conquer. Well, you have to remember that Northumbria at that time was a pretty substantial country that stretched from the Humber, over the Tees, the Tyne and The Tweed and included the land as far north as Edinburgh so it included what we now know as Yorkshire, Durham, Northumberland and most of Southern Scotland.

Very quickly the Vikings conquered the Yorkshire bit and parts of south Durham and created a kingdom based on the city of York, which they made their capital. For a few years that was as far as they got, but then in 875 AD they turned their attention to us up here in our North-Eastern corner. Under their leader, Halfdan, they invaded our bit.

They sailed into the Tyne and supposedly sacked the monasteries at Tynemouth and Jarrow and then, as evidence that they were more than pirates and raiders they stayed here; they settled in for the winter. They set up camp in Gateshead at the end of the Team Valley and waited for the next year's campaigning.

You might have expected them to spend the winter in Newcastle so they could go clubbing and enjoy the Christmas shopping but for at least two reasons that didn't happen. Firstly Newcastle didn't actually exist at that time so they were stuck with Gateshead and secondly, it seems to me that the North side of the river, our side, was still a step too far for them, a little too exposed and still firmly in the grip of their enemy – us.

The following year they kept going up the Tyne Valley, where they might possibly have destroyed Wilfrid's great church at Hexham, and over the next couple of years that remained the pattern, Halfdan and his Danes buzzed about biffing and clubbing and it has always been assumed that all of this buzzing and biffing included further attacks on Lindisfarne.

Certainly, later writers said that it did and in the museum on the island there is an extraordinary gravestone that was found in the Priory. It's known as the Battle Stone. On one side it shows the Day of Judgement – there is a cross and the sun and moon; penitent figures bow down beneath them. The other side is carved with a band of 7 tightly packed, possibly Viking, warriors, wearing chain mail and brandishing swords and battle

axes; you can almost hear their battle cries and imagine the terror that they must have created. It is a fearsome and apocalyptic image and it dates from this time – the late 800s

So, supposedly faced with threats like these, the monks set off again, still with the saint on their backs they left their island sanctuary, but this time they wandered much further afield. They went to Carlisle and to the West Cumberland coast. They set sail to Ireland but hit a storm and Cuthbert's coffin was lost overboard before being miraculously found again. The same thing happened to the *Lindisfarne Gospels*, which fell into the sea but were rescued undamaged. They went to the Isle of Whithorn, on the north shore of the Solway, for a while and drifted about like this for seven years before ending up at Chester-le-Street, where they stayed for almost 100 years, until they finally settled on Durham.

This story is usually told as evidence that the monks were escaping from the savage power of the Vikings but that just doesn't sound convincing. Throughout the 800s the Community of St Cuthbert had continued to get richer and more powerful. They had been granted land

Battle Stone, Lindisfarne.

and estates all over Northumberland and, as they wandered, they weren't moving away from the Vikings in a timid fashion, they were moving towards them. They moved south of the Tyne; they even travelled south of the River Tees into the heart of Viking territory. At one point they even went to York (or Yorvik), which was the capital of the Danish Kingdom.

They weren't running away from the enemy, they were meeting them, confronting them and negotiating with them. When they settled in Chester-le-Street, it was on land given to them by the Viking king Guthred, who went on to present them with more or less the whole of what it now County Durham. The impression I get from this story is not about a set of defenceless monks cowering away from attack and ultimately running away, but a confident and politically astute group who used their greatest asset, the body of their saint, as a source of power.

Meanwhile Halfdan was clearly aiming to take over the northern part of the former kingdom of Bernicia, the land north of the Tyne. For a short while he set himself up as ruler of the area and it seemed as if our Northumberland was going to become a Viking region like the lands further south but bizarrely it didn't happen and one of the bits of evidence that it didn't happen is to be found in the number of Viking place names to be found in Northumberland.

Before you ask, the answer is that there are hardly any.

You might recall how I talked about the way that the Anglo Saxons, when they arrived here in the 5th century, entirely replaced the existing language of the area and littered the landscape with place names in the Anglo-Saxon tongue. In the parts of England where the Vikings took over, the same thing happened. Yorkshire, for example is absolutely littered with Viking place names – hundreds of towns and villages whose name ends with "by" which was Scandinavian for a farm. There are hundreds more ending in "thorpe" and "beck" and "dale" and "fell"; Yorkshire is covered with Viking words for landscape features.

North of the Tyne there are virtually none. Walker and Byker just outside Newcastle are almost the only two places with Viking names. The "ker" part of both came from the Viking word "Carr", which meant a marsh, so Walker meant the marsh by the wall – the Roman Wall of course, which would have still been quite visible in those days. "Byker" is even more Viking since both bits of the word are Viking and mean the farm by the marsh. There are others, a few farms and villages around Rothbury and the Coquet Valley and near Bamburgh, which seem to be based on Scandinavian personal names, but by comparison to Yorkshire, or the Lake District and other areas that were entirely taken over by the Vikings, the numbers are miniscule.

Though there is one little mystery. In the Museum on Lindisfarne there are a series of stones which were dug up during an excavation in the middle of the later Priory buildings and they have been identified as Christian carvings made by in an Anglo-Scandinavian style. So presumably some of those Vikings did settle here in Northumberland, and presumably some of them were pretty quickly converted to Christianity. It just goes to show how little we know for certain.

Anyway, despite those few exceptions, in 877 Halfdan disappeared, killed somehow and somewhere, and the King that followed him was Guthred, the man who had presented so much to the Community of St Cuthbert. There is a story in one of the contemporary Lives of St Cuthbert that it was the saint himself who miraculously identified Guthred as the rightful successor to the throne of the Viking kingdom of York but meanwhile Northumberland, our bit of Northumbria, stayed Anglo Saxon, ruled from Bamburgh by Anglo-Saxon Kings.

It's all rather mysterious why this should have happened. Were the people north of the Tyne tough enough to keep the Vikings out, troublesome enough to make it not worth the bother of trying to control them? It's possible, even probable apparently, that the Anglo-Saxon kings in Bamburgh, or at least some of them, were puppet kings with Viking overlords further south but on the whole north of the Tyne remained a distinctively Viking-free zone. As far as Northumberland is concerned the Vikings came, batted around a bit … but never conquered and that makes the score …

Northumberland 1: Vikings 0.

5. THE NORMANS

I'll tell you what, writing this book hasn't made me like invaders very much. You might think that I went a bit soft on the Anglo-Saxon invaders because I could see that eventually they became A GOOD THING but it must have been pretty clear that I didn't think much of the Romans and definitely seemed to have felt that the Vikings were rather overrated, at least in terms of their impact on Northumberland. And now it's the Normans! Well, eventually, of course, they too turned into part of us so there's no point in getting too worked up, but initially, in 1066 when they first arrived, they seemed to have been pretty ghastly.

First of all they had no right to be here. I know that technically William the Conqueror had a possible, even a reasonable claim to be the king of England but so did Harold and he was already here, in situ and doing OK. England had been a relatively stable single kingdom for almost 150 years. It was among the first countries in Europe to achieve a settled status and a definite identity of its own. One writer says that '*The English had developed a settled identity precociously early among the European powers*'.

While most other bits of Europe were still struggling to achieve any sort of order, under a succession of competent kings England had developed an efficient set of laws and an organised form of taxation that people accepted. English writers were clear what they thought of the invaders. One contemporary writer (a man with a great name; he was a monk called Orderic Vitalis) wrote that the Normans had '*subdued a people that was greater, richer and older than they were*'. And it really was a rich country. In fact, in the years after 1066 when the Conquest was well under way, there's said to be plenty of evidence that Normans returning home across the channel were able to astonish people with the splendour of the clothes, the jewelled fabrics and the cloth of gold they had pinched from the English and the richness of the stuff they had looted and pillaged.

They showed that they were efficient looters and pillagers from the very start. Even before the Battle of Hastings, the moment they landed in England they used their battleaxes to slaughter all the cattle they could find and made themselves a major barbecue before building an emergency castle and burning down all of the villages round about; and in the years that followed, the looting and pillaging was remarkable because in an extraordinary way they took the lot – not just the treasure and loose change.

They pinched all the wealth to be found inside the churches of course but they went further. They pinched the churches too. They took over all the churches to the extent that the English clergy and bishops and such like were virtually all replaced in no time at all with Normans. They just got rid of them. There's a story about

Left: Warkworth Castle, originally built in Norman times but totally rebuilt in later centuries.

the main Norman churchman of those early years, a chap called Lanfranc, who imposed a new Norman abbot on a monastery in Canterbury. Of course, the English abbot had to be removed and there was resistance from the monks who were then imprisoned in chains; one of them was publicly flogged at the Abbey's gates.

When Thurstan, another monk from Normandy, was appointed abbot of Christ Church in Canterbury, he brought bowmen into the church in order to force the English monks to abandon their English ways of worshipping. The Normans did the same with landowners. By about 1072 almost all of the owners of all the estates, often members of families who had owned their properties for many generations, were chucked out and their possessions given to the newcomers.

It must have been a messy, piecemeal, chaotic process and there is no clear picture of how it happened, but over the next few years there was only one English bishop who managed to hang on to his job; all of the rest and almost all of the native aristocracy just disappeared. Lots of them went into exile. They went all over Europe, in fact a whole pile of them even ended up serving the Sultan in Constantinople! It's almost impossible for me to work out how the Normans did this because there weren't very many of them – 2000 knights supposedly along with their followers making perhaps an invasion force of about 10,000 to take over a local population of 2,500,000.

I suppose they could have done it by being nice and kind, offering everybody sweeties, but that's not what happened; they succeeded, as so many other invaders have done before and since, by being cruel and ruthless. From the start they were a bit on edge and that made them harsh. They hadn't really expected such a lot of opposition to their arrival and they were very jumpy and, like the Nazis in occupied France during Second World War, they were especially savage with anybody who tried to fight back.

As early as William's coronation, for example, which took place at Westminster Abbey on Christmas Day 1066, the Norman guards were startled by unexpected noises in the church; they were actually the shouts of the congregation acclaiming the coronation but the guards mistook the sounds for fighting so they responded by burning down London, which cast a bit of a blight over the occasion, and as they moved out through the kingdom they responded brutally to any resistance. They were very fond of castrating people for example, and cutting hands off, and blinding people, and often all three. But despite, or perhaps because of, this brutality there continued to be lots of opposition. One of the chroniclers of the time wrote: '*What were left of the conquered English lay in ambush for the hated race of Normans and murdered them secretly in woods and unfrequented places*'.

In the first few years there was almost constant resistance all over the country. but the most famous example of their ruthless savagery took place in the winter of 1069-1070. It was called The Harrying of the North and it involved a positive orgy of destruction in what we now call Yorkshire – the land between the Humber and the River Tees.

In 1068 William had been confronted by an almost perfect storm of opposition. There was a major revolt led by three northern earls and at the same time there was a Viking invasion. The Normans fairly quickly defeated the revolt of the earls but the Vikings turned out to be a tougher nut to crack so William came to a temporary arrangement with them by agreeing to leave them alone with a space to settle over the winter on the banks of the Humber. This might have looked like weakness but in fact it was a cunning wheeze because while the Vikings were putting up with a Yorkshire winter, William's forces systematically destroyed the whole of the landscape around them. They destroyed the whole of modern-day Yorkshire in a scorched-earth policy that not only punished the revolting English but was also designed to make the place incapable of supporting the Viking invaders. Everything went. All of the villages were destroyed; all of the stock and tens of thousands of people, perhaps as many as 150,000 people were killed. Some modern historians describe it as genocide.

Among the recently defeated Anglo-Saxon rebels was the earl of Northumbria. For a year or two part of

William's strategy for controlling the north was to appoint Anglo-Saxons as earls of Northumbria but as a tactic it turned out to be a pretty miserable failure. The first one he appointed was called Copsig but he only lasted about 6 months before he was murdered by his fellow Northumbrians. He was followed by Gospatric but he almost immediately joined a rebellion against William who clearly decided that enough was enough and appointed a Norman successor instead. He chose a man called Robert de Comines and a fat lot of good it did him. In January 1069, along with a force of 700 soldiers, de Comines marched north to Durham. The Bishop of Durham warned him not to come, telling him that there was a rebel army waiting for him but he went anyway and he was slaughtered. In Durham. It's hard to imagine, but his men were slaughtered in the streets and he was trapped in the Bishop's house when it was set on fire and he burned to death. That would definitely hit the headlines nowadays wouldn't it? It would probably be on the 10 o'clock news even though it happened in the North East, north of Watford and a very long way from London.

Mass Slaughter in the Streets of Durham!

So there we are; three or four years after the Battle of Hastings, slaughter was still commonplace and Durham was about as far north as the Normans had reached. You will have realised that so far there has been no mention of our modern county of Northumberland in this part of the story and that's because our Northumberland, the land north of the Tyne, was still a step too far for the invaders. It was not even certain that it was part of England.

One of the problems about invading England in those days was that it wasn't quite clear where it ended. The boundary was obvious on the south coast and down the east side because if you went too far you got your feet wet, but on the west there was no clear and accepted boundary between England and Wales and in the north the frontier had never been properly established.

Until fairly recently the North had been part of the Kingdom (and later the earldom) of Northumbria, which stretched from the Humber right up as far as Edinburgh, but by the time the Normans arrived that situation had become a bit more complicated. Northumbria, you might recall, had been made up from two earlier countries called Deira and Bernicia but by 1066, Deira, the southern bit, the modern county of Yorkshire, had been split off and made Viking territory, leaving the land north of the river Tees as the surviving rump of the old earldom.

Meanwhile … as they say in the movies … the Scots had become active and decidedly Scottish and over the previous half century or so they had taken the land north of the River Tweed as the basis of their new and emerging country. In 1016 (or 1018, depending on who you read) they had won the Battle of Carham on the banks of the Tweed and the river became the border between two countries.

So there we are. Scotland had nicked the northern bit of Northumbria, the Vikings had nicked the southern bit and that left the bit in the middle, the bit that we now call Northumberland and Durham still to be decided and even that was pretty complicated because for the previous 150-odd years Durham had increasingly become the property of the immensely powerful and politically astute monks of St Cuthbert and though they still owned land north of the Tyne, Durham (the land between the Tyne and the Tees) had become their heartland.

By 1069, as we have seen, Durham and its holy chaps, however powerful they might have been, had fallen to the Normans and in 1072 the invaders built a castle there so that left our little home in the North East as the last man standing. Where was it? Was it part of England waiting to be captured by the Normans or was it potentially part of the new expanding and energetic kingdom of Scotland?

I don't really think it wanted to be either of those things. The people north of the Tyne were just holding on to their … but actually I don't know how to end that sentence. I don't think they were necessarily holding out for independence but they definitely seem to have a strong sense of regional identity (just like Northumbrians do today) and were determined to resist too much outside control or even interference in their freedoms, so they hung on to their Northumberlandness. Ever since England had become a single country under Athelstan in the early 900s, Northumberland had been part of that country … but only just. The kings of all-England only just had control over the extreme north because Northumberland was still the territory of the house of Bamburgh and if its rulers were no longer kings, well, they managed to hang on in there as earls; they became the Earls of Bamburgh or sometimes the Earls of Northumberland and they continued ruling their little northern territory as sort of Viceroys for the kings of England. They weren't appointed by the king – they held their power by inheriting it. The independence of Northumberland was made even greater because large parts of it – the whole of Tynedale and Redesdale along with Hexham and the bit to the south, which is still called Hexhamshire, were all "Liberties" – places that had survived from way back in Saxon times where the king's writ didn't run.

So that was the situation in the 1070s. The Normans were sitting in Durham, knocking on the door to the south while the Scots were parked along the Tweed, knocking on the door to the North and in the middle there was us – a difficult and a dangerous area for invaders, still the territory of powerful men in some parts and still wild upland country in others and the whole lot was still more or less holding the assorted invaders at bay.

They were poised to take over though.

The Scots were definitely knocking at the door. The King of Scotland at the time of the Conquest was called Malcolm III. He was the son of King Duncan who had been murdered by Macbeth and he had, in his turn killed Macbeth. He had some possible claims to the whole of Northumbria because his wife's grandfather, Siward, had been the earl of Northumbria and Malcolm very much wanted to push the boundary of his new country further south beyond the Tweed and reclaim what he saw as his southern inheritance.

He quite regularly led invasions to make the point and we Northumbrians could quite easily have ended up as Scotsmen. We might even have preferred it. After all we had been part of the same country as the Scots for the previous 300 years and it might have seemed better to stay that way instead of falling victim to the new barbarians to the south.

The Normans, on the other hand, were clear that they wanted to keep the Scots under control and it was William himself who led the first Norman force into Northumberland. In 1072, on a punitive expedition against King Malcolm, he led his army across the surviving Roman bridge between what is now Newcastle and Gateshead and set off across Northumberland to get at the Scots. Like the Romans before him, he didn't stop here, just whizzed north up the A1 (still not dual carriageway he discovered to his horror) and kept on going right as far as the river Tay. On the way back home again there were floods on the Tyne and he had to turn inland towards Hexham before he could find a way of crossing the river.

For a while that seems to have been the only significant Norman visit to our county. They were firmly established in Durham but went no further. That was the situation that lasted till 1080, the year in which it all changed.

———————————

By 1080 there was a new man in charge at Durham. He was called Walcher and he came from Lorraine in eastern France. He'd been made Bishop after the massacre in 1070 and he had bought the title of Earl of Northumbria 6 years later. You get the impression that he might have been a good egg. I read a description of him that said that he was regarded as a "saintly, able and learned man" but unfortunately he turned out to be unlucky in several ways.

Firstly, King Malcolm and his Scots arrived on another of his raids. He launched another attack on Northumbria in 1079 and Walcher doesn't seem to have handled it well, so that for three weeks the Scots wandered round what we now call County Durham pretty well willy-nilly. There was the inevitable slaughter and pillaging and, when the Scots went back home with all their slaves and booty, there seems to have been a lot of anger at Walcher's failure to handle the situation better; but it was another problem altogether that led to

Walcher's downfall – a problem caused by one of his better qualities

Walcher seems to have tried to be a bit nicer in his relationships with the locals than lots of the other Norman leaders. He was surrounded by Normans, of course, who had all the best jobs and the castle was manned by French and Flemish soldiers like everywhere else, but Walcher also had quite a number of English connections. His Dean was English, for example, and his principal advisor was an English aristocrat called Ligulf and that led to jealousy among the Normans to the extent that Ligulf was murdered by two of Walcher's Norman followers, Leobwin his chaplain and Gilbert (one of the Bishop's own relatives), who burned down the house where Ligulf was staying at Newburn on the Tyne.

This was a big deal. Of course murder is always a big deal and even in those violent days it was a capital offence but in this case the situation was worse because it set up a feud. All of Ligulf's English relatives wanted revenge on his Norman murderers. Walcher did his best to calm the situation. He immediately opened negotiations with the aggrieved family and arranged a meeting with them in Gateshead – on a Saturday morning!

Good Lord!

I'm assuming that he chose Gateshead because it was the furthest north he was able to go – the effective limits of his control and I have heard suggestions that there was a mansion of the Earls of Northumbria there so he probably assumed that he would be OK … but Good Lord … Gateshead! We smug residents on the north bank of the river and those of us who have failed to find a Saturday parking spot at the Metrocentre would have warned him. Don't go to Gateshead on a Saturday morning, Walcher, it won't turn out well … and it didn't. The negotiations broke down – so they slaughtered him like they had his predecessor. It is said that he had 700 followers with him and they were all locked in the burning church and put to death.

William was cross as you can imagine. He sent his brother Odo, the Bishop of Bayeux, to exact revenge and he, being a really tough egg of a bishop, did just that. In a sort of re-enactment of the Harrying of the North, he laid waste to the land between the Tees and the Tyne to the extent that some years later, in 1086, when William's great survey of who owned what in his new kingdom, the Domesday Survey was carried out, most of the manors in Durham were described as 'lying waste'.

But while all of this was happening, on the North bank of the Tyne something else was afoot ….

Stockings, actually. Short ones.

Short stockings is another way of saying "curt hose"… curt for short, like when you're curt or short with someone and ho … you know what I mean … and "Curthose" was the nickname of Robert, William the Conqueror's eldest son. It was his father who had given him the nickname, whether because he was a short little man (a short-arse, as I rudely described him in another book) or ironically, because he was unnaturally tall as I have read in another source.

Whichever it was, he didn't like it. He seems to have been an extraordinarily sensitive young man (for a Norman) and fell out with his father and all his brothers because he thought they picked on him. In 1079, the year before the attack on Walcher, he had almost killed his father during a battle in Flanders and yet here he was, less than a year later, on the north bank of the Tyne, founding Newcastle. He repaired the bridge that his father had ridden over in 1072, built some sort of castle and founded Newcastle as a sort of bridgehead for the invasion of Northumberland.

The Normans had arrived!

Well, sort of arrived, but there isn't much evidence that they had any instant success. Their progress seems to have been so slow that it is hard to avoid the conclusion that in the wake of the Walcher catastrophe they were still facing major opposition from the locals. I haven't come across any hard proof of this but there is sort of negative evidence that bad things were still happening.

Take the position of Earl of Northumbria, for example. With Walcher dead it must have been really important to find a good strong successor but the man who was appointed in 1080, a chap called Aubry de Courcy, took one look at the job, immediately turned it down and dickied off back to Normandy, leaving the post unfilled for the next six years. It's not a good sign.

Another sign that things weren't going well is that nowhere in Northumberland features in the *Domesday Book* and the reason for that is that when the survey was carried out in 1086 Northumberland still wasn't fully part of William's new kingdom and in fact I think it's fair to say that it never was because he died the following year in September 1087 without ever having conquered Northumberland properly, which seems to make the score ...

William the Conqueror 0: Northumberland 1

It wasn't to last though because during the reign of his successor, his son William Rufus or William II, the Norman invasion of Northumberland finally began to take hold and by the time that Henry I, the one after William Rufus, died in the 1130s the process was probably complete. From the very end of the 1080s and the first half of the 1090s, Northumberland started to get shared out between major Norman families. You'll not be surprised to hear that it all went to chaps who were already rich, great magnates who had been the Conqueror's supporters before he even came to England and who all owned huge estates elsewhere in England as well. In return for all this wealth their job was to be grateful to their king, to help govern his kingdom and to support him against his enemies.

In the whole of Northumberland there were just a small handful of them – 15 of them according to one book I read, 21 according to another. Whatever, the whole county was given to just a handful of men. Alnwick, for example, was given to a man called Gilbert Tyson who had been William's standard bearer at the Battle of Hastings. Redesdale (and parts of lower Tynedale) became the property of a family called the Umfravilles. The Bolbecs were given land round Corbridge and Hexham, the Bertrams got Mitford; there were the Muschamps who had land round Wooler and the Roos were given ~~Australia~~ a pile of manors on the River Tweed and so on.

The chaps in charge were all given the title of 'Baron' and their estates became known as 'Baronies'. They were subdivided into manors. The Umfraville Barony in Redesdale consisted of 21 separate manors, most of which would have been tenanted by yet another Norman follower of the man at the top.

Once they had got round to divvying up the county, the changes they made to the Northumberland scene over the next century were extraordinary, really extensive, far more than I had expected when I started to think about it. They changed the place in really profound ways:

Castles

First of all the Barons all built castles, of course. That's what the Normans did. The Anglo-Saxons had never built castles but it was always one of the first things the Normans did. They weren't stone castles at first, though loads of them were later rebuilt in stone, but initially they were those typical motte and bailey castles you'll have seen in books, with a high, steep-sided motte (or mound) for the owner to live nice and safely on top of, and a larger, lower bailey surrounded by a ditch and a bank with a wooden palisade to protect the chaps. I've totted up how many of them there were in the county and I make it 18 but I might easily have missed some out.

There was a string of them stretching north from Newcastle up the coastal plain. Morpeth had one, and possibly two. There was one at Alnwick and Dunstanburgh and Bamburgh. Lowick and Wooler both had one and there was a string of them along the Tweed – at Berwick, Wark and Norham. Inland, the Tyne Valley and especially North Tynedale and Redesdale were well sprinkled with them. Loads still survive, either as earthworks or underneath the stone castles that were later built on top of them. Prudhoe was one and there were others at Styford near Corbridge, at Hexham, Gunnerton, yet another Wark (Wark on Tyne), Bellingham, Tarset and Harbottle ... but the finest of them all is the splendid, complete and utterly atmospheric motte and bailey castle at Elsdon. It had the good luck to be abandoned a few decades later and replaced by a new stone castle at Harbottle a few miles

Elsdon, motte and bailey castle.

to the east so doesn't seem to have had any later buildings built on top and it gives a remarkable impression of what these earliest of all English castles looked like … but its scale is so impressive that it also makes you ask how they managed to build so many of them, who did the building and how difficult a process it was.

Elsdon was the property of that family called the Umfravilles and if you read the books they always say something like "Elsdon Castle was built by the Umfravilles", as if Mr and Mrs Umfraville had done the job themselves, put their gardening clothes on, got the tools out of the shed and started digging, but obviously that wasn't the case. The effort must have been massive. The mounds were built with alternate layers of soil and stone to keep the banks stable and vast amounts of soil and rock and boulders had to be moved. Who did the work? How many builders were there and how long did it take? I'm just guessing, but I'm pretty sure there weren't enough Normans to do it so it must have been slave labour or at the very least an impressed work force of locals who built the castles.

Townships

But castles were just one part of the changes that were taking place. What was happening wasn't just a land grab; it was also a massive reorganization of the way the land was managed. The Normans didn't just take over the estates of the Saxon predecessors and give them to somebody else. What they did was re-configured the whole landscape – a process that required massive and unexpected levels of planning and involved dismantling the whole way the Saxons had managed the countryside.

I need to say that the process I'm about to describe didn't happen overnight. It's not clear when it started and it probably went on for the next century but the new Baronies were divided up into 'townships'. Townships could be quite different sizes from each other depending on the sort of landscape round about them, but they were almost all divided up in remarkably similar ways.

Each township had a village in the middle with farmsteads built around an open space or green. Most of the farmsteads were tenanted by serfs who weren't free but were bonded to the lord of their manor and each one had a farm of about 24 acres, There were some poorer people in each village too, cottagers who had just a couple of acres, not enough to live on, so they had to boost their incomes by working a couple of days a week for the Lord of the Manor or for the better off bondsmen with the larger farms.

Round each village there were three huge fields that were divided up into strips. In Northumberland the strips are called 'rigs', separated from each other by furrows. Each rig was about half an acre in extent and so each farmer would have a number of them dotted about the fields. They have all gone now, of course, replaced by later forms of farming, but the beautiful and ghostly outlines of these rig–and-furrow landscapes are one of the glories of our countryside, brilliantly clear in snow or in low evening sunlight.

I don't know about you, but I hadn't expected the Norman takeover to be so carefully planned or so fundamental. I was expecting to hear about big bad barons biffing the locals, chucking out the old Anglo-Saxon landlords and moving casually into their houses, not this systematic and pre-planned re-organisation of the landscape. I don't know who devised it, what level of administration there was. Whether it was done by local officials or national ones I don't know, but they certainly made changes to the shape of the English countryside.

And there was more ….

Churches

New villages needed new churches so loads and loads were built; most have been altered or rebuilt over the centuries but there are still enough to illustrate the amount of energy the invaders put into creating their new landscapes. There's a marvellous example at Old Bewick that I'm going to come back to in little while and there other beautiful surviving Norman churches at Seaton Delaval and high up on the moors at Thockrington. Edlingham, between Alnwick and Rothbury, is one of my favourites and so is Bolam in a beautiful landscape north of Belsay. Ancroft, just south of Berwick, has details that reveal that it was once much posher than it is today and there are a few which, despite

Thockrington Church.

The beautiful surviving Norman church at Edlingham.

all the wars that have happened since they were built, are still thoroughly Norman, ambitious and beautiful. Warkworth and Norham, both sheltered and protected presumably by the mighty castles beside them, and St Andrews, safe inside the walls of Newcastle, are the finest surviving examples we have.

And there was even more ….

Monasteries

The 12th century was the great period for the founding of monasteries in England and though Northumberland, situated up here on the wild frontier, never had the monastic riches of Yorkshire for example, there were still plenty of devout men and women who were prepared to seek out a life in the wilderness.

The two most important were monasteries that had been important back in Saxon times but had fallen out of use. Holy Island had always continued to belong to monks of St Cuthbert in Durham and right at the beginning of the conquest of the North East, in 1083, the Bishop of Durham, William of St Carilef, re-founded the monastery as an outpost from Durham. Ten year later, in 1093 the church at Durham started to be rebuilt in its present extraordinary form and at the same time work

Lindisfarne Priory: begun 1093AD.

The remains of Newminster Abbey, founded in 1137.

started on building a new church on the island. You'll know it. Everybody knows it well and loves it more, The ruins reveal that it was like a miniature version of Durham, a wonderful, rich confection of decorated pillars and arches.

Tynemouth was the next to be created. It had been hugely important in Saxon times too and was the burial place of a whole host of Saxon saints and kings, but it too had been attacked and destroyed by Viking raids. It was refounded in the 1090s by a man called Robert de Mowbray, the first successful Norman Earl of Northumbria. There'll be more about him later but he had fallen out with the Bishop of Durham so he offered the site to the Benedictine monks from St Albans.

And there were others. There were lots in Newcastle,

the Black Friars and the Grey Friars, a huge Augustinian nunnery and half a dozen smaller houses. Out in the countryside, Newminster just outside Morpeth was founded in 1138 and is one of the few that has kept any remains from the earliest Norman days. Alnwick Abbey followed in 1147 and Blanchland in 1165. They were all founded and paid for by rich chaps, local Barons who were buying themselves a bit of credit in Heaven at the same time as encouraging the settlement and civilising influence of religion on their lands.

And there was even more …

Planned or Planted Towns

The level of planning the Normans showed in the countryside was perhaps even more obvious in the towns, the boroughs they created. The Saxons, as far as I know, didn't live in towns but the Normans were different. In Northumberland, between 1080 when Newcastle was begun, to about 1200 at the end of the Norman period there were quite a lot of towns created.

I'll give you a list of the ones I can think of:

Newcastle, Bamburgh, Wooler, Corbridge, Norham, perhaps Rothbury and probably Wark-on-Tyne, Berwick, Alnwick, Hexham, Morpeth and Warkworth.

That makes 12 and there might be others I've forgotten about, but it seems an awful lot for an area where (a) there had been none before and (b) the population was extremely small.

Two of the towns, Newcastle and Bamburgh, were royal boroughs, founded by the king of England; both of them had the king as Lord of the Manor. Berwick was a Royal Borough too but it was founded by King David I of Scotland, so it was a Scottish borough in its earliest form. Hexham was founded by the church, by the Archbishop of York who was Lord of the Manor of the ancient Priory at Hexham, while Norham was created by the church

too, by the Bishops of Durham who still owned this northern edge of the county (and continued to do so, incidentally, until 1844 when it finally became part of the County of Northumberland).

The other boroughs were all started by individual Barons, eager to get some commerce going and create markets that they could use as a source of revenue. Some of the Boroughs (Morpeth, Hexham and Alnwick, for example) were much more successful than others and have survived ever since as proper market towns while others, including even the Royal Borough of Bamburgh, were less successful and have trickled along as villages, almost exclusively very nice villages, but villages nevertheless.

The extraordinary thing about these towns is how much planning clearly went into them. They didn't just

Warkworth with its perfect surviving medieval layout.

happen. It was obviously just like the planning process nowadays. You couldn't build what you liked or stick a conservatory or something on the back of your little farmstead or build a new one twice as big. Even in those days you had to dee what you were telt, pet!

The boroughs were all laid out in the same way, using variants on a standard plan with standard measurements. There was always a church or a monastery and a castle or a manor house. There was a market place in the centre and all of the houses that lined the main street were laid out on identical plots called Burgage Plots. They were all the same width with a house at the front facing onto the road or market place and with a long narrow strip of garden behind to provide space for the householders to keep a pig or a cow and grow vegetables for themselves. All the Norman boroughs in the country as well as in our county were laid out with identical burgage plots like these and often the old patterns still survive.

Right through the middle of Alnwick for example, from Narrowgate to the Hotspur Gate there are burgage plots; the north row in the centre of Rothbury is a terrific example; even in Newcastle where a millennium of vast development would appear to have changed everything, streets at the heart of the original town, streets like the Bigg Market and the Cloth Market, the bottom of Dean Street and The Close all still show the original pattern.

Of all the boroughs laid out by the Normans in Northumberland, by far the most successful (in terms of growth and economics at least) turned out to be Newcastle. I have written another whole book about the growth and development of Newcastle so I can't bring myself to do it all again in this book but it is worth saying that the speed and size of its growth was remarkable. Within a hundred years of the first steps made by Robert Shortysocks in 1080 the town had four parish churches, two of them, St Andrews and All Saints, at least a mile apart. There were a series of streets (Pilgrim Street, Westgate Street, The Bigg Market and Market Street for example) which still form the bones of the town today. There was a mighty castle and not one, not two but quite a lot of different markets. It was already a port and already one of the major towns of England.

But despite Newcastle's astonishing rate of growth it isn't necessarily the best place in Northumberland to look at the shape of a Norman Borough. That honour undoubtedly goes to Warkworth.

Warkworth is a town/borough/village that the visitor can look at from any angle without being irritated by the view. This is partly because its development has been restricted by its situation. Like the Cathedral and Castle at Durham, the town is squeezed inside the tight loop or meander of a river – in Warkworth's case the river is the Coquet and it curls like a serpent around the town. Across the river on the west side there are high wooded banks that have prevented extra development, while on the east side the river drifts towards the sea across peaceful and unsullied water meadows and marshes.

Between these outer reaches lies Warkworth, unsullied itself, and quite unchanged from its ancient shape. In fact it is so little altered that it if I had possessed a drone (instead of merely being one) I would have liked to fly my camera high above the town so that you could have seen its perfect medieval layout. This is because Warkworth is essentially what it always was, a single street of little houses that climbs steeply from the bridge and the church at the north end of the peninsular to the castle at the top of the hill. From my virtual drone you would have been able to see the still-surviving long thin gardens behind each house, the burgage plots by which the villagers supported themselves when the plan was first laid down in the 12th century; you would have seen that the single bridge is ancient and provided (in this county which was so dangerous and violent in times past) with a strong stone tower that could be locked in order to prevent those nasty rough people from the north, Alnmouth possibly or maybe Scotland, from dropping in unannounced.

My wandering drone would have dwelt for a moment or two on a number of special buildings – the beautiful early Georgian Bridge End House, for example but in the main it would have been satisfied to drift past pleasant 18th and 19th century houses and cottages that have replaced the original Norman cottages, noting how comfortably they sit beside each other. A number of them, you would have been pleased to note, have been

Exterior (left) and interior of St Lawrence Church in Warkworth.

altered or designed to let them minister to the pleasures of the flesh; there are several cafes here and at least a couple of good pubs. And there are shops too. If nicks are your thing or possibly nacks, well there are nicky-nacky shops aplenty, a couple of posh clothes shops, art shops and home-made jam shops, just the sort of places you want to drift past on your way to the bar lunch.

It's a nice town then but among these gentle pleasures there are two buildings that go beyond nice – one of them is great and the other is a masterpiece.

The church is the great one. It is dedicated to St Lawrence, who was one of those saints who give sainthood a good name. He was a deacon in 4th century Rome and, when the authorities demanded that he handed over his church's treasure, he gathered up all the poor and the sick people and said, "Here is the church's treasure". They put him to death for his cheek; in fact they barbecued him, grilled him on a gridiron.

So, a good saint and a great church. It is beautiful. It's large – the largest and finest Norman church in Northumberland (alongside Norham) and it is utterly rich in atmosphere and utterly rich in stuff – stuff to read and look at, stuff of all different periods, stained glass and carvings, monuments, pulpits and altar rails all of

the highest order.

So the church is great, but the castle at the top of the hill … well, the castle keep is a masterpiece but though it was begun in Norman times it has been so totally rebuilt in later centuries that I will have to come back to it in a later chapter.

Meanwhile… back in the early years of the Norman conquest of Northumberland, with all of the above changes still to come, of all the Norman administrators who became involved with Northumberland in those early days, there is one who emerges very clearly. He was that Robert de Mowbray who founded Tynemouth Priory and he was a proper toughie by all accounts, described by one contemporary writer as '*powerful, rich, bold, fierce in war, haughty, he despised his equals and, swollen with vanity, he disdained to obey his king*' – perfect material for Earl of Northumbria then. He became Earl in 1086 before William the Conqueror died and one of the first things he did was to rebel against the new King, William Rufus. William Rufus was the Conqueror's second son and de Mowbray revolted in support of the eldest son, Robert 'Short-stockings' Curthose. He lost and was punished, but not too much so that he kept his job as Earl of Northumbria.

This first rebellion took place in 1088 but it wasn't his last. In 1095 he led another revolt against William Rufus in support of someone else, someone insignificant whose name escapes me. This revolt was also a failure, but it included a series of events that made it memorable and proved finally that by that time there were Normans actually living in Northumberland.

By 1095 Robert was living in Bamburgh, in the old fortress of the Saxon Earls of Northumberland. He was married with children and the whole family were living there along with his followers and retainers. You need to know the name of one of those retainers, partly because it is a rather splendid name and partly because he is to play quite a significant part in the story. He was the Earl's Steward and his name was Arkle Moreal.

During the revolt, the fortress was besieged by William Rufus and his army built what was described as a marvellous siege-work, a timber fortress surrounding the existing castle. It was called (in rather chilling terms) Malvoisin or 'evil neighbour' and its purpose was to prevent anyone getting in or out but it apparently failed to do that because in fact Mowbray somehow managed to get out. Leaving his wife and family behind and old Arkle Moreal holding the castle in his name, he escaped and fled to Tynemouth. It's not clear what he was expecting to do but in fact he was captured and brought back to Bamburgh where the fortress was still bravely holding out under the control of Mrs Mowbray and the Steward who were refusing to yield.

King William, being a tough and a ruthless man, as kings tended to be in those days, wasn't in the mood to hang about so he displayed his captured prisoner on Malvoisin and announced that unless Bamburgh surrendered, Mowbray's eyes would be put out so Arkle, being a realist and recognising the inevitable, gave into the King and yielded the castle.

As it happens, Arkle Moreal was a pretty tough character himself and had played a huge role in another highly significant moment in Northumberland History. In 1093, a couple of years before the events recorded above, Malcolm Canmore (that's King Malcolm III of Scotland to you, of course) came south on yet another invasion in his quest to push the boundaries of Scotland further south and make Northumberland Scottish. He had reached Alnwick, which was the home, you will recall, of Gilbert Tyson, where he camped for the night and where he was surprised by a force led by Robert de Mowbray. In the battle that followed, King Malcolm was killed. The site where it happened is marked by a cross called Malcolm's Cross on the hillside just north of Alnwick Castle.

The man who killed the king was Arkle Moreal and there was a follow up to these events a few years later, which involved a very beautiful and isolated little Norman church just north of Alnwick in the greenest heart of Northumberland.

Old Bewick Church and the Queen of England

The church of the Holy Trinity at Old Bewick between Eglingham and Chillingham is a beautiful building in an extraordinary situation. It is a long way from the nearest village, in a churchyard that is almost surrounded by a stream called the Kirk Burn. 'Kirk' is still a common word in Scotland but not in England – it is an ancient word, pre-English, and it means 'holy place' and you get the feeling that this was always a holy place.

Our ancient ancestors often chose streams or springs at the foot of hillsides as the source of their worship and at Old Bewick, on the lip of a cliff just a few hundred feet above the churchyard, there are two Iron-Age hillforts. There is even an ancient style of bridge, a clapper bridge made of a single huge block of stone that crosses the Burn between the churchyard and the hillforts so it's not hard to imagine our prehistoric ancestors coming down to this dark, damp hollow on the edge of the hill to commune with their gods; it was probably a pagan religious site for hundreds of years before it was taken over by the Christians – but eventually this ancient holy place became a Christian church.

It's not clear when that happened but some of the stone in the west and the north walls is very obviously Anglo Saxon so there must have been a church there in the years before the Norman Conquest. Most of the building, however, is not Anglo Saxon because the church that is there today is an almost perfect example of a relatively small and extremely early Norman church that has barely been added to since. It is a perfect period piece, glorious inside – simple, severe and very, very beautiful. So how did such a lovely building end up in this isolated spot?

Well, now there's a question and it's going to get quite an extraordinary answer, an answer that will involve a man with a name like a horse, an earl, two queens, at least four kings and one possible murder and it starts in the pages of Shakespeare's *Macbeth*.

You might recall that in Shakespeare's play, when Duncan, the king of Scotland, is murdered by Macbeth, his sons Malcolm and Donalbain flee into exile to avoid the same fate. Eventually they return with an English army, Macbeth is killed and Malcolm becomes king in his place.

In real life Duncan was murdered in the year 1040 AD and Malcolm was crowned as King Malcolm III in 1058. A few years later, after the Norman Conquest, Malcolm married Margaret, who was a bit of a good egg, and was eventually made a saint, the only royal saint in Scottish history, and among her children was a daughter christened Edith, who became known as Matilda, or more commonly Maud … it is all a bit complicated.

Sadly, Maud's father Malcolm, as I've just been saying, was killed by Arkle Moreal at the Battle of Alnwick in 1093 and his body was taken to Tynemouth Priory to be buried

Meanwhile, in 1100 AD, the King of England, William II (or William Rufus as he is often known) was killed in suspicious circumstances. He was shot by an arrow while hunting in the New Forest. Among the hunting party was his brother Henry, the youngest son of William the Conqueror. When his brother died, Henry

Church of the Holy Trinity, Old Bewick: Early 1100s (restored 1866).

immediately left the scene and went to Winchester where he secured the Royal Treasury and had himself declared King the following day. He became King Henry I and you will not be surprised to learn that there are those who suspect that William's death was not a hunting accident at all and that Henry might have had something to do with it, though nothing has ever been proved.

Now, re-enter Maud (stage left). Maud had been sent by her mother to live in a monastery in southern England and had spent most of her life there, though she had never become a nun. She seems to have known Henry for some time and they may even have been in love with each other when they married in 1100 AD, shortly after his coronation. Genuine affection was probably a rather unusual situation for a Royal wedding in those days, but then Maud seems to have been an unusual woman – highly cultivated, pious, affectionate and well educated, while Henry showed signs of being fond of her and wishing to make her happy … which brings us (finally) to the church at Old Bewick.

At that time Old Bewick was part of the manor belonging to Arkle Moreal, the man who had actually killed Maud's father, and when he became king, Henry took all Arkle's lands off him and gave them to his new queen as some sort of solace and recompense for the loss of her father. She was known, alongside her love of poetry and music, to be very interested in architecture and had already been involved in building of a number of other churches, so she rebuilt Old Bewick – not with her own hands of course – she had the lads do it for her – but she made sure that standards were maintained and may well have employed the designers and craftsmen who were currently working on the new Castle and Cathedral in Durham (there is a carving on the Old Bewick chancel arch that is almost identical to a carving in the chapel at Durham Castle).

What she did next was interesting. She didn't want the church for herself or even the land round about it, what she really wanted was to do something for the soul of her father, so she gave the church and the land to the monks at Tynemouth Priory where her father lay buried. Actually, Tynemouth was a daughter house of the Abbey at St Albans and so the gift went to both places. This is what the contract that sealed the gift said:

Matilda of England, Queen, to Roger Bigot and all the King's Barons, English and French in Northumberland, greetings: Be it known that I have granted to God, St Alban and St Oswin and to Richard the Abbot, the land of Arkle Moreal to be possessed forever for the soul of my father …

There's more but that's the gist of it and that's how the church came to be so special and so beautiful – it was given to a queen by her husband as a gesture of love and built by a remarkable queen to protect the soul and memory of her father – no wonder it looks so good.

When he wasn't giving touching presents to his wife, Henry I was busy completing the Norman settlement of Northumberland and by the time his reign came to an end in 1135 things must have looked pretty settled. He had given a nice charter to Newcastle, which included some rights and freedoms to encourage the town's growth and development. He was generous but tough with his barons, giving them titles and land and whatnot but biffing them if they stepped out of line. His administrative skills were notable too and he developed an efficient financial system and increasingly accepted laws in the country.

The one thing he couldn't do sadly, was provide an heir that everybody was comfortable with. His only son (or at least his only legitimate son, he is reputed to have had 9 illegitimate sons and 13 illegitimate daughters) but his only male heir drowned when the ship he was in sank outside the harbour at Barfleur in Normandy with the loss of 300 lives. Apparently everybody on board, passengers and crew, were drunk and the boat hit a rock.

Henry was evidently devastated; he fainted on the spot when he was told the news. His wife, our Matilda, had already died by this time and in a bid to produce a new heir (and possibly because he liked her) he married again but there were no new children in his second marriage so he made his daughter (yet another Matilda) the heir to the throne. However, when he died, his nephew Stephen bypassed Henry's wishes and seized the top job and that led, pretty soon, to a ferocious civil war that lasted until Stephen died 19 years later in 1154 – it was a period sometimes called The Anarchy.

Norham Castle was on the front line in various disputes between the Scots and the English. The Keep dates from c.1157

Northumberland and Scotland during the Anarchy

I mention these events of national significance because they had a fairly short-lived but extraordinary effect on our county.

For a while we became Scottish!

In 1136, just after Stephen's coronation, King David I of Scotland invaded the North including Cumberland and Westmorland and of course Northumberland, where he besieged and captured loads of towns and castles including Wark, Norham, Alnwick and Newcastle.

That first invasion was inconclusive. His army was stopped and he had to give all of the castles back again but he wasn't away long. He had another bash two years later. In 1138 he was back with another army and recaptured most of the same castles.

Why did he do that? You must be asking.

Well, the ostensible reason, the legal justification if you like, was that he did it in support of Matilda. David was the son of Malcolm III who had been killed at Alnwick in 1093. His sister (Maud) had married Henry I, so her daughter, Matilda, was his niece. He had also grown up in the English Court, had been a close friend (and brother-in-law) of Henry and decided to support Henry's choice of successor. That was the ostensible reason and there was some justice behind it so there's no point in being entirely cynical about his reasons for invading.

On the other hand, it would be perfectly reasonable for you to be at least a little bit cynical because his motives were clearly a bit more complicated than that. He was a new, ambitious ruler of an expanding country. He is often described as "The King Who Made Scotland" and he clearly had an eye for the territory to the south of his new kingdom. Northumberland had been part of the same country as Scotland for hundreds of years and he wanted it back so when an excuse was available he took it.

That's two reasons why he invaded, but I suspect there was a third at least as big. Those early years of the 12ᵗʰ century were, in one respect, boom years in the north and the reason was silver. Suddenly, out of the ore fields of the Lakeland Fells and the North Pennines extraordinary quantities of silver began to be mined. It had always been there. The Romans had exploited the Alston mines for their lead but also for the riches of silver that came with the lead and in the 1090s William Rufus had founded, or refounded, Carlisle to exploit the mines in north Cumberland, but by about 1130 the riches were beginning to run out.

However, in 1133 news broke that fabulously successful new finds had been made, first of all near Caldbeck in Cumberland and later around Alston and the South Tyne and suddenly a bonanza was in progress. For the next 60 or 70 years there was nothing like it, not in Britain, or contemporary Europe and probably not in the world.

The bonanza came in two stages. First of all, from 1033 to the 1050s the main wealth was coming out of a mine called the Silverbeck Mine on the eastern slopes of the Lake District and then, when that started to run out there were new and equally fabulously rich veins of ore discovered in the North Pennines, in Northumberland and around Alston.

It seems pretty likely to me that David wanted that wealth to boost the coffers of his new kingdom, so he came and took it.

However, this second invasion was also unsuccessful so that should have put paid to his ambitions. David's army was defeated at a battle called the Battle of the Standard, which took place at Northallerton, but in a way that rather mystifies me he managed to do pretty well despite the defeat. In the treaty that followed he managed to hold on to Carlisle (where all of that wealth was, you will recall, and which he made the capital of Scotland) and he managed to get his son Henry appointed as Earl of Northumberland.

Hm?

I don't get it either. I suspect that the people on the other side of the table were so tied up in their civil war that they lost the plot, whereas David was more focused and determined. I think it's possible that they just wanted to get him off their backs and as (like so many politicians since) they didn't really care very much about the far North) they gave him Northumberland to keep him quiet.

Apart from the reasons I listed above, David had an extra bit of motivation – he thought Northumberland was part of his own inheritance. His granny had been married to a man called Waltheof who was the last Anglo-Saxon Earl of Northumberland and, despite losing the Battle of the Standard, David managed to persuade the English to give the title to his son!

It doesn't sound like a defeat, does it? And there was more. The treaty specifically banned David and Henry from Newcastle and Bamburgh, but those exceptions were soon overturned and the Scots were effectively in charge of the whole county. David was sufficiently comfortable in Newcastle that he founded the Black Friars while Henry, his son, almost certainly built himself a new castle and the splendid new church at Warkworth to rival the splendours of Bamburgh just to the North …

… so there we were, once again a de facto part of Scotland, and that's how it stayed until 1153, when David and Henry both died within a few months of each other. The new King of Scotland was Henry's son Malcolm. He became Malcolm IV but his nickname was Malcolm the Maiden, which provides a bit of a clue about what happened next.

The following year, in 1154, King Stephen died as well and his place was taken by Henry II who was certainly no maiden and in fact was geet tough as owt, as I believe they said in Newcastle at the time, so it wasn't too hard for him to persuade Malcolm to abandon the Scottish claim to Northumberland and that should have been that … but it still wasn't.

Malcolm wasn't well and he died early, at the age of just 24, and the crown passed to his younger brother whose nickname was at least as revealing as Malcolm's; he was called William the Lion and he was as sore as a gumboil about losing his Northumbrian inheritance, so once again the cycle of invasions began.

Prudhoe Castle Gatehouse: Early 1100s (upper floor added early 1200s). The castle was besieged by William the Lion in 1173 and 1174.

He invaded twice, in 1173 and 1174 and they were big-scale brutal affairs. He was clearly determined to hold on to his grandfather's gains. One of the places that he attacked on both occasions was Prudhoe Castle, which is right on the southern edge of the county so you can tell how far he got.

By 1173 castle technology had moved on a long way since the early motte and baileys of the early Norman period. Many castles had been built, or were in the process of being rebuilt, in stone. Alnwick Castle had been rebuilt in stone by 1157 and was already huge, as vast then as it is today. Bamburgh's great keep, which still dominates the skyline, seems to have been built about the same time and the vast and mighty tower at Norham Castle had been built by Hugh le Puiset, the greatest of all the great architectural bishops of Durham who owned the castle. Newcastle's magnificent keep was on the way up, though still incomplete, and all over the

county these wonderful symbols of Norman power were under construction.

Prudhoe Castle was one of them. Its splendid Gatehouse had already been completed earlier in the century and the curtain walls rebuilt in stone. The keep at the heart of the present castle was built at this time too, either just before or just after the building was besieged by William the Lion in 1173 and 1174. You might recall that this castle belonged to the Umfraville family and the owner at the time of the latest Scottish invasion was a man called Odinel d'Umfraville though I have to admit that I would have gone into hiding for life rather that acknowledge that my name was Odinel d'Umfraville.

You might think it's interesting that this relatively small castle on the southern edge of the county should have been targeted by William, but I think it is a question susceptible (as they say) of a ready explanation, which is that Odinel had been brought up in the Scottish court but had transferred his allegiance back to England and Henry and William was v. cross with him and besieged his castle… unsuccessfully. The Historic England guide book to the castle quotes a contemporary account of the siege by a man called Jordan Fantosme (another good name) who was the clerk to the Bishop of Winchester. The scene, at first, was quite splendid:

The king of Scotland had his pavilions, his tents and his marquees pitched there and he said to his noblemen: '*My Lords, what shall we do? As long as Prudhoe stands we shall never have peace …*'

But it did stand up and they failed to take it so they went home and came back to renew the siege the following year with their army enhanced by extra contingents of French and Flemish soldiers but old Odie was expecting them this time and he'd got the castle well stocked so it could hold out for a while.

While the siege was under way Odinel managed to slip out to gather support and he returned with … four hundred knights with shining helms … and after three days William gave up yet again but not before doing what besieging armies always do, I believe; he destroyed the castle's farmland, its gardens and crops and stripped the bark off the fruit trees and then set off back towards Scotland.

He stopped for a while at Alnwick, which turned out to be a great mistake. A detachment of his army. led by the Earl of Fife, set off to Warkworth which had, of course, been the HQ of his father, Henry, and a niggling thorn in William's flesh. The detachment is reputed to have forced 300 of the residents of the village into the church and burnt them to death.

What was it with churches and burning people to death? We have already heard about Walcher and the massacre at Gateshead and a few years later it happened again when King John came north to wreak revenge on one of the barons who had forced him to sign the Magna Carta; he came to Mitford and burned all of the villagers in their new parish church. It's a horror that seems to have gone on ever since. I've been to the village of Oradour sur Glames in central France where the Nazis did the same to the villagers in the Second World War

and I even noted that Hercule Poirot's back-story involved a similar incident in the First World War. Perhaps in the past churches were the only buildings big enough to hold all the people you wanted to burn, or perhaps, like the massacres in Mosques that have happened in more recent times, there is a special significance in defiling the place that your victims revere.

Meanwhile, back in Alnwick, William was caught in a surprise attack, at daybreak, in thick mist. The chronicler described the scene vividly … '*Now the battle raged fierce and hot on both sides; you could see many javelins hurled and arrows shot, the bold fighting and the cowards fleeing. There was great slaughter of the unfortunate Flemings, the fields were strewn with their bowels torn from their bodies …*'

William was taken prisoner. Just beside the entrance into Hulne Park, the Duke of Northumberland's great deer park and just two or three hundred metres from the castle gatehouse, is an inscription recording the event. If you look north across the fields from the stone you can see the monument recording the death of William's great grandfather, Malcolm III – it wasn't a lucky place for Scottish kings, Alnwick.

William was taken away to Normandy until a ransom was paid to buy his liberty and there is a story that when he was finally on his way home he was brought through Newcastle only to be met with a hail of stones and other abuse from the people of the town. I mention this story because it seems to me to mark the first time that the people of Northumberland made it clear that they weren't Scottish and it is true that the defeat of William the Lion did indeed mark the end of that desire to include Northumberland as part of Scotland. It wasn't until 1237 and under King Alexander the somethingth or other that the Scots finally renounced any claim to the county and the Border was legally established where it still is today, but after 1174 there was never another attempt to take over northern England and Northumberland finally and conclusively became a part of England … until a hundred years later when we all fell out again and started a war that went on for 400 years … but that's part of a later chapter and something to be looking forward to.

6. 13TH CENTURY

After more than a hundred years of struggles with the Norman Conquest, and after repeated attempts to make us Scottish, and after the capture and defeat of William the Lion in 1174, Northumberland finally passed into a long period of comparative and much needed peace. Of course peace was never total in the Middle Ages; war and rebellion were more or less a way of life and there was a brief flare up of nastiness early in the next century when King John came north to settle some scores with the barons who had forced him to sign Magna Carta, and the Scots, sensing that the English crown was a bit distracted, flexed their muscles once again.

Later in the century Simon de Montfort's rebellion, though it never affected Northumberland directly, unnerved the population of Newcastle enough to persuade them that they needed to wrap themselves up in some nice defensive walls. The owners of castles also continued to cast weather eyes over their defences and like nervous householders beefing up their burglar alarms today, made sure that they had added the latest security techniques to their properties, so new forms began to appear at almost all of the castles.

Newcastle got a complicated new gatehouse bristling with enough cunning wheezes to discourage Indiana Jones, and all over the county big rounded towers, inspired by the towers that Crusaders had seen in the Holy Land, were added to the curtain walls ...

... and of course, at a more ordinary level, people continued to be beset by all the normal unpleasantness that life always inflicts on us and probably affected more of us more often in those rough old days. For example, Barbara Charlton, writing about the North Tyne in the 13th century has a whole series of tales about how neighbours stole from each other as they always will and how court records reveal their habit of slaying each other with axes. She includes the hideous tale of a woman called Emma from Wauchope who was beheaded on the spot for some misdemeanour at Bellingham market ...

... and then there were those special difficulties that those of us who live in the North East have always had to put up with and which we continue to experience today – in particular the unpleasantness that we might call "the north-of-Watford syndrome" or possibly, to put it another way, the "grim-up-North" scenario. I have already had occasion in these pages to refer to the tendency of Newcastle United to appear last on *Match of the Day* and for BBC weather presenters to cover Northumberland with random left-over bad-weather and low-temperature stickers ...

... well that has been an age-old problem and one of the earliest examples of it raised its head in the first half of the 1200s.

You will recall that Robert de Mowbray, the first successful Norman Earl of Northumbria, because he was

Left: The waves at Tynemouth can still be as ferocious today as they appeared to the monks of St Albans in the early 1200s.

in dispute with the Bishop of Durham, gave the monastery at Tynemouth to the monks of St Albans and eventually, in the early 1200s a group of them came north to begin the rebuilding of their church. One of them, clearly a man without a northern bone in his body, was a bit shocked by what he found and wrote a letter back to his chums (or brothers) in St Albans, warning them what they would find if they came up to Tyneside for their hols. It was, in effect, an early Trip Advisor entry and (along with the Emperor Hadrian's poet, Florus) one of the first really bad tourist notices that the North East ever received. I'm going to quote a substantial chunk of it so you can get a flavour of what Southerners thought (and possibly still think) about us.

The letter still exists in the St Alban's Cathedral Library and you can imagine the whole thing as an answer to the question, "So what's it like up there in the North East? What's your accommodation like?" The answer isn't altogether encouraging.

"Our house is confined to the top of a high rock and is surrounded by the sea on all sides but one. Here is the approach to the monastery through a gate cut out of the rock, so narrow that a cart can hardly pass though...."

"…and the weather?" asks the innocent friend.

"Day and night the waves break and roar beneath the cliff. Thick sea frets roll in wrapping everything in gloom. Dim eyes, sore throats are the consequence. Spring and summer never come here. The north wind is always blowing and brings with it cold and snow and storms in which the wind tosses the salt sea foam over our buildings and rains it down inside our castle."

"Good lord! That sounds terrible! Is there anything else wrong?"

"Shipwrecks are frequent. It is great pity to see the numbed crew who no power on earth can save, whose vessel, mast swaying and timbers parted, rushes upon rock and reef."

"How awful! But what about the locals? I've heard that Tynesiders are very agreeable and friendly."

"The people who live by the shore feed upon black malodorous seaweed called shauk, which they gather on the rocks. The constant eating of it turns their complexions black ..."

"That can't be the only food they eat? Be honest, there must be plenty of local fruit and vegetables?

"In the spring the sea air blights the blossoms of the stunted fruit trees so that you will think yourself lucky to find one wizened apple, though it will set your teeth on edge should you try to eat it."

"It sounds desperate. Is there no nice food at all?"

"We are well off for food, thanks to the abundant supply of fish, of which we tire."

"Oh dear! I know the feeling. All those fish fingers. But surely down there by the seaside there is plenty of nice wildlife and lots of opportunities for bird watching."

"No ring dove or nightingale is here, only grey birds which nest in the rocks and greedily prey upon the bodies of the drowned."

"Heavens! Do you think we should risk booking there for next year?"

"See to it dear brother that you never come to so comfortless a place."

It's not the most enthusiastic endorsement of our beautiful north ever offered, is it, but there is a follow up. The letter didn't actually end there and the monk goes on to describe the new church, which has just been completed. He writes: '*But the church is of wondrous beauty ... Within it rests the body of the blessed martyr Oswin in a silver shrine magnificently embellished with gold and jewels ...*'

And it is. It is ruined now and the richly elaborate tomb of the saint has long been scattered, but the dramatic fragment of the great church that was built in

Tynemouth Priory, which features stained glass windows of Edward I and Edward II by William Wailes.

the early part of the 1200s and still stands proudly on the Tynemouth headland is indeed of wondrous beauty and in those respects, in its ambitious scale and beautiful simplicity, it is one of many wonderful 13th century churches in the county.

Most areas of the country seem to specialise in a particular period of church architecture; they are places to which you would go if you were especially interested in that particular period. You would head for East Anglia, for example, or perhaps Somerset if you wanted to immerse yourself in the great wealthy "wool" churches of the 15th Century, and you might head to Lancashire if you were looking for innovative uses of new materials – churches made of iron, for example or with terracotta details. The great abbeys of Yorkshire: Fountains Abbey, Rievaulx, Whitby, Byland Abbey and so on provide magnificent examples of the Early English Style of the 13th century. The Lake District, because of its isolation over the centuries, is a wonderful area to explore simple and humble little chapels.

Well, Northumberland is rich in 13th century churches. It falls short of North Yorkshire in terms of its abbeys but there is no shortage of parish churches built during this window of peace in the 1200s.

A few of them are great. I have already mentioned Tynemouth but Hexham is another, richly decorated and richly furnished. Brinkburn is yet another beautiful building in an exquisite setting by the River Coquet near Rothbury. It is a little older than the others, still with hints of Norman architecture about its arches. These are the great ones, but round about them are lots and lots of smaller and simpler but still beautiful and surprisingly ambitious parish churches, many of which have a characteristic that seems to be quite typical of Northumberland and not so common elsewhere – a lot of Northumbrian churches have Anglo-Saxon features on the one hand, and they have 13th century features on the other but there's nothing in between. It is as if the Norman Conquest passed them by. There is a whole heap of churches like this in the Tyne Valley – Ovingham, the two churches at Bywell, Corbridge and Warden all have fascinating survivals from Saxon times, nothing from Norman times and big and quite splendid rebuilding from the peaceful years after 1200.

Ovingham is a fine example. The tower is Saxon; it is high and dramatic, but the rest of the church is a large, complete and very perfect Early English building from the 1200s with a positive forest of pillars and Gothic arches inside. St Peter's church at Bywell is another, with big and important Saxon remains, but its chancel is a

Brinkburn Priory 1190-1220 (restored 1858).

fascinating bit of 13th century building, so much of a period piece that it feels very odd to modern eyes. It is extraordinarily tall and narrow, almost too narrow for its height and the windows are long, thin lancet windows, again excessively narrow and elongated. I have to admit that it is one of my favourite bits of medieval church architecture – but then I love them all; Bamburgh is superb, its chancel a piece of pure architecture and not just a building. Hartburn has another of the remarkably narrow chancels contrasting in the strangest way with

the broad, airy, pillar-forested nave, Haltwhistle is complete and very perfect … there is something so typically Northumbrian about these 13th century churches. They don't shout their glories like churches in other places and other periods; they never have spires or grand contemporary towers, but there is an intensity about them that can seem almost oppressive but deeply spiritual as well.

Eee! I could go on. If I was standing in front of you I probably would go on; you wouldn't be able to shut me up. What a joy it would be for us both, but the basic point that I would be making would always be the same, that the 13th century churches are a powerful reminder of the window of peace that occurred in the 1200s.

And the churches aren't the only bit of evidence. The county was settling down to a more normal way of life. More and more land was being taken into cultivation. Villages such as Elsdon and Harbottle, high up in the county close to the Scottish border, were given permission to hold markets. Markets and annual fairs developed in towns throughout the county – at Alnwick, Wooler, Haltwhistle, Hexham and lots of other places.

Towns expanded. The population was on the rise. There are plenty of surviving 13th century manor houses as well. Because of what happened in the following century, a lot of them were later turned into castles but if you look at them carefully you can tell that they started off as houses and only became castles later on. Off the top of my head I can think of at least 10 houses where this happened. Shortflatt Tower, Welton Hall, Halton Castle, Belsay Castle, Chillingham Castle were all like this and a particularly good example is Aydon Castle, just north of Corbridge. If you visit it nowadays (and you can, because it belongs to English Heritage and is open to the public) you find a beautiful little castle with castle walls around the outside and lots of other castle-y features. It was given permission to get turned into a castle (Licence to Crenellate) in 1305, but at the heart of the building is a typical, unfortified medieval manor house with a great hall and kitchens and a private wing (or solar) for the personal use of the lord and his family; this house was already there in the 13th century and was only defended later on because of what happened next….

St Peter's at Bywell, with typical 13th century lancet windows.

Hartburn church's fine 13th century chancel.

Dogtooth and nailhead decoration at Whalton church.

....and what did happen next is that a little girl died quite a long way from Northumberland.

Her name was Margaret and she was the granddaughter of Alexander III, the king of Scotland. Alexander had a long and successful reign; he was married to another Margaret who was the sister of King Henry III of England and together they had three children – two sons and a daughter (also called Margaret) who married the King of Norway. From that reasonably normal family situation and from the point of view of a king who needed to produce an heir to the throne, all seemed well, but quite suddenly poor old Alexander's life fell horribly apart. His wife died. Both his sons died before they had produced any children and finally his daughter died in childbirth leaving Alexander with no family at all and no heirs except Margaret, a

new-born baby girl living with her father in Norway. He declared her as his heir, despite her age; it was the only thing he could do but just to be sure he got married again to see if he could produce a more direct successor and lo and behold, his second wife became pregnant. A good ending? Not a good ending! In 1286, before the baby was born, indeed while Alexander was on the way to visit his pregnant wife, he fell off his horse and was killed! To complete the story, in the event his second wife's baby was either still-born or miscarried so that left little Margaret as the last man standing, or at least the last baby toddling, since she was only three by the time all of these tragedies had occurred.

Obviously, little Margaret couldn't be expected to rule the country at her age, so six Guardians were appointed to do the job for her, but there was another character in the story who was determined to play a part. This was Edward I, King of England. Alexander's first wife had been Edward's sister, which, I suppose, gave him a bit of a vested interest; but more important than that, the kings of England were always convinced that they had higher status than the kings of Scotland and though the Scots were independent and determined to remain that way, Edward was equally determined to increase his power and influence; so he came up with the wheeze of marrying little Margaret to his own son, little Edward Caernarvon, the Prince of Wales, who was also just three at the time. His idea was to use these two tiny tots to bring about the union of the two countries of Scotland and England (under the control of the English, of course).

The negotiations for this marriage were complete in 1290 when the potential bride and the potential groom were both seven years old and little Margaret set off from Norway in the care of the Bishop of Bergen and headed towards Leith, where all the dignitaries of Scotland and England were waiting to greet her. Unfortunately she never got there. There was a terrible storm and the ship was blown wildly off course until it reached South Ronaldsay, hundreds of miles to the north in Orkney, where the little girl died, supposedly of sea sickness, in the arms of the Bishop of Bergen. Her body was taken back to Norway and she was buried in the same tomb as her mother in Bergen Cathedral.

So there you are! And we think we've had it hard. Who would be a king … or a queen … or especially a tiny little royal pawn trapped in the ruthless cruelty of international diplomacy?

So that's what happened next, but what happened after that (next next) brings the story closer to home and introduces the dreadful theme of Northumberland's suffering over the next few centuries.

This is how it panned out.

With the Little Maid of Norway dead, Scotland needed a king pretty desperately, so adverts were put in all the local Chronicles and things and 13 people applied for the job. The interviews took place in Berwick on Tweed and the man who chaired the interviewing panel was Edward himself (because he was the sort of boss king and whoever got the job would be expected to bow down before him).

I believe the interviews went much the same as they've been going ever since. I presume the interviewees had to give a presentation – probably a PowerPoint since they were applying to be kings – and eventually the panel retired to discuss its choice. It turned out that there were really just two candidates in the running. The other eleven were no-hopers but Robert the Bruce (remember that name) and John Baliol both had pretty good claims to be chosen.

Edward (and the rest of the panel) chose John Baliol who came from Barnard Castle in County Durham, but who got his claim to the throne from his mother who rejoiced in the name of Devorgilla (if it's possible to rejoice in such a name). She was a granddaughter of the great King David, so John Balliol came from a good lineage.

There were conditions attached to his appointment. Edward made it absolutely clear that he himself was to be top king and that not only would JB have to pay homage to him, but the Scots would also have to support the English in their overseas wars and other foreign policy adventures. You might think that this was a bit of a cheek and typical English arrogance, and there are several million Scots who would probably agree with you. At the time, though, possibly to make sure he got the job, John Balliol agreed to Edward's conditions.

I say, "at the time", but in the event that's not what happened. The first act of homage took place when Balliol knelt down before Edward (in Newcastle incidentally) but a couple of years later Edward pushed Balliol too far. He made outrageous demands that the Scots join his war against the French and provide money to fund it, so John Balliol not only ignored the request but he went one step further and signed a treaty with the French.

Edward was miffed … and when a king like Edward I gets miffed it's better to look for the door.

He leapt into miffed mode. He declared Balliol a traitor and set off north with the intention of wreaking revenge. His army passed through Newcastle and arrived at Norham by the River Tweed on 29th March 1296. The following day, the 30th March, his army sacked Berwick, which had been founded by the Scottish King David (John Balliol's grandfather) half a century before and was at that time the most important port in Scotland. The slaughter lasted for two days, during which Edward's army killed something between 4000 and 17000 of its inhabitants.

You often hear rather similar stories about such events, stories that may be true or may be just urban myths, but they are undoubtedly memorable. People said that there was so much blood flowing in the streets of Berwick during those two days that it turned the wheels of the water mills. They said that for centuries afterwards, if you dug a hole two feet deep almost anywhere in the town you found human bones.

After the sacking, Berwick was going to change hands between the two countries time and time again; it was going to retain a tactical and symbolic importance; it was eventually going to end up as a beautiful Northumbrian town – but it was destroyed for ever as a great Scottish city and it was never again a great port. That's how brutal the English attack was.

But Edward's fury and revenge against John Balliol wasn't to be satisfied by destroying just one town. On the 29th April he marched north and won the battle of Dunbar and then, during that spring and summer, with apparent ease, he drifted around Scotland capturing all the main castles and putting his own men in charge and replacing the Scottish Government with one of his own and then he left, he dickied off to fight another war on the continent, leaving the chaps in control, apparently confident that Scotland was done and dusted – but of course it wasn't.

Almost immediately the Scots began to fight back and who can blame them? The same year, later in 1296,

there was a whole series of sporadic but savage retaliatory raids south into Northumberland. They reached as far as the Tyne Valley where Hexham was among the places burned. The name to remember is ~~Mel Gibson Braveheart~~ William Wallace, who was responsible for this immediate fight back and even more for what happened the following year.

In the autumn and early winter of 1297, the Scots revolted in a serious way. There were at least three separate revolts but the one that involved us was the one led by William Wallace. On the 11th September he rather unexpectedly won the Battle of Stirling Bridge (partly because the English commander, the Earl of Warenne, slept-in and missed the beginning of the battle).

Emboldened by that success, Wallace set off south with a substantial force including, apparently, a fearsome band of warriors from Galloway, and spent five weeks destroying virtually the whole of Northumberland and large parts of Cumberland as well. It was an utterly devastating raid. The Northumbrians panicked; people fled to Newcastle or any other walled or well defended place, leaving the countryside virtually deserted. A contemporary account says that the people '… *petrified with fear evacuated the countryside of their wives and children and all of their household goods, sending them to Newcastle …*'.

The roll call of villages that suffered catastrophic losses included places like Yeavering, Hedgely, Doddington, Hethpool, Akeld, Alnwick, Felton, Rothbury, Woodhorn, Stamfordham … actually I might have just as well said that virtually the whole county was devastated – except Newcastle.

Oddly, Wallace arrived at Newcastle, which was defended but not totally, its town walls were still incomplete in 1297 and the castle was relatively sparsely garrisoned, but he never attacked it. Instead he went off to Carlisle, which he also failed to attack, before coming back and burning down Hexham, and Wylam and Prudhoe and then, with winter seriously beginning to bite, he turned north and set off back home.

But while they were still destroying the Tyne Valley there is one quite revealing story about the Scottish raiders who seemed to have been a particularly wild and hairy bunch. Apparently the weather was dreadful and the River Tyne was in full spate, so when the Scots were burning down Wylam on the North bank of the river, the men from the village of Ryton on the opposite bank, feeling safe behind their flooded river, jeered at the Scots who, being Scots, leapt into the water, swam across to the other side, burned down Ryton and killed everybody in it.

After his 1297 raid on Northumberland, William Wallace only came back here once. He continued to be a rebel in his native Scotland and a thorn in the English flesh for a number of years until 1305, when he was captured, taken to London and put on trial for treachery. His rather splendid reaction to the charge was, "I could not be a traitor to Edward for I was never his subject" but he was still found guilty and executed.

First of all he was stripped naked and dragged through the streets behind a horse. Then he was hanged drawn and quartered which means that he was hanged by the neck but taken down before he died; his genitals were cut off and his bowels removed and burned in front of him while he was still alive. Finally, he was beheaded and his head was displayed on London Bridge but for his last appearance in Northumberland, one of his limbs was nailed up at Newcastle!

There is a moral there somewhere. But the moral for Northumberland was that the 13th century, which had seemed reasonably normal for so long, ended in disaster and the disaster was going to continue for an extraordinarily long time

The Border Wars are often described as the 300-years war and having started in 1296 they certainly lasted until the Union of the two crowns in 1603, but some people would say that the war lasted even longer than that since there were several follow-up wars in the 1600s and the last recorded battle was a skirmish called The Crookham Encounter that occurred as late as 1685.

Others would point out that there were two major rebellions by the Scots in 1715 and 1745 so perhaps the war was still bubbling along nicely into the middle of the 18th century, and some would even point out that the desire to be independent and free from English control has never left the Scots and that perhaps the conflict is

William Wallace, depicted here in stained glass, led a devastating raid on Northumberland in 1297.

with us still … but however long the wars lasted, Northumberland was going to suffer because of them, and whose fault was that?

Edward's.

That's an opinion of course. It's my opinion. I recognise that in the 13th century there would have been plenty of people who would have disagreed with me and put the blame on the Scots. After all, they would have said, John Balliol broke the treaty he had signed on being made king; he reneged on his promise to pay homage to Edward, so it was his fault … but who's going to blame him nowadays when we've come to realise that liberty is more important than life? The Scots wanted freedom and the English didn't want them to have it, so there was a whole heap of nastiness still to come. It is going to be explored in gory detail in the next chapter.

7. BORDER WARS

War A (1296-1328)

The war that started in 1296 and included the grotesque and brutal killing of William Wallace is called 'The First War of Scottish Independence' and it went on for 32 years until a treaty was finally signed in 1328.

At the beginning, while Edward I was still alive, the English tended to be in the ascendency and so almost all the action took place north of the Border. Edward was another of those kings whose nickname was quite revealing. Actually he had two nicknames; he was called 'Longshanks', I imagine because his shanks were quite long, and he was called 'The Hammer of the Scots' because there seem to have been few things he liked better than hammering Scotsmen, so for the first few years of the war the only tramp of military boots in Northumberland was the sound of English armies marching north in "Scot-Hammering" mode until, by 1304, the English were pretty well in control of the whole country; but eventually even the toughest hammer gets worn out and King Edward began to fade. He was up here when the final fade occurred in fact.

In 1307 he arrived with another army, first of all to Newcastle, where he stopped for a while to get in a bit of shopping, and then along the Tyne Valley towards Cumberland. He stopped for a few days at a place called Bradley Hall which is a small hill farm nowadays in an intensely romantic situation on the slope of the Whin Sill, below the Roman Wall and just beyond Housesteads; it's difficult to imagine there being a house there big enough for an army to stop or for a king to sleep.

From there he crossed over into Cumberland and stayed for a while at Lanercost Priory near Brampton before moving on, first to Carlisle and then out onto the wild bleakness of Brough Marsh on the Solway where he died, and where today an achingly isolated monument marking the place of his death still stands. In my youth I used to cycle out from Carlisle with a flask and my bird book in my backpack and sit beside this monument musing on history and the fate of kings and surrounded by sky and salt marsh, in a landscape that somebody described as possessing a kind of transcendental monotony.

Edward's death didn't happen in Northumberland, of course, and you'll be asking why I have gone on about it and the answer is that Edward the First's death changed everything because his successor, Edward II, that little Edward Caernarvon who never did get to marry the Maid of Norway, wasn't half so potent a military leader as his dad and by chance he was suddenly confronted by a Scottish King who was, to quote king Lear, "every inch a king".

Robert the Bruce was a tough egg. Like William

Wallace before him, he had been a freedom fighter for a number of years but in 1306 he went further and seized the throne and was quite determined to resist the claims of the English to be overlords of his country. He certainly wasn't prepared to sit and wait for the enemy to come to him, so before long, and devastatingly, the people of Northumberland found themselves on the receiving end of an extraordinary explosion of violence.

They were invaded twice in 1311, for example. In August, the Bruce arrived with a full army and savaged the heart of the county. They took vast amounts of booty away with them, burnt down anything that was standing and took no prisoners – anybody who tried to defend themselves was put to death.

A month later the Scots were back again with an even larger army and as a result even more destruction. On this occasion the Northumbrians recognised the inevitable and raised £2000 to buy off the enemy. £2000 was an extraordinary amount of money; the annual tax bill for the whole of Newcastle was only £100 so the county probably thought it had bought itself a bit of time but no … you don't get rid of tough eggs as easily as that and early in 1312 R. Bruce reappeared demanding yet another £2000.

You're probably asking yourself how he got away with it, why there was no equally powerful English army available to stop him.

It's a good question and there are several answers to it.

First of all, the border is a very long way from London but not very far from Edinburgh. The two sides of the border, even today, are quite different places. If you drive up the A68 over Carter Bar on the way to Edinburgh the English part of the journey is through wild, rough, open moorland. Farms are few and far between, villages non-existent, sheep quite common. But cross the Border and descend down the other side and you quickly find yourself in a very different landscape. You find yourself in the Home Counties in fact, the Scottish Home Counties, well wooded, mixed arable and pastoral farming, substantial and prosperous small towns and villages. In those days the differences must already have existed and it was certainly a great deal quicker for a Scottish army to reach the war zone than for an English one …

… and anyway, which English government, then or now, could really be bothered with the extreme north? Then as now the London establishment had no real interest in the North. One of the books on my shelves says that '*the attitude of Central Government was often extraordinarily detached and disengaged.*' And even if they did get stirred up there was literally very little they could do about it because there wasn't enough money in the King's coffers to keep a standing army protecting the border just in case an attack came and it took ages to enlist a temporary army and march 300 miles from London. By the time they got here any raiding Scottish force would have been long gone.

So the border region was literally left to its own devices by the national government. The nearest branch of the National Government was to be found 150 miles south in York. North of that there was no real control. There were castles, of course but they were only of limited use in protecting the area. If an attack came, any garrison at the castle was stuck inside while the invading army had the choice of stopping and besieging them or walking on past, waving gaily at the inmates watching glumly from the walls. The castles looked great of course, they still look great and we love their daunting splendour, but they were rubbish at controlling invasion.

The weaknesses I've just described weren't peculiar to this particular war, of course. They had existed for hundreds of years. In Norman times, when Scottish kings like Malcolm and David and William the Lion wanted to attack Northumberland, they could do it willy-nilly because there was no similar army to stop them. Since Norman times the English government had abandoned responsibility for protecting the northern border and left the locals to defend themselves.

To be fair the locals did have a system to help them do it. The system was called The March Laws. 'March' is an old word meaning a border and the Anglo-Scottish Border was organised into two – the East March and the West March (a third one, the Middle March, was added later). The King appointed Wardens of the Marches and it was their job, using their own money and local men, to provide for the defence of the border. The Scots set up the same system on their side and a whole structure of local laws developed which were, as far as I know, unique in Europe. It was the only international border that was managed at an entirely local level. The Wardens would meet on 'March Days' and attempt to settle any disputes. They could fine people and compensate others. They could execute people there and then for March Treason – for helping the other side, for example, or even marrying a woman from the other side without the specific consent of the Warden. But the one thing they couldn't do, because they didn't have the manpower to do it, was stop a full-scale attack by a Scottish King and his army.

So there were lots of devastating raids. I have no doubt that invasions in the other direction, by the English into Scottish territory, were devastating too but it seems to me that there was an extra element of terror involved in the Scottish raids on Northumberland (and Cumberland). From the time of Edward I, English soldiers had been paid to fight. Knights got a shilling a day, archers 4d and ordinary soldiers 2d but as far as I can tell Scottish soldiers got nothing. They came because they were motivated by a passionate belief in their country and hatred of the enemy … and because they got to keep anything they could loot. I suspect that both of those reasons made them particularly fearsome.

Eventually of course, after the Scottish attacks had been going on for several years, Edward II got going and set about fighting back on a national scale. In 1314 he came north with a proper army, supposedly the largest English army to ever attack Scotland but unfortunately not the most successful and he got himself totally thrashed at the Battle of Bannockburn.

Double thrashed, maybe triple. The King himself only narrowly escaped with his life. He managed to get to the coast and escape back to London while the rest of the English forces were utterly routed to the extent that you might have expected the English king to recognise that his claim to be the overlord of the Scottish king was dead in the water. But no. Medieval kings weren't like that and Edward refused to give up his claim, so the war dribbled on intermittently but savagely for another 14

years. In 1315 Northumberland was invaded again and in 1318 Berwick was besieged and, after holding out for several months, fell to the Scots once again. At the same time the massive fortress on the Tweed at Norham was besieged for almost a full year and though parts of the outer castle were occupied by the Scots for a few days, it managed to hold out, which was brilliant and must have frustrated and irritated the Scots no end … but it didn't do much to help the rest of Northumberland, which had been left utterly exposed by the rout after Bannockburn and was suffering terrible hardships.

The people of Bamburgh, for example, wrote to the king begging to be let off their taxes because their lands had been '*once again captured and laid waste so that they were utterly burned to the ground*'. Newcastle was no better off. Their lands had been '*so utterly laid waste by the enemy that they can earn no income from them.*'

So the war in the years after the awful and humiliating defeat at Bannockburn was continuous and absolutely unremitting. You can't imagine that the situation could get any worse, but it did, or at least it got no better, and not just because of the war. The weather was appalling with torrential rain and savage winters. For year after year between 1315 and 1322 in Northumberland (as well as all over Europe) there were dreadful harvests; cattle and sheep were dying and people were starving. On top of that the Scots just kept coming. Without any opposition they could overrun Northumberland and keep going down through Durham almost as far as York

The English king, meanwhile, was having his own version of a dreadful time. His favourite, Piers Gaveston (who was also possibly his lover), was murdered by his Barons; he split up with his wife; there were a whole series of revolts against him but still he refused to give up his claims in Scotland so still the war went on. In 1322 he invaded Scotland again with another enormous army but because of the appalling weather he couldn't feed his men; they were starving so they had to slink off back home, humiliated and having achieved nothing. The Governor of Norham Castle, Sir Thomas Grey, wrote: '*The Scots were so fierce and their chiefs so daring that it was no otherwise between them as a hare before greyhounds*'.

…And then Edward was murdered in 1327. He was captured in Wales, taken prisoner to Berkeley Castle and murdered, possibly with a red-hot poker in a grotesque reference to his relationship with his possible lover Piers Gaveston. So that was it. His son took over and became Edward III; in 1328 the Treaty of Edinburgh-Northampton was signed, recognising the right of Robert the Bruce to be undisputed King of Scotland and the First War of Scottish Independence was over. After 32 years.

Yee Ha! Peace in their time. Edward II dead; Robert the Bruce died the following year in 1328! Northumberland was safe again!

For a few minutes!

War B (1332-1357)

The new Edward, Edward III, was just 17 when his father died, and in his minority England was effectively under the control of Roger Mortimer, his mother's lover. Edward immediately had him killed, started to rule for himself and almost as fast started the Second War of Scottish Independence!

At the beginning, the Second War of Scottish Independence seemed to be just an internal Scottish struggle, though its roots were deep in the events of the previous half century. When Robert the Bruce died, his son and heir, David, was only 5 years old and so Edward Balliol, the son of that John Balliol whose refusal to pay sufficient homage to Edward I had set the whole thing in motion, seized the chance to reclaim his father's throne for himself. His claim started a civil war in Scotland, which he lost, and he fled to England where he persuaded Edward III to support him in exchange for yet another promise to recognise the English king as his overlord (just as his father had – what goes round …).

So Edward became involved in Scottish politics once more. He did this partly because he was eager to avenge his father's humiliation at the Battle of Bannockburn, partly out of a sense of damaged English pride and partly because the treaty that ended the 1st War had never been popular on the English side because lots of nobles who had lost their estates in Scotland, considered themselves "The Disinherited" and wanted a chance to get them back.

All of these things happened in 1332 and the following year Edward marched north and laid siege to Berwick (again). The town was strongly defended so he left part of his army to continue the siege and carried on north to capture Edinburgh in the hope that the Scots would be persuaded to give up all of their resistance. That ploy failed (is that a surprise?) so Edward came back to Berwick to get on with the siege.

Meanwhile, the Scots, far from giving up, followed Edward with a large army but instead of attacking the English directly they had a cunning wheeze. Edward had left his wife Philippa (who he loved) in Bamburgh Castle, so the Scots sneaked round Berwick and laid siege to Bamburgh in the hope that the threat to Philippa would be enough to make Edward back down. It wasn't enough (love didn't go that far), so towards the end of July 1333 the two armies met in battle at Halidon Hill just outside Berwick.

I'm not a great man for battles but Halidon Hill has some features that captured my interest. Firstly, I happen to know that the Mayor of Newcastle, Richard de Emeldon, was killed there along with another 59 of his townsmen, but secondly the battle was the first recorded use of a military tactic that was going to make English armies the most successful in Europe for almost a century, including the great and famous victories over the French at the Battles of Crecy and Agincourt.

Before Halidon, the main tactic for winning battles had been to have teams of heavily armed mounted knights with 9-foot long lances charging at the enemy infantry – an invincible force until the Scots came up with the idea of the 'shiltron', which was a circular mass of men, each with an even longer lance or spear, which meant that the charging horses were suddenly confronted with an apparently impenetrable line of lances 14 feet long and they didn't like it. They hesitated, lost momentum and became vulnerable. But at Halidon Hill, Edward, advised by his Northern adviser Sir Gilbert Umfraville, turned to archers as the new weapon of choice. All armies had archers, of course, but normally the archers had to provide their own arrows, which were hard to make and expensive to use, so they tended to use them sparingly; but under Edward, the archers were provided with a relatively endless supply of arrows and they used them in massed ranks of longbows, which turned out to be an absolutely devastating weapon.

So there we are. Another war and even more blood and guts on the fields of Northumberland. This war lasted for the next 25 years. It started with the English victory at Halidon Hill (accompanied, of course, by yet another siege and slaughter at Berwick itself) and it went on from there. Because Edward mark III was a bit more proactive than mark II, more of the action took place over the Border in Scotland but wherever it happened one thing was absolutely clear … nobody ever won and within a year of being thrashed on Halidon Hill the Scots were back in the ascendancy and back on the attack.

The trouble from the English point of view was the French. Edward had already started a war (which turned into The Hundred Years War) against the French in a bid to hold on to his continental properties and so he was distracted. He was like the Nazis desperately trying to fight battles on their western and their eastern flanks towards the end of WWII, so he was always in danger of taking his eye off us up north. The French and the Scots recognised this, of course, and became allies as a result and in 1335 the French sent boatloads of military supplies to Scotland and raised a force 6000 strong that would be available to come to Scotland if they were needed. Very soon they were needed, and they did come, though on this first occasion they attacked Carlisle and the rest of Cumberland instead of Northumberland.

And then the tables turned again. On 6th August 1346, Edward's army won the Battle of Crecy against the French, putting that particular enemy out of commission for a while, so Edward turned his attention back north again where the Scottish King, David II, had raised an army and marched south into England in support of his French ally. They had passed through Northumberland in the usual way but avoided Newcastle for once. They crossed the Tyne and on 17th October they were brutally defeated by the English in the Battle of Nevilles Cross just outside Durham.

In the 1960s I trained to be a teacher at Nevilles Cross College and as a student I would sometimes go to the CIU Club by the traffic lights (where beer could be had at 11 pence a pint) and sometimes to the Nevilles Cross Pub on the opposite corner, where they served a rather odd grey pie that could be made a more respectable brownish colour by the addition of HP Sauce. The road between these two drinking places was (and still is) called Red Bank, supposedly because it became a river of blood during the battle in 1346.

And that should have been that, but of course it wasn't; the war should have been over but it dribbled on for another 11 years with fluctuating patterns of ascendancy and in the course of it terrible things happened:

Take the Battle of Nesbit Moor for example.

Nesbit Moor took place in 1355. It wasn't terribly important in the big scheme of things and it isn't remembered as much as many of the other battles of those endless wars, but one thing happened there that is definitely worth knowing about. The Scots won. That's not the interesting thing; in wars like this you win a few and lose a few but at Nesbit Moor the Scots won and most of the English troops were taken prisoner. Now you probably know what happened to prisoners in medieval wars – nobody wanted the expense of keeping them in prison so the ideal solution was to ransom them – sell them back to their own side and make a bob or two out of the deal.

That's what happened here except that alongside the Scottish troops at Nesbit there were the French troops that I mentioned before and one of them bought all of the English prisoners off the Scots – this was nice for the Scots, who got their rewards without having to put in any effort, but it wasn't so nice for the English because the buyer didn't do it to let them free or to make a profit; he did it because his father had suffered at the hands of the English and he wanted revenge; so he bought the lot and put them all to death.

Wars are like that.

The following year, 1356, Edward was back again to seek vengeance for the death of his troops. There was no proper battle, no one was defeated, but he engaged in an event which became known as The Burnt Candlemas.

Candlemas takes place on 2nd February and it is an important day in the Christian calendar. It celebrates the purification of Mary, 40 days after the birth of Jesus. In more ancient times it also celebrated the mid-point of winter, the point at which the light begins to return and ceremonies on that day are made beautiful by the use of candles …

… but the Burnt Candlemas, Edward's revenge, was marked by a 'chevauchee', a scorched-earth policy where all crops and livestock, all usable land and all buildings were burnt or flattened by bands of mounted men riding though the countryside destroying anything in their way. It has become a common enough strategy in the centuries since, but it seems to have been invented in the 1300s. And it worked. Along with the inevitable siege of Berwick that followed (yet again) and without a battle being fought, it brought the Scots to their knees and led to the Treaty of Berwick and the end of the Second War of Scottish Independence.

———————————

During this Second War of Scottish Independence when such terrible things had already happened, another event occurred, unrelated to the war, which was even more terrible if that's possible to believe.

In 1349, in the midst of it all, Northumberland was struck by the Black Death and about 50% of the population died.

It seems inconceivable that such a dreadful thing could have happened and not just in Northumberland; the same thing happened everywhere else, in Britain, throughout Europe, Asia and evidently much of Africa; half the population of the world died in one single and devastating pandemic. There's no comfort, of course, in the fact that everybody else was in the same boat – shared misery isn't any better than any other type of misery and so Northumberland, in the middle of the 1300s as the Second War of Independence was coming to a close, was a pretty dreadful place to be.

And yet …

I am normally quite fond of writing 'and yet …' because the words indicate a perhaps unexpected twist in the story, which is the case here, but the twist on this occasion is pitifully depressing because despite all of that misery, all of those varied ways that Northumbrians had found to die, nothing changed on the border line and I have to write …

War C (The next 100 years and more)

It just went on and on and on.

The plague went on. There were four more outbreaks in the next 50 years and by 1450, more than 150 years after the wars had started, the population of Northumberland was much lower and wealth was far lower than it had been at the beginning. And still they fought!

I read one account of those years and the writer said that after the Treaty of Berwick in 1352 '*the relationship remained uneasy and cross border conflict remained endemic.*' "Uneasy" would have seemed an odd word to choose if you were a resident of Northumberland at that time. In the reign of Richard II, for example, the county was invaded by full-blown Scottish armies in 1380, 1385, 1387, 1388 and 1389. It got no better during the reign of Henry IV, which involved battles at Humbleton Hill near Wooler in 1402, at Yeavering in 1414 and Wark on Tweed in 1419.

And then of course there was the War of the Roses in the 1460s when the county became a battlefield in an English civil war between the Yorkists and the Lancastrians with battles at Hedgely Moor near Wooler, at Hexham and at Bamburgh which was attacked by Henry VI in 1464 and became the first British castle to be defeated by gunfire. Throughout this particular war the Scots continued to be involved, sniping on the sidelines and actively supporting one side or the other (I can never remember which). And so it went on until 1513 when the Scots were finally defeated so utterly at the Battle of Flodden that for long period in the 1500s the full-scale international confrontations began to fade away and there were no major battles at all.

Why did they do it? Why didn't they just stop? Why didn't it all peter out?

There were clearly reasons why it should have done.

On the one hand it made life for the ordinary people intolerable and dreadfully interfered with the commercial and economic life of the county. On the other hand, the more powerful people had a pretty odd and equivocal attitude towards their enemies. Lots of families had estates and interests on both sides of the border and continued to hold them or periodically swapped sides when their interests dictated they should.

Even at the top the relationship was odd. The sisters of several English Kings married Kings of Scotland (Edward III's sister was married to the son of Robert the Bruce, for example) but instead of fostering friendship and nice family nights around the tele the war just went on and on. Why was that?

Well, there were lots of reasons. Obviously kings and their ambitions played a big part. In the 1400s Henry IV, and his son Henry V, renewed the English claim to be the overlords of Scotland while the Scots, in their turn, seemed equally determined to reclaim their ancient lands south of the Tweed (us!) as part of Scotland and all of that kept the intensity as high as it had ever been.

But you can't help thinking that there was more to it than that. It seems that war was just what people did, it's what they expected and they spent their whole lives at it. I'm talking about posh people here, knights and members of the aristocracy; I'm not sure whether to include ordinary people in the same way; I don't really know what their attitude to war and fighting was but the chaps at the top seemed to have lapped it up.

Take the Percys, for example. The Percy family acquired Alnwick Castle in 1307 and they very rapidly became top dogs in the county. They started off with 3 or 4 "Lords Percy" until the1350s when the 4th Lord Percy got promoted and became the 1st Earl of Northumberland. After that there was a long line of Percy Earls that came to an end late in the 1600s and since then there have been 13 or 14 Percy Dukes of Northumberland and I'll undoubtedly come back to talk about them again later on but the "Lords Percy" and the first 4 Earls of Northumberland all lived through and were heavily involved in the Border Wars. Even a casual flick through the description of their lives in the guide to Alnwick Castle makes clear what their lives were like:

Henry, the 1st Lord (1309-1315) distinguished himself in the Scottish Wars (we are told) and had been rewarded with further lands as a result by Edward I. He was involved in the murder of Piers Gaveston and was captured at Bannockburn and subsequently ransomed. His son and heir …

Henry, the 2nd Lord (1315-1352) spent practically his whole life in the Scottish wars but still found time to go and fight lots of other wars in France and Flanders. He was at the Battle of Nevilles Cross in 1346 and made a tidy profit out of the prisoners he took there, a profit that he turned into architectural magnificence in the shape of the two splendid octagonal towers that form the entrance to the keep at Alnwick. He died in 1368 and was replaced by his son …

Henry, the 3rd Lord (1352 1368) who, even before he succeeded to his estates had been at Crecy and just managed to get home again in time to be at the Battle of Nevilles Cross. He took part in Edward III's savage "Burnt Candlemas" that I wrote about a little while ago and as the guide book says: "For several years after this he was continuously employed in warfare either on the Border or in France, He was then succeeded by …

Yet another Henry … what a surprise. They were all called Henry until the arrival of the 7th Earl in the middle of the 16th century who was called Bert … that isn't true actually, he was called Thomas but I was trying to think of an amusing name for an earl so I do apologise if I have offended any earls called Bert.

He was succeeded by …

Henry, the 4th Lord who received a bit of a promotion and became the 1st Earl (1368-1409). The 1st Earl, along with his son Henry (or Harry) Hotspur are among the high points of Percy and Northumbrian aristocratic fighters. The Earl had been everywhere, fighting everybody but eventually settled down to a spot of nice local Border warfare so he didn't have to commute so far. In 1377 he "led an army of 10,000 men into Scotland … and ravaged the lands of the Earl of March". The following year he took his son with him to besiege Berwick Castle. The castle only had 48 defenders and I think they were all elderly men but they managed to hold out for eight days before surrendering and being

The towers of 1346 at Alnwick Castle

Battle of Homildon Hill in 1402) and started "The Rising of the Percys" that led to Hotspur's death at the Battle of Shrewsbury in 1403.

But in Northumberland Hotspur's most famous escapade took place at the Battle of Otterburn in 1388 – at least not actually at Otterburn itself because Hotspur's part in the actual battle didn't go very well; his forces were defeated and he himself was taken prisoner and had to be ransomed – but the prelude to the battle showed him in his true colours and those colours were wild and impetuous. They were the colours of the ideal chivalric knight.

What happened was this. Under the command of James, Earl of Douglas, the Scots had launched an invasion. They had ravaged Northumberland pretty thoroughly and then moved on down to Durham to engage in a spot of ravaging down there as well and then, on the way home, hearing that Newcastle was only being lightly defended they came to try their luck on Tyneside. Meanwhile, when he heard about the Scottish invasion, the Earl of Northumberland decided he would stay in Alnwick to try and intercept the Scots on their way home and he sent both his sons, Harry and Ralph, to defend Newcastle, so when the Scots arrived there was a fantastic scene, a scene of pure chivalry. It was a classic medieval confrontation but it was also utterly male, the sort of masculine aggression and pride that's still constantly on display today. For example …

… once, when I was a teacher, I went on a biology field trip with quite a large group of students, probably 15-year olds, and we were down by a river. There was a single tent on the other side of the river and a couple of boys tending a camp fire. One of the boys in my group recognised one of the boys across the river and pointed at him. He said, "I know him" and the boy he was pointing at jumped to his feet and shouted, "Who are you pointing at?" and waded straight into the river until it was deep enough to come up to his neck but he kept on coming, on his own, towards a group of about 30 teenagers and 3 teachers. We were all completely dumbfounded as he strode out of the water, walked straight up to the boy who had pointed at him, and put the nut on him.

put to the sword. It was at this event that the Earl's son, Harry (as it says in the Alnwick guidebook) '*greatly distinguished himself and earned the soubriquet of "Hotspur"*'. You'll be surprised to hear that he was only 12 years old at the time. What on earth was he doing there? He should have been at school; maybe he was at school; perhaps he was doing a Key Stage 3 project called "National Curriculum Pillaging", but whatever the motivation was, you've got to wonder what a 12-year old had to do to distinguish himself at putting elderly defenders to the sword.

You probably know that Harry and his dad became major players on the national stage, popping up in Shakespearean plays and what not. In 1399 they deposed Richard II and paved the way for his successor, Henry IV to usurp the throne, but a few years later, in 1402, they had fallen out with Henry (over something piffling to do with some ransom money for three prisoners that Hotspur thought he was due after the

Alnwick Castle from the meadows.

That's effectively what happened by the walls of Newcastle in August 1388; it was just a bit grander and the people involved were a bit posher; and on horseback.

The scene is vividly described in the ballad called *The Battle of Otterbourne*. First of all, Douglas arrived and like the boy by the river he didn't mess about. He rode straight up to the walls and shouted out his challenge

And he marched up to Newcastle
And rode it round about:
O wha's the lord of this castle,
Or wha's the lady ont?

The scene took place outside the North Gate of the town so you might imagine Douglas on his horse, outside Fenwicks or perhaps somewhere a little higher up Northumberland Street, possibly Sports Direct. So, anyway, he shouted out and inevitably it was Hotspur himself who replied from the walls.

But up spake proud Lord Percie then,
And O but he spake hie
I am the lord of this castle,
My wife's the lady gay

He wasn't prepared to accept the taunts of a man like Douglas and so immediately he leapt into action

He took a long spear in his hand,
Shod with the metal free,
And for to meet the Douglas there,
He rode right furiouslie

And they met in single combat outside the North Gate of the town – the walls probably lined with locals and defenders, presumably baying for blood like the crowds in the Gallowgate end at St James' Park, and the Scottish invaders doing the same at the away-supporters end; they had a jousting match, in full armour, riding on richly caparisoned horses and with pennons fluttering in the breeze. Douglas won; Hotspur fell and Douglas

117

had one last dig. He said (in medieval Scottish), "If it had just been the two of us, on our own with nobody watching on, I'd have had you; I'd have finished you off" or, as the ballad puts it a touch more poetically:

> *Had we twa been upon the green*
> *And never an eye to see*
> *I wad hae had you, flesh and fell*

But instead of killing him, in one dramatic insulting gesture, he ripped Hotspur's personal pennon from his lance and away he rode mocking and threatening to fly the flag from the battlements of his castle back in Scotland. Hotspur wasn't the sort of man to take that sort of thing lying down – well, obviously he had to take it lying down because he had just been knocked off his horse in full armour, but he certainly wasn't going to put up with it and that led to the impetuous night-time pursuit of his foe and the wild, ill-planned confusion of the battle that followed, to the defeat of the English

army, the capture and ransom of Hotspur himself and the death of Douglas.

I don't know how common scenes like this were, but they certainly weren't unknown and I suspect they happened quite often. 50 years earlier, in 1338, a Scottish knight called Alexander Ramsay was present at a siege of Berwick and he wrote that there was "a jousting tournament" outside the walls of the town, that's how he described it, as if it was some sort of game, like the football match between English and German soldiers in no-man's-land during the Christmas truce in 1914, except that in 1338 two of the English knights were killed and one of his own kindred, a knight called Sir William Ramsay, was fatally wounded.

But the classic example of the way that for many in those days, war and romance were linked together is to be found in the story of Sir William Marmion and what happened during the siege of Norham Castle in 1318.

Marmion was a tournament knight, which means that he used to go jousting. Tournament knights were the sporting superstars of those days, the premiership footballers of medieval Europe and you know what sporting superstars are like – they have an eye for the ladies.

So, at a tournament, in Lincoln I believe, Marmion fancied a maiden and attempted to plight his troth with her, but she was evidently a good girl and would not let any naughty plighting take place. She clearly fancied him though and sent him a golden helm, which he doubtless saw as a good sign. I think if a girl gives you a golden helm you could reasonably expect that you were in with a chance. She also said that if he did the most dangerous deed in the kingdom he would be free to plight away. Good grief; if it had been me I would have run a mile because I'm not very fond of dangerous deeds – but not Marmion, he was made of tougher stuff, so he went to see the proper authorities on chivalry and they told him what many have discovered since. They said, if you want to go somewhere really dangerous, Marmion, go to Northumberland, that's the most dangerous place in the Kingdom. So he did. Somehow he managed to get in to Norham Castle despite it being under siege by Robert the Bruce's forces and you would have thought

Berwick: The White Wall, 1297-8. The Water Tower rebuilt. c.1540.

that was that but no … it wasn't enough for Marmion. He decided he had to attack the entire Scottish army single handed so he put on his golden helm and his armour, got on his horse and charged out of the gate at the west end of the castle which still bears his name today. Needless to say he got beaten to bits and his chums had to risk their lives to come and rescue him.

What a plank, you might think but that's not what they thought in those days; they recognised Marmion as an ideal and a perfect knight and it is an ideal that stuck. 500 years after the events at Norham, Sir Walter Scott retold the story (though he transposed it into something that happened at the battle of Flodden, 200 years later than the actual date). This is what he says about the warriors of Northumberland in those days

… the Borderer: bred to war,
He knew the battle's din afar, and joy'd to hear it swell.
His peaceful day was slothful ease
… but war's the Borderers game.

It's an exaggeration, of course. Even to the chivalric knights it wasn't just a game. The ballads of those days have moments of real pain and tragedy as well as glory; their tone is often sombre and harsh and while they celebrate deeds that are filled with pride and courage their tone is often bleak. The *Ballad of Chevy Chase,* for example, the greatest of all the English ballads, is said to be based on a battle fought high up the valley of the River Breamish, inevitably between a Douglas and a Percy. The Percy on that occasion might have been Hotspur's son, the 2nd Earl, and the events of the day are filled with a passionate chivalry. The leaders look superb…

Earle Douglas on his milk-white steed,
Most like a baron bold

…and they fight with fantastic energy and honour. They have swords of "tempered steel" and the blood is always trickling down their faces like rain. They keep going against all odds even when everything seems lost…

For Wetherrynting my harte was wo
That ever slayne should be
For when both his leggis were hewyne in to
Yet he kneeled and fought on hys kny

(Or to put it another way, to use the language of the 18th century editor who wished to make it all more comprehensible, a little less sombre …

For Widdrington needs must I wail
As one in doleful dumps
For when his legs were smitten off
He fought upon his stumps

… and a great deal more Monty Pythonesque)

And when they die, they die magnificently, uttering ringing testimony to their followers' bravery and their enemies' nobility. In the poem, the Douglas and the Percy fight an extraordinary single combat until one is dead and the other dying, at which point Earl Percy takes his enemy's hand …

Jousting at Alnwick Castle.

Then leaving life, Earl Percy tooke
The dead man by the hand;
And said, Earle Douglas! For thy life
Would I had lost my land

It's all wonderful stuff, thrilling and glorious but the poem ends on a more sombre note, which reminds us that it isn't just a game. I love this poem in its entirety, but I love most of all the simplicity and sadness with which it ends…

Of fifteen hundred Englishmen
Went home but fifty three
The rest in Chevy Chase were slaine
Under the greenwood tree.

CASTLES

I made a radio programme once about Alnwick Castle and in it I was able to interview the then Duchess of Northumberland. We sat in the castle's splendid library and she was very nice and polite so being a clever and fearless journalist I asked her the probing question: "What's the worst thing about living in a castle?"

And she said, "By the time you get from the kitchen to the bedroom your hot milk's gone stone cold." I felt for her pain of course, but the reason that I mention her here, amidst all this talk of Border wars and Percys and Douglases is that she was, of course, a Percy, the wife, if I remember rightly, of the 12th Duke of Northumberland, but she had been born a Douglas and raised in a castle on the Scottish side of the Border. In the interview she described herself lightly as the victim of the last Border raid. We smiled, of course, in the shared knowledge that she was joking, that we have come a long way since those times, that there are no Border raids and no victims any more.

As it happens, the castle that she lived in shares her whimsical connection with the violent past. It is an extraordinary vision of the Middle Ages. You might recall that back in Norman times it was almost the same size as it is today way but since then, in the later Middle Ages, the curtain walls were enriched and glorified with a bristling ring of towers. I've already mentioned the splendid octagonal towers that were paid for out of the proceeds of the Battle of Nevilles Cross but alongside those there is a terrific 14th century gatehouse with a long and dramatic barbican in front of it. The battlements of the castle are topped with stone figures of pretendy defenders that could never have fooled any attackers with half an ounce of sense. The ones there now are 18th century replacements, but there must have been similar figures in earlier times and they were atrotropaic figures which isn't a word you hear often, or indeed ever. It means that they weren't meant to look real but were intended to be magical, to ward off evil influences (and Scotsmen).

They look great. The castle looks great, a dream of its chivalric past and we love it of course, and go to visit it in our thousands. I was there recently with my granddaughters and we were thrilled. The Harry Potter films were partly filmed at the castle and the youthful wizard (or his stand-in) was there when we went, teaching people to play quidditch in the Inner Bailey.

On the field below the castle, alongside the River Aln, we watched a jousting tournament in a scene enriched by decorative Medieval-style pavilions and fluttering pennons, the thunder of hooves and the gleam of polished armour. It was all very exciting and hugely decorative but fortunately (unlike at the jousting outside the walls of Berwick in 1338) nobody died and you won't be surprised to hear that at the quidditch match nobody actually flew. It was all a sumptuous fantasy which is to a certain extent exactly what we are hoping to find when we visit a castle.

Which makes us locals lucky, because Northumberland, for obvious reasons, is absolutely oozing castles. The architectural historian Niklaus Pevsner described it as THE castle county of England and we are rightly proud of them. They are the one positive thing to have emerged out of all of those years of war. You might well have a favourite among them, many people do; I have an American friend who lived in

The 14th century keep at Warkworth.

Northumberland briefly in the 1980s and she still maintains stubbornly that Dunstanburgh Castle belongs to her and her alone. Few people can fail to fall beneath their charms. It is a little recognised but definite fact that nobody has ever approached Bamburgh for the first time from the north and come round the corner and seen the castle, laid out below in all its glory, standing proud upon its magnificent rock, without going OOOOoooo!

For pure architectural splendour the most remarkable of all the castles is Warkworth which (you might recall from an earlier chapter) was probably started by Henry, the Earl of Northumberland and son of King David of Scotland, back in the mid 1100s, but it became a property of the Percy family in 1332.

Dunstanburgh Castle, c.1314.

Did you spot that I wrote "a" property and not "the" property because the Percys were a remarkably powerful family and had houses all over the place. We all know about Alnwick Castle, of course but there were lots of others. They had houses in London obviously, but then who didn't, and they had a town house in Newcastle. Prudhoe Castle was one of theirs as well, but they also had other major castles dotted about all over the place.

In the Middle Ages none of these houses were lived in all of the time. There might have been a skeleton staff to keep them safe, but most of the time they were empty of people and stuff and the household processed between them at different times of the year. And what a process it was. There would be great trains of carts and servants carrying all of the family's possessions – hangings for the walls and all the furniture, cooking utensils, clothes, even the windows. This lot would go on ahead to get the place ready for the lord while he came along in a second procession of astonishing grandeur. He would be splendidly clad on a richly caparisoned horse, surrounded by his wife and family, pages and other servants would be running along beside them, and behind the family came the lord's riding company.

If you have read or seen Shakespeare's *King Lear* you might recall that when the king gets old he decides to divide his kingdom up between his three daughters. He gives everything away to them and in return all he wants is that he should be allowed to keep a hundred knights to ride with him as he stays with each of his daughters in turn. It is a disaster. In no time at all, in a single scene in fact, the daughters cut his allowance of knights down to fifty, then twenty five, ten, five and finally none. He is left with nothing.

Well, the Earls of Northumberland who built Warkworth and all those other castles had their knights as well, their Riding Establishment who rode in procession, wearing the Percy livery and badge, a visual symbol of the lord's power and invincibility. In the 1500s, about the time when *King Lear* was written, Henry Percy, the 5th Earl of Northumberland, went nowhere without 66 knights at his back. That's how powerful the owners of Warkworth were.

One of them, another Henry, the 1st Earl, built the great tower or keep that dominates the top of the hill. He built it in the 1390s and it is this building that is considered to be one of the masterpieces of English Medieval architecture.

Most Medieval domestic (and castle) architecture is quite informal and irregular, with buildings fitted in wherever there was space for them. They can be exciting and beautiful of course but they aren't planned and organised like a formal piece of architecture is.

Warkworth's keep manages to do both of these things. It is thrilling to look at, soaring and dramatic, but it is perfectly organised as well. All four sides follow the same pattern and inside is a perfectly planned rich man's house. It has a great hall with kitchens next to it. There is a chapel and withdrawing rooms for the family. The basement has servants' quarters and storage and in the centre there is a taller tower that acted as a light well and collected rainwater to flush the toilets. It is a bit difficult to appreciate these things nowadays when the walls are bare and the rooms unfurnished, but all the experts agree that it remains one of the greatest houses ever built in the Middle Ages.

What they don't agree about is what it was for. There was already a complete house in the grounds of the castle with a vast Great Hall and splendid lodgings for the Earl, so why did he need another? Some have suggested that it was where the family went when they kept "secret house", when they retreated to be on their own for a few weeks and sent most of their followers home for a holiday.

Others have suggested that it was meant as a family home for Harry Hotspur, the Earl's son who had been born in the castle. Or maybe it was mainly about showing off. All over Northumberland in the late 1300s there was a taste among the posh and powerful for building great towers; it was just something you had to have – like lions on your gateposts nowadays or a conservatory in the back garden. Perhaps the 1st Earl was just determined to have the best status symbol of them all.

If that's what he wanted, that's what he got.

But beyond the great castles, the palaces of the greatest magnates, the county has dozens of other

Halton Castle, above, and, Welton Hall, below, were built as normal manor houses before becoming fortified buildings.

castles, not so vast and not so prominent but still fascinating and massively powerful, the fortresses of the next rank of aristocratic families.

Occasionally they are free-standing towers like Langley Castle, a vast compact mass of castle, on the southern edge of the Tyne Valley a couple of miles south of Haydon Bridge. Langley is a towerhouse – literally a house in the form of a tower. It contains all the elements that a medieval house was supposed to have, kitchens, great hall, a solar or great chamber, bedrooms and toilets (or garderobes), but instead of laying them out next to each other like in a normal house, they are all scrunched together, hunched around each other and on top of each other. The kitchen is on the ground floor, the great hall above and above that, on the top floor, is the solar, the private room into which the owner and his family could retreat away from the very public life of the Great Hall for a little bit of privacy. The chapel and the bedrooms are in the surrounding towers that emphasise each of the corners of the house, except for the south-west tower which is where you went to the toilet. It is one of the greatest toilet towers in Europe in fact. On each floor there is a companionable row of four stone seats under pointed arches with banks of great stone chutes down through the thickness of the wall to a stream diverted to flow under the corner of the building, which would carry the oojah away down the hill (presumably onto someone else's property).

Almost as huge as Langley are the towers at Chipchase Castle and Belsay. Both are wonderful to look at, romantic in their profiles with battlements projecting beyond the face of the wall and resting on rows of richly carved corbels; the corners are higher and rounded and again resting on moulded corbels. Inside they are both empty and unused now but there is plenty of evidence of their former use and their former glory. Chipchase still has a portcullis controlled from a chamber above the entrance. Belsay's great hall has vestiges of the wall paintings that must have made it look splendid in the past. Both towers are complex, like Langley, cleverly fitting all the relevant rooms into their compact forms.

I'll have to be a bit careful here because there are dozens of fortified buildings of this type and unless I keep a grip on myself I'll still be rabbitting on about them for pages and pages and I would find that you had all sneaked off to make cups of tea and left me talking to myself, but there are four broader, general points I'd like to make before I leave them behind.

The first point is that none (or possibly virtually none) of these slightly smaller castles started off as a fortified building. All of them (or maybe virtually all of them) were begun in the 1200s or before and had existed

The vast compact mass of Langley Castle.

as more normal manor houses in the years before the hostilities started. Welton Hall, Halton Tower and Aydon Castle, all in a loose row along the north side of the Tyne Valley are just three of many examples of this development. The core of Aydon Castle is a typical medieval house such as you could find elsewhere in the country. It was built in the 1280s or 1290s. It has a great hall on the first floor with a kitchen at one end and a solar and private apartments at the other. All of it is undefended but in 1305, when it was clear that the war was here to stay, it received its "Licence to Crenellate", its official permission to turn itself into a castle with battlements (or crenellations). That's when it got the inner and outer curtain walls that protect it.

The second point is that virtually none of the towers appear to have been built to stand alone. In the past they used to be called "Pele Towers" and the assumption was that most of them were built as free-standing towers when the wars started and later on, when things had finally settled down, the owners added new wings and more spacious accommodation. But no! That was not thus, as they say. That isn't what happened because in virtually every case it's pretty clear, after close examination, either that the towers were added later to existing buildings to provide more security when the danger arose, or that they were attached to other buildings from the start, buildings that have either disappeared or been altered in later centuries.

Halton Castle is an excellent example of this. From the front, and from outside, its high, dramatic 14th century tower, built of Roman stones, looks as if it is obviously the oldest part of the building and the beautiful 17th century wing attached to it is evidence of the changes that happened later but in fact, behind the tower, and behind the facades there is clear evidence of the 13th century house that was there before the tower was built. The owners had a nice house in fact, but when the wars started they added some extra protection. I did much the same to my house in the 1980s. When it seemed as if a general call had gone out to the local criminal community that you could get nice things easily if you went to the Grundy's house I added a burglar alarm and generally beefed up my defences. That's what they did in the 14th century.

The third point I want to make is that these buildings might have been put up or altered in a war zone and at times of profound insecurity, but you wouldn't know it to look at them. They don't hide away. They are bold sticky-uppy buildings, high and prominent in their landscapes, proud of themselves when you might have expected their builders to cower away and hope to be un-noticed by passing armies.

Edlingham Castle, on the moors west of Alnwick is a good example. A few years ago, Edlingham didn't exist as a castle, it was thought of as no more than a fragment of a tower surrounded by a few grass-covered mounds of fallen stone. But now it has been excavated and a whole, small but beautifully formed little castle has emerged from beneath the grass, with a gatehouse and a cobbled courtyard and curtain walls. It is an amazing transformation, but for me the most amazing part of all is to be able to see into the shattered walls of the main tower, where it is clear that the great hall on the first floor must have been magnificent. The ruins reveal a great

Ruined Great Hall at Edlingham Castle.

stone-vaulted chamber, two storeys high with a richly decorated fireplace against the wall. Hollywood couldn't have come up with a better vision of the Middle Ages, and yet here it is, in Northumberland, high and isolated on the moors, a few miles from the Scottish Border.

Who'd have thought it?

And fourthly? They are beautiful. Splendid. Romantic. Atmospheric. In every case their stonework is intensely characterful, rough, weathered and immensely strong. My own particular favourite is Halton Tower, though you can only see it from an angle from the nearby churchyard, but all of them give tremendous satisfaction. Northumberland doesn't have mellow and picturesque, half-timbered medieval houses like Kent or Suffolk. But it does have these martial masterpieces.

And at a slightly lower social level there are lots and lots of smaller but still enthralling towers of a similar type. In 1415, Henry V ordered a survey of the fortifications in Northumberland and it listed 78 towers and they were followed in the next few decades by at least another 35. Loads of them survive in some form or other – complete, in ruins, incorporated into later buildings. An interesting group of them are traditionally known as Vicar's Peles – towers associated with parish churches to provide safe (or at least a bit safer) accommodation for the vicars and perhaps emergency accommodation in times of danger for the parishioners too. The tower in Whittingham has an inscription (added in 1845 when the tower was restored) which begins with the words: '*This ancient tower which was formerly used by the village in times of rapine and insecurity …*'

There are similar "Vicar's Peles" at Corbridge, Alnham, Embleton and Elsdon. They were needed, of course, because of the general level of 'insecurity' but more specifically because churches weren't safe. You

Vicars Pele at Embleton.

would think they would be, that holy places would be in some sense sacrosanct, but how often have we already seen in this story examples of people burnt to death inside their churches and I am sure that the examples we know about were just the tip of the iceberg. I can think of lots of bits of evidence that it happened regularly.:

- Many of our church buildings have reddened stonework in their outer walls which is evidence that the sandstone has been burnt.

- In the garden of Lilburn Tower near Wooler there is a beautiful ruined church, a ruined 13th century church whose walls stand only a few feet high. It has never been rebuilt since it was desecrated in the 14th century with its priest murdered at the altar.

- Beside the beautiful little church at Kirkharle in the upper Wansbeck Valley, there's a monument that tells how Sir Richard Loraine was slaughtered by the Scots while returning from his private devotions in 1483.

Stories like these must constantly have been a worry in people's minds. Some churches (Kirknewton, Bellingham and Corsenside, for example) were vaulted in stone to make them more fireproof. Some, quite a lot probably, had no windows at all – until the Victorians came along and restored them, they were just bare stone boxes. Others had strong stone-vaulted porches or towers with no windows low down and no ease of access.

Vicars Pele, Corbridge.

Defensive walls and Priors Tower at Hulne Priory.

The ruined chapel at Liburn Towers. It was desecrated and abandoned during the Border Wars.

One church, the Norman church at Ancroft in exposed and dangerous country just off the Great North Road and just south of Berwick, had its west end converted into a towerhouse. It has a massive stone-vaulted ground floor, a spiral staircase and little slit windows further up – it is a church/castle in fact.

And sometimes the whole religious site was turned into a fortress. Tynemouth Priory is a fortress as well as being a monastery and military defences were added to Lindisfarne Priory, but the best example is at the Premonstratensian priory in Hulne Park outside Alnwick. There, the whole monastery has a tough, unembellished, entirely undecorated wall about 15 feet high around the whole site. Inside the wall the monastery is glorious but the surrounding wall is like the wall around a modern gaol and the only original entrance is through a low dark tunnel that looks like the entrance to a dungeon.

So that's the situation up to about 1500. Can I sum it up? I'm not sure I can. There were some people who did OK some of the time and some families who did alright most of the time, but it clearly wasn't nice. For ordinary people, there were fewer of them than there had been 200 years before and their lives were worse; and for the well-to-do ... well I don't think many of them came up here for their hols.

There was one man, though, who did come to Northumberland on a brief visit. He was an Italian called Aeneas Silvius and in 1435 he went to Edinburgh by boat on a secret mission for the Pope. In fact he was made Pope himself in 1458; he became Pope Pius II and has the reputation of being one of the most urbane and civilised Popes of the Renaissance. He came from a small town called Corsignano, south of Siena in Tuscany and when he was Pope he rebuilt it as a little Renaissance masterpiece and called it Pienza after himself. When his mission to Edinburgh was complete, he travelled back through Northumberland disguised as a merchant and he had some interesting things to say about his journey. He said that the men were in terror of the Scots which isn't all that surprising, but he also said something a little more unusual about the women. He said they were reluctant to let him sleep alone because that was the custom of the country. Hmm! Of the county itself he summed it up in just three words. He said it was, uninhabitable. uncultivated and horrible.

Time to dip my toe into the adventure of the next chapter.

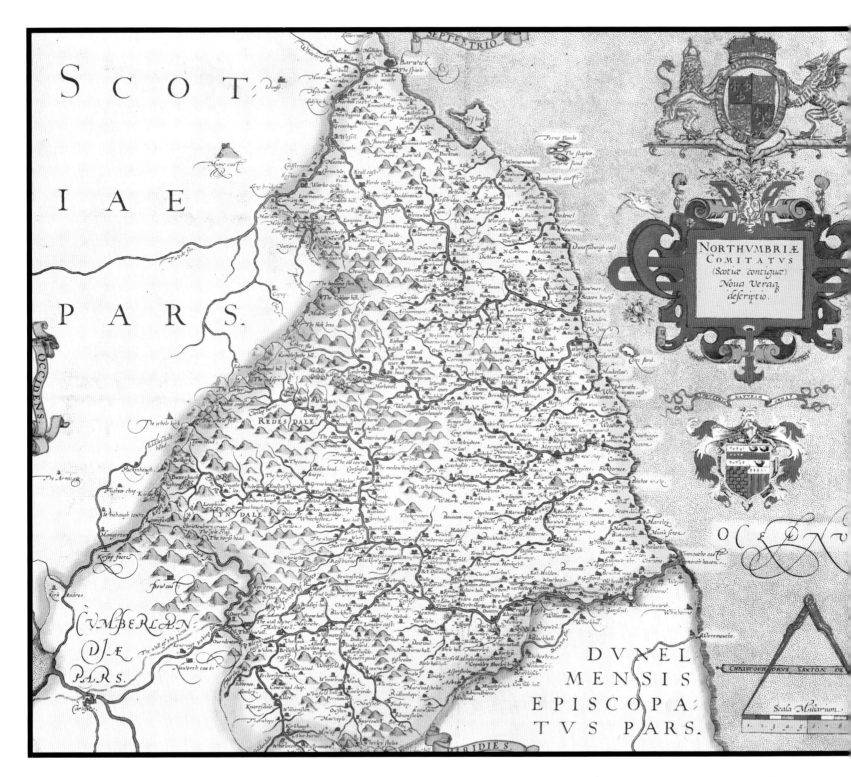

Sexton's 1576 Map of Northumberland.

8. THE 1500S

The bus driver, John Renton, who I mentioned in the first paragraph of this book, had previously been a policeman and at one stage he had been stationed in Wooler which is where I met him one morning in the spring of 1984 on the first day of my life as a Listed Building Fieldworker. I had dropped into the station to warn the police that I was in the area and would be calling on isolated houses, so if anybody was suspicious of my presence the police would be able to put their minds at rest. John Renton turned out to be interested in what I was doing and waxed historical for a while, outlining some of the old buildings in the countryside around Wooler that I might well come across. In return I mentioned an old house that I had just driven past about a mile south of the town on the A696 and he said,

"Oh yes! We've had bother there. That's where we had them Scots camping."

I didn't follow. I thought maybe it had been some Scottish revellers on their way south on Glasgow holiday week, or a gang of rowdy Celtic Supporters returning from a match in England, some recent act of civic disorder, the sort of thing a Wooler policeman would need to concern himself with, but no … it turned out that he was talking about the encampment set up by King James IV and the Scottish army in the days before the Battle of Flodden in September 1513. They have long memories, Northumbrian policemen, let that be a lesson to you.

As it happens, James IV was the last monarch to set foot on Northumberland soil for almost a hundred years. In the previous 300 years kings of various nationalities had been ten a penny. You couldn't join a queue in Greggs to get your (vegan) sausage roll without finding that a king of England or Scotland had pushed in front of you, but after 1500 that all changed and you might have hoped, like I am sure the people of Northumberland must have hoped at the time, that the change had come about because the warfare between England Scotland had finally come to an end or at least begun to fade away.

But no, sadly you are going to have to live with conflict for a few pages yet. However, the nature of the warfare was about to change in character and that change was brought about by the invasion of the county by James IV in 1513.

What happened was this.

In 1513 Henry VIII had started a war against the French and was doing particularly well, so the French king, Louis the somethingth or other, wrote to his old (auld) ally the Scots, begging them to invade England in order to distract Henry and take some of the pressure off the French. He accompanied his letter with a ship load of weaponry and a bag full of money (14000 French crowns). The trouble was that the Scots were at the time trying to recover from another recent and difficult war and anyway the king, James IV, was married to Margaret

Tudor (who was Henry VIII's sister) so he was a bit reluctant to get involved in yet another confrontation with his brother-in-law. Eventually, though, he gave in to the bribery and on the 11th August he declared war against the English and crossed the Border with a force of 40,000 men, a whole heap of excellent cannon that he had recently bought from the Dutch, and his massive siege cannon, Mons Meg, which was quite easily capable of reducing castle walls to rubble …

… which is what it did. The first thing the Scots did was to lay siege to Norham Castle and use Mons Meg to pulverise the weakest point in its walls from across the river Tweed. As it happens Norham Castle hadn't ever shown a great deal of weakness in the past and it was apparently the only Northumbrian Castle never to have been taken by the Scots, but on this occasion the Scots were helped out by an English traitor who had sneaked out to tell them where the weakest parts of the castle were.

The plan of attack worked well and after six days it was all over and Norham had been captured and the traitor came to claim his money. James, ever the honourable king, paid him the promised amount and then immediately had him put to death for being a traitor. Rupert Matthews, from whose book, *Northumberland Battlefield Walks* I pinched all this information, says the place beside the castle where the traitor was killed is still called Hangman's Field.

The ease with which Norham had been taken was a clear warning sign to all the other strongholds in the area and nearby Etal Castle, Chillingham and Ford Castle gave in straight away. James stayed for a few days at Ford. Being a king with 40,000 soldiers behind him, he got the best bedroom (even though he was unlikely to have booked in advance). The tower where he stayed is still called King James' Tower and the rather beautiful bedroom is still called (rather predictably) The King's Bedroom.

Sadly for James, though, this little holiday in Ford Castle was the high point of his brief visit to England because it all went hideously downhill from there.

With the English army approaching under the command of the Earl of Surrey, James arranged, in that curiously civilised way they had in those days, that they would fight the battle on the 9th September. They didn't actually agree where the fight would take place, but James decided on Flodden Ridge, just west of the village of Branxton. He settled there at the top of the hill, looking down on a marshy valley with a little stream in the middle and waited for the English to arrive. From the Scottish point of view, it looked like it would work to their advantage. They were higher than the English position so could keep an eye on what was going on. They had their backs to Scotland and the border was close by, so if they were in trouble they weren't likely to be trapped without an escape route. However, in the event, no bit of the battle went right for them while the English had two strokes of luck (or skill) that allowed them to take the day.

The Scottish tactics involved dividing their army into tight phalanxes of men armed with 14-foot lances. Those at the front of each phalanx had their lances horizontal, pointing straight at the enemy, while those in the ranks behind held the lances more aloft so they could quickly step forward if the man in front fell. Each phalanx was tightly packed and contained about 8000 men, so close together that even if those in front were scared as they approached the enemy, they were driven on by the men behind.

It was a formidable formation and should have worked … it was a tactic that had worked all over Europe and at Flodden it **did** work at first. The phalanx on the left wing of the Scottish position drove into the English force opposite them and caused them to break. The Scottish phalanx worked so well that the English turned and fled and the Scots, convinced that they were the victors, broke ranks and started to chase after them … but the English had a surprise up their sleeves. They had held back the cavalry wing of their army. It was under the command of Lord Dacre and it was waiting out of sight at the rear of the action and just when the Scots thought they had won, and in the pursuit of the fleeing Englishmen had lost the tightness of their formation, the cavalry suddenly appeared, created havoc and total panic and completely destroyed that section of the Scottish army.

Meanwhile, in another part of the battle, the English had a stroke of luck (or skill). In the centre of the battlefield James himself was in command of another phalanx of about 8000 men and rather bizarrely had placed himself right in the middle of his men; perhaps the idea was to show the troops that he was with them but there was clearly a danger that he was not in a position to have any overview of what was going on and in no position to make any key tactical decisions.

However, at first it all seemed to be going well. The King's phalanx advanced with devastating force but then they were unlucky, or not careful enough, or not capable of responding to changing circumstances because part of the English army under the command of Lord Stanley arrived late at the battle and, unnoticed in the midst of all the stuff that was going on, they were able to sneak round behind the Scots and launch an attack on James' phalanx from the rear. The Scots were entirely trapped. A great body of pike-bearers was a powerful weapon when it was advancing but the soldiers were so tightly packed that they had no chance at all of turning round to meet an attack from behind. They had supposedly trained to be able to wheel round and change the direction of their attack, but the English charge happened too quickly and they were utterly destroyed.

In fact, over the space of a couple of hours, the whole Scottish army was utterly destroyed. James, trapped in the heart of his phalanx, was killed too, along with 24 earls and other lords, two abbots, two bishops, one archbishop and 10,000 men. I would say, as the books normally say, that the English did better because they only lost about 2000 men, but I don't suppose that would have been much comfort to the families they left behind.

As for James, he never got back to Scotland in any way at all. Not even dead. His body was taken to Newcastle to be embalmed and then sent to London. In an act of ironic brutality his bloodstained clothes were stripped off and sent to the King of France as a reminder of what happens to people who resist the English and he himself was displayed for public entertainment before being taken and buried in Surrey … and for Scotland, it was all a catastrophe. The flower of Scotland, as the song says, had been destroyed and it was going to be more than a hundred years before a full-scale Scottish army crossed over into our county again.

So with full-scale war against the Scots out of the picture at last, you might have hoped that our much-troubled county would have finally settled down to be just another part of England, typical of the country as a whole, but of course it didn't turn out that way. You don't get rid of the effects of 300 years of war as easily as that. There may have been no more major, international confrontations or incursions, but for the rest of the 16th century and beyond, the county, well, at least the hills in the north and north-west of the county and the valleys that bisect them, Tynedale and Redesdale in particular, remained a hotbed of smaller scale, localised, informal violence. The 1500s were the days of The Border Reivers!

A 'Reiver' was someone who 'reives'. The word 'reive' (or 'reave') was an old northern word meaning 'to steal'. We still use it, for example in the word 'bereave' which means to steal a life. Another old border word that is still in use was the word 'mail', which meant 'rent'. They used to talk about whitemail, which was the normal, legal tax or rent that you would pay to your landlord and then they would talk (as we still do nowadays) about 'blackmail' which wasn't legal at all; so the Borderers have given us the words 'bereave' and 'blackmail', which is quite revealing about what life was like in 16th century Northumberland.

What life **was** like was hard, especially up in the hills to the north and west of the county. 300 years of brutalising war, neglect by national and local government, a system of inheritance that constantly divided land up equally between the sons in a family, so ensuring smaller and smaller farms and estates, poor land and a harsh climate – all of these led to the emergence of the 'reivers', who lived by raiding, cattle rustling and sheep stealing.

They raided fairly indiscriminately – across the border into the next country or across the ridge into the next valley. You might expect the attacks to be all against the Scots, but attacks on the neighbours were also common. In 1570, for example, Alnwick and the villages round about it were attacked and effectively laid waste by a force of borderers from the hills and in particular from North Tynedale and Redesdale.

What you didn't attack were people who shared the same name as you. The people in the hills were organised in clans – except that they didn't call them 'clans'. They were called 'surnames' or 'graynes'; 'kin-groups' is another phrase that gets used. If you happen to be called Armstrong or Elliot, Graham, Charlton, Fenwick or Forster, Robson or any of the other old Border surnames you can be pretty sure that your ancestors used to spend their time nicking cows and sheep from their neighbours. These are all still incredibly common names in the North East. I recall a class I taught in Felling a number of years ago that included two Elliots, three Fenwicks, a Robson and four Forsters. They all used to steal sheep from each other.

The sheep stealing and cattle rustling (not in Felling – that bit was a lie) could be a small scale activity or it could take place on a huge scale. It involved all social classes from peasants to leaders of the family groups and even members of the ruling elite.

One story, one of the best known stories, is the story of the Charlton Spur. The Charltons were (and remain) one of the most important groups in North Tynedale. There are posh Charltons and not so posh Charltons and

among the posher are the ones who live in a country house called Hesleyside, just outside Bellingham. I was involved in the listing of the building (including, I blush to have to tell you, listing a fountain on the lawn, which the then owner, Major Charlton, had constructed out of a demolished pigsty the previous year. He was surprised to find he'd made such a good job of it) and when I was there I was shown the Charlton Spur and Dish – a plain pewter dish bearing an ordinary iron spur such as might have been worn by John Wayne.

The story is that if there was nothing left in the larder, the Mrs Charlton of the day, instead of bringing food to the table, would appear with the Dish and the Spur. The message was obvious; she was telling her husband to get on his horse and bring back a cow! You can see a stirring painting of this scene, painted by William Bell Scott, in the Central Hall at Wallington.

At a lower social scale is the story of Barty Milburn of the Combe and his neighbour Corbit Jack, both of whom lived a little higher up the valley in the wildest of wild country north of Tarset, seven or eight miles north of Bellingham. Barty had his flock of sheep stolen in a Scottish raid, so with his friend Corbit Jack he set off on a 'Hot Trod' after the thieves. If you declared a Hot Trod and set off within 6 days of the original offence, you were allowed to put a piece of burning turf on the top of your pike or lance and you could legally cross the Border in pursuit of the baddies. That's what Barty did.

It was probably autumn because autumn was the most popular time for raids – the evenings were still long and there was no danger of winter snows, the stolen animals were strong and fat on summer grass so they could travel further and faster, which made a successful conclusion to the raid a bit more likely.

So far, Corbit Jack and Barty come out of this bit of the story pretty well but what they did next wasn't quite so worthy. It's about 15 miles from Tarset to the Scottish Border and when they got there, on the far side of Carter Bar, they lost the trail but they didn't want to come home empty handed so they stole a random flock from someone else. They shouldn't have done that, it put them in the wrong and they were on their way home when they were overtaken by the rightful owners of the

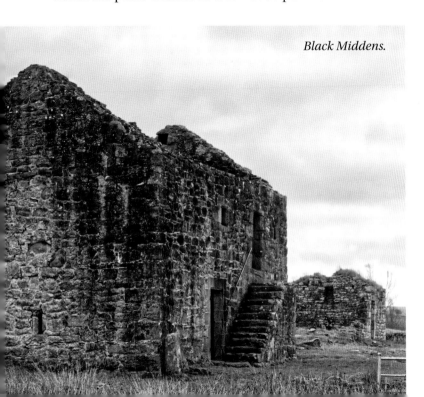

Black Middens.

Raid on Hollows Tower painted by Pete Armstrong.

sheep they had taken. There was a fight and Corbit Jack was slain but Barty dealt with the Scots single-handed. He killed one of them with ease and the other he struck so hard that *'his heid sprang alang the heather like an onion'*. He took his fallen neighbour over his shoulder and driving the sheep before him, made his way home.

I can't resist these stories. I can't say with any certainty that they're true, but people have been telling them for a very long time. Here's another one:

A party of Robsons from North Tynedale crossed the Border and stole a flock of sheep from the Armstrongs in Liddesdale. They brought them home without realising that they were diseased with the Scab, which infected the Robsons' own flock. Furious, they went back to Liddesdale, murdered seven Armstrongs and left a note saying: '*The neist time gentlemen cam to tak their schepe they are no to be scabbit.*'

Sometimes the raids were less about little acts of local meanness and more like a full-scale military operation. In 1583 one of the Liddesdale Armstrong, William Armstrong, who was known as Kinmont Willy, led a band of 300 reivers into North Tynedale where they stole: 140 cattle, 60 horses and 500 sheep.

They also burnt 60 houses and killed 10 men!

Mind you, that was nothing; in 1544 an army of English Borderers savaged the whole of the Scottish side of the Border. They are said to have killed 403 Scots, taken 816 prisoners, stolen 10,386 cattle, 12,492 sheep, 1296 horses, 200 goats … and so on.

Occasionally, or sometimes (I don't know how rarely this happened), the raids were closer to being international in origin, government policy rather than private opportunism.

In 1587 there was a Scottish raid into Tynedale that led to the partial destruction of Haydon Bridge. It was carried out by a band of 400 attackers led by the same Kinmont Willy I mentioned above.

The special significance of this raid was that in February of that year Mary Queen of Scots had been executed on the orders of Elizabeth I and it's possible that the Scottish King, Mary's son James VI, wanted to make at least some sort of response to the death of his mother, so the Haydon Bridge raid, which took place in October, may well have had official or semi-official Scottish Government blessing.

The notion is that he wanted something to happen that would hurt the English but, for reasons that will become clearer a little later in this chapter, he didn't want a full-scale international incident. So he made it look like a raid; you could turn a blind eye to a raid and blame it all on the uniquely local roughness of the Border Reivers … and it wouldn't lead to outright war.

So the scale of the conflict could be small and local but still vicious, or it could be huge and brutal and even more savage and that's what it was like for the whole of the century. Between 1510 and 1603, as many as 1145 separate raids (or about 12 a year) have been recorded, but the assumption is that scores, possibly hundreds of the smaller raids were never recorded, which meant that it was a hard life in the Border hills during the 1500s.

Mind you, it may have been hard at the time, but nowadays, how we love imagining the hard lives of the past, how we romanticise them, and one of the glories of the hills and valleys of north Northumberland is that they don't look or feel as if they have changed very much since those days so it's quite easy to picture what life might have been like.

I'm not sure that I have ever mentioned this to you, but I used to be a Listed Building man. In the 1980s I was one of four people responsible for surveying the buildings of Northumberland, Tyne and Wear and County Durham but just two of us covered the bulk of the county of Northumberland.

I was particularly lucky with the area that I was made responsible for because it included the whole of the Border line, the North Tyne Valley and Redesdale and almost the whole of the Cheviot Hills – the wild north and west of the county in fact, the very land of the Border Reivers. I had 6" to the mile OS Maps to guide me and my job was to visit every building and structure marked on them. It was an extraordinary experience. Isolated farmhouses and cottages, ruins at the heads of valleys, sheepfolds on the high sides of mountains, monuments on the hilltops, all had to be visited and assessed to decide whether they were worthy of being listed. I found myself exploring (alone) through the wildest of wild places, heading for places with remarkable names like Hell's Sike and Villain's Bog. I'm not absolutely certain what a Sike is but I passed one in the Kielder Forest that was called Pissing-Down Sike; there was a Barebottom Plantation and a house called Skirl Naked.

I am a timid little man and always have been, so working in the wildest and most isolated parts of the Northumbrian countryside, while always thrilling, could sometimes be a bit of a challenging experience for me. One of the problems was that there were just so many animals there and of so many different types. I met them all, it seems to me, and ran away from most of them.

To be fair to myself there were some that you would have run away from too. For example, I was concentrating on taking a photo of a ruined tower called Little Swinburne Pele in remote country just off the A68 when I felt something warm on the back of my neck. Imagine my surprise when I turned and found a big white Charolais bull standing immediately behind me. It had pleasantly warm breath and, to be honest, a mild and gentle look about its eyes so it may well have approached me in a spirit of friendship but I was unwilling to take the chance and broke a number of long-standing records in my eagerness to get away.

OK, bulls are one thing but even sheep on the hills can give you a nasty look and who knows what cows are thinking of when you pass them; horses, of course, are big and curious creatures and on the open moors they have a tendency to spot you from a good distance and charge up to make your acquaintance. Owners will tell you that they are just being friendly, but they love to nibble and their hooves are hard (the horses', that is, not the owners').

And beyond the animals there were the people. I was a born and bred townie who had watched the film *Deliverance* so I harboured an unspoken but deeply felt notion that people living in wild places could turn out to be wild themselves

For example, I went to a house deep in the forest once, deep, deep, deep in the Wark Forest way beyond Stonehaugh. The trees were tall and dark and I was expecting the worst – perhaps not orcs or trolls, maybe not even Hansel and Gretel and gingerbread houses, but wall-eyed rednecks at the very least, and savage dogs straining at the leash. In this state of mind I arrived at the house, sat quietly in the car for a moment or two among the dark trees to give the dangers time to reveal themselves and then slowly and reluctantly got out and went to knock on the back door of the house ….

It was full of women laughing a lot. There were women everywhere who had emerged from houses even deeper in the forest, tempted by the dangerous lure of coffee and, if I'm not mistaken, biscuits. One lady had even come from Cumberland, along forest tracks from near Gilsland and because the ways were so rough she had come out for coffee on her tractor.

It was brought home to me by experiences like these, how utterly normal life actually is in the distant hills these days, but looking at it, looking at the emptiness and the wildness, the roughness of the stone and the entirely unadorned simplicity of the buildings it was (and remains) impossible for me not to be reminded of what it used to be like in its savage past, so what I was looking for, what I was really hoping to find as I visited these wonderful places, was the 16th century. I wanted to uncover more and more vestiges of the world of the Border Reivers. Sometimes the landscape was so redolent of the past, so rough, empty and wild that I found myself imagining that I was actually in the past. I remember a long and isolated walk up a narrow valley, heading for a house marked on the map as "Yearning Hall" and whether it was the gloriously suggestive name of the building I was heading for, or something about the closed hills around me, but I lost myself in a fantasy of being there 400 years earlier, alone, helpless and exposed to attack by reivers.

It didn't happen of course, but on at least one occasion I thought for a brief moment that I had actually found the reivers or more to the point, that they had actually found me. This was another long and solitary walk on the hills north of Alwinton, near an abandoned farm called Old Puncherton. I had seen nobody for ages and heard nothing but the calling of sheep and found myself in a place with a jumble of old dry-stone walls, the view closed in by a low hill that obscured the path to the north, when I heard the thunder of hooves. I believe John Wayne had similar experiences from time to time, and unless I'm much mistaken Alan Ladd also. They would both have been unsettled and I was too, especially when a fast-moving posse of riders swung round the base of the hill and skittered to a halt around me. In an instant I was surrounded by large snorting horses topped by smaller snorting riders; I would have given them anything. They could have taken all of my sheep if I'd had any but of course they wanted nothing; they were just a group of young people out on a ride from a riding school in the forest at Kidlandlee. Nice, friendly and excitable.

As it happens, neither of those walks provided any discoveries of a listable nature. Yearning Hall turned out to be a ruined 19th century cottage and Old Puncherton was atmospheric without meeting the criteria set by English Heritage. They were wonderful places … but not what I was looking for…

… because what I was looking for were bastle houses!

For those who aren't familiar with the title, "bastle-house" is a description applied to a class of buildings which appeared in their hundreds on the Anglo-Scottish Border in the later 16th century and continued to be built into the 17th century. I think that up to now over 200 have been identified in Northumberland alone and there are others in Cumberland and on the Scottish side of the Border.

When they were first built and until quite recently

A Charolais bull keeps a watchful eye on John at Little Swinburne Tower.

all sorts of words were used to describe them. They were sometimes called 'castles' or 'peles'; 'stone house' was another common description. The word 'bastle' was also used but it was used sometimes to describe different classes of defensible buildings as well, so nowadays, to keep things a bit more simple, the word 'bastle' is used in a more limited way to describe a very particular sort of structure.

The word itself presumably comes from the French 'bastille' because these are defensible houses, little fortresses, 30 or 40 feet long, about 20-odd feet wide, two stories high and with immensely strong walls made from huge blocks of rough-hewn stone. The walls are almost always over 4 feet thick and, while there are some variations, their appearance is quite remarkably consistent. Almost always they have two doorways – one to the ground floor and the other to the upper floor. The upper floor was where people lived and sometimes it has had a later stone staircase added to it, but originally, and in many cases still, the only way up would have been by a ladder that could be pulled up after you.

I personally would not have liked that because, as I sit here writing these words, I am 73 years old with an irritatingly sore left hip. So I can really imagine how little I would have enjoyed the sight of a gang of hairy Scotsmen approaching at speed as I hobbled towards my handmade and rickety ladder.

But with the ladder pulled up and the door closed there would have been some level of relief because the walls were so thick and the windows tiny. The door was secured with one or two stout oaken drawbars that slid into deep tunnels in the thickness of the wall. Relative security then, but not comfort or, I suspect, all that much confidence. The dream must have been that the attackers would be in too much of a hurry to hang around and that you yourself would probably not have enough possessions to make it worth their while beating the door down …

… except for the animals of course, which is what they would actually have come for. The animals would have been downstairs, protected by a similar door and with even smaller windows or none at all. Some of the bastles had strong stone vaults over the ground floor.

Those that did always seem to have had a little hole in the middle so that the person who locked the ground floor door could be pulled up to the relative safety of upstairs. The hole through the vault at Hole Bastle near Bellingham is 14 inches square so whoever was given the job of getting the animals safely locked in – well, let's just say it wouldn't have been me. Among bastles as a whole the stone vaults are relatively rare but the ones that don't have a vault have a ceiling almost, or even possibly more impressive. They are made of huge close-set timbers, almost whole tree trunks, oppressively heavy, like something trolls might build. If they existed. Which they don't …

In most cases, but not always, the doorway into the ground-floor byre is to be found in the gable-end of the building while the upper doorway was in the middle of one of the longer side walls. The ground-floor doorways are among the most exciting features of the bastles. Sometimes they have huge, roughly-arched stone door heads, as primitive as you might find in an Anglo-Saxon church. Often they have relieving arches of stones set on edge to take the weight of the wall above. They look great.

And then there are the walls themselves.

There's nothing, to my mind, quite like the sensation of getting close to a bastle-house wall. There is nothing pretty about them; they virtually never have any architectural features or signs of sophistication. They are the plainest things in plainland, but seen from close-to they are massively impressive. They don't even have foundations but are built on a plinth of huge boulders to provide some stability. The scale is cyclopean and the roughness speaks volumes for the age in which they were built.

It is worth remembering that they were being built at the same time as palaces like Longleat or Burghley were being built in counties further south, and when Elizabethan or Jacobean manor houses were being built to grace civilised lives in a peaceful country. But up here, in the wild northern uplands, war had been more or less continuous for about 300 years and violence was still endemic, so a class of buildings emerged to cope with the danger.

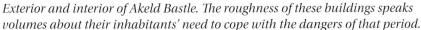
Exterior and interior of Akeld Bastle. The roughness of these buildings speaks volumes about their inhabitants' need to cope with the dangers of that period.

It was a unique architecture (assuming that "architecture" is an appropriate word to apply to these extraordinarily primitive structures). They're unique for the reasons I have just given, because the ground floor seems to have been given over to animals while the people climbed a ladder to the upstairs room, pulled the ladder up behind them and hoped to hold out until the danger passed. Nowhere else in Britain does this arrangement appear to have developed.

Most of the bastles were to be found in the remote and isolated valleys in the hills but there are others far beyond the wild places in the depth of the hills. It is true that many of the best examples of them are found high in the valleys of the North Tyne, the River Rede and the Coquet north and west of Rothbury, but there are many (and used to be more) much lower down the Tyne and along the South Tyne at places like the village of Wall and Haltwhistle, at Chesterwood near Haydon Bridge, at Ridley near Beltingham and in considerable numbers around Bardon Mill. There are some (and used to be more) along the upper reaches of the Wansbeck, at Cambo and Kirkwhelpington for example. Closer into Newcastle there are examples as near to the city as Black

Callerton beside Ponteland and an excellent example at Eltringham on the banks of the Tyne just west of Prudhoe. They also exist in large numbers south of the Tyne where there are clusters of them on the moors of Allendale. Outliers exist all over the county, even on, and close to the coast so it seems clear that the danger of violence was present everywhere.

Before my chum Peter and I were given the job of listing the buildings of Northumberland in the early 1980s, only about 70 bastles had been identified – in a survey by the Royal Commission on Historic Monuments, which had been carried out in 1970. Earlier books barely mentioned them at all. The 1st edition of Niklaus Pevsner's Northumberland volume in the 'Buildings of England' series, which was published in 1956, mentions a few but not with any sense of what they were like as a group or how they differed from other defensible buildings.

Bastles, as we know them, were too little and ordinary, too deeply vernacular to interest proper architectural historians in those days. But we loved them and sought them out voraciously. We found lots – some complete or relatively complete, others surviving as

Hole Bastle, Bellingham.

Woodhouses Bastle.

Gatehouse Bastle, Tarset.

parts of later buildings. Many existed only as fragments, the lower few feet of walls, isolated or retained as bits of later field walls, but wherever they were and whatever was left, they were instantly recognisable, another tick in the box, another jolt of excitement.

Not only are these extraordinary buildings unique to our area, they are also the oldest in the county that were the homes of ordinary people.

In other parts of the country there are medieval farmhouses that were the homes of fairly ordinary people; there are even, from time to time, medieval cottages and hovels that were the homes of the genuinely poor; but here in Northumberland there are no such buildings, they were too mean to have survived and only these bastle-houses remain as evidence of what life was like. Even they, rough and small as they are, were probably the homes of relatively important people in the local community because the massiveness of their construction, the huge and formidable size of the boulders with which they are built, must have required a vast amount of effort and organization.

Nobody knows where they came from or who invented them. Nobody knows how they were built – whether each family built their own or whether there was community effort involved. Nobody really knows when they first appeared. In 1541 the government conducted a survey of all the fortifications in the Borders but it made no mention of bastles. Instead it described immensely strong wooden houses with turf-covered roofs as defence against fire but none of these houses have survived and none have even been identified in excavations so they seem to have been replaced by the bastles later in the 1500s.

What's not clear is the precise date at which they started to appear. Only three or four of them have dates carved on them and the dates are very late. There's one in Cumberland from the 1590s but the two or three dated examples in Northumberland all have dates from just after 1600. Woodhouses Bastle near Holystone has '1602' carved on its doorhead, and there's a very odd inscription over a doorway in Falstone, just below the Kielder Dam. The house was extended in the 1700s so the original bastle doorway is now inside the present house. Its inscription is quite hard to read but it seems to be dated 1604 followed by the first 10 letters of the alphabet minus the I. Very curious. Could the owner or the builder not read but thought it would look impressive to have some writing over the door? I don't know, but I did feel that it was evidence of the very primitive lives being led there in that time – but the dates **are** curious and there are some writers who suggest that the bastles were all built in the 1600s, about the time, or even after England and Scotland were finally united under James VI of Scotland after the death of Queen Elizabeth.

I find that hard to accept. As buildings they are so clearly meant for defence against the sorts of attack that took place in the 1500s that it would seem bizarre only to start building them when the need for them was beginning to decline. The irregular violence of the Borders didn't finish in 1603 when Scotland and England were united under King James (the sixth of Scotland and the first of England) but it gradually began to fade away and become more local, whereas the bastles are stark monuments to a world where there was no security at all. So I'm sticking to the traditional view – that they were built from the second half of the 1500s onwards. So there!

When the bastles were built is not the only question about the world of the Border Reivers. There is also the question of how long the violent and brutal lifestyle continued. There is a lot of evidence that it kept going at some level for ages and ages, long after both sides of the Border had been united under one king. After James VI became King James I of England in 1603 he launched a harsh and ongoing campaign against the reiving families. He issued a royal declaration against them that said: '*Proclamation is made against all rebels and disorderly people, that no supply be given to them, their wives or their bairns and that they be prosecuted with fire and sword*'

Hundreds of the worst offenders were rounded up and transplanted into Ireland with threats of execution if they came back to the borders. Acts of Parliament were passed making their lifestyle illegal, and specifically outlawing the use of ransom and blackmail. These Acts continued to be renewed periodically throughout the 1600s but Beryl Charlton, in her history of Upper North Tynedale, has examples of the ongoing violence that happened despite the new laws and her account suggests that the families were deliberately thumbing their noses at the authorities. She tells of a raid into Tynedale by the Scottish Elliots and Armstrongs that took place in 1611. This is what she writes: '*the day after this raid a detailed list of those who had suffered was compiled by Sir William Fenwick, Keeper of north Tynedale: his account is horrific*:

– Lyell Robson, of the Small Burne, shott in at the harte with a single bullott, and slaine.
– Elizabeth Yearowe of Stannishburne, shott with twoe bullettes through both her thighs, the right thigh broken asunder with the shott, and slaine
– Walter Robson of the old side, hath his left arme broke asunder in twoe places with twoe bullettes
– Mary Robson, wife to James Robson, called Blakehead, is shott with five haile shott in her breasts.
– Elizabeth Robson, wife to Jeffray Robson, beinge great with chylde, is hurte verie sore in the head with the stroke of a peece ...'

The list goes on, but the point is clear ... the violence went on too – for a very long time. A hundred years later there were still things happening in the valleys that harked back to the days of the Reivers. The best known of them is the story of The Long Pack.

In Bellingham Churchyard there is a gravestone lying on the grass; this is The Long Pack and it refers to a story from as late as 1723 when Colonel Ridley, who lived at an attractive early Georgian house called Lee Hall, a few miles south of Bellingham, had gone to London and left the house in the care of three servants.

One day a pedlar called at the house and asked for lodgings. He was refused but he begged to be able to leave his pack behind so he could collect it the following morning. During the evening, Alice, one of the servants, got worried and convinced that she had seen the pack move, so one of the other servants took his blunderbuss and fired it into the pack and they were shocked and appalled to hear a dreadful groan and to see blood oozing out of the pack. Inside they found a dead man with a whistle around his neck and they realised that they had discovered a plot to rob the house. They summoned help and at midnight blew the whistle. Raiders rushed out of the woods to be met with a hail of gunfire. Several were shot, but in the morning all evidence of the attack had been spirited away – except the body in the pack, which was buried, under a grave that looked like a pack, on the unconsecrated north side of the church.

While the story may well be true as told, the stone itself, the Long Pack, is actually a rather high quality 13th century grave cover pressed into reuse because of its pack-like shape. Meanwhile, Bellingham church itself shows evidence of the continuation of the violence after the Union of the Crowns. The church had been built in the 13th century (though it may well have its origins hundreds of years earlier in the time of St Cuthbert) but it was badly damaged by a Scottish raid in the 1500s (we've seen in the past, being a church was no security against attack) and for many years it lay roofless and unused until it was restored in about 1609, years after Scotland and England had been united. The interesting thing about the restoration is that the church was given a heavy, powerful, protective stone-vaulted roof. It seems clear that the builders had no confidence that the church would be any safer in the future than it had been in the past, so they made it into a sort of fortress.

So the violence went on, right though the 1500s and for many years after. Even as late as 1597 there was a general feeling among those in charge locally and in London, that Northumberland, or more specifically the Border was more or less ungovernable.

In that year there was a report sent to Queen Elizabeth that listed all the ways that life in Northumberland was worse than anywhere else and you won't be surprised to hear that in the eyes of the south we were pretty rubbish up here. The church had let us down, education was in a dreadful state, the court system was under awful pressure and wasn't working properly, JPs weren't doing their job, fines weren't being collected and punishments not carried out. Local officials were corrupt. Law and order was terrible. Custodians of castles weren't living in them (while presumably still collecting their wages). It was like something you would read in the *Daily Mail* – or perhaps more accurately it resembled the way that rather smug self-righteous English people tend to think of other countries that they see as less civilised than their own.

That's the way it was. People in charge and people from down south had a tendency to think about Northumberland as if it was a place apart, not really part of England at all (you're right, nothing changes).

It's not that the picture in the report painted a totally false picture; the situation up here certainly had been dire for a long time but there is evidence, and especially evidence provided by the historian Diane Newton that by the end of the century, perhaps by the 1590s, perhaps even by the time that Elizabeth was reading the report, that the situation was beginning to get better.

Celebrated artist Joseph Crawhall depicted The Long Pack.

One of the bits of evidence that Diane Newton talks about is murder rates as revealed by court records. She is able to point out that by the end of the century murder rates in Northumberland were no worse, and in some cases better, than in other counties. Sussex, for example, which seems a rather nice, gently respectable county nowadays, had substantially more murders than Northumberland. The figures for the years 1597-1604 were as follows:

Northumberland	*18 murders*
Hereford	*12 murders*
Sussex	*26 murders*

She goes on to point out that in the years before 1597 all of the murders recorded in Northumberland had been committed by members of the Reiver community, but between 1597 and 1604 only one of the 18 was committed by them. The figures do suggest that things were at least beginning to settle down.

Who can tell? It had certainly been as rough as hell and maybe it was beginning to be a bit less so.

Meanwhile, as all of this extraordinary stuff was going on, largely up in the hills, other things were happening as well, and by 'other things' I principally mean the struggles and conflicts associated with religion. In the 1500s the whole country, in fact the whole of Europe was racked by struggles about religion and Northumberland was no different from everywhere else.

Henry VIII broke away from the Roman Catholic Church in order to be able to divorce his first wife, Catherine of Aragon, and marry Anne Boleyn. The break with Rome, along with his Government's chronic shortage of money, also led to the Dissolution of the Monasteries and lots of people hated the direction the country was going in, so in 1536 revolts sprang up against the King in many parts of England – but the principal revolt, the one called The Pilgrimage of Grace, actually started in Northumberland.

It was led by two members of the Percy family – not the head of the family because Henry, the 6th Earl of Northumberland, stayed in the background, but his two brothers, Sir Thomas Percy and Sir Ingram set the whole thing going. They brought their own followers into the fray and gathered a certain amount of support among the more conservative Catholic families elsewhere in the county including some lesser landowners like John Heron, who was the owner of Chipchase Castle in Tynedale.

In fact, they seem to have been quite remarkably proactive in persuading their neighbours to join in because, being Percys and having the power and influence the name gave them, they summoned all the gentry of Northumberland to Alnwick Castle, trapped them inside the walls and insisted that they signed a declaration in support of the revolt whether they wanted to or not.

As part of the recruitment drive, Sir Thomas turned up in Hexham market to seek support. Now, as it happens, Hexham Priory was one of the first religious houses slated for dissolution under Henry's new policy and it was one of the places where there was serious resistance to the King. When Henry's Commissioners turned up to close down the Priory they found 20 of the Canons waiting for them on the roof of the Abbey Gatehouse and they weren't behaving in a monk-like way at all. They were led by a chap called The Master of Ovingham and they were all bearing weapons, clad in armour and supported by crowds of locals from the town.

The Commissioners (being men of sense and discrimination) backed off. It was a critical moment in the history of Henry's revolution but ultimately it led nowhere. The Pilgrimage of Grace flared briefly and then fizzled out. The two Percys fizzled out too. Thomas was arrested and executed in the Tower of London; Ingram spent the rest of his life in the Tower.

Lots of ordinary people were fizzled out as well and as was the way in those savage old days, thousands of them were executed including lots in Carlisle and in Durham, but not very many, surprisingly enough, in Northumberland, which got off relatively lightly by comparison to other places. The following year, in 1537, the Commissioners came back to Hexham and the Priory was dissolved after all.

Religious conflicts between Catholics desperate to hold on to the old religion, and Protestants equally determined to reject any sort of control from Rome continued throughout the rest of the century and Northumberland continued to be at the forefront of the struggle.

After Henry VIII had died and his son Edward VI had died tragically young, Mary Tudor came to the throne. She had remained staunchly Catholic and set about using repressive measures to force people back to the old religion. She burnt people to death if they opposed her – over 300 of them in the five years she was on the throne and among her first and most notable victims was Nicholas Ridley, the reforming protestant Bishop of London who came from Northumberland. He was born near Haltwhistle, at a house called Unthank Hall some of my books say, but I have always believed he came from another Ridley property, Willimoteswick Hall near Bardon Mill. I don't know who's right.

When Mary died in 1558, her half-sister Elizabeth took over and she leapt off in the opposite direction; she re-introduced the Protestant faith. People can't have known whether they were coming or going. This time it was people clinging on to the old Catholic ways who were being executed.

In Northumberland lots of the gentry, and especially the Percys, were still firmly Roman Catholic and in 1569 they rebelled yet again, this time against Elizabeth. Lots of people thought that Elizabeth was illegitimate because they believed the marriage of her mother, Anne Boleyn, to Henry had not been legal, so they wanted to replace her with another Mary, Mary Queen of Scots, who was a Roman Catholic.

This rebellion was called The Rising of the North or The Revolt of the Northern Earls and one of its two leaders was Thomas Percy, the 7th Earl of Northumberland. I suspect that religion was only one of the things that led him to revolt. I think that people like him, other Percys and earls for example, thought that they had been sidelined by central Government and they wanted to get back the local power that they had lost. But whatever was driving Henry P, his rebellion failed and he fled to Scotland where he was captured and returned to Elizabeth to be hung, drawn and quartered.

His brother, who might have been a Catholic sympathiser as well but claimed not to be, was allowed to succeed to the title. He became the 8th Earl of Northumberland but was later arrested on suspicion of treachery and sent to the Tower, where he was subsequently discovered dead in bed with three bullet holes in his chest – evidence, I believe, that somebody didn't like him.

Opposition to all of these religious upheavals was met by very different responses in different parts of the county. While the cheesed-off rural aristocracy and the

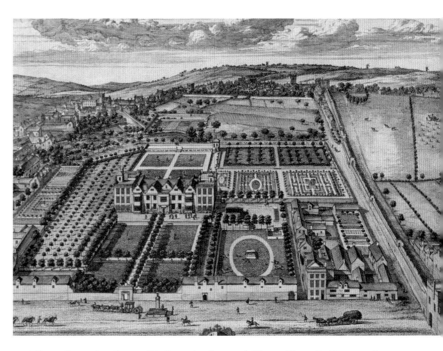

The tudor splendour of Robert Anderson 's Newe Place in Newcastle.

more conservative country districts tended to support the rebellions, middle-class Newcastle took virtually no part in them. In Newcastle nobody protested particularly during the Dissolution of the Monasteries, for example, when the Town's many religious institutions were closed down, because by the time it happened there weren't many religious people living in them anyway – the old monastic ideal had been fading for decades and Newcastle had sort of left the old medieval religious life behind and was more concerned with other things.

It was concerned with trade, for example, and particularly with coal. In the course of the 1500s the town increasingly cut itself off from the old concerns. It cut itself from the ongoing violence of the border country when, in 1564, its Guild of Merchant Adventurers made it an offence for any of its members to employ as an apprentice anybody from the Reivers' strongholds of Tynedale or Redesdale and, in disputes over coal, the town turned against the Catholic Church too.

The Church was the principal owner of coal mines

in the area; the Bishop of Durham had mines all along the south bank of the Tyne and the Bishop's jetties on the Gateshead side of the river where he exported his coal were repeatedly burned down by the merchants of Newcastle who wanted total control over the trade on the river.

With the Prior of Tynemouth they went several steps further. The Prior owned most of the pits on the north side of the river and for hundreds of years there had been bitter conflict between Newcastle and the communities downstream (including North Shields) for control of the coal and the right to export it. Newcastle took some pretty extreme measures. In 1267, for example, Mayor Richardson and the rest of his corporation sailed down the river as far as North Shields and burnt it down, while in 1510, as part of the ongoing struggle for control of the river, a large group of Newcastle townsfolk, along with the aldermen and many of the principal people in the town, gathered in Jesmond with the intention of murdering the prior. They failed, but that's what it was like.

So by the 1500s, Newcastle had become a place apart from the rest of the county – dominating, even bullying its neighbours, absolutely determined to be top dog while cutting itself off from the rest of the county. In the course of the century it became a hugely important trading city. Its merchants controlled all the increasing amounts of coal that were vital to London and the rest of the country. Its shops stocked goods from far off places, from the Mediterranean and even the Philippines. Its streets were lined with splendid three- and four-storey half-timbered houses with shops on the ground floor and living accommodation above the shops.

The most impressive of all the Tudor houses in the town by far was built by a man called Robert Anderson. He was a member of the town's elite, a coal owner and a merchant, and in 1563 he bought the two largest religious houses in the town – the huge Benedictine Nunnery and the Franciscan Friary, which had stood side by side, roughly on the site of Grey's Monument and present-day Grey Street until they had been dissolved in the 1540s. In their place he built himself a house which

Northumbrians still felt the need for defensive buildings like Elsdon Tower, as opposed to the stylish Tudor houses of Newcastle.

he called Newe Place. It was gigantic – a beautiful Tudor design, set in a huge walled garden bounded on the east by Pilgrim Street and on the north by the town wall along the line of what later became Blackett Street. It had the reputation of being the finest house in England within the walls of a walled town. It has gone now along with all the other Tudor houses, swept aside by later waves of development, but its former splendour is a stark reminder of the differences that existed between Newcastle and the rest of the county …

… because you will be astounded to hear that in the whole of Northumberland … good grief this is a bold thing to say and it probably isn't true. I've probably forgotten something and people will write and tell me off … but I'm going to be rash and say it anyway … because in the whole of Northumberland outside of Newcastle there are virtually no houses at all that were built between 1500 and 1603.

Elsewhere in England there are dozens and dozens of magnificent trophy houses (sometimes they are called 'prodigy houses') from Tudor times and especially from Elizabethan times; and there are thousands of mellow farms and picturesque manor houses from the same time. They are among the glories of English architecture. Hardwick Hall, Longleat, Montacute, Burghley House … fantastic places … but Northumberland has none, not one 16th century house!

It had rich people who you might have expected to build nice houses for themselves in those relatively peaceful times; it even had fabulously rich and powerful people like the Percys, but in the 1500s they didn't build themselves country houses, they continued to live in their castles. People did that in other parts of the country as well, of course, but in other counties those who chose not to build brand new houses tended instead to add new wings and new fronts to their old warlike castles to bring them up to date for a new, gentler age.

If you have the strength and determination to keep with this story into the next chapter you will discover that the well-to-do began to dip their toes into the brave new world of domestic comfort and alter their castles in far greater numbers in the decades after 1603, but in the 1500s they just didn't do it. You get the sense that nobody had the confidence to pull down their defensive walls or lower their drawbridges – as if war was so deeply entrenched in the local psyche that the need for protection trumped a desire to be modern.

They even continued to build new castles throughout the 1500s. Posh Northumbrians clearly felt the lack of security enough to keep on building themselves towers or little castles like they would have done in previous centuries. Elsdon Tower, beside the church at the head of Elsdon village green, is a good example. It stands alone and has thick walls, a stone-vaulted basement and battlements, hardly distinguishable from the great towers built at places like Belsay and Chipchase in the 1300s, and yet it was built in the second half of the 1500s. The reason was fairly obvious. The village had experienced two catastrophic raids by Scottish Reivers in the 1570s, so security was still the top priority.

There were quite a lot of similar buildings. Another late tower-house, one of my favourites actually, is a house called Coupland Castle in a beautiful situation, close to the River Glen, between Wooler and the Border.

Coupland Castle.

The tower has been added to (very successfully) in more recent centuries but the original building, which looks Scottish in style and is constructed out of wonderfully coloured. rough volcanic boulders from the Cheviots, is still absolutely defensible in character, even though it was probably built as late as 1595.

And despite the lack of official war there was even one full-scale and very proper official Royal castle built in these years. It is one of the greatest of all the Northumbrian coastal castles. Lindisfarne Castle on its extraordinary rock was only begun in 1549-50.

Meanwhile older castles and towns were adding new and more sophisticated defences to their walls – just in case as it were. They were adapting to artillery, the new weapon of choice, which had allowed the Scots to take all those Northumbrian castles with such ease before the Battle of Flodden.

In the course of the 1500s all of the defended places on the Border line were strengthened. Wark and Norham Castles and the old medieval walls at Berwick got new defences. They all were given bulwarks and casemates for cannon; they all had new gun loops to allow defenders to fire from protected positions.

Lindisfarne Castle, one of the greatest of all the Northumbrian coastal castles. Work only started on it as late as 1549-50.

The same new defences were added to Harbottle Castle which isn't even on the Border line – it lies more than a dozen miles south of the Border in the valley of the River Coquet. Harbottle was originally built in Norman times by the Umfraville family and throughout the bad times of the 14th and 15th centuries it had performed a stern purpose as a garrison and a defence against any attack. It had also been a house, though, and remarkably, in the early 1500s it became for a while a royal residence. After the death of James IV at Flodden, his wife Queen Margaret had remarried and become pregnant; however, because of opposition to her new husband she needed to flee across the border into Northumberland. For a while she stayed at Harbottle and it was there that her baby, Margaret, the mother of the future Mary Queen of Scots, was born.

But of all the new defences built in the second half of the 1500s the Tudor ramparts at Berwick were the most important. The town's medieval walls had been

16th century walls at Berwick.

begun in 1296 by Edward I as soon as he had captured the town and they were completed a few years later by Robert the Bruce.

These medieval walls were added to in the 1540s by a couple of extra towers designed to be effective in the new world of artillery fire. One of them is a mighty bulwark down by the river bank at the end of a spectacular section of medieval wall; the other is an even more powerful fort called Lord's Mount, which formed the north-east corner of the medieval town walls. That one, Lord's Mount, is supposed to have been designed by Henry VIII himself and it is immensely strong – circular with hugely thick walls and deep casemates for cannon. It faced north from Berwick towards Scotland and it was a whole new step in the development of fortification – but it was as nothing by comparison to what was begun about 20 years later.

The Elizabethan Ramparts at Berwick, which were begun in 1558, were the most ambitious (and by far the most expensive) defensive scheme created in the whole of England in the 1500s. They cost, in total, £128,648 5 shillings and 9 pence. (Actually it wasn't ninepence but ninepence halfpenny but I couldn't find a way of typing that on my computer).

However many half pennies were paid out though, it was a formidable amount of money but it was felt to be necessary because Elizabeth's government was nervous. They had just lost control of Calais, the last English outpost on continental Europe, there were French troops in Scotland and the serious possibility of a new war against the Scots. In the event the war never happened and the fortifications were never fully finished but they were, and they remain, the most remarkable example of the new Italian-inspired defensive thinking in Britain and among the greatest examples in the whole of northern Europe. They are also fantastically atmospheric to walk round. They wrap up the town and give it a wonderful sense of enclosure. They are the last serious castle walls to be built in Northumberland, about 500 years after Robert Curthose's castle at Newcastle and a full 300 years after the Border wars started in 1296. Fantastic as they were, they were never tested in anger and in 1603, just a few years after their construction was abandoned, the English and Scottish crowns were united under one King. James VI of Scotland became James I of England as well, bringing conflict between the two countries to an end for ever … maybe!

I have mentioned 1603 innumerable times in the course of this chapter and hammered home the fact that James VI (of Scotland) became simultaneously James I (of England) but I feel justified in going on about it partly because it was such an odd thing to have happened, and partly because it was going to have such a dramatic effect on Northumberland.

First of all, the oddness. In 1603 Queen Elizabeth died. She left no heirs. Her predecessor, Mary Tudor had left no heirs and Edward VI, the ruler before Mary, had left no heirs. All of Henry VIII's children were now dead and there wasn't an heir between them, so the only person left with any connection to the Tudor royal line of succession turned out to be James VI, the King of Scotland. How on earth did that happen?

Well, his great grandmother had been Henry VIII's sister. She was Margaret Tudor, a daughter of Henry VII who had died in 1509, 96 years earlier. Margaret was married to James IV of Scotland who had invaded England in 1513 and been killed in the Battle of Flodden. Her descendants had all been bitter enemies of England and included her granddaughter, Mary Queen of Scots, who was beheaded by Queen Elizabeth. James VI was the son of Mary Queen of Scots and her second husband, Lord Darnley.

So that was the man they chose. He had already been king of Scotland for 36 years when he got the England job. Like all Kings of Scotland he was a recognised enemy south of the Border and Elizabeth had already spent £128,648 5s 9d (and a halfpenny) on the walls of Berwick in order to keep him and his armies out of the country. Isn't that amazing? Don't you think that it is incredible that the rules of succession were (and possibly still are) so strict that you have to appoint a recognised enemy to the top job if there's nobody in front of him?

By 1603 it had been obvious for decades to everybody (as well as to Elizabeth herself) that the Queen was not going to leave an heir. It was obvious to James that when she died he was going to be the last man standing. That situation was sort of semi-officially recognised as early as 1586. when English and Scots negotiators spent a week in Berwick negotiating a friendship pact between the two countries. The Treaty of Berwick was signed on 6th July and in it both sides agreed that they would help each other if either side was invaded by a third country. By 1586 both England and Scotland were mainly Protestant countries and they were both worrying about the French and the Spanish, the two great Roman Catholic superpowers who were desperate to make Great Britain Catholic again. At the same time, Elizabeth was desperate for some sort of heir, a secure line of succession so the country wouldn't fall into chaos after her death. She also knew that she was on the verge of executing James' mother, Mary Queen of Scots, so she was probably trying to soften the blow for James, while he had clearly set his heart on eventually becoming king of England and was prepared not to make too much of a fuss about his mother's death.

What a tangled web we weave, as Shakespeare put it. But at least the beginning of the reconciliation between the two countries began in Berwick, which time after time had flipped between the two countries and which, for hundreds of years, had suffered with such intensity in the Border Wars.

In the end, in 1603, the people of Berwick were still terrified that it might all kick off again. When the Queen died, Sir John Carey, the deputy Governor of the town, wrote in panic to Sir Robert Cecil. He didn't know what to do or what line to take. He didn't know whether James would arrive in peace or with a hostile army but in the event it all passed off peacefully. Sir Robert Carey (the Deputy Governor's brother) rode north with news of the Queen's death. He stopped, for example in Morpeth and Alnwick, to proclaim James as the new King. Berwick greeted James with a massive multi-gun salute and it was all over. Within a couple of years James had abolished the Border and taken to calling Northumberland one of "The Middle Shires" but you will have to wait until the next chapter to find out how successful all of that was.

9. 17TH CENTURY

In my study, at the end of my desk as I write, there is almost always a book called *Archaeology in The Northumberland National Park* by an archaeologist called Paul Frodsham. Actually it's not just by Paul Frodsham because lots of other archaeologists have contributed specialist articles to the volume. I have used this book endlessly while writing my own stuff and I desperately hope I haven't misrepresented too much that I have read. Anyway, having just finished that last chapter, I immediately opened ANNP (as we in the Grundy study call it) to dip my toe into whatever happened next in the story of our county and on page 111 came across chapter 8 entitled *From Trauma to Tranquillity: The post-medieval period (1603-1901)*.

I was encouraged by this. I seemed to have been writing about trauma for such a long time and desperately felt the need for a bit of tranquillity. This was the stuff, I felt, to give the troops.

Not only that. Page 111 has a photo on it, an aerial photo of some interestingly random field shapes dotted around on a bleak-looking moor. Imagine my delight when I read the caption to the picture. It read:

Enclosures at Yearning Law

I do hope that you can recall my long, lonely and over-imaginative walk through a wild Border-Reiver landscape towards Yearning Hall; well Yearning Law was the hill that loured above me as I walked though those splendid and solitary places near Blindburn in the valley of the Upper Coquet. The head of the valley was the Border itself and Scotland no more than a mile or two away. If you want to get a sense of what it's like, you could do no better than look up "Yearning Hall" on Google because some kindly soul has posted a collection of terrific pictures of it.

The cottage that still stood relatively intact when I was there in the 1980s is now a broken-down ruin – but picturesque. In one of the photos there is a herd of wild goats on the hillside behind the cottage looking more like creatures you would see in the Himalayas than the Cheviot Hills. It's a marvellous place but the reason I mention it now is because ANNP says that the random field shapes in the aerial photograph probably represent shieling settlements from as early as spring 1604.

You'll have to think back right to the beginning of this book if you need to remember what a shieling is. I wrote in Chapter One how for hundreds, possibly thousands of years the people of the hills had spent the winters deep in the valleys and moved up into the hills with their livestock as the weather improved. You might recall in that first chapter that I speculated whether the practice had already started in prehistoric times and even in the worst of times during the 1500s it had never gone away. The Elizabethan traveller and antiquary William Camden came to Northumberland in 1590.

Left: Chillingham Castle.

Unsurprisingly, one of the things that struck him was how dangerous the county was. For example, he was hugely impressed by the remains of the Roman Wall but couldn't get to see the central section of it round Housesteads because it was still the haunt of dangerous men; but he did get to see evidence of transhumance. He wrote about … '*Ancient Nomades, a martiall kind of men, who from the moneth of Aprill unto August, lye out scattering and summering (as they tearme it) with their cattell in little cottages here and there which they call Sheales and Shealings*'

The 'little cottages' were shiels or shields and the areas round about them, where the animals grazed in the summer, were known as the shieling grounds, the places reserved by each family for their particular use and even now bearing their original names. You can see them all over the OS maps of the hills. They often include family surnames like Bellshield, or Ridley Shield, which would have been the shieling grounds of the Bell family and the Ridleys.

In the worst of times through the 1500s the practice of transhumance and therefore the use of the shieling grounds had not disappeared, but it had become reduced in area and in the most dangerous places near the border it had been abandoned altogether and one of those dangerous places, one of the wildest bits of all was Upper Coquetdale, the area around my Yearning Hall.

But what happened next was interesting. When King James took over his new extended role in 1603, he immediately declared the Border redundant and launched his offensive against the Border Reivers. The effectiveness of his policy was obviously patchy, and I have already written about how the roughneck lifestyle trickled on right into the 18th century, but some things happened immediately.

Within a few months, lands and lifestyles that had been threatened through the hardest of times of the previous century began to get back to normal, and that normality included the practice of transhumance, so the shieling grounds of Upper Coquetdale, which had been a virtual desert, were suddenly repopulated in the months after 1603. Paul Frodsham even suggests that the area might have been repopulated by Scottish settlers from across the Border but whoever was using the land, it must have felt like an encouraging return to normality.

And it wasn't alone. Quite suddenly there were all sorts of changes taking place. Before 1603, for example, and ever since the beginning of the wars, Borderers had occupied their farms by something called "customary tenure", which meant that they got the property cheap on condition that they promised to be available to fight for the authorities in times of war, but quite suddenly in 1604, customary tenure was abolished and replaced by normal leaseholds like people had elsewhere in the country.

I'm not saying the change made a great deal of difference to the living standards of ordinary Northumbrians, because it didn't – many of them still lived in the most basic accommodation but at least it was a start, a little sign that Northumberland was ceasing to be just a war zone and was instead taking on the habits and laws of the rest of the country.

One of the most obvious signs of change is that the posh began to move on from their castles and build houses that presented a gentler, more domestic face towards the world. In the first third of the 1600s a number of families built themselves Jacobean houses or altered their existing castles with new Jacobean extensions. There aren't a lot of them that still exist, five or six in total, though there were probably quite a lot more that were rebuilt again in later centuries, but those few are worth thinking about because they are evidence of a new mood, a new confidence that insecurity was a thing of the past.

The first one to be built, at least the earliest that I know about, sadly no longer exists or possibly was never fully completed because I've never seen a picture or a proper description of it but it was a house that was being built on the site of Berwick Castle as early as 1607 by a man called Lord Dunbar.

When you think about the history of Berwick, the horrific and repeated traumatic experiences that it had seen over the past 300 years, it's a big deal that someone would come along and build a peacetime house on a site that previously had seen nothing but war. On top of that it seems to have been a house that made its domestic point in a pretty ambitious way. There are only two things I know about it. In Holy Trinity Church there's a chest that incorporates a series of quite excellent Jacobean reliefs. They are dancing maidens, quite lively and beautifully carved and they came from Lord Dunbar's house. The other thing I have read about it is that it had a long gallery. If you have visited any of the great Elizabethan houses of England, you will probably have come across long galleries. To put you in the picture if you've never experienced one, they were galleries, if you see what I mean, and they were long. It's not completely clear what they were used for but I think the assumption is that people walked up and down them as a way of taking exercise. There may have been other uses; perhaps they played indoor bowls in them or had group pilates sessions or three-legged races but whatever they did they were very impressive rooms; because they were invariably high up at the top of the house and very long they were also excellent viewing platforms.

According to Mark Girouard, the longest long gallery in the country was reputed to be the one at Worksop Manor in Nottinghamshire, which was demolished in the 1760s. It was 212 feet long and 36 feet wide. That's a big room – and you can imagine how it must have galled its owner, Lord Shrewsbury, to get a letter from a chum telling him that the new house being built at Berwick by George Home, the 1st (and only) Earl of Dunbar, would make it pale into insignificance. '*Worksop gallery was but a garrett in respect of the gallery that there would be*' was the way he put it.

Lord Dunbar was a new man in Northumberland. He was one of James I's men, a very useful servant to the king. One of his jobs was King's Commissioner for Ordering the Borders so he was the man who started to sort out the Border Reiver problem and to be going on with, just in the year 1604 alone, hanged 140 '*of the nimblest thieves in all the Borders'*.

He went on to become Chancellor of the Exchequer (a job he made a few bob out of) and among other tasks he was given the contents of Queen Elizabeth's wardrobe to dispose of. He didn't divide them up between the corporation dump and a charity shop like he would have done if he'd been disposing of my wardrobe; instead he sold them for £60,000. She must have had a few nice bits and pieces, Queen Elizabeth. I'm not sure how far £60,000 went in those days but his new house in Berwick with its enormous long gallery only cost him £20,000, so presumably the old Queen didn't do her shopping at Primark.

I'm not sure that Lord Dunbar's house at Berwick was ever finished because he sadly died in 1611 but he was (or would have been) the only newcomer among the Jacobean builders of Northumberland. All the others were members of ancient Northumbrian families who had owned their properties for centuries.

The first one to go up was a new wing and entrance to Belsay Castle, which was erected (as it says in an inscription above the door) in 1614 by Thomas Middleton and Dorothy his wife.

The Middletons had owned Belsay since the 1200s, in fact by 1278 they already had a posh enough house to provide a bed for Edward I when has was up here on his hols. They lost the property for a while in the 1300s after one of the family revolted against Edward III and was hanged, drawn and quartered, but they got it back in 1379 and built the fabulous tower that still forms the main feature of the castle today.

That 14th century tower looks as if it stood alone but it probably didn't. Nobody knows what other buildings there were round about it but there must have been something because there are blocked doorways on the first and second floors that must have gone somewhere. One suggestion is that they opened onto bridges that led to a detached building. Whatever was there, though, Belsay was always a great building and the Middletons were a classic Northumbrian family – constantly involved in the wars and the governance of the Border. They became Lords Lieutenants and High Sheriffs of the County and were Wardens of the Marches and MPs and things – they were a busy and significant family.

Thomas Middleton, the builder of the new house (along with Dorothy his wife of course) was no different from his forbears. He hadn't expected to inherit the estate but his elder brother died unmarried and he took over. The life that he led didn't seem different from what had gone on before. At various times he was a magistrate and a High Sheriff. Throughout his life he still had to deal with typical Northumbrian problems. In 1618, for example, while he was a magistrate, he had property stolen by John Charleton, one of the notorious North Tynedale Clan, and quarter of a century later nothing much had changed; by 1643 he was a Commissioner in Northumberland responsible for '*sequestering notorious delinquents*' … (what a lovely phrase that is incidentally… So what do you do for a living, officer? I sequester notorious delinquents, your honour.)

So in some ways life doesn't seem to have changed a great deal for Thomas, but his house tells a different story. He built an extension to his tower which wouldn't have seemed out of place anywhere else in the country at that time. It was completely up to date. Instead of tiny little gun loops like the lower floors of his castle had, he gave the new house large mullioned-and-transomed windows (even on the ground floor) and an elegant Classical porch with an arched doorway flanked by pairs of Classical columns; there's a lush, well-carved heraldic crest above with the date and the names of the builders. It's ruined now and roofless but its quality is still clear. It is well-built, welcoming and accessible, with no defensive references at all – clear evidence that by 1614 the Middletons at least were confident that the wars were finally over.

The next family to drag their ancient castle screaming into the modern world was the Grey family of Chillingham Castle.

Like the Middletons, the Greys had been around since year dot and had started out in the 13th century with a single large tower as their manor house. (Inevitably King Edward I stayed there in 1298; the man was obsessed; he clearly couldn't keep away from Northumberland; I've heard rumours that he even had a caravan at Seahouses.)

In the 1300s the Greys turned their solitary tower into a full-blown castle with a courtyard in the middle. From this castle successive generations of Greys ruled over the extreme north-east of the county. There wasn't a job they didn't do or a position they didn't hold. They were present at all the battles and their castle was on the front line of Scottish raids on innumerable occasions and that's the way it remained until the arrival on the scene of Ralph Grey in 1552.

In many ways Ralph was a typical chip off the old Grey block. There was barely a single official Northumbrian pie into which his thumb had not been stuck. He was on loads of Commissions. He was involved in a Commission against Piracy and another aimed at '*Suppressing Malefactors*' (rather similar to sequestering notorious delinquents I imagine). He conducted a survey of Border Castles and was Deputy Governor of Berwick. Actually he was quite often a deputy-something-or-other; unlike his predecessors in the family he never quite made the top jobs and there were two reasons for that. One was that he was a bit of a closet Roman Catholic at a time when Elizabeth was making that an unhealthy thing to be. He was known to '*harbour Jesuits*', which was a sure-fire way to be overlooked for the top jobs.

The other reason he tended to get overlooked was that he had rubbish relationships with his neighbours. Feuds; he had feuds with his neighbours, especially the Selbys of nearby Branxton. In 1597 he took part in an abortive duel against one of them in Berwick churchyard and subsequently attempted to murder him. That sort of thing tends to get noticed. However, he did one thing really well and that was that he played a useful and significant part in smoothing the transfer of power to James I when Elizabeth's life began to fade.

The question of the succession was still a really contentious issue and there were lots of secret negotiations going on and Ralph was part of them. His house, so close to the Border and well off the beaten track, was a good place for sneaky meetings and he was actually distantly related to the Scottish Ambassador to the English court. He was called The Master of Gray and in the final year of Elizabeth's life he was a regular visitor to Chillingham as plans were made for a smooth transfer of power when the time came …

… as it did … and because the arrangements had been well made, in 1603 there was no bother. King James arrived in Berwick with no opposition and was

Chillingham Castle. In 1617 it was the scene of a rare peaceful visit by a Scottish king.

welcomed into England before his similarly peaceful and relatively triumphant progress through the country to London. Significantly (from our point of view) one of the first things he did in England was to go to the end of Berwick Bridge and turn plain old Ralph Grey into shiny new Sir Ralph Grey.

That entire story is merely a precursor to describing what happened next to Chillingham Castle, which was that its warlike demeanour was softened in Sir Ralph's time by the addition of interesting domestic features.

Two things were changed. First of all, a new entrance front was created on the north side of the castle. It's quite grand; for Northumberland at that time it's very grand with big windows and a frontispiece with classical columns on three floors and carved beasts with shields on the parapet. There's a short flight of stairs up to the doorway, which leads through into the courtyard where there is quite an impressive arrangement of stairs and balustrades and decorative stuff. It was faffed around with a bit in later centuries but the original 17th century bits include seven rather crudely carved and badly worn statues, one above the door into the Great Hall at the top of an external staircase and the other six attached to the wall on either side of the stairs.

These statues are the Nine Worthies – well they would be if they had all survived; as it happens they are seven of the Nine Worthies

The Nine Worthies were first described in the Middle Ages, but they were still very popular and influential throughout Europe in the Renaissance. They

Chillingham Castle, with its statues of the Nine, sorry, Seven Worthies.

were all heroes who represented ideals of chivalry; three of them were pagan heroes from Classical times (Hector, Alexander the Great and Julius Caesar); three were Jewish heroes from the Old Testament (Joshua, David and Judas Maccabeus; I had to look him up); and the final three were Christian heroes including King Arthur, Charlemagne and Godfrey Bouillon (who sounds like a soup or a stock cube). Each one of them was associated with a particular chivalric virtue like strength and courage, judgement, wisdom and courtesy.

The question about these alterations and additions to Chillingham Castle has always been when they were built. On earlier occasions when I have written about these things I have been rather coy about their date, attributing them to the early 1600s in a vague sort of way,

but I have recently read a convincing article by a historian called Anna Brunton. Its title is *The significance of the Worthies of Chillingham Castle* and in it she makes a really strong argument that the alterations were probably done to prepare the castle for a visit by James I in May 1617.

The history of English country houses is full of extraordinary changes made to welcome the arrival of a monarch. It's not uncommon nowadays to redecorate a bedroom or have the front room sofa covers cleaned for the arrival of guests but some of the changes made to welcome kings and queens were so great and expensive that they ruined the owners, especially if the monarch never bothered to turn up but at Chillingham he did. James arrived at the castle on May 9th and that afternoon he knighted Edward Grey, Sir Ralph's brother. The idea is that he would have entered the courtyard and ascended the staircase to the Great Hall until he was on the same level as the Worthies. It would have been a symbolic compliment, a sly suggestion that the king possessed all the great qualities shown by the heroes of old.

I don't think the case has been proved beyond doubt – but I bet it's right and it's a nice symbol for a new world. In the past, the arrival of a Scottish king near the border would have been a source of fear and led to rebuilding and strengthening of a warlike nature, but by 1617 such a visit led to an increase in the peaceful, decorative and more sophisticated arts.

A few years later, in 1621, another castle transformation occurred. It happened at Chipchase Castle in North Tynedale, which was a property belonging to the Heron family. The estate had been acquired in 1348 by Sir William Heron who built another of the great towers of Northumberland. It's a little rougher and tougher than the tower at Belsay, which might reflect the demands of its more exposed and dangerous location deep in the North Tyne valley and on a key route into Scotland.

The Herons, like the Middletons and the Greys, were yet another typical Northumbrian family but if anything even a bit more so. The castle's website (it's a wedding and events venue as well as a house nowadays and it has a really pretty website with good info and beautiful pictures) … the castle's website goes so far as to describe the family who built it as *'A hot-tempered race, regularly in trouble with the authorities'* and that is a good description – especially when you look at their behaviour in the 1500s; the merest snapshot of their activities will reveal what I mean:

1536: John Heron joined the rebels in the Pilgrimage of Grace.

1537: he was accused of the murder of Roger Fenwick.

1540: took part in an unofficial raid into Scotland.

1550: the Herons of Ford were involved in a terrific feud against the Manners family of Etal Castle with pitched battles and incursions and all sorts of violent activity.

1587: accused of being involved in and possibly even encouraging the Scottish raid on Haydon Bridge.

You might ask yourself how such a troublesome family would get round to building a beautiful and harmonious extension to their house.

Answer: they died out.

In 1591 the direct family line died out and the estate passed into the 6-year old hands of Cuthbert Heron, the cousin of the last owner. He continued to be the owner until his death in 1655 and when he was 36 built the house that stands today.

I love this house, I need to tell you, and will brook no criticism of it and I have two stories to tell that relate to it.

Firstly, in the 1980s when I was a listed building man (have I ever mentioned that?) the day arrived when I had to go and list it. I arrived in a bit of a state partly because an elderly lady in a nearby village, seeing me in her neighbour's garden, had mistaken me for a burglar and attacked me. There's not a lot a respectable building lister can do to defend himself against the attacks of an elderly lady, especially one who is so clearly heroically defending her village and her neighbours, so I had withdrawn in rather poor order and set off to Chipchase where I had an appointment.

On the way I got a puncture (well, actually my car did) and I had to lie on the ground beneath it to attempt a repair. It was raining heavily so I arrived at the castle looking a little the worse for wear. When I got there, I found that a shoot had been taking place on the estate and the shooters were having lunch in one of the front rooms. Soup was being served by waitresses in little black dresses and white pinnies. I was greeted gracefully but not invited in so I sat in front of the house in my damaged car and my damaged clothes and ate my sandwiches in the rain as the smell of game soup wafted out into the air.

There isn't a lot of point to that story except that my life hasn't often brought me into contact with the world of the county set and it seemed appropriate that I should have been a bedraggled observer and not involved in their revelries.

The second story took place in Malaga in southern Spain, where I had gone for a winter break. What a lovely place it is incidentally. I was walking along a main shopping street when, in the window of a gentlemen's outfitters, I saw a poster that shouted not just Englishness but the wilder and rougher version of Englishness that is so characteristic of Northumberland. It was an advert for a Barbour Jacket and showed a rather splendidly craggy chap standing in front of an equally craggy Chipchase Castle. There was only a tiny fragment of the castle on display, but to a man who had eaten sandwiches in the rain outside it, instantly recognisable. I stood among the Spaniards, transfixed by the rough beauty of my native land – he said a bit too portentously.

What Cuthbert Heron created was the most impressive Jacobean house in the county. It has a richly-decorated Jacobean porch, dripping with slightly OTT classical details and on the roof there are curly bits and lots of statues standing on the decorative parapet. Inside, it was altered a lot in the 18th century, so there's not much sign of its original décor but it does have one remarkable fireplace which deserves a mention. This is what I wrote about it in another book. I said that it was

… A re-erected, extremely sumptuous Jacobean fireplace with four allegorical figures, a large relief of Father Time with the four Elements, and biblical as well as other small reliefs.

It sounds good, doesn't it? It **is** good and extraordinarily well carved. I described it as re-erected because the room it's in is now rather a fine Georgian room but also because it was probably brought to Chipchase from elsewhere. It was probably brought from Newcastle.

The three Jacobean houses I have described aren't quite the only ones I could have mentioned. I could have included Ford Castle and possibly the much smaller Welton Hall, just off the military road, where a medieval house was given new details in 1614. I could have talked about Denton Hall, the Roman Catholic Bishop of Newcastle's house built in 1622 on the western edge of the city and there may be others, but instead I must say a word or two about Newcastle itself because by the time the modern Jacobean world was beginning to take root in the rural parts of the county it was already thoroughly present in Newcastle.

The Chipchase fireplace is one of a series of similar works, dated from about 1630, which were created in Newcastle. There may have been more once but only three of them survive now, as far as I know and only one of them is still in the city where they were carved; it's in the Merchant Venturers Court in the Guildhall down on the Quayside. It is, like lots of Jacobean designs, more than a touch grotesque; part of its decoration is a portrayal of the Judgement of Solomon, which shows Solomon brandishing a sword while holding a naked baby upside down by its heel; it's not the sort of decorative motif that most people would choose to have permanently in their front room; it would definitely put you off your cocoa, but it is magnificently carved.

Another of the fireplaces used to be in a pub called The Beehive Inn, also on the Quayside until it was demolished; it then travelled about a bit and got lost and almost broken up but now it is safe, beautifully restored and on display in the Bank Room at Beamish Museum.

The other is the one in Chipchase and I mention all three of them because, apart from being carved in Newcastle, they are works of international quality and sophistication and alongside them there are enough surviving bits and pieces from the same period to suggest that Newcastle was not only a thoroughly modern place but also had access to high-end art and

Jacobean fireplace in Newcastle's Guildhall.

Chipchase Castle.

culture. There's an exquisite little chapel of 1634, which is part of Trinity House just off the Quayside; it's a mass of well-worn timber and gleaming wooden decoration and feels like the inside of a ship. There is a terrific monument in St Nicholas' Cathedral to the Maddison family, which dates from 1632 and is elaborately carved and vibrantly coloured. There's a splendid plaster and painted ceiling of these same years in a former merchant house under the High Level Bridge (it's a restaurant called The House of Tides nowadays and my wife reminds me with some bitterness that we have never been there).

There must once have been lots of other things that have been swept away in later upheavals but what is left is clear evidence that Newcastle, along with the rest of the county, was beginning to come out of its medieval past and was, by the standards of the day, a wealthy and successful place.

Coal, of course, was the reason it was doing so well.

Earlier in the previous century almost all of the coal mines near the Tyne had been owned by the church,

specifically the prior of Tynemouth on the north side of the river and the Bishop of Durham on the south and if the merchants of Newcastle already had a pretty firm grip around the throat of the coal trade and controlled who could sell it and buy it, who made most money out of it (them!), they still weren't yet in control of the whole process; but that began to change after the Dissolution of the Monasteries, and when Elizabeth came to the throne the mines (like all the other monastic possessions) were effectively nationalised and belonged to the crown.

Her cunning wheeze was to lease them all back to private individuals and make her money by taxing the leases. There was a bit of to-ing and fro-ing in the situation but by 1600 the whole process was in the hands of the Newcastle merchants. You couldn't make any money out of coal unless you were one of the favoured Newcastle merchants. They were known as the Company of Hostmen and they were in charge of the whole caboodle; they owned the mines; nobody else could sell the coal but them; they owned the boats that exported it and nobody could arrive from elsewhere to do trade on the river without going through them.

You would, of course, have to recognise that the merchants of Newcastle did nothing out of the kindness of their hearts; they were completely ruthless in the protection of their monopoly. It was an attitude that had been going on for a very long time. You might recall the story of the Mayor and corporation of Newcastle burning down North Shields in 1267 and the attempted murder of the Prior of Tynemouth by the people of Newcastle early in the 1500s.

Well, I came across an extraordinary example of their ruthlessness in an exhibition in The Old Low Light Heritage Centre on the Fish Quay in North Shields, which showed the same remorseless determination to stay in control in the 1600s. The exhibition was called "Shields v The Toon" and it told the story of a ship that went aground off North Shields in 1646.

The captain, Henry Harrison, managed to get safely to shore and he employed a local ship's carpenter called Thomas Cliff to free the ship, beach it and begin repairs. You might think this was a reasonable thing to do, it being his ship and all, but when news reached Newcastle, a posse was sent down river to arrest Thomas Cliff and cast him into prison because no ships carpenters were allowed to operate on the Tyne except the Newcastle Company of Ships Carpenters. There was a fracas as the arrest took place as there so often is and Cliff's wife and daughter were beaten up, to the extent that his wife Anne died of her injuries. Even in those days there were court cases of course, six years of them in fact, but nobody was ever punished and perhaps more to the point, Thomas Cliff never worked again. He had dared to challenge the monopoly of Newcastle – and lost.

It wasn't enough to keep a savage grip on what you'd got, of course. You needed to keep on getting more – so in addition to all that, once the Newcastle merchants owned the mines, the amount of coal being dug up began to increase massively. For some reason the church had controlled the volume but there was no holding back a Geordie merchant so, encouraged by the crown (who got five bob a chauldron, which was a huge amount in those days) the town's economic power and sophistication was going from strength to strength.

But alas it wasn't to last. I started this chapter rejoicing in the arrival of 'tranquillity' to replace the 'trauma 'of the preceding centuries and so far I have been bravely trailing the few green shoots that suggested that peace and comfort was going to be the way forward … but it wasn't to last, and from the middle of the 1630s for the next 20 or so years so much was going to go wrong. In a moment I will be talking about not one, not two but **three** brand new and unexpected wars that affected the county, but first I need to spend a few moments looking at the dreadful outbreak of plague that devastated Newcastle in 1636.

Plague was a feature of life and death in the 16th and 17th centuries. There had been major outbreaks in 1546, 1583 and 1604, but the worst of all in our part of the world was the one that struck Newcastle in 1636.

Actually, and almost inevitably it had first appeared down river at Tynemouth and North Shields the previous year, 1635, because it was brought to the Tyne on board a ship and the communities at the mouth of the river were likely to meet it first. North Shields was described as being 'almost depopulated' and the effect on Newcastle when it took hold there at the beginning of May 1636 was entirely devastating. The first cases occurred in the overcrowded area of Sandgate down by the river and its progress through the town can be measured by the rise in the number of burials that were recorded by the town's churches.

From Sandgate it moved up-river to Sandhill, where the centre of local government was situated and where the houses of the rich stood. A little later it had caught hold in the upper town until, by August, the whole town was in its grip. Dr Jenison, a local preacher, wrote that '*it increaseth, it rageth, runs and spreads like wildfire*'.

Dr Jenison went on to publish lists of the burials that took place that year in each of the town's four parish churches. Newcastle had a population of about 10,000 and in normal times there would be about 50 funerals a month in the town as a whole, but by May that year were over 50 a week and by the end of July each of the parishes was burying 4 or 5 a day and sometimes as many as 15 or 16.

As it happens I am writing these words in April 2020, in the midst of the Coronavirus Lockdown with no certainty about how the situation that prevails at the moment will end, so I can understand and empathise with the fear that must have frozen the people of Newcastle in those days; but even now, with all of the uncertainties that surround me I am not expecting a catastrophe like the outbreak of 1636.

Last night I stood outside my house, and at a decent distance from my neighbours clapped to show my gratitude and respect for the services fighting to protect us; in 1636 there was nobody to do that, nobody official to provide the services and nobody understood what needed to be done so that when the epidemic burnt itself out at the beginning of December that year, an estimated 5,631 people had died, just over half the people in the town, one out of every two people in Newcastle had passed away. In terms of simple numbers that figure has clearly been surpassed many times in the history of the world, but as a percentage of a local population, it can't often have been beaten.

But there are similarities. In the present outbreak it is impossible not to be aware of the good things that are happening as well as the tragic ones. Last night's clapping and outpouring of gratitude was a wonderful expression of community feeling and there are so many other, similar things happening. People are watching out for their neighbours, checking on them and shopping for them; workers are still working, collecting the bins, stocking the aisles and caring for the elderly. Social media is awash with affectionate and brave determination to keep in contact; witty, creative and heart-warming messages abound. We are surrounded by evidence that people are in this together and it sort of makes it bearable.

To be honest, it was a bit like that in 1636 too. There are many horrific and stereotypical images about plagues, about the fear and the selfishness, the fear of dying alone, rejected and shunned – but that isn't the impression you get when you read about the Newcastle plague in 1636. People must have felt those things but they seem to have tried their hardest to do things right. Households attempted to self-isolate and boarded up their doors and windows, but it was also clear that people broke the rules and took personal risks in order to help the dying – they sat beside their friends and held their hands, they took in the children of neighbours who had died. There's no evidence of crime; no houses left abandoned by death were looted and when lawyers recorded the wishes of the dying for their wills, they recorded more love than desperation – how much the dying dreamt about their unborn children and how desperately they longed to be buried beside a husband or *'soe neare unto my deare mother and sister as conveniently may be'*. Even those whose job it was to keep the official records attempted to insert some humanity into their lists. The Parish Clerk at St Andrew's Church added little facts to show that these bodies were not just names to him but the names of people he knew, people who needed to be remembered: he wrote the name of *Robert Toddericke which had the honch back* and *Gorge the Fiddler*.

———

And then, as if a devastating plague wasn't enough, in 1640 a Scottish army led by General Leslie crossed the River Tweed, marched through Northumberland, fought a full-scale pitched battle in Tynedale, routed an English army and, with no particular difficulty, captured Newcastle and Tynemouth. They occupied Tyneside for a year. That was a bit of a turn-up for the books considering that in three hundred years of Border warfare neither place had been captured once and this attack came after more than half a century of continual peace.

What happened was this. In 1639 Charles I (the son of James) was having bother with the Scots. He wanted them to be a bit more English and, in particular, he was determined to force them to accept a nice Church of England Prayer book, which had been devised by his religious advisor, Archbishop Laud. He was equally determined to insist that the Scottish Church should be ruled over by Bishops like it was in England and use the same sort of religious ritual that Laud was busy re-introducing in England. Well, the Scots determination to do none of those things was implacable; the vast majority of them had become puritans and Presbyterians and they wanted none of that ritual which smacked of a return to the Popery that had been cast away almost a hundred years earlier by Henry VIII; so they said no and a rebellion ensued which is usually known as The First Bishops' War.

It was serious enough that the king decided to leap up to the North East to take control of the situation himself. He arrived in Newcastle on 5th May with what is described as "a gallant army". It was all very splendid and he stayed in the town for 12 days and was apparently magnificently entertained by the Corporation. He even knighted the Mayor and the Town Clerk before going on to Berwick but in the end he wasn't needed. There were a few skirmishes and a very few deaths in Scotland but the two armies that faced each other across the Tweed near Berwick never came to battle and the whole thing seemed to have been settled by a treaty rather deliciously called The Pacification of Berwick.

If only it were that easy. Pacifications rarely are in my experience and on this occasions Charles continued to take an uncompromising stance so a few months later, in 1640, the whole thing flared up again – except that this time there was no faffing around with armies facing each other across the Tweed. In a cunning wheeze General Leslie led his troops across the river a few miles upstream from Berwick at Coldstream, bypassed the English army entirely and charged south through Northumberland like a bullet, heading straight for Newcastle.

Newcastle wasn't a random choice of target for the Scots. They came here because they wanted control of the coal, which they could use to finance their army and, perhaps even more importantly, to hold London hostage and cut off a major source of income to the king, because by this time the king was used to getting two shillings tax for every chauldron of coal exported from the Tyne so if he lost that, the assumption was that he would have to give up on his demands on the Scots. So Newcastle was a natural target.

However Newcastle had long been surrounded by a pretty impressive ring of defensive walls, which had actually been strengthened in 1638, especially on the northern edge of the town so the Scots should have been faced with a formidable problem – except that they were led by General Leslie who was pretty formidable himself and his fiendish plan on this occasion was to avoid attacking Newcastle from the north. Instead he decided to cross the Tyne and attack from the south, so he headed for the first available crossing point upstream from Newcastle, which was the ford at the village of Newburn.

Newburn was defended by an English army that had rushed out of Newcastle when it became clear what was happening, so the two sides confronted each other across the Tyne. I have to say that it seems to have been no contest. The English army was massively outnumbered (3500 against 20000), they were out-gunned and the artillery that confronted them was brilliantly placed on high ground (and even on top of Newburn church tower) so they were entirely exposed on the flat marshy land south of the river.

They were also a rubbish army. The King had raised them hurriedly in the south of England and they had been neither paid nor trained. They were notoriously ill-disciplined and created havoc with violent disorder in all of the towns they passed through on the way north. Lots of them deserted and others mutinied and two Roman Catholic officers were murdered by their own men. So it's not altogether a surprise that they were routed or that the English commander, Lord Conway, made the decision to abandon Newcastle altogether, leaving it invitingly open to Leslie and his troops.

There's some evidence that the Scots were received reasonably well at the beginning, but you can't expect an army of 20,000 men to occupy a town with a population of 10,000 without tensions rising so there were lots of problems. It was all very well that the soldiers were under orders to pay for stuff they needed and that looting was prohibited, but there were still plenty of ways to offend the natives. The cavalry were allowed to commandeer fodder for their horses, for example, and soldiers were permitted to pillage any houses where the occupants had fled. And perhaps more importantly the demands of General Leslie himself were pretty imperious. He insisted that the corporation had to provide billets for 2000 men and the town had to pay him £200 a day to cover the wages of his army. On top of that he demanded a loan of £40,000. These were vast sums of money in those days and he made it even worse by seizing control of any crown property in the town and (worst of all, I imagine, as far as the Corporation and the merchants who ran it were concerned) he confiscated all the mines and all the coal so nobody local could make any money any more.

So it's no surprise that the people disliked their occupiers. Their pride had been hurt by the ease with which they had been outsmarted at Newburn and even if the Scots avoided the worst excesses of invading armies they were still hated. One Alderman of Newcastle (who was a puritan himself and might have been expected to accept the puritan Scots on religious grounds) summed it up: *The soldiers are intolerably insolent in their discourse, slighting the King's army and indeed the whole nation'.* He described them as *'a viperous brood so freely received into the belly of the country'* and worried that they were likely to *'eat through the bowels of their fosterers.'*

And of course they didn't just occupy Newcastle. They were after everything Tyneside had to offer. Tynemouth Castle and the remains of the former priory had long been the Tyne's first line of defence and a major trophy in itself. Since the Dissolution of the monasteries it had become part of the vast Percy estates and the Percy who was Earl of Northumberland in 1640 had actually been born and raised in the castle. Charles himself had even been for a mini-break there in 1633 on the way to his coronation in Scotland and whoever controlled Tynemouth Castle effectively controlled the river and even access to Newcastle. In the years before 1640 its defences had been chronically neglected and there were regular complaints by the people of Newcastle that it needed to be kept in good repair. Well, in 1640 the Scots took it in hand and by doing so they were protected from attacks by the king from the sea and they had good communication routes back home to Scotland.

The Scots stayed on Tyneside for a year and then left in August 1641 having achieved their aims but their success went on to have really profound consequences for the country as a whole because by seizing Newcastle's coal and denying the King his usual tax from it they had put fantastic pressure on the Royal finances and the only thing Charles could do was to recall Parliament and ask for more money, but he was denied. Instead of giving the king what he wanted, the members of the Parliament unanimously voted to control him and that led directly to the civil war. The country divided between those Puritans who wanted a "root and branch" reform of religion and those who supported the king and wanted to retain the bishops and the existing prayer book – the structures of the Church of England.

Rather surprisingly Northumberland chose to side with the king. I say "surprisingly" partly because the character of the county, and especially Newcastle, nowadays seems to me to be rather bolshie and independent and partly because that seems to have been its quality in the centuries before the civil war as well. The Newcastle merchants, in particular, had spent hundreds of years getting their own way as often as they could. They didn't even like the King all that much; they had argued for ages about taxes with him and lots of people in the area were puritans and disapproved of his religious policy … and yet Northumberland, along with Cumberland became one of the few major areas in the country to declare their support for the King.

Isn't that an interesting thing?

Why did they do it? Well, there seem to have been lots of reasons. Northumberland had plenty of Puritans in it – but there were fewer than in many other places. More people had clung on to their Catholic faith in the northern counties than happened elsewhere – but more important than that was the county's recent year of humiliation under the Scots. You have to remember that Northumberland had been part of a hostile border with Scotland for hundreds of years and all of those old antipathies were revived by General Leslie's occupation.

Everybody knew that the puritan merchants in London and the south had encouraged and applauded the Scots in their attack because the invasion weakened the King, but in the North the old enmities had been re-awakened and when the civil war started the Scots were once again on the puritan side – so Northumberland went the other way.

The war started in 1643 but for once the North East wasn't immediately involved. For a few months the war mostly happened down south but then there was an agreement called *A Solemn League and Covenant* signed between Parliament and the Scots and that placed Tyneside (because of the strategic importance of its coal) firmly at the heart of the action.

In January 1644, the Scots arrived again with General Leslie (now elevated to the title of Earl of Leven) once again the commander. This time, however, he actually arrived rather slowly; there was less of that charging across the county like a Pendolino express train and more of the old Morpeth Crawl.

First of all the Scots occupied Berwick in September and then spent the autumn and winter mustering on the Border. According to the "Solemn Agreement …" there should have been:

18,000 Foot soldiers
2,000 Cavalry
1,000 Dragoons (whatever they were)

But in the event there were slightly fewer, possibly about 14,000. Because they were Covenanters and Presbyterians, the soldiers' instructions were the same as they had been in 1640 when they last occupied Newcastle. Each troop was accompanied by a Presbyterian minister, which meant that swearing, plundering and whoring were all forbidden and the soldiers weren't allowed to make any insulting remarks about the king. This was because Charles was not only the king of England, he was also the king of the quite separate Kingdom of Scotland so he was *their* king, the king of the invading army and those in charge wanted to make it clear that they weren't *rebelling* against him but merely trying to draw the his attention to the error of his ways.

On 19th January 1644 the Scottish army left Berwick, heading south on their way to Newcastle. They passed Alnwick, where there should have been a Royalist force waiting for them but it withdrew in front of them so they moved straight on. It took them a long time to get anywhere though because the weather was rubbish; there had been snow followed by a thaw and the road became flooded and impassable so they didn't reach Morpeth until 28th January – 9 days to cover about 40 miles – and they were stuck at Morpeth for several more days.

What must it have been like for the Northumbrians to watch this slow and laborious trudge across a landscape they knew so well? Because there's no record of any fighting it's not the sort of incident that gets mentioned in history books very much, but for the locals, whatever their politics, it must have been a deeply unsettling experience. Those with Puritan sympathies might well have felt exhilarated, while those who supported the King (and especially those who still clung on secretly to the dangerously forbidden Catholic faith) would have experienced fear – but for all of them it must have been a momentous but worrying experience.

The delays caused by the weather meant that General Leslie's army was late arriving at Newcastle. It arrived on the same day as, but a few hours after, a Royalist force led by William Cavendish, Marquis of Newcastle, arrived to strengthen the town's resistance – though even without those new men, the town was in a better shape than it had been the last time the Scots had arrived.

For a start Newcastle had a new mayor who was a tougher egg than had been in charge in 1640. He was an interesting chap called Sir John Marley who had started his working life as a coal-fitter and alehouse keeper but worked his way up until he had become one of the leading Hostmen and worth about £4,500, which was a bob or two at the time.

He was a royalist and ardent anti-Presbyterian and he had been knighted after the Bishop's War for his opposition to the Scots and when the Scots arrived this time he was resolute and despite only having about 1500 defenders to hold the walls against an army of 30,000, he denied them access to the town. He had already strengthened the defences, built a couple of additional forts outside the walls, made the ditch more difficult to cross and cleared away all of the suburbs on the north

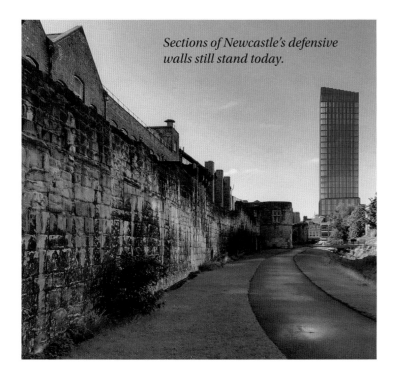

Sections of Newcastle's defensive walls still stand today.

side of the town so that any attackers would have no cover to help them. He had also sunk a series of ships in the river to prevent a parliamentary attack from that direction and when Leslie sent a message demanding that the town should surrender, Marley replied with a certain degree of arrogance and quite a bit of courage, *'His Majesty's general being at this time in the town we conceive all the power of government to be in him'* and he refused to open the gates.

For the time being Leslie didn't faff around trying to force the issue. He left some of his men loosely besieging the town and clearing up pockets of local resistance in Northumberland and Durham while he set off south (via Ovingham) with the rest of his army where they took lots and lots of towns until, on 2 July, they took part in the crushing defeat of the King at the Battle of Marston Moor.

Marston Moor left the whole northern half of the kingdom in Parliamentary hands … except for Newcastle, and Newcastle had to be taken quickly because no coal had reached London for ages and the city was desperate for it. There was a report that *'many*

poor have perished, being unable to buy fuell' and others had taken to burning parts of their own houses.

So General Leslie came back and the second siege of Newcastle began. Initially it sounds more like a civil engineering job. The records reveal that 3000 countrymen were *'summoned to bring mattocks, spades and shovels and labour in the trenches'.*

For me, the extraordinary thing about this siege was that it happened here, in our town – all the significant events occurred in places where we go for walks or sit and drink coffee. The Scots captured the fort at Shieldfield (just along from The Biscuit Factory); they dug mines under the walls near Pilgrim Street and beside Newgate, at White Friars (on the northern edge of the present city centre) and at Sandgate down near the river. They built bastions and temporary batteries and pounded the town with artillery fire.

During Victorian restorations at St Andrew's church, cannon balls were found lodged in the walls of the tower. They're still there, resting on a window sill in the church – smaller than I had imagined they would be but no less lethal. At one point the town wall by the church was blown up and *'the defenders suffered dreadfully trying to block this up'.*

I have to admit that I have always had quite a specific image of sieges. I have imagined long periods of silence, hunger and tense waiting for the final attack to begin but the reporting of Newcastle's siege gives a very different picture. One Parliamentary correspondent with the attacking forces wrote: *'The enemy from the castle doth mightily annoy us with their great artillery but the Scots are casting up with incessant labour what works they can….In the meantime our pioneers are as busie at works underground as our cannons are playing above it. The endeavours of both sides are indefatigable and in the thick clouds of smoke the thunder of the cannon are perpetually disputing …'*

There must have been sallies and attacks to repel; we know this because prisoners were taken who were to play a role in the final act. Propaganda played a part too; pamphlets purporting to be *'from a well wisher'* were thrown over the walls to try and tempt the defenders into surrender.

But there were also endless attempts to resolve the situation without any more violence. Letters flew between the attackers and the defenders. On 7 September, for example, the Scots made a plea for surrender... 'we earnestly incite you to the end that further Effusions of Christian Blood may be prevented ... acquit yourselves like rational men'.

They didn't even get a reply to that one so Leslie wrote again saying 'we desire you to prevent those Evils which cannot longer be avoided ... the citizens and soldiers', he said, 'may be safe and the town, being preserved from ruin, may enjoy the Fruits of settled peace'. He finished the letter by telling them that if they failed to act, 'you then may expect the extremities of war.'

This time Sir John Marley wrote back with extraordinary coolness. He said: 'We have received your letter wherein you require and summon us to give up and surrender the town, alledging divers Reasons, mixed with Threats to move us, all of which we have well weighed and considered and so now return this answer, That we declare to the world that we keep this Town for the use of his Majesty.'

That's quite impressive, isn't it, and his next letter, following a day of failed diplomacy was perhaps more impressive still. It was a more emotional letter, sadder, a little petulant. It's clear that Marley knew that the time had come and there was no more room for negotiation and he ended bitterly by urging the Scots to 'think of some other course to compose the Differences of these sad distracted Kingdoms and annoying us who never wronged any of you.'

One curiously modern form of warfare is said to have emerged during the siege. According to Newcastle's 18th century historian, John Brand, General Leslie sent an ultimatum to the mayor, threatening to blow up the tower of St Nicholas' Church if the gates weren't opened immediately; Marley's response was to set up a human shield. According to Brand he 'immediately ordered a certain Number of the chiefest of the Scottish Prisoners to be carried up to the Top of the old Tower and placed below the Lanthorne and there confined'. He said that the tower was indeed a beautiful object, but that Leslie should know that 'the moment he destroyed the beautiful Structure, he should bathe his hands in the blood of his countrymen'.

The tactic might have saved the tower but it didn't hold back the inevitable. By now the mines were ready. Two of them had been detected and flooded by the defenders but two remained, packed with explosives and ready to go and at 3 o'clock on 19 October the attack began simultaneously in a terrifying variety of places. Mines were blown up under Sandgate and White Friars causing the walls to collapse and there were further breaches of the gates all round the town – at Pilgrim Street on the east side, at Closegate (down by the river in the south-west corner of the walled town) and at Westgate.

The Scots poured in and for a couple of hours there was terrible carnage through all the streets we know today. The casualties were to be found on both sides and one Scottish source almost praised the defenders who 'left nothing unessay'd to repel the fury of the assault.'

In fact the most vivid accounts of the fighting that I have found have come from the diaries of Scottish soldiers. One, called Lithgow, wrote about, 'the thousands of musket balls flying from our faces like to the driving hailstones from a Septentrian blast, the clanging and carving of naked unsheathed swords, the pushing of broughing pikes crying for blood, the carcases of foemen lying like dead dogs in the groaning streets'.

The names of many of those dead "foemen" are recorded in the Parish records. They included:

Ather Herron ... bured ... which was kild with a grenad
George Fishbourne bured ... which was kild by ye Skotes at the Spittl
Edward Mylburne bured ... which was kild in Pilgrim Street by the Scotes at the skirmes

The fighting continued for two hours until the defenders finally capitulated in the Bigg Market – except for a group, which included Mayor Marley, who had retreated into the castle and held out there for a further two days until 21 October. Tynemouth Castle held out for a few more days until 27 October when the siege of Tyneside finally ended and the river was entirely in the hands of the enemy.

You might think that the occupants of Newcastle

had put up a pretty impressive resistance and that they had been well led by their Mayor and I might think that you are right, but the Scots were scandalised by Marley's behaviour. Euen Lindsay, a soldier in the Earl of Loudoun's regiment wrote that Mayor Marley, '*having threatened to use Scots prisoners as human shields, promptly quit the defence and scuttled to the castle ... it remains a mystery why this creature was not put to the sword as custom permitted following an unnecessary storming.*'

But he wasn't. Marley's subsequent history was quite interesting. He had quite clearly been a thorn in the Scottish flesh. Having been knighted for his resistance to them in the Bishop's War and having humiliated General Leslie at the beginning of 1644 *for 'refusing the fair proposition urged for the surrender of the town'*, he had gone on to lead Newcastle through a major siege but, instead of being sentenced to death as Euen Lindsay thought he should have been, his possessions were all sold and he was exiled to the Netherlands.

Sadly, when he was abroad, he seems to have behaved with rather less glory. He was penniless, and in desperation he offered to disclose his fellow Royalist exiles' plans to the authorities for £100. But when it was all over, when the Puritan Commonwealth had come to an end and the Restoration of the Monarchy had occurred, he returned to Newcastle, regained his seat as an Alderman and was elected an MP.

But that was a long way in the future. In the meantime the Scots stayed in Newcastle as occupiers for almost three years – until 30 January 1647. They seem to have been quite pleased with themselves and eager to publish their kindness and clemency, suggesting that there had never been a town captured in a siege where there had been less cruelty and plundering or more mercy involved. You might want to temper this rather self-satisfied view of things with the information that it was only the houses of the rich that were protected from plunder and the Scottish soldiers (poor old things) had to make do with what they could loot from the houses of the poor who were given no protection at all.

It's not quite clear to me what the situation was like in the town when the siege was over because not a lot seems to have been written about it, but I suspect that the atmosphere was pretty volatile. The Scots were in charge – subsequent events were to demonstrate that forcefully – but they weren't the actual rulers of the town. The old Royalist members of the Corporation had gone, cast aside, exiled like Mayor Marley or brooding darkly in the background, and their places had been taken by a new group of men who were sympathetic to the parliamentary cause. These people must have been in the town all the time, unable to express their religious or political sympathies while the town as a whole had gone Royalist but now they emerged and took over. Most prominent among them was a man called John Blakiston who became the mayor in 1645.

He was a local mercer, a coal merchant and a Hostman. He was also a puritan, a passionate puritan, totally opposed to the church reforms that the king and Archbishop Laud were introducing and in fact he was so vociferous in his criticisms of the changes that he was excommunicated by the Archbishop. (Incidentally, he was also an enthusiastic supporter of emigration to America and his son went on to become the Governor of Maryland). In 1640 he had been elected as the town's MP. How odd for such a man to have been, nominally at least, representing a town that had chosen exactly the opposite position to his own, and how satisfying it must have felt to have watched things turn full circle and to find himself in power.

But there were others who would have felt no such satisfaction. William Grey, Newcastle's first historian, who published his *Chorographia* in 1649, took exactly the opposite side to Blakiston. He was passionately Royalist and prepared to be pretty forthright about the victors. He described the Scots as '*a mercenary nation, for any nation for money*' and wrote that there are three things you can find anywhere in the world, '*a Scot, a rat and a Newcastle grindstone*'.

Ouch!

What an extraordinary situation – you can imagine that victorious Scots, triumphant Parliamentarians and disappointed Royalists were all mingled in a bitter whirl of conflicting emotions and into this maelstrom came another, entirely unexpected element. Suddenly, on 13 May 1646, the king became part of the mix. He was here

Mural by James Tucker that shows King Charles I entering Newcastle.

because he had finally surrendered outside Newark, but rather than fall into the hands of the Parliamentary forces that he clearly feared, he had given himself up to the Scots who brought him to their Northern stronghold.

In the Laing Art Gallery there is an early 20th century mural by James Tucker that shows King Charles I entering Newcastle. The town has been painted so that it looks like somewhere in Renaissance Italy. The residents who are bowing down before the king are elegant Renaissance figures while Charles himself looks every inch a king – calm, controlled and dignified.

The contemporary description of his arrival makes the event seem grand and powerful, not unlike its depiction in the Laing. He walked into the town, across the bridge from Gateshead along a lane of muskets and pikes. There were bonfires, bells, drums and trumpets and he was guarded by 300 horsemen, those closest to him bareheaded. If he did behave with the dignity of the picture it was a good performance because he is described as having been '*reduced to a condition in the last degree disastrous and melancholy*'. And for all the show of respect, he was still a prisoner, still on foot and completely surrounded by enemy troops. He might have hoped to find friends in this loyal town but a proclamation was issued saying that '*no Papists or Delinquents*' were allowed to approach him.

The town he entered was still clearly a war zone. There were sunken ships in the river below the bridge, the defensive walls were breached and broken, the mines beneath the town had been flooded. St Andrew's, one of the four parish churches in the town, was battered and broken. The suburbs beyond the walls had been burned and destroyed. It was a town without trade; for four years the coal business had virtually stopped. It was one of Newcastle's lowest moments.

The King remained in Newcastle until January 1647 when the Scots handed him over to the Parliamentary forces. Actually Cromwell's forces bought him. They paid the Scots £200,000 for him – an absolutely vast amount of money. Presumably that was the going rate for a king. A few days later the Scots themselves withdrew and Newcastle's extraordinary involvement in the civil war came to a close.

And away from Tyneside … well who knows how much disruption had gone on. I'm not really clear about how much action Northumberland saw in the first civil war. I know there was a battle at Corbridge in 1644 when a Royalist force led by a man called Sir Marmaduke Langdale (they knew how to name people in those days!) drove off a Scottish army trying to cross the Tyne; there was another engagement the same year at Ovingham where the Scots successfully managed to cross the river; for a few years Blyth became the main supply port for the Scottish army so there must have been lots of coming and going along the roads between there and the Tyne. Holy Island had a castle and a useful harbour too and it changed hands several times over the next few years. Berwick inevitably was a focus of activity.

And when the first civil war drew to a close there were still two more civil wars to come. The second one followed the execution of the King and went on in 1648 and 1649 while the third, which was mainly between the Parliamentarians and the Scots lasted from 1650 to 1652. Throughout these years and later, right through the 1650s the situation in the whole country remained incredibly volatile with a constant maelstrom of Royalist resurgences and parliamentary retaliation.

In Northumberland, Tynemouth and the Tyne, in particular, continued to be involved. Danny Lawrence, in his book on North Shields paints a complicated picture of how the castle changed hands time and time again over the following few years. He tells the story of a Parliamentary soldier called Lt Col Lilburn who was in control of the castle in 1648 but who suddenly decided to change sides. He dismissed all his men, released all his prisoners and put out an appeal to local Royalists to rise up and help him hold the castle. Some did, but a force of parliamentary troops arrived from Newcastle and took it back again. Lilburn himself was executed, obviously, and his head stuck on the castle walls to encourage the others.

Parliamentary forces and Royalist forces played tiggy in this sort of way around the Tyne for a while and, of course, it was the locals who paid the price. Danny Lawrence's book includes an estimate from one significant resident, Ralph Gardiner of Chirton on the outskirts of North Shields, about how much the whole sorry story had cost him. He claimed that he had suffered greatly at the hands of all the different armies. He said that:

The Royalists had cost him £500
The Scots £400
Parliament £200

A total of £1100 which is supposed to represent about £2,000,000 in today's money.

I have sort of run out of steam about these civil wars but I have two final tales to tell, one huge but far too little known, the other small and intimate, a bit puzzling and worth a glance.

The first took place in 1650.

By 1650 the Parliamentary forces had fallen out with the Scots over the precise nature of the religion that each of them followed; they had also, in the wake of the execution of Charles I, almost immediately crowned his son, Charles II, as king of Scotland and as a result there was a real fear among the Parliamentary rulers in London that the Scots were going to invade England, so Oliver Cromwell (like lots of other unscrupulous leaders before and since) decided to pre-empt the Scottish attack and invade Scotland instead.

The invasion led to the Battle of Dunbar in which the Scottish army was once again led by General Leslie who had played such a huge role earlier in the conflict. This time he lost. Cromwell won the battle convincingly and took a vast number of Scottish prisoners. Some of them, who were older or badly wounded and therefore deemed to pose no threat, were allowed to go back home but a huge number of men were held and force-marched out of Scotland, across Northumberland en route to Durham where they were to be held in the virtually abandoned Cathedral until decisions could be taken about their future.

These few years of the civil wars were sandwiched in Northumberland by Scottish armies heading south from the Border. Each of them was a force that was or had been led by General Leslie. In 1640 his army had sliced through the county with clinical skill towards Newburn and the capture of Newcastle. The march in 1643 was a re-match, slower and more methodical, but ultimately once again successful – but for the Scottish soldiers in 1650, the march was a different experience altogether

Five or possibly six thousand men were in the column that had to walk the 100-odd miles from Dunbar to Durham but only 3,000 of them reached Durham alive. The rest died on the way.

Some, nobody knows how many, died in Alnwick Castle where they were kept for several days in the open air, in the Middle Bailey of the Castle. Many seem to have dropped down dead by the roadside. They had gone hungry into the battle and eaten virtually nothing in the days after. At Tweedmouth on the outskirts of Berwick, where they spent the night in the rain in a field, they were given a biscuit each and a handful of dried peas. As they left Alnwick there was another biscuit to keep them going for two days until they reached Morpeth where they were held in a large walled garden beside the castle. In the garden they are said to have gorged themselves on raw cabbages and made themselves violently ill; nobody knows how many died there either. In Newcastle, the survivors spent the night in St Nicholas Church where a further 140 are said to have died before the rest were taken on to Durham.

In Durham many more died and were buried in the Cathedral grounds, others were sent off to work as slave labour in local industries and the rest were eventually deported to the North American colonies where mostly they survived and have left descendants who are passionately concerned to follow up this extraordinary story. And it is extraordinary, isn't it? That Alnwick and Morpeth and the Great North Road should have been littered with the corpses of thousands of prisoners seems inconceivable but there is also a terrible irony in the story. So much passion, so much commitment, certainty and hope went into the civil wars but so little came out of it. The religious belief that started it led to the brutality at the end; the political desire to replace the monarchy had already been replaced by a new monarchy, friendship and treaties had turned to warfare and hatred.

It was all so sad and ultimately pointless, but then, when is it not?

My other little story also starts in 1643 with a man called John Swinburne of Capheaton Castle. He was a much-married man and had relatively recently married his third wife, a lady called Anne Blount, who had given birth to a baby also called John. John the father was a committed Catholic and a Royalist and had already distinguished himself in the service of the King during the Bishop's Wars. There is clear evidence that Charles I was intending to knight him for his services, but before this could happen he was murdered, at Meldon of all tiny, beautiful and peaceful Northumbrian places, by Captain John Salkeld, an equally passionate Parliamentarian supporter from Rock Hall in North Northumberland. Throughout the county and throughout the country such small-scale private battles were increasingly common and it is reported in many places that Catholic families felt under threat from the passionate Puritanism that was driving the war. For one or both of these reasons the story goes that the baby, John, his father's only heir, was taken to France and left in the care of a monastery.

The story, as far as I know, started as a family legend but emerged into the air in John Hodgson's *History of Northumberland*, published in 1827. Hodgson was the vicar of Kirkwhelpington, which is just about 3 miles north of Capheaton and he was a friend of the Swinburne family who continued to live at Capheaton in the 1820s as they still do today. His version of the story is quite short and I have a mind to quote it in its entirety. This is how it goes: '*He was sent while a child to a monastery in France where a gentleman of the Radcliffe family* (who came from Dilston near Hexham and were related to the Swinburnes) *accidentally visiting the place recognised in his face the features of the Swinburne family. On enquiring of the monks how he came there? The only answer they could give was that he came from England, and that an annual sum was remitted for his board and education. On questioning the boy himself it was found, however that he had been told his name was Swinburne which, with the account of his father's death and his own mysterious disappearance in Northumberland, induced the Superior of the house to permit him to return home, where, in an inquest specifically empanelled for that purpose, he identified himself to be the son of John Swinburne and Anne Blount by the description he gave of the marks upon a cat and a punch bowl which were still in the house.*'

You might think that there are some odd bits of this story. You might want to know who was paying the money and where his mother was (actually she had remarried and moved south to live with her new husband, an officer in the Parliamentary army). You may be wondering what the instantly recognisable

Swinburne features were. Did he have the Swinburne nose, or the Swinburne's pointy chin? I have met Swinburnes of more recent generations and I can reveal that they didn't seem to me to have markedly odd characteristics in any way. Above all you may be surprised that the memory of a cat and a punch bowl were considered sufficient evidence for a court of law to declare him the heir to the family estates – but that's what happened. He came back, passed the test and in 1660 was knighted by the newly installed King of England, Charles II.

I like this story because it has a nice romantic sense of derring-do, a bit of mystery and because of what happened next.

What happened next is that Sir John (as he now was) pulled down his family's old castle and built himself a mansion in a brand-new style. It was started in 1668 and completed in 1672 and it was the first house in Northumberland by an architect whose name is known.

He was called Robert Trollope. He was born in York and lived in Gateshead in a house roughly where the south end of the Redheugh Bridge is nowadays. The house that he built for Sir John Swinburne is fascinating in a cheerful, richly decorated, slightly provincial Baroque way. There are really entertaining carvings on the door surround and curly pediments all over the place. Baskets of carved stone flowers decorate the walls and there is a strangely beautiful sundial. Some of the carvings hark back to the Middle Ages (the sundial has a surround of dog-tooth ornament, a motif that was common in the early 1200s), others are modern and Classical – but offbeat (for example, the four giant pilasters that separate the windows have wildly exaggerated rustication – that means that they are really bumpy and sticky-outy – and that makes them entirely typical of the Baroque architecture of the period all over Europe).

Capheaton wasn't the first strangely decorative building Trollope is known to have designed – he was responsible for a very lively and decidedly peculiar new Guildhall in Newcastle, which was built in about 1655; its exterior was rebuilt later but a lot of Trollope's remarkable interior decoration survives, but Capheaton was his first known house. There's a painting of it in the

Halton Castle, given an exquisite new façade in the 1690s.

house that shows it in its complete and original form, and especially the walled formal garden that framed the south front. In the painting the Swinburne family is greeting friends who have arrived in some splendour with a carriage drawn by two horses and a number of servants with horses. The family has left the house and come down to the front gate to meet their visitors. The ladies of both families are standing politely watching and waiting but Sir John is greeting his neighbour more formally, bent over, half kneeling and kissing his hand.

I was told once that the scene was supposed to honour and represent the arrival of the family who discovered Sir John in France and transformed his fortunes but nobody seems to say that any more so I'm not going to mention it, forget I said it, but what I can say with certainty is that the image shows Capheaton as a secure and confident place, filled with civilised touches and graciously formal manners – posh people behaving like posh people were doing all over the country.

All around Capheaton, and indeed all over Northumberland, a burgeoning collection of new aristocratic houses began to be built in the years after Sir John's new creation. Several of them were almost certainly designed by Robert Trollope. Callaly Castle is a huge and complicated building between Alnwick and Rothbury. It has facades all over the place but the main entrance front on the south side is distinctively Trollope-ish and hugely entertaining.

Netherwitton Hall is another probable Trollope House and so is Bockenfield, north of Morpeth, and its near neighbour, Eshott Hall (where my daughter got married you might, or possibly might not be interested to know). There were lots of others. Several families round Capheaton took the plunge too. The Loraines at nearby Kirkharle built a new house and were very soon engaged on a massive taming of the wild landscape around their house. A few miles west, at Bavington, the Shaftoes got into the same mood. The wonderful Wallington, a couple of miles north-east of Capheaton was under construction in 1688.

All of those examples went on to be massively altered and extended in the next century and will really feature in a later chapter, but the movement started in the later years of the 1600s. The splendid 14th century tower at Halton Castle, just north of Corbridge, is another example; it was given an exquisite new façade in the 1690s. In Newcastle the last few decades of the century saw reconstruction and a new sophistication to the extent that when the great traveller, Celia Fiennes visited the town in the 1690s she said that it was more like London than any other town in the country and she specifically praised the lofty and elegant brick buildings.

Few buildings of the period have survived the seismic changes that occurred in the next couple of centuries but one that has is Alderman Fenwick's House on Pilgrim Street – inside and out an elegant gentleman's residence of the 1690s.

I started this chapter panting like a hart after cooling stream of tranquillity but the 17th century has turned out to have included an inordinate helping of trauma too. I had hoped to end it on a moment of calm-ish normality but I find, to my dismay, that I have somehow omitted to include the stories of three people I have long been a bit keen on; so before I dip my toe into the waters of the 18th century I'm going to add a little detour to look at the lives of three 17th century women who all lived in turbulent times.

Alderman Fenwick's House on Pilgrim Street is a surviving example of Newcastle's growing sophistication during the 17th century .

10. THREE 17TH CENTURY WOMEN

1. Katherine Babington

This is the story I was going to tell you. I've been telling it in this form for half a lifetime. For a long time I felt I was the only person telling it but nowadays it's all over the place, in books and on websites. I read an almost identical version of it in the local paper recently under the headline, '*Sad end for bold beauty who was locked in tower*'.

The "bold beauty" was Katherine Babington and this is the story I would have told.

In the 1660s she was married to a man called Philip Babington who, among other things, had been an officer in Cromwell's army and Governor of Berwick. The Babingtons were both puritans and they lived in a house called Harnham Hall, which is on a hilltop about a mile from Bolam Lake.

She had the reputation of being startlingly beautiful. When I told this story, I used to dramatise her beauty by saying that she stopped the buses when she went shopping in Newcastle. I thought I was exaggerating but more recent versions of the story include the details that magistrates in Durham passed an order that she wasn't allowed to sit in the window of pie shops in the city because she caused crowds of bystanders to stop the traffic. This is something, to be honest, that has never happened to me.

Anyway, the story goes that being a puritan she was offended by the local vicar, the vicar of St Andrew's church at Bolam and persuaded, or paid, the son of the local blacksmith to pull the vicar out of his pulpit. As a result, she was taken before the ecclesiastical court and excommunicated. She was ordered to stay inside her house and was denied the right to see any man but her husband (a fearful punishment, my wife tells me, for any woman).

So there she stayed, locked away until she died in 1670, when she suffered a final indignity. She was denied burial in the church's graveyard, so her husband created a tomb for her, dug out of the crag on which their house stood. It's there still, cut out of the solid rock with a stone-vaulted ceiling. It is, I have to tell you, an extraordinary place. The tomb itself is empty now because, according to the story, the body was defiled and the bones scattered by thieves in the following century so they could take the lead coffin in which she lay. Two inscriptions do survive though – one clearly original and one probably made some time later, though it too was recorded as long ago as the early 1800s. The original one is carved in stone and reads:

Here lyeth the body of Madame Babington who was laid in this sepulchre the 9th September 1670

Beneath it is a verse which she is reputed to have written herself. It reads:

> *My time is past as you may see*
> *I viewed the dead as you view me*
> *'Or long you'll lie as low as I*
> *And some will look on thee.*

The other inscription is painted on wood and if you have read a lot of memorial inscriptions, seems touching but a little more conventional

> *In hopes of future bliss I lie*
> *Though I would have been pleased to live, yet was*
> *Not displeased to die*

The rocky outcrop above the entrance to the tomb is topped with a wall that is almost as extraordinary and atmospheric as the tomb itself. It is high and long and built of beautiful local sandstone and on top of it there use to be a series of Janus-headed busts, which means that each has two faces back to back. They were made later than the tomb, probably in the early 1700s, but their strangeness adds to the sense of mystery.

I first became acquainted with this story in the early 1980s, sitting in the kitchen of Harnham Hall with the then owner, a man known by everybody as Farmer Wake, whose story was almost as strange as Katherine Babington's; his life had the same complicated social and religious mix as her history. He had been born, apparently, in a cottage at the foot of the hamlet of Harnham; the cottage had gone down in the world, so that by the time I met him, his birthplace had become a cowshed while he, from humble beginnings, had set off in the opposite direction until he owned the big house on the top of the hill.

As we talked, guests arrived; a group of Buddhist Monks in wellies and saffron yellow robes (or possibly deep red – it was a long time ago) came to join him for lunch. In this place where religious intolerance had been the most famous thing ever to happen, with the tomb of an excommunicated woman in the rock beneath the house, he had allowed one of the other houses in his hamlet to become a Buddhist Monastery and befriended the monks to the extent that they came daily to share their lunch with him. One, I recall, was a Canadian monk and another from Germany. The others I am not sure, but they all sat together on the ancient high-backed settle in the kitchen in a quiet and companionable way, 4 yellow (or red)-robed monks and one elderly Northumbrian farmer. It was a privilege to be there.

At one side of the kitchen fireplace there was an alcove with a built-in glass-fronted cupboard and from it Farmer Wake took out two small panes of old glass which had clearly been inscribed by somebody scratching them with a diamond ring. One of the pieces of glass had written on it:

> *Philip Babington, September 5th 1666*
> *Katherine Babington, September 7th 1666*

The other pane was inscribed in the same way. It read:

> *How vain is the help of man. Katherine Babington. Omnia Vanitas. June 9th 1670*

"Omnia vanitas" means 'all is vanity', or to put it another way, 'everything is meaningless'. We know that she died on 28th August in that year, a mere 10 or 11 weeks after those words were scratched on the glass. She was only 35 years old when she died and it seemed to me that there was (and still is) an unbearable sadness carried in the whole story.

However, though the sadness can't be denied, it does seem that coming back to it now, Katherine's actual story must have been a little different from the one I have been enjoying all these years.

First let me tell you a bit more about her.

She was a puritan, a Presbyterian, and her puritan connections were as impressive as they come. She was born in London in 1635, the eldest daughter of Sir Arthur Hazelrigg who was one of the main military leaders of the Parliamentary forces in the civil wars. He ended up, first of all, as Governor of Berwick and then later, at the end of the first civil war, in the critical post of Governor of Newcastle. During the second civil war he was constantly needed to protect the Tyne from continued

Royalist attacks. He was a big deal and his daughter would have grown up in the presence of all the big cheeses of the puritan world – Cromwell, Fairfax, all of them.

She married twice. Her first husband was another significant puritan and Parliamentary soldier called Colonel George Fenwick of Brinkburn near Rothbury. He was an interesting chap. With his first wife he had emigrated to America in the 1630s and founded a colony at the mouth of the Connecticut River. He built a fort there but came back home after his wife died.

In the war he fought for the Parliamentary forces before becoming (like everybody else it seems) the Governor of Berwick. He was the man responsible for building Berwick's remarkable parish church. He married Katherine sometime in the early-ish 1650s. She must have been really quite young and the marriage didn't last long because he died in 1656 when she was only 21 or 22 years old.

She didn't marry again for several years, until 1662, in fact, when she married Philip Babington (yet another governor of Berwick; presumably that was where she met him).

So that's her background – a thorough and deep-seated puritan life. The question is what happened next; how did she move from newly married in 1662 to a rock-cut tomb in the garden eight years later?

Well the first thing that is clear is that she never paid the son of the local blacksmith to pull the vicar of Bolam out of his pulpit. That had happened long before she was

Harnham Hall .

on the Bolam scene, probably about 1646 when she was 11 years old. The historian John Hodgson, writing in 1825, makes it clear that there were two distinct excommunications, both of them involving the same vicar of Bolam, the Reverend Foster, who seems to have been a fiery and mean-spirited little man. This is what Hodgson has to say about the first excommunication: *'Mr Foster certainly carried his grudge and resentment against the Whigs for the treatment he met with during the commonwealth, to a great length. The registers notice that he refused burial to a son of the Bolam blacksmith who pulled him out of his pulpit when he was first ousted from his living.'*

That quote clearly implies that he was ousted from his church twice.

Around that time there were two great periods of turbulence as far as vicars were concerned. The first was during the civil war and the Puritan rule under Cromwell that followed it. The main driving force behind all the warfare was the organisation of religion. The king had been determined to reintroduce ritual into the church and to ensure that the whole country accepted the control of bishops.

The Scottish Presbyterians and the Parliamentary puritans, on the other hand, were determined to get rid of all the old pomp and church ritual which they saw as harking back to the Roman Catholicism that had come to an end in Henry VIII's time. When the Scots were in Newcastle, for example, there is a description from one of their puritan English supporters about how they broke down the altars and the communion rails in churches, how they took away the ancient vestments used in the town's ceremonies and smashed the stained glass and religious statues.

And of course they got rid of the vicars too and replaced them with puritan preachers who were more to their taste. The same things happened everywhere and it seems likely that the Reverend Foster fell victim to the same forces. It is likely that being "pulled out of his pulpit" might have been a literal event but also a metaphor for losing his place in the church when the puritans took over.

The second great moment of change in parish churches went in the opposite direction. It occurred after the monarchy had been restored. Charles II's Restoration happened in 1660 and two years later, in 1662, he passed the Act of Uniformity, which meant that every vicar had to sign a promise to accept the rule of bishops and to use the Book of Common Prayer and the forms of worship that had been laid down by the Church of England. Thousands refused. In the country as a whole at least 2000 vicars with puritan sympathies either walked out of their churches or were ejected from them.

One of the most notable was a man called Ralph Ogle who was the vicar of Berwick. He was quite a notable figure in the Northumberland church and the authorities tried to bribe him by offering to make him a bishop but he was having none of that. He owned an estate at Bowsden, which is near Lowick, a few miles SW of Berwick, and he started to conduct services there. He held them in the open air, an absolute rejection of the sort of ritual that was being reintroduced into the churches by more high-church and traditional vicars, often vicars like Bolam's Mr Foster, who came back out of retirement to take up the livings they had lost during the wars.

Stuff like this was happening everywhere, but Berwick and Ralph Ogle seem especially relevant to what happened in Bolam. Philip Babington had been (the puritan) Governor of Berwick. Katherine's first husband had been responsible for rebuilding Ralph Ogle's parish church in Berwick. The newly married couple must have shared the general Presbyterian hatred of what was happening to their religion and something seems to have happened at Bolam that led to her excommunication. It seems probable to me that the Reverend Foster got his church back after 1662; it seems even more probable that he fell out with the Babingtons and something happened in 1664 that led to her been summoned before the Ecclesiastical Court. Nobody knows what she did or said. John Hodgson says … *'for some reason or other being prosecuted by the Spiritual Court (…she…) was excommunicated, a sentence about that time very frequently denounced upon dissenters for contempt of court.'*

Whatever she did, and whatever happened next, only three things are known. In 1666 the couple shared a pane of their window to express their togetherness. It was still part of a front window when John Hodgson was writing in the 1820s. In 1670 she scratched again on the window but the tone of her message this time was not of love but of despair. Did she know she was ill and had little time left? Or was it some broader more existential despair about the way the world (and her church) was going? And then, in late summer she died. She was only 35 years old and could not have been expecting to go so soon. She died on 28 August and was interred in her rock-cut tomb 11 days later on 9 September.

It doesn't seem a long enough time for her to have been refused burial and for her husband to have devised a whole new way of interment, to have cut the rock and set aside part of their garden to receive her body. The arrangement seems more pre-planned than that, It seems to me that in the same way that Ralph Ogle and the others preferred to abandon their churches and worship in the open air, something similar might well have happened in the Babington household … better to be buried at home than to lie in the ground of a corrupted church.

This is what John Hodgson had to say at the conclusion of his brief section about the life (and death) of Katherine Babington: '*One of the Hazelriggs, a relation of Mrs Babington, was about the same time buried in a field near his house in Swarland, and it has been shown that Mr Horsley had himself entombed in his own orchard at Milburne Grange. The Quakers and Presbyterians indeed became prejudiced against a churchyard burial. They objected to the use of ritual for the burial of the dead and chose tombs and sepulchres for themselves.*'

I think he's right. Whatever she did to the Vicar of Bolam, I think she was buried in her own garden not because the vicar refused to bury her in the normal way, but because she wanted to be.

There are connections between Katherine Babington and my second 17th century woman – not that they ever met or even knew about each other but both were concerned in their way with the conflict that was occurring in those days between the puritans and those who followed the old religion.

2. Grizelda Cochrane - Highwayperson Extraordinaire

Shortly after his wife died, Philip Babington rented out one of the farms on the estate to a Scotsman. I don't think this arrangement would have pleased the vicar of Bolam very much because the tenant turned out to be a Scottish Presbyterian minister called William Veitch, who stayed there for the next four years. Not only did he stay there but he started preaching there, holding increasingly popular open-air meetings. People came from all around; there were Presbyterians, Anabaptists, all the different sorts of dissenters that the vicar clearly couldn't bear. It must have made him boil, which would have been a good thing; he sounds like a man who deserved to boil.

William Veitch was in England because he had had to flee from Scotland where there was a terrific Government backlash going on against what were thought of as 'rogue' or 'renegade' ministers. The punishments meted out to these Presbyterian ministers who abandoned church organisations, church buildings and rituals and conducted services in the open air were really severe and he was one of the most prominent of them so he had fled to Northumberland (along with lots of other preachers in similar situations).

At first he had taken an alias (he settled in Newcastle for example calling himself 'Mr Johnson', which was his mother's maiden name). He was really fond of Newcastle incidentally and thought the people there were extremely kind, which made him, as you can guess, a man of taste and discrimination. But however nicely he was treated in Newcastle, those years from the 1660s on were very dangerous for 'vagrant' preachers like him and he was constantly at risk of being caught and arrested in England almost as much as in Scotland.

In his memoirs there is a terrific account of a moment at Stanton Hall near Morpeth, where he was living at the time, when a troop of heavily-armed soldiers came to arrest him. They divided into two; one group of them came through the main gates and across the garden, another group broke down a postern gate in the garden wall and arrived at the back door before his wife had a chance to bar it properly. They forced their way in but despite being heavily pregnant she was able to delay them while he hid. The memoir says: *'He got into a hole within the lining of a great window which had been made on purpose, for the whole room was lined with wainscot.'*

And they failed to find him on this occasion. He was advised to make himself scarce for a while, so he set off like a sort of modern-day Cuthbert to preach to people in other parts of the county. In particular he went off to the hills, among the naughty rough border folk in North Tynedale and Keilderhead, around Carter Bar and the top of Redesdale and he was chuffed to bits by the *'wonderful success the preaching of the word has had by ministers retiring there under persecution.'* He says that the Scottish Presbyterian ministers have been able to almost extinguish '*those feuds, thefts and robberies that were so natural to the place'*. In the past, he says, the people of the hills had set off riding all night to steal, but now that they have heard the word they travel all night to hear the gospel.

So you can tell that the atmosphere in Northumberland was quite volatile in these decades – with a powerful and growing band of Presbyterians on one side, especially among the ordinary people, and the Establishment on the other side, the Government of James II, the latest of the Stuart Kings, like his father and grandfather before him sympathetic to the Catholic faith. The two sides feared and hated each other and the authorities were unremitting in their attempts to arrest the preachers who they saw almost like we might see terrorists nowadays.

One of the main thorns in the Presbyterian side was a soldier called Colonel William Strother, who came from Fowberry Hall near Wooler. He was Deputy Lieutenant of Northumberland and an active agent of the Scottish council responsible for apprehending ministers who had taken refuge in Northumberland. He was the officer in charge of the attempt to arrest William Veitch at Stanton Hall and he was in command at a minor battle called The Crookham Affray that happened in 1678.

In 1678, in Scotland, the Covenanters, the Presbyterian army, was in open revolt against the government and the fighting threatened to spill over into England as well when a troop of Presbyterian soldiers arrived in Crookham, near Ford, two or three miles south of the border, which is where they clashed with Colonel Strother's men. They lost. Two of the Scots were killed, including Robert Morley, the officer in charge.

In broad terms the Crookham Affray wasn't a very significant engagement except for two things. Firstly it turned out to be the last battle to take place on Northumbrian soil between regular soldiers from Scotland and England. It was, in a sense, the last battle of a war that had started with Edward I and William Wallace in 1296, 400 years earlier. That is something isn't it? 400 years!

And secondly it was remarkable because the people of Crookham sided entirely with the Scots. Crookham and Ford and the surrounding area were a hotbed of religious dissent and the Scots were wined and dined when they arrived. During the fighting the villagers, all of them Presbyterians, climbed on the haystacks and the roofs of their houses and cheered on the invaders; and when it was all over and the defeated Scots had fled, the people of Crookham refused to join in the hue and cry as it was their supposedly patriotic duty to do.

Which brings me finally to Grizelda Cochrane.

In 1685 all the pent-up opposition to James II turned into outright rebellion. There were two separate revolts; one led by the Duke of Monmouth in the South-West of England and the other led by the Earl of Argyle in Scotland. Both attempts failed and lots of the rebellious leaders were tried and, in some cases, executed. For once, Northumberland was not involved.

Except in the case of Grizzy Cochrane.

Grizzy Cochrane was the 18-year-old daughter of John Cochrane of Ochiltree, who was the second son of the Earl of Dundonald. I think that made her quite a posh lass. Her dad had been of a rebellious disposition for quite a long time and he had been exiled in the Low Countries to avoid punishment, but he came home to join the Earl of Argyle in 1685. He was captured, tried and condemned to death in Edinburgh. However, the execution required the King's signature before it could

be carried out and that had to be sent from London by horseback in those primitive days before emails made executions so much easier to arrange. So, before the King's warrant arrived, John Cochrane's father and his chums were desperately trying to have his conviction overturned but their attempts were having no success …

… until the entry of Grizzy into the story.

The story goes that having heard her grandfather and his companions expressing the hopelessness of the situation, she went immediately home, climbed up to a servant's room in the garret and nicked his clothes. She needed a gun, of course, and even in the 17th century few 18-year-old girls had access to one of those so she nicked a gun as well – and she nicked a horse too - an especially frisky one that a lesser highwayperson would have avoided at all costs and she set off south for Northumberland in order to hold up the postman and intercept the King's message.

She rode all night and passed through Berwick before morning and took up a position where she could stop the mail.

The place she chose for her ambush turns out to be quite difficult to identify. In guide books it is called "Grizzy's Clump" but where G's Clump was isn't altogether clear. I always thought it was a tight little clump of firs or Scots pines on a small circular hillock right beside the A1 near the turn-off to Fenwick, south of Holy Island. On the OS Map it's called Bamburgh Hill, probably because it provides a clear view of Bamburgh Castle. However when I wrote about that a year or two ago I got a letter from somebody at Belford Local History Society to the effect that the clump was further south, near Buckton, just about where the old A1 branches away from the modern road on its way towards Belford. Scottish websites tend to be even less precise and say that she lay in wait on the bleak Tweedmouth Moor near Berwick, dressed like a stripling in a coarse jerkin and cloak.

Wherever it was, however, she waited until she heard the post arriving, leapt out and threatened the post rider, pinched his sack and rode off back to Edinburgh.

It was a very brave thing to do – but sadly

Grizzy's Clump, just off the Great North Road.

unsuccessful. Her father's defenders were unable to persuade the judge to change the sentence and another letter from the king was sent for; so a couple of weeks later off she went again. Actually one of the first versions of the story doesn't say she went, it says that on this occasion '*she wended her solitary way dressed in palmer's weeds*' (whoever Palmer was and whatever he was doing dressing in weeds).

On this second occasion she took a different approach and leapt out with gun blazing, which startled the horse to the extent that it fell over and she thought she had killed it. But she hadn't, so she rode off taking the mailbag and the rider's horse with her.

I do believe that you can get into a lot of trouble for shooting at a postman and stealing his mail (and his horse) but on this occasion she got away with it and the plan worked. The highwayperson was never identified by the authorities and before the courts could get a new warrant from the king John's friends managed to get him pardoned. He went on to live for a long time – until 1691 or 1701 or 1707 or after 1707, depending on which version of the story you read. Grizzy herself married somebody called Ker and lived for ages, only dying in 1748 when she was 83.

So that's the story of Grizelda Cochrane, a hero of the Puritan revolution and a general good egg, but I happen to know that you, because you are nasty cynical people, are thinking that there are quite a lot of questions to be answered before this story can be taken at face value.

1. Why did she ride all the way to Northumberland to do the deed instead of waiting somewhere close to Edinburgh?

2. How did she know what time the postman would be coming past? He had to ride all the way from London to Edinburgh. It took him days and days to make the journey so how on earth did she know what time (or indeed what day) he would pass her clump?

3. Did she jump out and try to rob every rider who came along just in case she missed the key man? Perhaps the postman always sang the same merry tune or his horse had specially recognisable horseshoes.

4. Having been robbed once why did the postie not change his behaviour for a bit to make it more difficult for future Highwaypersons?

5. How did anybody know which day's postbag the King's warrant was in? You know what kings are. Sometimes they will sign a death warrant immediately and get it straight back into the post but sometimes it just lies there in his inbox. Most of the kings I write to are like that. You can't rely on them for speedy responses.

6. Does anybody know for certain that this story happened?

Well I hope it did. There are lots of written versions of it, including one long (and relatively awful) 18th century ballad, but I need to be honest and tell you that there are other accounts of John Cochrane's life that don't mention Grizzy's exploits at all – but I hope she did what the story says. There's another brave dressy-uppy woman to come in the next chapter of this book and Northumberland has a number of other remarkable women to come in the remaining years but Grizelda is one of my favourites. As a dad with daughters of my own, I have a vested interest in their willingness to leap heroically to my defence. They haven't needed to yet, but they might one day and it is my dream that they will take G. Cochrane as their model.

3. A much married ~~lady~~ girl

There's one more 17th century lady I want to write about. I say 'lady' but in fact I want mainly to write about what happened to her when she was a girl.

She didn't live in Northumberland, in fact I'm not sure she ever even visited it, but she did own a pretty large amount of it. She was a Percy, the daughter and only child of Josceline, the 11th and last Earl of Northumberland, who died when she was only three years old, leaving her as the owner of the whole Percy fortune, which included vast estates in Northumberland, Yorkshire and Cumberland; she owned lots of Sussex, including Petworth, which had been the family's principal home for almost a hundred years. She owned Syon House in Middlesex and the huge and utterly desirable Northumberland House on the Strand in the middle of London.

The only bit of her family's ancient inheritance that couldn't be passed down to her was the title – it wasn't possible for a girl (or a woman of course) to become an earl, but instead she immediately became a Baroness so that her title became Elizabeth, Baroness Percy and she was, quite simply, the richest toddler in the country. This is the way that one recent website described her:

The entire Percy property and fortune with the exception of the title itself passed to her - making her the most eligible spinster in England.

I don't know about you, but I don't generally find myself looking at a three year old and thinking, "She looks like a most eligible spinster". I might think that she looks like a bit of a handful or a little sweetie pie but rarely, in fact never, have I looked at a little girl and said that she looked like a most eligible spinster.

The trouble was that she was commoditised from the start, in particular by her grandma, the widow of the 10th Earl, a grotesquely grasping figure who almost instantly wrestled her away from her mother. She lost the battle and spiralled away from the family to marry again a few years later leaving Elizabeth to be trussed up and delivered to market when she was ready.

She was evidently ready (at least in the eyes of her

Elizabeth, Baroness Percy.

granny) by the time she was 12 years old and she was married off to a 20-year-old called Henry Cavendish, Earl of Ogle, who was the son of the second Duke of Newcastle. Rather bizarrely they swapped names. She became Lady Ogle and he became Henry Percy. It was a condition of any marriage she might have that her husband became a Percy in order to keep the family name alive.

It wasn't a successful marriage, or long. One of the histories I read said, "owing to her age it was probably never consummated". The thought that it might have been consummated is so grotesque that it should have been expressed differently. You would want to assume that given her age it couldn't have been consummated. But whatever happened in the bosom of the family, it didn't happen for long because within a year her husband had died, leaving her as a 13-year-old widow…

Enter stage left, husband number two.

On the 15th November 1680, when she was 14 years old, she was married to a man called Thomas Thynne who was 33 years old and a member of Parliament. The History of Parliament Online website paints a picture of a quite awful man. It says, '*Despite his notorious lack of intellectual capacity he demanded a secretaryship of state*'.

In 1680 it says he '*spent the summer in pursuit of a bride suitable for his wealth*'. He had been pursuing her ever since her husband had died earlier in the year and he was eventually able to buy her by paying £10,000 to a man called Richard Brett, a sort of wheeler-dealer businessman who was married to Elizabeth's cousin and who arranged the whole deal.

Even by the standards of those days it apparently seemed a sordid deal. Charles II described Brett as a '*fool and a knave*'.

Thynne turned out to be as hateful as you might imagine, she was miserable, and the marriage lasted no time at all. Within a few months she had run away from him. With a servant to help her, she went to Dover, hired a rowing boat and rowed over to Calais from where she made her way to Amsterdam and cast herself on the mercy of the British Ambassador.

Meanwhile … there was yet another man on the scene. He was a Swedish adventurer called Count Karl von Konigsmark and he either desired her 14-year old body, or her centuries-old wealth, or both, so he had Thomas Thynne attacked in his carriage on Pall Mall and murdered! He had employed three hit men to do the deed. They were all captured, tried and executed but Konigsmark himself got off, almost certainly on account of a bribed jury.

So that's two down and one to go but before she could be married again, probably sometime in 1680 when she was still 14, she had her portrait painted by Sir Peter Lely, the principal court portrait painter in England.

Her picture shows quite a pretty girl, clearly young with a rather naive and unsophisticated hairstyle. So far so good; but she is also wearing an expensive dress with a daringly scooped neckline revealing a shocking amount of décolletage for a young girl. It is really quite disturbing. She is a dressed-up, sexualised schoolgirl and it isn't nice.

And then along came Charles Seymour, 6th Duke of Somerset. He tried twice to get her but she said no. But he finally got his way and in 1682, when she was 15, they were married. He was 21, a bit older than her, but not excessively.

He was a ghastly man, controlling, domineering and violently proud. Even though she had brought him great wealth and status she received neither affection nor gratitude in return. His nickname has always been 'the Proud Duke' and one story about him (which I lifted from Mark Girouard's book *Life in the English Country House* will be enough to illustrate what he was like.

He used to eat all his meals under a canopy. This was a fashion that had been common for great lords in previous centuries but it was wildly old-fashioned by the later 1600s. Worse than that, as he ate all other people present had to remain standing until he had finished. On one occasion he fell asleep in the middle of his tea and one of his daughters, who was pregnant, took the opportunity to sit down for a moment. He woke up and saw her and immediately reduced the amount she was going to be left in his will by £20,000! That's the sort of man Elizabeth had for her third husband.

But with all these dreadful experiences behind her and an ongoing life filled with coldness and unhappiness, she did alright for herself. She became a great favourite of Queen Anne, Lady of the bedchamber and lady of the Queen's Robes and if she never personally experienced her Northumbrian Estates, well her son Algernon did. When he became an MP in 1708 he chose to be the Member for Northumberland, a position he retained until 1722 when his mother died and he became Lord Percy and moved on to the House of Lords. He was given the title of Baron Warkworth and eventually made the Earl of Northumberland, a title that had been in abeyance since 1670 when his grandfather had died.

So when Algernon died in 1750 his daughter, Elizabeth (the granddaughter of the Baroness Elizabeth Percy) inherited the lot and decided to restore Alnwick Castle and live in it, the first Percy to have done so in almost a hundred years. In 1766 her husband was made the first Duke of Northumberland so she became the first Duchess and a very remarkable one she was.

But that's a story for the next chapter.

II. 18TH CENTURY HOMES & GARDENS

The 1700s were a sort of catchy-uppy time in Northumberland. This was the time when at last the county started to become a more normal part of England instead of some wild enclave on the further edges of civilization. Lots and lots of fine Georgian country houses were built surrounded by more and more fine Georgian landscapes. The owners and builders of these splendid places weren't always quite as fine themselves – they were Northumbrians after all and we would expect no less of them – but they were often interesting, odd and sometimes disreputable, definitely worth talking about.

The countryside beyond the mansions changed too. Vast areas of wild waste were taken into cultivation and tamed; open land was enclosed, the poverty of the county was increasingly turned to productivity; new farms were built that were going to turn out to be one of the distinctive glories of the county and with them went new and improved housing for more ordinary people. Lots of our towns, too, developed a more genteel and Georgian face and new roads improved the links between them. Ports were built that allowed for trade and increased the county's contact with the rest of the world.

The industry that was going to dominate the world's perceptions of us developed too. There had been coal mining for centuries and glass manufacture for decades by the time the 1700s started but in parts of the county those industries and others were going to become a dominant feature of our future.

And even our past began to become a part of our future (he wrote mysteriously). Northumbrian architects, builders and clients found it difficult to ignore the wild and woolly past and the county is richer than most others in Georgian Gothic buildings – modern structures that hark romantically back to the medieval past – and that led to the beginnings of 'heritage' tourism too – visitors who came specifically, as they do today, to explore the region's rough, historic past. Sir Walter Scott was among the first and the most famous of them. Where travellers in the past would have done their level best to avoid the wildness of the Cheviot Hills, in 1791 he came on holiday with his uncle and stayed in a farmhouse in the hills where he wrote this letter home:

'I am very snugly settled in a farmer's house ... in the very centre of the Cheviot Hills, in one of the wildest and most romantic situations ... we are amidst places renowned by the feats of former days; each hill is crowned with a tower or camp or cairn, and in no situation can you be nearer more sites of battle ... My uncle drinks the goats whey here, as I do myself ever since I understood that it was brought to his bedside every morning at six by a very pretty dairy maid.'

Left: Sir John Vanbrugh's masterpiece, Seaton Delaval Hall.

All day we shoot, fish, walk and ride; dine and sup on fish struggling from the streams, and the most delicious heath-fed mutton, barn-door fowl, pies, milk-cheese etc all in perfection, and so much simplicity resides among these hills that a pen ... was not to be found about the house, even though it belongs to a considerable farmer, until I shot the crow with whose quill I write this letter.'

So those are the themes that are going to be explored in this chapter – gentrification and gentility, taming the wilderness, a toe into the tide of growing industrialisation, all with just a sprinkling of that wildness that never seems very far beneath the surface in Northumberland.

I'm going to start, for reasons that will become obvious in the light of the list I have just written, with Seaton Delaval Hall and the Delaval family who built it and lived in it.

Langleeford - scene of Walter Scott's holiday letter.

Seaton Delaval

The Delaval family had come over from Normandy (presumably from the very nice town of Laval on the eastern edge of the region) with William the Conqueror and they had been given land in Northumberland where they stayed, unnoticed by me, for the next 5 or 600 years. The ones that form the basis of this part of their story were born at Dissington Hall, near Ponteland just to the north west of Newcastle.

One of them was called George. He was an Admiral and from a moderately impoverished start made a bit of a fortune out of the navy and in a pretty brilliant diplomatic career, so in 1716 he was able to buy Seaton Delaval Hall for £5000 from one of his relatives who had gone bankrupt. There was an old house on the site, but he decided straight away to improve it or demolish and build something new. He hired Sir John Vanbrugh and building began in 1718 and went on until 1728, by which time both the admiral and his architect had died, leaving behind a masterpiece.

There aren't many architectural masterpieces in Northumberland. There are some very good and lots of very exciting buildings but not many that would deserve the title 'masterpiece'. The Keep at Warkworth Castle could be one and possibly (from a future century) Lord Armstrong's Cragside, but I don't think anywhere else fits the description – except Seaton Delaval, so it deserves a little bit of attention.

The architect, Sir John Vanbrugh, was a very interesting man. He was a soldier and a spy who became a hugely successful playwright and then suddenly, out of nowhere became the greatest architect of his age. Most architects start small and cut their architectural teeth with Lego™ and Playdoh™ and stuff but Vanbrugh's first building, his very first building. was the huge and utterly splendid Castle Howard in North Yorkshire and he was responsible for the absolutely gigantic Blenheim Palace. Those are two of the greatest buildings in the whole of the country.

Seaton Delaval is tiny by comparison to those vast palaces, though it's bigger than my house and, I imagine, yours, but it is nevertheless Vanbrugh's masterpiece; it was his last building and it was already old-fashioned when it was begun. It's in the Baroque style, that rich, overcrowded, excessively dramatised version of Classicism that had been fashionable in Britain and most of Europe in the previous century, but in 1715, an architect called Colen Campbell published "Vitruvius Britannicus", which introduced into the country a much smoother, calmer style of Classicism, which has become known as the Palladian Style. The new style instantly became the go-to style for country houses in Britain so Seaton Delaval looks wild and exaggerated by comparison to other new houses in the county. It's a restless, romantic masterpiece with giant porticoes all over the place and bristling with sticky-outy bit of surface decoration. The basement on which it rests has bands of muscular, bulging rustication and it is all theatrical and passionate. It's hard to describe but I don't think you would be likely to apply the word 'pretty' to it. What you could say is that it was powerful and that it certainly doesn't look like any other house.

Sir John Vanbrugh

What seems to have happened is that Vanbrugh (who lived in Greenwich), just seems to have responded to the place, to Northumberland, to the wild sea and the wild northern skies. He seems to have loved the north. He described it as being far better than what he called "the tame sneaking south" and it is an amazingly northern house. It's like a re-interpretation of a castle tower, all compact and powerful, jutting up into the sky with turrets and things all round it.

Inside … well there isn't a lot left of inside because it was destroyed by a catastrophic fire in 1822, but the scale and shape of the shell make it clear that it can never have been a cosy house. Domestic comforts were clearly less important to Vanbrugh (and presumably his client) than grand statements.

And the grounds were no different. There were formal gardens immediately round the house, which were re-created in the 20th century and they are absolutely gorgeous but beyond them was a vast landscape of enormous dead straight rides and avenues that stretched out into the distance. An avenue a mile long went straight as an arrow from the south front of the house and though it has now gone and been replaced by farmland, the obelisk that marked its southern end is still just about visible in the distance.

So, it was a big, uncomfortable but magnificent house and if the building was extraordinary, the family who lived in it matched their home. Hardly any of them led a normal conventional life or had a conventional death. The Admiral went first. In 1728, before his house was even finished, he fell off his horse and was killed. He had no offspring so he left the house to his nephew, Captain Francis Blake Delaval, who had made a fortune in the navy by capturing enemy ships. He already owned another estate, at Doddington in Lincolnshire which was the home of his wife Rhoda.

Together (I assume it was together; you're never quite certain what happens in marriages) together they had 12 children who were wild and undisciplined. They have been described as the "Gay Delavals" but their behaviour stretched the notion of gaiety to new limits.

They did gay things like bringing in strolling players to provide entertainment. They drank and gambled and had mistresses and things (but then who didn't) and they played practical jokes on their visitors. I hate practical jokes. I was once handed an almost red-hot teaspoon by a boy called Sandy who laughed merrily at my discomfiture and I have hated his memory ever since.

It's bad enough staying in other peoples' houses without having to worry what they were going to do to you next, but the Delavals loved a good jape. They had a bedroom where the walls could suddenly be removed to reveal you when you were getting undressed for bed. They had a bed which, while you were asleep, could be lowered into a bath of cold water or raised so that you woke with your face pressed against the ceiling. They were clearly a hoot.

When the Captain died in 1752 (fell down the stairs outside the south door, since you ask) the house was passed down to the most extreme of all his children, another Francis. He may well have been charming and entertaining, but he also seems to have been a bounder and a cad (as we say in Gosforth). He was awash with mistresses. He tricked an elderly widow into marriage and frittered her money away on gambling and other women. He became an actor in London! Need I say more! His debts grew so many that after a few years of being in charge of the household he swapped with his younger brother John, who was more sensible than he was. Sir John Hussey Delaval took over the house while Francis received an annuity, which he spent with enthusiasm. He seems to have spiralled out of control in London until 1771 when he ate a vast meal and died of a stroke, alone except for a single servant.

But even sensible John had a wild edge and a little sprinkling of tragedy about him. He only had one son who, when he was 19, tried to rape a chambermaid and she kicked him in the balls with sufficient venom that he died of shock. His father, obviously, was devastated by grief but what could he do about it? He couldn't make it go away; he couldn't punish his son and of course he couldn't punish the girl since she had correctly been defending herself. What could he do? What would you do? Well what he did to assuage his grief was to take an axe and chop down all of the trees on his estate before going down to Doddington, his other estate in Lincolnshire, to chop down all the trees there as well. Presumably that got it out of his system.

So … quite a family and quite a house but they spread way beyond Seaton Delaval and had ramifications all over the county as well. It was a Delaval owner of Ford Castle who built the beautiful Gothic forecourt to that house. Another of the Ford Delavals, Sir Francis Blake built another extraordinary Gothic house called Twizell Castle right on the border, just above the River Tweed near Cornhill. It is ruined now and strangely atmospheric, but it was five storeys high and built entirely of stone. Every room right up to the top floor was given a stone vaulted ceiling. It seems that that Sir Francis was a bit obsessed by fire and made his house as

Ford Castle.

Twizell Castle.

fireproof as possible. He also made it as expensive as possible and he was declared bankrupt before it was complete. He fled to Edinburgh where different financial rules allowed him his liberty and is supposed to have sneaked back into England from time to time to revisit his stone albatross.

So they were quite a family – but they were clever too and among the first serious industrialists in the county. For centuries the coast from near Blyth almost to Whitley Bay was a source of salt. Salt pans stretched for miles and it was the Delavals who controlled that production. They owned coal mines too. The coal was used partly to heat the salt pans and boil the sea water until only the salt remained – and partly it was exported. At first it was exported from a small natural harbour called Hartley Haven, just east of the house, but it was difficult to enter and had a tendency to silt up, so in the late 1600s the Delaval of the day came up with a cunning wheeze. He built a sluice gate across the narrow end of the harbour, where the stream that created it flows in, and when the tide was at its highest the sluice gate was closed so that a massive weight of water was held behind it and then, when the tide was at its lowest and the harbour was just exposed mud flats, the sluice was opened and the weight of water rushed through the harbour, scouring away the silt that was constantly in danger of choking the haven. It was brilliant, and it worked, and that's why the place is called Seaton Sluice nowadays

Later on, in the 1760s, with the original harbour still proving small and difficult to enter, Sir John came up with yet another wheeze and that was to excavate a straight cut through the headland to the sea. It was (it is, because it is there still and very impressive too) 9 metres wide, 16 metres deep and 275 metres long, There was a lock gate at each end so that it could be filled at high tide and a dozen or so ships could ride out any weather and get loaded without interruption. It was a really clever and a really sophisticated solution for an 18th century harbour. It all looks quite small to our modern eyes but by the time that Sir John made the extension the family had extended their areas of concern. They had copperas works, iron works, limekilns and a brewery but most of all they added glass making to the coal and the salt pans. In 1762 they opened the Royal Hartley Bottle works, which became the largest such manufactory in the country. By 1771 it was exporting, from this relatively tiny little harbour, a total of 1,740,000 bottles a year!

So there you are, the Delavals – wildly creative, the owners of an architectural masterpiece, brilliant and innovative entrepreneurs, a hint of caddery and a splendid dash of tragic bad luck. They seem like a useful introduction to 18th century Northumberland.

Seaton Sluice .

...and now for someone completely different.

In 1716, the year that Admiral George bought Seaton Delaval, a son was born to a quite ordinary, in fact possibly quite humble tenant farmer called William Brown, and his wife Ursula. The Browns seem to have come from Redesdale but by 1716 were living and farming at Kirkharle on the estate owned by Sir William Loraine, a man who featured in the last chapter when he was mentioned as one of the people who were improving their estates. The new baby was the fifth child out of four sons and three daughters born to the Brown family. He was christened Lancelot but you can call him Capability.

Royal Hartley Bottle works c1890.

Capability Brown, as you know, is the most famous and influential gardener that Britain has ever produced. He is also, almost certainly, the most famous and influential person ever to come from Northumberland. He didn't actually invent, but he developed and perfected the uniquely English style of the Landscape Garden, which is the only artistic style of world-wide significance ever to have been invented in Britain.

You know the style as well as you know his name because the two go together like chicken and baskets – the great swards of grass that sweep right up to the walls of country houses, punctuated with clumps of trees and mirrored lakes, sheets of serpentine water; the belts of trees that frame the house or stop the distant view. It's a style that emphasises the forms and shapes of the natural landscape and it is gardening on an immense scale.

Capability Brown is known to have created about 270 gardens in the course of his life of which more than 170 remain still worth seeing today. There is hardly a big house that you can think of that doesn't have its Capability Brown garden - Castle Howard and Blenheim palace, Stow, Petworth, Burghley, Belvoir Castle, Montacute, Hampton Court – wonderful landscapes around marvellous houses. It has been calculated, I think, that he was responsible for transforming the appearance of half a million acres of England, which is roughly the size of an average sized county. But as we know, size isn't everything, quality matters too, and his gardens are not only big but also superb in our national landscape and so important to our imagination that he changed the way we think about our green and pleasant land. His work went on to influence every single landscape gardener since, in Britain and all across the world.

He was personally important too. He ended up running a vast organisation. By 1760 he was in charge of 20 foremen, each of whom was responsible for a gang working on a different garden. He became friendly with many of the aristocrats for whom he worked. One of his daughters married the highly successful 'society' architect, Henry Holland. He wasn't the only man from relatively humble stock to make it big in Georgian society of course; even in those far-off days there was enough flexibility that talented people in all sorts of walks of life were able to rise through the ranks; there were men like Dr. Johnson, the artist Joshua Reynolds and the writer Tobias Smollet. Adam Smith, the economist, was from a fairly ordinary background and so was our own, our very own, Lord Collingwood.

I'm not saying they were all from poor backgrounds, these people, but they weren't from the aristocracy; they were relatively ordinary. Many of these men settled in London and many of them knew each other. CB was a chum of the actor David Garrick, for example, but his reputation also allowed him to be a close friend of three prime ministers including William Pitt. When he died in 1783, following an asthma attack in the street on the way home from a dinner party, he was extensively mourned. One evening before the funeral there was a knock on his door and when his wife went to answer it she found King George III on the doorstep; he was on his own and he had popped round to pass on his condolences.

So … a life of extraordinary significance … but he was born in a cottage or a small farm on the Kirkharle Estate in the valley of the upper Wansbeck, two or three miles from Wallington. He started off being taught by the parish clerk in the local church before moving on to a school in Cambo run by a man called Thomas Gastle. He seems to have stayed there until he was 14 (some say 16), which was a long time in those days (the immensely famous Admiral Collingwood left Newcastle's Royal Grammar School when he was only 12) and after leaving school he started to work as a garden boy for Sir William Loraine.

It's not clear what his job was at Kirkharle but there was plenty to do. Sir William was involved in a massive amount of planting, for example he is reported to have planted 24,000 trees including chestnut, beech and oak, 580 fruit trees and 500,000 quicksets (for setting hedges). That's a lot of plants. As it happens, the day before I wrote those words I went to Cowells, my local garden centre of choice, and bought three smallish bedding plants, a terracotta pot, some peat-free compost and a jar of plant food and I had to have a little lie down after paying the bill, so obviously there was a great deal going

Bavington Hall, possibly an early design by Capability Brown (inset).

on in those days and Sir William couldn't have planted the lot himself so one assumes that CB was involved in all sort of bits of it.

When I go there, to Kirkharle I mean, which I do regularly since it has a coffee shop that is a rich source of cheese scones, I find myself wondering how much of the landscape round about he was involved in. It's not easy to tell because, in fact, he came back later in the century to work on the estate again, as a mature gardener and a famous man, and most of the landscape immediately round Kirkharle probably dates from that time; it looks like classic Capability Brown with grassy swards and clumps of trees and what-not, but as I walk in the nearby lanes, I seem to come across ghosts of the earlier landscape too, places where there is a real patina of age with embankments of massive boulders and huge surviving ancient trees in rows like avenues.

The historian, John Hodgson, who has already featured heavily in these pages, became the vicar of Kirkwhelpington, the parish next door to Kirkharle, and knew many people who remembered Capability Brown. He is determined to give CB the credit for much of what is visible. He writes, '*The magic hand of Brown contrived to throw the sweetest charms into the fields of the place of his nativity*' but he also goes on to say that Sir William loaned his employee out to work for his neighbours, the Shaftoes of Bavington Hall.

The Shaftoes had owned Bavington for many years but they had lost it briefly when one of them was tried for treason after taking part in the 1715 Jacobite Rebellion. Their attainted property had been bought by a relative, the Admiral George Delaval of Seaton Delaval who featured earlier in this chapter. In a protective sort of way, he held on to the house for them and when he died in 1728 he bequeathed it back to them and sometime after that the returning Shaftoes began to make improvements to the house and grounds. Nothing is certain about this, but it seems possible to me that the young Lancelot Brown might have had a hand in what was done.

I say this because in front of the house, towards the south, there is a huge landscape that has many of the features of a Capability Brown landscape – but a bit cruder and more mechanical, as if it might have been a bit of a first go. Immediately in front of the house is a lawn that ends in a ha-ha and beyond that is a huge unbroken sward of grass that sweeps away towards a hill in the distance. Either side the grass is guarded by double avenues of trees and in the middle, off centre and quite picturesque, is a clump of trees. At the end of the grass, and not visible from the house, is a lake that is now managed by the Northumberland Wildlife Trust, but which probably originated when the sward and the surrounding land was drained in the 1730s. It's a ghost landscape now. It hasn't been part of the Bavington Hall garden for ages and ages but you (or at least I) have to wonder whether it is an early work of CB, a demonstration of the early promise that perhaps prompted Sir William Loraine to lend him out to his neighbour.

The lake at Bavington ties in with CB's early development as a gardener in another way. Apart from planting, Sir William was doing something else that was going to be important in CB's later life. He was, as they put it at the time, *'draining the morasses'* on the estate.

Even now we know that the boggy bits of Northumberland can be the boggiest places in bogland, so that the only way to move across undrained land is to leap from tussock to tussock like a ballet-dancing hippo and in those days anybody who wanted to make their estates financially viable needed to make them a great deal drier, suitable for sheep if not for arable crops. CB used his ability to control water as a key part of his design skills throughout his career so that does suggest he became interested and perhaps skilled in water management early in his working life at Kirkharle (and Bavington).

As a result of this, when Sir William completed the improvements on his estate in 1738, the 22-year old Brown went off to Lincolnshire with a letter of introduction from Dame Anne Loraine, Sir William's second wife, to her relatives who lived near Boston. At that time, and in that area, there were huge moves afoot to drain the fens, so, from the point of view of both his existing experience and his future life, it was a really useful place to develop the next stage of his career. He stayed there for two years and acquired two things – experience and a wife. He met, courted and married Bridget Wayet, who was a daughter of the local squire and sister to a drainage engineer. His marriage to Bridget lasted 44 years until his death in 1783 and they had nine children, which is not a bad record!

From Lincolnshire he moved to Buckinghamshire (bearing Dame Anne's introductions to her father on this occasion) and within a year he was working as an under-gardener at Stowe. From there the rest is history – he leapt upwards and onwards (yet another hippo) into the gardening stratosphere.

There are those who cast doubt on some elements of this story; principally there are some small-minded misery-guts who can't accept the possibility that a lower-class person can achieve great things. There are always mutterers who suggest that he must have been posher, perhaps, they snigger, he might have been the illegitimate son of Sir William or even something scandalous to do with Dame Anne. How, they ask, could a boy from a little village school achieve so much?

Pshaw!

It was a school of good standing, as the historian Dorothy Stroud wrote and *'there was no foundation for the jibes his jealous rivals were later to make about Capability's lack of education'*.

And as for the idea that he was secretly from higher birth …

Pshaw again!

The family, as a whole, did well. His brother John became a surveyor on the Kirkharle estate and eventually Sir William's land agent. He went on to marry Jane Loraine, a daughter of the big house. Another brother, George, became a stonemason at Wallington. He spent his life there and progressed to become the Wallington estate mason-architect, working alongside major architects like Daniel Garrett and James Payne, who provided designs for the Blackett family. So unless

Alnwick Castle with Capability Brown landscape.

the Brown family were serial providers of illegitimate sons, the idea of Lancelot's illegitimate origins are ludicrous.

A more insidious attack came from his rivals in the architectural and gardening community. They accused him of being *'bred a gardener'* and therefore of lacking a painter's eye because he had never studied the great masters of landscape. His most passionate critic, William Chambers, revealed naked class prejudice and said that *'Landscape gardening in this island is abandoned to kitchen gardeners, well skilled in the culture of salads.'* He said that such men (though he meant CB) *'emerge from the melon grounds to take the periwig and turn professors …'*

Pshaw to the lot of them – he was an ordinary bloke from Kirkharle who achieved extraordinary success and it is worth asking (a) what Kirkharle gave him and (b) what he gave back to the land of his birth.

The (a) bit seems straightforward – Kirkharle and the Loraines gave him the time and the opportunity to develop his skills and the connections to set him on the road to greatness. But there was more. You just need to walk the lanes and fields of the beautiful country of the upper Wansbeck valley to realise how its beauty must have soaked into his soul as he walked the three miles to school and as he roamed and played – because those bits of Northumberland are a Capability Brown landscape in waiting – a wild, broad vista of low rolling hills, clumps of trees and accidental lakes. All he had to do to make it suitable for the great mansions of southern England was tame it a bit. That's what Kirkharle and Northumberland gave him – his style.

And that's exactly what he gave back to Northumberland – over the rest of his life he kept on coming back to the county and helping to accentuate its beauty. The county is filled with Capability Brown-style gardens. He wasn't the maker of them all but lots of others were influenced by him.

One group stretching out in all directions from the village of his birth forms an almost continual line many miles long. It starts at Belsay. On the north and east side of the Belsay Castle is a classic landscape garden, rarely seen by visitors who come to the later gardens around the house but very beautiful. Capheaton Hall next door has another Brownish garden, which includes a distinctly CB-style lake. Then there is Kirkharle itself and its neighbour Bavington. Kirkharle flows across the A696 into Littleharle and then to the gardens at Wallington,

Belsay Castle with surviving 18th century landscape garden.

which stretch on for miles and miles, as far as Rothley Lakes on the edge of the great wilderness of Rothbury Forest and the Simonside Hills.

Wallington is one of Capability Brown's two great contributions to the Northumberland landscape, the other is Alnwick; both were done quite late in his life and both are rather different from the way we expect his gardens to look and the way they have tended to be elsewhere in his life and elsewhere in the country. I'm going to describe what that means at Alnwick in a moment but first of all I want to say something about …

Wallington and the Blacketts

There was a medieval tower and mansion at Wallington belonging to the Fenwick family who owned the property until 1680, when it was bought by a Newcastle merchant called Sir William Blackett.

… I hope you spotted the significant clause in that last sentence. I wrote that Wallington was bought "by a Newcastle merchant".

In this chapter so far we have had an unusual mixture of origins and social class. The Delavals were old aristocracy, part of the ancient elite class of Northumberland who, in the course of the 1700s moved off in a new direction and became not just landowners but also industrialists, men of trade, making their new money from coal mining and glass manufacturing, shipping and trade generally.

Lancelot Brown, on the other hand, started in the working class and used his practical skills to launch himself into the sort of stratospheric social situation where a king could call on his widow to offer his condolences. Things were changing by the time the 1700s came along and the history of the Blacketts of Wallington is yet another illustration of the flexibility in social class that was possible in 18th century Northumberland.

The first William Blackett started off as a merchant in Newcastle in the 1600s and made a fortune based on hard practical things like shipping, coal mining and lead. He wasn't satisfied with that, of course. Wealth is a nice thing in itself, I believe, but not enough unless it leads to

power and very soon William wasn't just a rich merchant but had become the Sheriff of Newcastle and then the town's MP. He bought and extended a gigantic house called Newe Place (and later Anderson House) inside the walls of the town and before he died (in 1680) he achieved some other key signs of success. He became a "Sir" after being knighted by the king and he started a dynasty with a succession of sons to carry on the family name. He was on the way towards leaving the middle class behind and joining the big boys but there was still one more step to take.

Nowadays, if you're successful in business in a city like Newcastle you tend to buy an expensive house in town or in the suburbs but pretty soon you want something else as well so you acquire a place in Beadnell perhaps or a second home in Spain or southern France. I'm not knocking it, incidentally; that's what I would have done if I had ever achieved financial success and it is what people like the Blacketts started to do by the end of the 1600s. To be successful you needed more than money and power; you needed the trappings of old money, you needed to join the elite old families in the countryside; you needed a country estate.

So, in 1688, Sir William, the second baronet, bought Wallington off the Fenwicks. He immediately pulled their house down and built a new one twice as good. It was square with sides 120 feet long and a courtyard in the middle. It had sash windows, which were quite a new invention at that time, and so the new house looked similar to the way it looks now but just a little bit plainer and simpler.

That second Sir William had the reputation of being a good egg – popular in the North East and popular in London where he was seen as a highly effective MP, but sadly he died in 1705 leaving yet another Sir William, who was only 16 at the time.

This third Sir William Blackett was not just young, he was also a bit of a lad. He liked a drink for example and the evidence of history is that he liked the ladies – or at least one lady, which is a different thing.

When I was listing buildings back in the 1980s I came across a farmhouse near Berwick that was clearly quite out of the common run. It was, it still is, a

A view of Wallington Hall from Shaftoe Crags.

substantial, carefully built, symmetrical house with sash windows and a tall pyramid roof, an almost perfect example of a house from the early 1700s. You could find similar houses in the same style at the same time all over the country and even in sophisticated old London. Inside it has strong, simple but beautiful decoration of the same period, all made out of carved wood. There are a couple of panelled rooms and a powerful staircase.

You don't usually see stuff like that among the farmhouses of Northumberland. They are normally plainer by far and not as old, so this house was a bit of a mystery until research revealed that it had been the home of somebody who was significant to a rich and powerful man. It was, in fact, the home of a lady called Elizabeth Orde, who was the mistress of the third Sir William, the naughty old Blackett. His illegitimate daughter, Elizabeth, grew up there and it seems likely that it was Blackett money that built the house and that the solidly splendid décor was a reflection of what Wallington had looked like at that time.

191

So, Sir William the third was a bit of a lad.

He did the respectable thing though and got married. He married a lady called Barbara Villiers and the National Trust's Wallington guide book gives a pretty extraordinary account of the wedding. Apparently, it was a custom to give a pair of kid gloves to each wedding guest in those days and at Sir William's wedding 1086 pairs were handed out. As part of the celebrations there was a party on Shaftoe Crags, a wonderful outcrop a couple of miles south of Wallington. The guide book says that there were bonfires, and '*a drink-maddened crowd danced to the sound of the pipes*'. There were lines of bottles on the rocks and each time they drank a toast to the bride and groom they smashed the glasses and started again. It was a rave in fact. Nowadays there would be stories in the *Daily Mail* and a disapproving tone on *Look North*.

You don't last long if your lifestyle is like that and in 1728 Sir William died, apparently relatively unregretted by everybody (except, presumably the glass and bottle makers). The marriage that started so noisily doesn't seem to have been very successful because there were no children and his wife remarried almost immediately after he died.

There was a twist though. His will had a twist in it which reveals something a bit deeper than the drinking and roistering suggests. It suggests that Sir William had a desire to ensure that his family and his family name survived.

In his will he left Wallington and the whole of the Blacketts' Northumberland estates to a nephew called Walter Calverley from North Yorkshire. The bequest came with a condition that within a year, Walter had to take the name 'Blackett' and get married to Sir William's natural daughter Elizabeth Orde – oh! and he had to accept his uncle's £70,000 debts, which seems like a hell of a lot nowadays but which was a colossal amount in those days.

The nephew was only 21 at the time but he accepted the challenge – he changed his name to Walter Calverley Blackett, married his cousin and settled in Wallington, where he turned out to be an interesting man. In some ways he was very nice; a fair-minded and

Elizabeth Orde's house near Berwick.

generous employer who looked after his workforce in good times and bad. In other ways he was a bit of an oddity. The National Trust guidebook (published in 1994) quotes a letter that had recently been discovered in the Alnwick Castle archives, written by someone called P. Poynings. P. Poynings says that Sir Walter was very fond of the ladies but that he restricted his amours to '*servant maids and women of that class*'.

He loved food a lot (or even a lot of food) but did not drink excessively; he chose to be constantly surrounded by a house-load of guests but to take no pleasure in them. He always went to church but always fell asleep through the service. The conclusion that P. Poynings drew is that '*having completed his fine mansion, park, follies and gardens*' he seemed to '*have lost his zest for life*'.

He certainly made a fine mansion. He started the remodelling of his house in 1738 using an architect called Daniel Garrett whose alterations of the existing building were relatively small on the outside, but subtle and beautiful; he rebuilt the south front in an understated but intensely satisfying way. The inside was transformed. Oh! What a job they made of it. Sir Walter went the whole hog. He installed a colony of Italian Stuccatori on the estate. Stuccatori were workers in stucco – fancy plasterers to you and me – and this particular gang were led by two brothers called

Franchini, or sometimes Lafranchini (their motto: The Franchini mob: we'll get you plastered). The work they did was fantastic, in the Rococo style, absolutely up to the fashionable minute and absolutely top notch in quality, as good as could be found anywhere else in Europe.

You see what's happened here with the Blacketts at Wallington. In no more than a couple of generations, the family of a well-to-do Newcastle merchant had managed to establish itself at the very top of the architectural and social tree in Northumberland. It was a position they never lost. Even though Sir Walter had no surviving children he was able to pass on his creation to a close female relative who was married into the ancient Trevelyan family and they took over the place and lived in it for more than two centuries until it was handed over to the National Trust.

Wallington is the greatest example in Northumberland of how industrialists and merchants joined the rural elite but it certainly wasn't alone; all sorts of others were on the same road – brewers, coal-owners, bankers all sorts of merchants were at it. In 1781 a Newcastle furniture manufacturer called Robert Lisle built himself a lovely house called Acton House near Felton. Belford Hall, which is a splendid Palladian Mansion built in 1754, was the creation of Abraham Dixon, the son of a master mariner who had bought into the landed gentry in 1726. Gosforth Park, which now forms the basis of the grandstand at Gosforth Park Race Course, was built in 1755 by the Brandlings whose money came from collieries. The county has masses of examples of similar stories – especially if you keep looking at houses built after 1800. The Lawsons were able to build their fabulous Longhirst Hall because of the coal underneath their land. The Cooksons at Meldon Hall ran chemical industries, the Bigges at Linden were mine-owners – all of these and lots of others were built on the proceeds of trade and industry and especially on mineral wealth.

But Wallington was the top of that particular list and Sir Walter Calverley Blackett, as well as making his house magnificent inside and out, created a glorious estate around about it.

The earliest things he did in the 1740s and 50s would all have involved the Brown family of Kirkharle – but not Lancelot 'Capability' Brown; instead it would have been his brother George, who was the estate master-mason at Wallington, who would have assisted James Paine as he designed the Clock Tower to the north of the house and the gorgeous bridge over the Wansbeck to the south. George Brown probably helped when Sir Walter laid out a deer park at Rothley Crags, two or three miles north of the house. He would certainly have been involved in the folly that was built there; it is a mock ruined castle with a two-storey tower in the middle, flanked by castle walls and pavilions at each end.

The word is that visitors to the house would come up here, sometimes dressed in medieval clothes. The men, dressed in pretendy armour, would ride about chasing deer in a picturesque fashion, cheered on by the ladies in their mock-mediaeval wimples, who were having a picnic beneath the (phoney) walls of the (phoney) castle.

So the Wallington landscape was well on the way to being remodelled even before Capability Brown came to add his mark in the 1760s. But when he came he did lots. In front of the house he gave the grounds the usual swardy clumpy vista that we have come to expect from elsewhere, but it is smaller than he normally made and

The Clocktower at Wallington.

the natural landscape where it lies is much less altered than he normally does. It forms the short steep hill from the house down to the banks of the fast running River Wansbeck. Unusually there is no lake visible from the house, though there are lakes all over the place in the landscape as a whole. Four of them are to be found nestling calmly and secretively in the beautiful woods that flank the house and two others (Rothley Lakes) are miles and miles away to the north, at the end of long, winding rides that follow the lines of streams and emerge on to open moorland. There's a wonderful kitchen garden too, in a steep and dramatic valley, protected by the woods behind it and with unexpected and beautiful glimpses of the real landscape beyond its walls.

The remarkable and highly original thing about this garden is how little CB has chosen to change and control the real nature that lies beneath his design. He seems to have reached a stage in his career when he realised that the garden and the landscape were both part of the scene. It didn't matter where one ended and the other began. Parts of the Wallington landscape are quite minimalist, almost invisible gardening.

And finally Alnwick (and its first Duchess)

At Alnwick, a few years after he had worked at Wallington, Capability Brown did the same thing; he created his usual swardyclumpytude in the valley in front of the castle. It is glorious, lush green and as grassy as they come (he never planted simple grass incidentally; all his swards were planted with a mixture of 27 sorts of grass seeds to give the effect of natural variation) but once again there is no lake. There was going to be one. He was going to dam the River Aln and create one, but that year, 1771, was one of the wettest on record. On Tyneside the Tyne rose to prodigious heights and washed away the old Tyne Bridge having already destroyed all the bridges in Tynedale except the one at Corbridge. You might have heard the story of the baby in its cradle that was washed away when the houses on the Tyne Bridge collapsed into the river, only to be picked up unharmed by fishermen several miles out to sea). So

at Alnwick CB was persuaded that it would be dangerous to attempt to dam the river and he just adjusted it instead, a series of weirs were built to keep it calm and placid – all very Capability Brown-ish …

… but upstream he took a different approach.

Upstream is Hulne Park which, since medieval times, had been the deer park of the Earls of Northumberland. It is quite vast. It might even be the largest space in England that isn't crossed by a public road. Or it might not. I may have made that bit up; but it is big. These days you can go into it free of charge as long as you don't drive in or take a dog in, and as long as you are out by sunset. If you haven't been there yet, well, that is a very good thing and you should stick to your record because those of us who do like to go like it to be as quiet as possible.

The last time I went was on a beautiful late autumn day. There had been early-morning mist that was clearing as I arrived and the colours were still vibrant and glorious. There were sheep about and two splendid bulls safely glowering at me from behind a stone wall. There were pheasants everywhere, hundreds of them, iridescent and brilliantly coloured, but there were virtually no peasants to interrupt my solitude. Actually I did meet a couple of rather nice peasants from Yorkshire who had rented a cottage in Alnwick for a week and there was a youngish female peasant with whom I chatted briefly before she strode past me through the trees. I even met one of the Duke's workmen who wasn't at all peasant-like. He had a posh pick-up and a leaf blower with which he was keeping the park's roads and verges clear of leaves as he had done, he told me, for the past 25 years, because Dukes, as I am sure you know very well, like their roads to be nice and tidy.

And there was me, of course, a born peasant, on my way to visit the incomparable 18th century folly called Brizlee Tower.

I need to explain.

In the distant past, as I say, Hulne was a deer park. As long ago as 1244 King Henry III presented 12 fallow deer does and five bucks to the then owner and eventually there were said to be 1000 head of deer within the park walls. In the 16th century, Princess Margaret, the

Hulne Priory and (right) Brizlee Tower.

daughter of Henry VII, was taken hunting there by Henry Percy, the 5th Earl of Northumberland. She apparently enjoyed herself immensely and shot a doe with her crossbow. You didn't mess with princesses in those days.

In the 1600s, Hulne passed through some difficult times. Assorted members of the Percy family were extravagant and went bust or got into bother with the king and at times Hulne was almost lost. For a while it was even leased off to local businessmen for mining and quarrying purposes but it was rescued in the middle of the 1700s by the first Duke of Northumberland along with the first Duchess who wanted to transform the wild and neglected park into the sort of landscape garden that posh families required in those days. They brought in two helpers: L.C. Brown of this chapter, and Robert Adam, among the greatest architects of the time, who was already busy transforming the interior of the castle for the Duchess.

We think we know about Capability Brown. We expect him to provide mirrored lakes and green swards of lawn littered with clumps of trees, the sort of gardens that he created all over the country, but that's not what he did at Hulne. He made something much, much wilder and Northumbrian than he did anywhere else. The landscape was described as "a desert" when he arrived and it was almost as wild but more accessible and exciting when he finished. He created variety by planting woods in some places and in other places beautiful meadows along the river banks. Sometimes he took advantage of the topography and opened out vast vistas of the distant hills; at other times he closed off the distant views altogether and created pathways and ridings through dense woods.

In many 18th century landscaped gardens, the pathways and vistas end at specially built classical temples and other bits of fantasy history but Hulne is different in this respect too because at its heart is an extraordinary and absolutely genuine historic building. It's called Hulne Priory and Capability Brown and Robert Adam used it as a marvellous focus at the heart of the park.

It was built in 1242, the first English property of the Carmelites or White Friars, and it still survives, not completely but to an extraordinary extent. It's on a beautiful promontory high above the River Aln and it is still entirely surrounded by a 12-foot high wall, which was built to defend it at the height of the Border Wars.

Inside the wall there's a mighty 15th century tower and immensely romantic ruined walls, into and among which Capability Brown and Robert Adam scattered equally romantic mock Gothic buildings. There's a beautiful summer house, a host of stone monks lurking among the stones and there's even a Gothic toilet decorated with arrow slits so the Duke (or the Duchess I hope) could sit on the loo and repel boarders. All houses should have one.

The Priory is a fantastic place, an unmissable place, but I have visited it on many occasions, so on my last trip I climbed instead to the highest point of the park, to the extraordinary Brizlee Tower, designed by Robert Adam as a memorial to Elizabeth, the first Duchess, who died in 1776. It is a beautiful building in a beautiful place. The views are perfect. You can see the sea and you can see the Cheviots and you can enjoy everything in between – Northumberland's wildness and vastness is laid out below you.

The path that leads to it takes you past a strange and wonderful fantasy walled garden and a bizarre 18th century stone figure of a monk standing among twisted tree roots at the foot of a sandstone outcrop. There are little ponds among the trees and they were thronging with wildfowl as I passed. The woods were alive with the whirring of pheasants' wings and to complete my adventure I was greeted by a rainbow that almost certainly had a pot of gold at the end.

But I may be wrong....

Which leads me finally (in this chapter) to....

Elizabeth Percy, first Duchess of Northumberland

Halfway up Brizlee Tower is a terracotta medallion of Elizabeth the first Duchess of Northumberland. She looks nice. She is shown in profile and looks quite realistic. She has a slightly double chin and a slightly hooked nose but she also has a gentle smile on her lips and the gentleness can be seen in her eyes too. Her husband, the first Duke, has a medallion as well, further round the tower. His profile is facing towards hers. He looks nice too, more serious, in fact quite earnest, but his picture also looks like a portrait of a real person, there

Dukes like their roads nice and tidy.

The 1st Duchess of Northumberland on the Brizlee Tower.

is nothing idealised about either of them. In her diary, in 1757, she recorded how real she was and how similar she was to him: '*My Lord weighs 12st 13L'*, she writes, '*12st 9L'*. A big lass, as the song goes, but a bonny lass.

All of that might be untrue. It's possible that I have made them sound nice because I want them to be nice and that because I have always liked them.

She was the granddaughter of Elizabeth, Baroness Percy (the one who married the relatively ghastly Duke of Somerset in the late 1600s). Her father (who seems to have been a really nice man) was allowed to take the redundant title of Earl of Northumberland.

Her husband was a politician and statesman called Hugh Smithson. They were married in 1740 and, in the terms of the time were a most unusual couple. It was a love match, or as one recent writer has described it '*a scandalously unfashionable love match'*. They also had a highly unusual relationship. Instead of her immediately taking a back seat in their activities as women were expected to do, they were much more like equal partners and as you will see from the rest of my account of her life she continuously pushed back the boundaries of what women were supposed to be and do. This is what the historian Laura Mayer wrote about her: '*As a patroness, travel writer, scenic tourist and political campaigner Elizabeth crossed and re-crossed the boundaries of feminine propriety.'*

She was, not to put too fine a point on it, a bit of a joy.

After their marriage the couple initially lived in his family estate at Stanwick Hall, a house near Richmond in North Yorkshire, which has sadly been demolished, but when her father died in 1750 his daughter (because he had no sons) inherited all the Percy estates except for Petworth and it's because of what happened next that I want to spend a bit of time talking about her.

As always when one of the Percy lasses inherited all the family wealth, her husband was required to take on the Percy name and in the case of Sir Hugh he also took over the title of Earl of Northumberland, which had been given to his late father-in-law. His advancement didn't stop there though. He was a successful and a useful politician and became a favourite of George III as well as holding the very important and sensitive role of Lord Lieutenant of Ireland for a number of years and for this the king created a new title and in 1766 he became the first Duke of Northumberland which made Elizabeth the first Duchess.

But before all that happened there was one other change that was going to be a big deal in the future development of Northumberland itself.

They were going to bring the Percy family back home to Alnwick!

So there they were in 1750, after the death of her father, fabulously wealthy, houses all over the place including the splendid old Syon House by the Thames on the outskirts of London (which the family still owns, incidentally) as well as Northumberland House in the middle of the City, which was one of the grandest houses in the whole of London (but which was demolished in 1874 to make way for Northumberland Avenue) … oh and Alnwick Castle, which at that time was a decaying ruin near the Border, 300 miles from anywhere. In 1750 it was almost 200 years since any Percys had actually lived there but that is what Mr and Mrs Percy decided to do.

Almost immediately they set about restoring the castle with a view to making it their principal seat. In the present music room there's a painting by Canaletto, done just after 1750, which shows the condition the buildings were in when they inherited the place. It is clearly the Alnwick we still know but in a very different state. The walls are broken in places and there are trees growing out of the battlements. There are odd turrets and towers in the background that no longer exist. The banks below the castle leading down to the River Aln are rough and unkempt, and so is the river itself – a rocky, turbulent country stream. However, it is a wonderful painting and to our eyes it depicts a beautiful and romantic place …

… and amazingly that is exactly how it seemed to its new owner too and she immediately set about making it habitable.

I say 'she' because I am completely convinced that it was Elizabeth who was responsible for bringing the Percys back to Alnwick and that she was the one who undertook its restoration.

That's what I'm saying, but it's not what people used to say.

All of the stuff written in the past about the restoration of Alnwick, including the description in the edition of the Castle Guidebook that I must have bought a few years ago, gives the credit for the move north and the changes that took place in the castle to her husband (Hugh Smithson, as was). Elizabeth gets barely a mention. I'll re-write that – Elizabeth doesn't get a mention at all. He is described as carrying out a '*Long-cherished scheme of restoring Alnwick Castle and fitting it up as a residence for his family'*.

But at the time it was clear to everybody that it was *her* plan. She was captivated by the romance of her ancient and warlike ancestors. She called them '*her braw, rough ancestors'* and her love of her family's heritage led her to resurrect ancient Northumbrian customs, while the castle enthralled her. In her diary she described seeing it '*on an elevation that gives great dignity to its appearance and in ancient times rendered it a most impregnable fortress'*.

Right, that brings me back to Elizabeth and Hugh

Percy. I wrote a moment ago that they were more like equal partners than most 18th century married couples and one way the equality shows itself is in the restoration of their properties. They had inherited two magnificent country houses – Alnwick and Syon House and they each seem to have had one of their own which was their responsibility. Hugh took charge of Syon while Elizabeth made the decisions about Alnwick.

They both used the same architect – the great Robert Adam. He started off working at Syon for Sir Hugh, so until he was available to come and dedicate himself to Alnwick the basic building work was done by the very excellent James Paine. Adam came and supplied the details and the interiors when his work was done at Syon. Both houses seem to have been completed by about 1766 but they were very different from each other in almost every way. It was all a question of style

In the middle of the 18th century there were two different styles available to clients and architects – there was the gothic style and there was the classical.

In those days it was quite rare for anybody to look at an old gothic building and like it or recognise its beauty. For example, an architectural critic called Robert Morris wrote this about the totally gothic Westminster Abbey which we tend to agree nowadays is quite a nice building, but to him: '*It appears only a heavy, lumpish, unrefined mass of material jumbled together without design, regularity or order.'*

Hm! Not at all pro-gothic and the dominant style at the time, the dominant architectural style throughout the 1700s, was the classical style. That was the go-to style for almost all important buildings, and on the whole the gothic was only used for minor buildings – garden buildings and follies and things like that – which brings me back to Elizabeth and her husband, Hugh.

At Syon, Hugh chose the neoclassical style, of which Robert Adam was probably the country's greatest proponent, and he created one of the finest neoclassical interiors in the country. If you can seek out a picture of the anteroom that Adam designed for Syon in about 1760 you will be mightily impressed. It has wonderful marble columns bearing gilded life-size copies of antique statues, the ceiling is rich and magnificent, the floor richer and even more magnificent. It's not a comfy room; you couldn't imagine curling up on the sofa and watching *Midsomer Murders* in it, but it is definitely amazing.

Meanwhile at Alnwick, Elizabeth went for the Gothic style because it seemed more appropriate for a medieval house but she also wanted a style that suited her taste. She visited lots of other people's new houses around the country and quite often she didn't like what they'd done.

Sometimes she didn't like the excessive decoration, all the curly bits and pieces, at other she was irritated because the library was too dark – she thought a library should be about the books and that meant that you should be able to see them. She wanted a nice modern kitchen as well. One of the problems with the gothic style in the 18th century (and sometimes later as well) was that it was associated with darkness and mystery. Jane Austen's *Northanger Abbey* was a satire on the modern taste in gothic houses, which were gloomy and filled with strange chambers and underground passages, mysterious cupboards and curious old chests. Elizabeth wanted none of that. If she'd been living nowadays I suspect that she would have had picture windows and bi-fold doors and what not. She wanted a comfortable, light and airy home and that's apparently what she got.

I say 'apparently' because it's not there any more. It was ripped out by her great grandson, the fourth Duke in the 1850s and replaced with the heavy, impressive Italian-style decorations that the castle has today. To his Victorian eyes her playful, light-hearted gothic seemed merely lightweight and unworthy so he took it away; there don't seem to be even any pictures of it and only a few fireplaces and some furniture remains – except in Hulne Park.

In Hulne Priory, next to the gothic toilet with the arrow slits, is quite a large, two-storey gothic summer house that was designed by Robert Adam and it provides clues about what the castle itself might have looked like. It's not lightweight at all, in fact it's charming. The windows are big and richly decorated; the interior décor is light, airy and festive. If even a garden room can be as nice as that then I bet the castle itself was a stunner. I'm

The Summer House at Hulne Priory.

sure I would have loved it – but it doesn't really matter. The fourth Duke's changes were and remain, terrific. What matters more than the decorative choices that Elizabeth Percy made are that she made them at all. The thing that matters now is that she and her husband took the decision to make the castle habitable and come back north. It was a decision that has had an effect on the county ever since – as we will see.

At the time, though, her design choices were panned – in particular they were panned by the writer and politician Horace Walpole, who clearly didn't like her style of gothic. He thought it was flippant and inaccurate by comparison to his own gothic Strawberry Hill at Twickenham and he thought she was flippant as well. He described her as "junketaceous", a word I had to look up. It seems to mean light and frothy and frivolous like a whipped-up milk pudding. He was really horrible about her. He called her a '*jovial heap of contradictions*' and said that her appearance was '*more vulgar than anything but her conversation*'.

His criticisms have stuck and been echoed by later critics too. I've just quoted the accusation that her work was actually done by her husband but other writers have taken a contradictory but equally insulting line; even relatively recent writers have accused her of wasting her husband's money on Alnwick, despite the fact that the money had come from **her** inheritance and he wouldn't even have had any money, or become an Earl, or a Duke, if he hadn't married her. Snarl, snarl, grumble grumble!

You have probably realised this, but I really like her. I've been reading a recent re-assessment of her by Laura Mayer but I first came across an old copy of her diaries decades ago and was fascinated by her energy and independence. I've been reading them again recently, downloaded from the internet and I have been just as impressed. She comes across as intelligent, adventurous and splendidly outspoken. She said that she had '*a longing to enjoy my liberty*' and she did. She went off travelling on numerous occasions without her husband and had all sorts of adventures.

Without a single Eurostar train or Easyjet flight she popped over to Paris, across to Geneva and the Alps (where she met Voltaire, incidentally, who gave her a melon and a pineapple). She travelled down the Rhone to Avignon and Marseilles. She didn't do it all exactly on her own, hitch-hiking or on a bike, she had some servants with her, but she often left her husband behind her – and she had a great time, an adventurous time. She took a risk crossing the Channel from Dover in a monstrous storm on one trip and when she was going down the Rhone there had been serious floods; she had to cross the River Drome using a bridge that had been half washed away and she crossed one of the other rivers without a bridge at all, struggling through the swollen waters.

In Paris in the spring of 1770 when she went to the marriage of the Dauphin to Marie Antoinette she was present at a catastrophic firework display that occurred in the Place de Concorde several days after the wedding, when thousands were crushed and injured and over 150 were killed. Her coachman was warned to flee before the horses were crushed to death, but he said he cared less for the horses and more for the suffering all around them. He attempted to rescue a dreadfully injured woman, but she died shortly later. She describes how '*people walked over the dead bodies just as in a battle*'. Carriages were covered with desperate people who climbed all over and inside them to escape the crush.

At the wedding itself we get a different side of her –

an amused, waspish, intelligent eye commenting on the social whirl. The bride and groom were both 15 years old but she says that the girl looked '*very fine in diamonds. She is little and slender; I should not have taken her to be above 12 years old*'. She is quite funny about the young groom. She describes how he blushed up to his eyebrows and refused to look at his bride when he put the ring on her finger   .

She was often very forthright about people. In Paris she went to see an opera called *Castor and Pollux*, which she said had cost £5000 to stage. One of the singers had five different costumes and three different hairdos in the course of the performance. She was called Mme Arnauld and the Duchess reveals that '*this lady was kept by the Duc de Auragne*'. She went to a party at Versailles and among the guests were '*trois filles do joie de la derniere magnificence*'. Her friends and neighbours back in Northumberland didn't escape comment either. This is what she had to say about the Lady M … S … '*I now begin to fear that the Lady M….S…. of whose good behaviour to her husband I had conceived a very high opinion, was not quite so proper as I could wish and I feared that she had discovered that Sir Matthew White Ridley was younger and handsomer than her husband.*'

Mind you, sex was everywhere. She was good at spotting it. In the Elector's court at Bonn she says. '*Dress is not carried to great height but intrigue is, to the extent that a virtuous woman is almost as rare as a Black Swan. All have their lovers and too many of those of their own family.*'

Eee, I could go on. Every page you turn to has stuff that grabs you but, you know, even this diary (which wasn't published until centuries after her death) gets criticised. She has been accused (by mainly male critics) of producing mere lists of the names of people she met. Nothing could be further from the truth. She has an eye for everything and especially for landscape, of which her descriptions are not only exquisite but also passionate – the view over the Saone at Lyons towards the Alps – the Rhone Valley at Vaucluse, the Quay at Marseille, are beautiful pieces of travel writing and passionate evocations of the world around her. She loved the landscape around Alnwick with the same enthusiasm. She loved to go out for rides in her carriage, for example, and is said to have identified 93 favourite rides in the estate round her castle.

So that's Elizabeth, first Duchess of Northumberland. She's one of my favourites and significant. Her decision to bring the Percy family, with all its wealth and power and influence, back to Northumberland, has had an impact ever since, not least because it left us with a castle to love and since I'm not going to come back and talk about it again I'm going to finish this section with a few words on how it has fared since then.

First of all it still looks pretty impressive.

If you drive north up the A1 past Alnwick the road curves round the east side of the town. It goes down a bank, across the River Aln and back up the other side of a little valley. To the right is a pretty Capability Brown landscaped hillside with clumps of trees. To the left should be the castle, but can you see it? You cannot. Bushes of various types, osiers perhaps or maybe hawthorn, obscure the view so that drivers who know that there is a castle lurking just out of sight and who are desperate to catch a glimpse of it have been known to break their own necks in a worthy but vain attempt to see over the branches – but all to no avail. Just once, just for a second, immediately before the slip road that leads to Denwick and all points east, the bushes disappear, the view opens out and Alnwick Castle is briefly on display. It's a breathtaking moment. Strangulated cries come from passing cars and no wonder, because Alnwick Castle has become everybody's dream castle. If you asked a child to design a castle, Alnwick is what she would design. Or he, if it was a boy child you had asked. It is like a living embodiment of the Middle Ages.

When you get closer to the castle, the excitement in no way diminishes – it would remain drop-dead gorgeous if you were to look at it under a microscope. The closer you get, however, the more complicated it becomes, the less simple and childlike. It has been here a long time and lots of generations have left their mark upon it so that it is no longer a pure and simple surviving medieval structure though a lot of it is suitably old. There are 12th century bits and lots from the 14th century. The 14th century stonework is especially gorgeous – big and

soft and well worn. You could fall in love with it. The outer gatehouse dates from that time and so does the wonderful barbican in front of it protecting the approaches to the gate. There is a Percy lion flaunting itself rampantly on the front of the gatehouse, revealing levels of rampancy that verge on the embarrassing. Later Percys, and specifically the fourth Duke in mid Victorian times, as we know, rebuilt vast areas of the castle and his machine-cut stone is clearly identifiable as well.

Since 1307 when they first came, a lot of assorted Percys have lived here. There were a whole heap of lords Percy, for example and then ten Earls Percy, and since 1750 it has been the home of the Dukes and Duchesses of Northumberland – Percys to a man (and woman). I interviewed one of them once – a duchess, and asked her, with the sort of originality that has made me the journalist I am, what it was like living in a castle. She said it was very nice but that there were disadvantages. Because of the distances involved, she said, her hot milk had often gone cold before she got to bed. On the same occasion, I recall that I and my little team rang on the door bell at the main entrance to the castle keep and the door was opened by the Duke himself. It was all very nice and jolly. We conducted the interview in the library beside a huge and splendid television with a remarkably extensive collection of videos in a revolving Regency bookcase beside it. An unfinished game of Scrabble was laid out on an occasional table and there was a tempting array of bottles on a silver salver beside it. A fire roared in the enormous fireplace. I thought to myself, I could handle this, I could live here, perhaps I was born to be a member of the aristocracy; but then the Duchess made her crack about the hot milk and the whole edifice crumbled. The sadness of wealth became clear to me and I was reminded of the joys of living in my little terraced house where the distance from kitchen to bed is so small that it is possible to scald your mouth on the hot milk several hours after lying down.

On the other hand, the walls of my little terraced house are not hung with Turners and Van Dycks and Titians, with paintings by del Pombio and (my favourite) Andrea del Sarto, whose self-portrait has the saddest eyes imaginable. My great-great-grand whatsit never invited Canaletto up for the weekend so he could paint my house. I have no inlaid cabinets from Versailles and no ancestors who were ladies in waiting to Queen Anne or who were Lord High Admiral of England. My ancestors in the 19th century didn't bring in Italian designers and craftsmen to produce a neo-Renaissance palace of astonishing sumptuousness (sumptuosity?).

It *is* an astonishing place, Alnwick Castle. I can't think of any other private house like it for the range and quality of art on display or for the richness of its decor but ever since it was remodelled by the Victorians there have been those who haven't liked the style, who have thought of it as an inappropriate display for a medieval castle. In 1860 the *The Alnwick Mercury*, quoted the architectural magazine *The Builder*, which said of the interior decorations, '*We believe them to as elegant and flowing as Italian art can be. But we are not reconciled to seeing them pervade the ancient home of the Percys'*.

I don't share this critical opinion. In my opinion the décor is rich but it is wonderfully done; the rooms are vast but comfortable the art is of the highest possible calibre but entirely accessible. The carved wooden panels in the reveals of the windows are miracles of elaborate carving but the view beyond the glass is even more beautiful, the simple muted beauty of the Northumbrian landscape.

12.   1715 ONWARDS

In 1965 I came across to the North East from Carlisle to train as a teacher and one of the first things I did was go to a folk concert at the Theatre Royal in Newcastle. I remember nothing about it except one electrifying moment when a singer called Bob Davenport came and stood all alone at the front of the stage, stuck his finger in his ear and sang

> '*Farewell to pleasant Dilston Hall*
> *My father's ancient seat*
> *A stranger now must call thee home*
> *Which gars my heart to greet*'.

The song was *Derwentwater's Farewell* and he sang it entirely unaccompanied, on a darkened stage, pinned in place by a single spotlight. The drama was intense, the tune exquisite, the words passionate and tragic. I wasn't sure how hearts got 'garred' but the alien dialect words just added to the mysterious power of the song. That moment and the song have stayed with me ever since. I would sing it for you now if you were here, and if I could sing, but you're not, which is a good thing because I can't.

The song is about James Radcliffe, 3rd Earl of Derwentwater who lived at a place called Dilston Hall between Hexham and Corbridge. He took part in the Jacobite uprising of 1715, was captured, taken to London to be tried, and was executed the following year. The words of the song purport to be the Earl's own, spoken on the night before his execution. He is filled with sadness and longing for the home that he will never see again:

> '*No longer by the banks of Tyne*
> *Will I walk in autumn grey*
> *No longer hear in the early dawn*
> *The laverocks break the day*'

'Laverocks' are curlews, incidentally, whose plaintive call is still part of our heritage today because the bird is the symbol of the Northumberland National Park.

He thinks about those neighbours who shared the fated rebellion with him – George Collingwood, brave Widdrington, Forster, Shaftesbury and Errington – and he regrets their lost dream as well as his own.

> '*If thou and I must lose our lives*
> *Our king must lose his crown*'

And then inevitably his thoughts turn to his family – the wife who persuaded him to take part in the ill-starred revolt and the baby he will never know

Left: Alnwick Castle at sunset. Photograph by Alan Wright.

'And fare thee well my lady dear
Ill, ill thou counseld'st me
Now never more will I see the babe
That smiles upon thy knee'

And as the dawn approaches and the dreaded day arrives the song ends beautifully. It is filled with regret for what he has done, foreboding for the day to come and yearning for the land he has lost. This is how it goes:

'And fare thee well my bonny grey steed
That carried me ay so free
I wish that I'd been sleeping in my bed
When last I mounted thee

The warning bell now bids me cease
My trouble's nearly o'er
Yon sun that's rising from the sea
Shall rise on me no more

Albeit that here in London town
It is my fate to die
Oh carry me to Northumberland
In my father's grave to lie'

Dilston Castle, the home of the Radcliffes.

*James Radcliffe,
3ʳᵈ Earl of
Derwentwater.*

The Radcliffes were an ancient Cumbrian family. There are memorial brasses of some of their ancestors in Crosthwaite Church on the outskirts of Keswick and they had extensive estates in that area but over time, by marriage, they got equally vast estates in Northumberland as well. They owned huge mineral rights in the north Pennines, and lots of the Tyne Valley, including most of the North Tyne. They owned the parish of Simonburn, which was reputed to be the largest parish in England. It stretched from Simonburn right up past Bellingham, beyond Falstone and Kielder to the border line. They owned equally huge estates in the north-east of the county as well, round Wooler and south of Berwick.

They were, as you can tell, a pretty big deal with connections through marriage to almost all the major families in the county. They had been given the title Earls of Derwentwater in the early 1600s by James I and settled at Dilston Castle at that time. In the 1620s James Radcliffe's grandfather built a impressive new Jacobean house that incorporated parts of the medieval castle.

The chapel at Dilston Castle.

They had always been a Roman Catholic family and held on to their faith throughout the wars of religion that convulsed the 1600s. In the grounds of the new hall they kept hold of one of the few churches in the country that continued to be a Roman Catholic place of worship and it was their ongoing dedication to the old religion that led the third Earl to his tragic fate in the 1715 rebellion.

────────

In 1965, when I first heard the song, I knew nothing about the 1715 rebellion. I knew much more about Bonnie Prince Charlie and the 1745 uprising but I had barely heard of the '15, so just in case you are in the same boat, I am going to spend a couple of paragraphs telling you how it came about and what happened. I need to start in 1688.

In 1688 James II, the son of Charles II, was on the throne. There were already two things that people disliked about him – firstly that he was a practising Roman Catholic in a country that was largely protestant and secondly that he was a firm and somewhat abrasive believer in the Divine Right of Kings; having recently executed one king (Charles I) and recognised that loads of others had absolutely no light of divinity shining out of them, the country no longer approved of that; and then suddenly there was a third reason to be wary of

him. In June that year he had a son and people realised that he had started a potential dynasty of Catholic monarchs so they chucked him out; he was deposed in what became known as The Glorious Revolution and replaced by Mary, his protestant sister who was married to William, the Prince of Orange.

Some of the Catholics in the country refused to accept this outcome and many conservative-minded people were reluctant to accept a foreign-born ruler like William so from that moment there was a Jacobite movement dedicated to reversing the revolution that had occurred in 1688.

Northumberland and Tyneside were particularly rich in aristocrats like the Radcliffes who had held onto their Catholic faith, so the North East became one of the hotspots of revolt. Nationally there were a number of small uprisings and one actual invasion. In 1690 England was invaded by the French; guess where it took place. Guess which was the scene of the last foreign invasion of English soil and which was the last place in England to be captured by foreign soldiers … the answer is Widdrington! In 1690 a French force landed in Druridge Bay and plundered Widdrington. In 1697 there was another plan to start a rebellion with an invasion through Newcastle but it was discovered by government spies and the principals were arrested before it could take place.

Throughout all these years the deposed court in exile was living at St Germain in Paris. James II died in 1701 and his son James Francis Edward became the 'pretender' to the English throne, surrounded by exiled devotees and supporters, among them James Radcliffe, the future third Earl of Derwentwater, who had been sent to France by his father to be a companion of the young Prince. The two young Jameses were cousins actually, or sort of cousins. Our James was the son of an illegitimate daughter of Charles II. Our James and the royal James were evidently best buddies as they grew up together.

But then, in 1705, our James came into his inheritance when his father died, and in 1709 Queen Anne gave him permission to come back to England. He was 20 years old and he decided to settle on his

Northumbrian estates, which he had never seen before. He liked Dilston and soon began to replace his grandfather's Jacobean mansion with a shiny new Queen-Anne style house. In 1712 he got married to Anna Maria, another devout Roman Catholic who he clearly loved. The letter he sent to her just before he died started *'My Dearest Worldly treasure'* and in a letter to his parents-in-law, he said '*In giving me your charming daughter you have made me the happiest of men.*' So it was all going really nicely. He was popular, the locals liked him and this is how the writer, Tobias Smollett described him: ... *kind, courteous, generous, hospitable, tolerant of other religions, he treated friends, neighbours and tenants in the same charitable way'*

He was an accomplished musician and, it seems, pretty nice to look at – *'slender, not tall but with grey eyes and a charming smile'.* He also had a very cute pet spaniel that appears with him in his portrait and you can't help trusting a man with a nice little dog.

In 1713 Anna Maria gave birth to a son called John and was soon pregnant again and everything in the Dilston garden seemed to be not only hunky but also dory.

However the storm clouds were gathering; James' fate was sneaking up on him. This is how it happened.

William and Mary had both died and been succeeded by Mary's younger sister, the equally protestant Queen Anne, who had a very successful reign but suffered dreadfully in her personal life. She is thought to have become pregnant 18 times but 12 of the pregnancies ended in miscarriages or stillbirths. Of the babies who survived 5 died before they were 2 years old

In 1690 a French force landed in Druridge Bay and plundered Widdrington.

which just left her with one son who finally died when he was 11. Her husband, who she loved, died before her and she finally died herself in 1714 with no heirs. The country was desperate to find a protestant successor so they chose George, second Elector of Hanover, a man with absolutely no interest in or connection with England and who spoke no English; he just happened to be a protestant and a great grandson of James I. He was the best they could come up with, so you can understand why the Catholic Jacobites with their Tory supporters, convinced that the country would be willing to reject such a choice, started their rebellion.

It was a rebellion that James Radcliffe had no choice but to join. The English rebels were mainly centred on Northumberland and the third Earl was by far the most important, wealthy and powerful Roman Catholic and known Jacobite in the area, so he was fated to take part.

The song implies that he was reluctant to do so and his wife had to persuade him …

> *'And fare thee well my lady dear*
> *Ill, ill thou counseld'st me*
> *Now never more will I see the babe*
> *That smiles upon thy knee'*

… and there was a legend at the time that, like Lady Macbeth, she had almost forced him into action, claimed that he was dithering, and to shame him she threw down her fan and demanded his sword in exchange – but there is no evidence for that; his position meant that he was forced by circumstances to make his stand alongside the rebels.

It was a disaster. The whole uprising was a disaster – badly planned and pathetically run. Nothing went right. The rebels had expected to be supported by the French, but Louis XIV died just before it started so there was no help there. There were bits of armies raised in Northumberland but nothing like as many as they'd hoped for. They were supposed to join with others from Scotland but the leaders were generally incompetent and totally failed to communicate with each other so it just fell apart. It was all very sad and I can't bring myself to explore the sorry inadequacy of the actual campaign but they drifted about for a couple of months, ended up in Preston of all places and were comprehensively defeated by forces loyal to the Government and King George.

James Radcliffe was captured and taken to London. He was only 25 years old. His new house wasn't yet finished; his little son was just a baby and his wife was pregnant, his whole life was ahead of him but it came to a hideous end, beheaded on a scaffold on Tower Hill in front of thousands of people. His wife had lodged with him in the Tower in the weeks before his death and she and others had begged the king for a pardon but it never came. For some reason most of the other leaders were reprieved but he wasn't. He was offered a pardon if he would renounce his faith and his opposition to the Hanoverian Dynasty but he refused and on the scaffold he made a speech of tremendous dignity, declaring his eternal loyalty to James III, his rightful sovereign. It went like this:

> *'I die a Roman Catholic; I am in perfect charity with the*
> *world, I thank God for it, even with those of the present*
> *Government who are most instrumental in my death. I*
> *freely forgive such as ungenerously reported false things of*
> *me; and I hope to be forgiven the trespasses of my youth by*
> *the Father of infinite mercy, into his hand I commend my*
> *soul'*

Then his head was cut off and it was all over.

In the song he prays that his body will be borne back to Tynedale and buried in Hexham's "holy towers" alongside his father; but his father wasn't buried in Hexham and neither was James. His embalmed body, with the head neatly sewn back on again, was brought back to Dilston where he was interred in the family's private chapel among his ancestors

Anna Maria never returned to Dilston, in fact she settled in Brussels, never remarried and died five years later. The babe that smiled upon her knee died when he was 19, of complications following an operation to have a kidney stone removed. Only the unborn baby survived to live a relatively full life. She was called Anne.

So that's James Radcliffe, third Earl of Derwentwater, nice bloke, nasty end – but the story didn't end there. After his death, the Derwentwater estates were seized by the Government. They should have passed to young John but he died before reaching his majority and the only other possible heir was James' brother, Charles, but he was barred because he had been part of the rebellion too, so the Government held on to the lot. In what seems like an ongoing, mean-spirited act of revenge they demolished his house in the 1750s, but before that happened, in 1735, they handed the rest of the estate to the Commissioners of Greenwich Hospital as a means for that naval charity to fund itself.

Over the years that followed, the Hospital Commissioners made a number of decisions when it came to their northern estate that have had a lasting effect on our county; the oddest decision relates to the group of new parishes they created by dividing up Simonburn Parish in North Tynedale.

Simonburn was a huge parish serving a wild and wildly under-populated country and that was the way it stayed until 1818 when the great parish was divided up by Greenwich Hospital into seven smaller ones called Simonburn, Humshaugh, Wark, Bellingham, Thorneyburn, Greystead and Falstone. Five brand new churches were built, while in each parish new vicarages were built or major restorations took place. The conditions they placed on the new parishes included the requirement that their vicars should be ex-naval chaplains and that they should have been graduates of Oxford or Cambridge Universities.

Why did they do it?

They did it because once the wars against the French had come to an end following the Battle of Waterloo (in 1815) the navy no longer needed to be as big as it had been so they suddenly had a whole heap of surplus navy chaplains they didn't quite know what to do with; so rather artificially they created jobs for the boys up here in Northumberland.

It wasn't entirely a successful operation. These men had been used to the cut and thrust of Navy ships or the life and bustle of barracks in Portsmouth and Plymouth; their wives, I imagine, were used to dancing quadrilles in the Officers' mess and, understandably they found it difficult to transfer to the wilds of North Tynedale, which might have been a nice place but undoubtedly lacked life and bustle (or quadrilles). At least two of the ex-chaplains went mad under the strain. Archdeacon Singleton who visited one of the new parishes in 1832 wrote: '… *Mr Rennell the rector is in confinement as a lunatic in Newcastle. Mr Rennell, as far as I can hear was an orderly and temperate man which Mr Burdon, a fellow sufferer from the neighbouring living certainly was not!'*

A year or two later the Archdeacon described visiting the Reverend Edward Brice and his wife at Thorneyburn. Now even today, Thorneyburn is pretty remote. It's beyond Bellingham. For heaven's sake it's beyond Tarset and even Greenhaugh and you can't say much more remote than that. There are barely any houses in view, let alone next door. It's a quarter of a mile from the nearest house and a mile at least from the nearest village. The Tarset Burn and its mini ravine cuts the church off from almost everywhere. There's moorland and rough pasture all around – and this is where he went to meet the Reverend Ed and Mrs Brice, recently arrived from Portsmouth. Unsurprisingly he found them cheesed off … '*they seem but little satisfied with the absolute seclusion of their very pretty rectorial house and garden. To be sure I saw it under a summer sun, whilst the poor lady detailed with horror her lively remembrance of two SNOW BLASTS'*

The Archdeacon was convinced, as most people have been since, that the Commissioners made a mistake in building this number of churches. There wasn't even any population to support them. Thorneyburn couldn't muster more than 40 people on a Sunday, while Greystead never seems to have had a congregation larger than about 20. But they did. All of these new churches were built, along with rather spiffing new rectories, huge gardens, excellent stables, carriage houses and outbuildings in the most …

I was going to say, '… *in the most beautiful Regency style*' and indeed the houses and outbuildings and such are really lovely. They were designed in 1818 and they are very simple and very elegant but also spacious and generous. They have big sash windows and fine-cut

Humshaugh Church.

stone walls, roofs of beautiful Lakeland slate. The detective story writer, Edward Grierson, who lived in one of them for more than a quarter of a century, wrote, *'they are well found and shipshape, though mine is somewhat infested with bats'*.

They were designed by Greenwich Hospital's tame architect, a man called H.H. Seward, who had been trained by Sir John Soane, and whose principal works are all down south but about whom there is one remarkable fact that I would like to share with you – while the first of those H's stands for a nice conventional 'Henry', the second H in his name stands for 'Hake'. What would you have done to your parents if they had called you Hake?

For all his pedigree, Hake's churches couldn't really be called beautiful. They are beautifully built and very spacious. They are even quite nicely proportioned – but they are, unmistakably, very plain. There is nothing blissful about them, nothing fancy, and you could imagine them being designed at that time in one of the workaday new industrial suburbs that were springing up around the big cities – but they seem so odd up here in the remote seclusion of the moors. They are little pieces

of civilised urban design plonked down in the wild North East. Rough grass, bracken and heather press up against beautifully made garden walls. Elegant wrought iron work rusts picturesquely in the northern weather. To be honest they fascinate me, these odd little islands of southern England on the northern fells, but thinking about the difficult lives that must have been lived in them, I can't help coming to the conclusion that Hake and his masters had little sense of what you need, either in architecture or in life, to be Northumbrian.

Apart from this odd little group of churches, the rest of the Greenwich Hospital estate was agricultural land and for quite a long time after being given the estate the commissioners seem to have done very little with it, but in 1807 they made a visitation to their northern property and from then on they became proactive and enlightened landlords.

I have written elsewhere (in the following chapter) about the terrific new farms and labourers' cottages they built in the 19th century so I'll not go on about them here except to say that Greenwich Hospital owns them still, lots of them anyway; stuff has been bought and sold since then but the Greenwich Hospital Northern Estate still measures about 7,800 acres almost all of it farms in the Tyne Valley around Haydon Bridge and in the north of the county south of Berwick. All of them are tenanted and many of them, according to the Greenwich Hospital website, have been tenanted by the same families for many generations.

Cottages at Cheswick East House Farm were provided by Greenwich Hospital in 1808.

Right now, what were we talking about? Ah yes! The 1715 Rebellion. Cast your mind back, if you would, to the song about the Earl of Derwentwater and the list of his fellow rebels, to George Collingwood and brave Widdrington and so on. Do you recall seeing the name 'Forster' among them? Well that was Thomas Forster who was one of the two MPs for Northumberland. He wasn't a Roman Catholic but he was a member of the Tory party and a convinced Jacobite so, because he was important, a member of a prominent family but not one of the unpopular Catholics, the other plotters thought he would be a good figurehead and might draw in other non-Catholics to join the revolt. This meant that despite having no military background he was put in charge of the rebel Northumbrian forces.

He didn't do well – but then why should you expect him to? He was indecisive, missed opportunities, was let down by his fellow rebel leaders and, like the Earl of Derwentwater, ended up being captured after the Battle of Preston and taken to London for trial and possible execution.

So who was he, and where did he come from?

Well, the Forsters, like the Radcliffes were an old Northumbrian family, involved in all the heavy stuff the county had to deal with. For more than a hundred years they had been Constables of Bamburgh Castle and one of them, Sir John Forster, had been a long-running, effective, but notoriously corrupt Warden of the Middle March in Elizabethan times. By 1715 there were two main branches of the family – close neighbours and closely connected with each other. Firstly there were the Bamburgh Forsters, who were responsible for Bamburgh Castle but since it was largely in ruins probably lived in Bamburgh Manor house next door to the church. And secondly there were the Forsters at Adderstone Hall, a house at Lucker, about five miles north-west of Bamburgh just off the Great North Road.

I'm afraid that quite a lot of the Forsters were called Dorothy and two of those Dorothys are central to what happened to the family in those days and you are going to have to pull yourselves together and pay attention or you'll never be able to tell them apart.

The first Dorothy was part of the Bamburgh branch of the family. She was the youngest child of Sir William Forster of Bamburgh and his wife (also called Dorothy but you can forget about her). Daughter Dorothy was born in 1673, one of 9 children in the family. She was apparently nice and I've seen her described as *'fair, blue-eyed and charming'*. Locals called her *'Pretty Dolly Forster'*. She certainly caught the eye of Nathaniel, Lord Crewe, the Bishop of Durham, because he fell for her and asked if he could marry her. The problem was that he was 40 years older than her, but despite that he seems to have been heartbroken at the refusal. He did, however, go away and marry someone else for a while but a few years later, when his first wife died unexpectedly, he came back and asked again. This time he was accepted, despite the fact that she was 27 and he was 67. Oddly, possibly even bizarrely (I'm never very sure about these things), oddly it seems to have been a love-match and the word on the street was that they were happy together.

However, there were tremendous sadnesses in Dorothy Crewe's life as well, because her family had been extraordinarily unfortunate and by the time she got married, the whole of her immediate family had died. Of her eight siblings, three had died young and one of her

Portrait of Lord Crewe at the Deanery in Durham Cathedral.

older sisters had died unmarried. Her brother John died in his twenties in 1699 and her eldest brother William, who was MP for Berwick, died the following year when he was just 21. Her sister Frances, who had married into the Adderstone/Lucker side of the family and who I'm coming back to in a moment, died in 1697 and that left just Dorothy and one brother, Ferdinando, who became

Monument by Dorothy Forster in Bamburgh Church.

the head of the family – and then he died too. In 1701, when he was 31 year old he was murdered by one of his neighbours, a man called John Fenwick from Rock Hall, which is no distance at all from Bamburgh. The two of them had an argument and stepped outside to settle it when Ferdinando tripped or slipped and as he lay helpless on the ground John Fenwick ran him through with his sword. Fenwick was executed on the site of the murder but that didn't bring Dorothy's brother back, so she was left as the last of the Bamburgh Forsters standing.

A few years later, in 1711, she erected a monument in Bamburgh church to the memory of all her brothers and sisters. It is a beautiful and moving object, very simple but exquisitely carved. It is laid out like a list in an exercise book with all the names down one side and what happened to them down the other and finally, at the bottom, she added herself, the only sibling left alive. This is what she wrote:

SHE

'Being the Only one Remaining of the Family
Set up this Monument in Memory of her dear
Brothers
As the least respect that Could be paid them
For their True Affection
To the Church, Ye Monarchy, their Countrey &
Their sister
AD 1711'

She didn't know, of course, that four years later she was going to join them – but that's a sadness that was still to come.

I have a feeling for this family. It was full of sadness but time after time its members revealed their tender and sentimental attachment to their loved ones.

Set into the floor of Bamburgh church, just a few yards from Dorothy's memorial, is the gravestone of her sister Frances, who had married into the other branch of the family and become the wife of Thomas Forster of Adderstone. I'm going to quote this one too because though it's a bit rougher in design (and spelling) I think its message is beautiful. This is what it says:

'Here Lyes Interred the Body of Mrs FRANCES
FORSTER wife of
Mr THOMAS FORSTER of Lucker
(Having lived in Great Happinefs
and Intire Affection Man and
Wife the Short Space of Tenn
Yeares, Three Monthes and Fifteen
dayes and had Issue three son's
and foure Daughters) Departed this
life ye 15th Daye of October AD 1697'

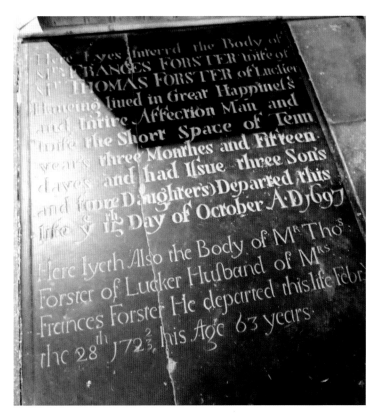

Monument to Frances Forster in Bamburgh Church.

One of those three sons of Frances Forster was the Thomas Foster who went on to lead the rebellious forces in 1715 but before he did that he had a bit of a stroke of luck. The whole of the extended Forster family's estates were bankrupt after decades of excessive good living and gambling, so there was nothing left when the murder of Ferdinando meant that the property had to be divided up. Half of what there was went to Auntie Dorothy from Bamburgh, who was now married to Lord Crewe, and the other half went to Dorothy's nephew, Frances' son, Thomas.

They would all have been ruined, but Lord Crewe stepped up into the breach, paid off the debts and bought up the estate. It cost him a bit of a fortune (£20, 697 to be precise) but it saved his wife's family's honour and her heritage from destruction – yet another example of the unexpectedly caring nature of this group of people.

And there's more – some of it sad and touching and some extraordinarily noble. Here's the sad bit first.

In 1715, after the Battle of Preston, when Thomas Forster had been captured and led off to London to be tried, news of the disaster reached his aunt and it killed her. She had convulsions and died there and then, on the spot as she heard the news. She was 42. How remarkable is that? I can't help associating Auntie Dorothy's death with the tender emotions of the gravestones in Bamburgh church. This was a woman, I can't help feeling, who had suffered so much family pain that she couldn't handle another disaster among those she loved – so she died.

The other Dorothy, the one I haven't mentioned yet, took a different approach.

The other Dorothy Forster was Thomas Forster's sister and she also revealed a passionate family connection. Her response to Thomas's arrest wasn't to die of shock but to go down to London (Grizzy Cochrane style) and rescue him.

There are three versions of Thomas Forster's escape from Newgate Prison. Some writers don't mention Dorothy at all. In these versions the implication is that Thomas did it all on his own in clever manly style, he didn't need a woman to help him. I imagine these writers as having had the romance sucked out of their souls at birth by a pitiless fate. There are others who say that Dorothy set off from home in Northumberland with a local blacksmith in tow and somehow, when they got to London, the blacksmith managed to make an impression of the key to the cell and they let her brother out. That's a version that appeared in an article written in 1837 and it's better than the first version but only just.

So that leaves the third version; the one I have always heard and like best is that she went to the prison to visit her brother day after day with her female servant in attendance until the guards were so used to them that they were almost invisible. And then … this is the cunning bit … one day Dorothy went alone but wearing the servant's clothes beneath her own. In the cell Thomas dressed in the servant's clothes, walked calmly out of the tower alongside his sister, got on Eurostar or a boat or something and was in Paris in a couple of days.

How cool was that? He stayed in Paris for the rest of his life until he died there in 1738, when his body was brought back and buried in the family vault in Bamburgh Church.

The interesting thing about these two stories that emerged out of the 1715 rebellion is that they both produced a legacy that has resonated in Northumberland ever since. When the Earl of Derwentwater died and his possessions were handed over to Greenwich Hospital it started a process that continues to have impact today and something similar grew out of the tragic events that blighted the Forsters at that same time.

When it was all over, and the Forsters were no more, Lord Crewe was left holding the lot. He was devastated by the loss of his wife and sat regularly mourning by her grave. In Bamburgh he started a process of restoring the castle and then, when he died six years later in 1721, having no family of his own, he left the bulk of his wealth as a charitable trust called the Lord Crewe Trust which emphatically still exists today.

There were five trustees whose job it was to spend the Trust's money and I have read that the amount of money they were responsible for was £1312.13s.6d p.a., which is just about enough to have your eyebrows plucked nowadays but was a massive amount in those days. It was used mainly for the benefit of clergy in the Durham Diocese – helping out those who were having a hard time, vicars retiring and needing help to find a retirement home, sending promising sons to university and stuff like that.

In those terms it still exists. It has been paying out continuously for 300 years and there is still a fund available today to help local vicars and their families. I know of one family who have been able to take their children away on holiday thanks to the trust and I am sure that many of its original concerns are still being met, but from the start there was always money left over that had not been given out and the trustees began to extend the range of charitable activities that they supported. The name to know, the Chairman of the Trustees who had the biggest impact in this respect, was a man called Dr. John Sharp.

John Sharp, it seems to me, must have been a lovely man … no that's not enough, he seems to have been a wonderful man and he came from a remarkable family. His father, Thomas, was an Archdeacon and a nice man too, an interesting and charitable man. He was the vicar of Rothbury and in the 1720s he built a tower called Sharpe's Folly on a hill above the town. He built it partly to satisfy his interest in astronomy and astrology but mainly so he could provide paid employment for local workmen, struggling in a time of hardship. He became the first Chairman of the Lord Crewe Trust until he died in 1758 when his eldest son, John, took over from him.

John Sharp (he also took over his father's role as Archdeacon of Northumberland in 1762) was the vicar of Hartburn, but to be honest he spent an awful lot of his time and an awful lot of his personal fortune at Bamburgh. He continued the restoration of the castle that had been begun by Lord Crewe, which was a good thing. He restored the Keep for example and made it habitable; but much more impressive than his architectural work was the way he pushed the Trust into new, adventurous, necessary and quite extraordinary charitable directions.

For the next 30 years, until he died in 1792, he oversaw and partly funded a remarkable range of philanthropic initiatives all based physically in Bamburgh Castle.

At the east-end of the castle is a windmill, for example, or at least the body of a windmill, its sails aren't there anymore, but it was built in the 1760s to grind corn that could be provided free to the poor in times of emergency and at intervention prices the rest of the time. In later years other things were added to what was available – there was barley and beans, peas oats and rice and in later years, after his death in 1792, the shop became more varied still and sold all sorts of necessities at reasonable prices.

Dr Sharp set up schools as well. After 1772 there was a free school for the children of the poor and a sort of special school to prepare poor girls to work in service.

There was an infirmary too, where poor people could get state-of-the-art medical treatment. John's brother, William, was surgeon to King George III and helped supply the infirmary with all the latest stuff. There were syringes – which of course imply vaccination and John Sharp's infirmary was among the first places to try vaccination against smallpox. They conducted trials, adverts for which were stuck on the church door to find people willing to take part in the experiments. There were other oddly modern things too – one was a mysterious 'electrical machine' for example and I was also fascinated to read (given that I am writing this in the midst of the Covid 19 lockdown when the provision of ventilators for the NHS has been such a national obsession) that his brother provided the infirmary with special bellows to give patients … to give patients what?

You are expecting me to say that the bellows were designed to provide respiration for patients with breathing difficulties like the ventilators in use these days but that's not how medical innovation and understanding works and the Bamburgh bellows were invented for a very different purpose!

They were called Resuscitation Kits and they were paid for by the Royal Humane Society, which was founded in 1774 as the Society for the Recovery of Persons Apparently Drowned.

The kits were needed at Bamburgh because the Lord Crewe charity was heavily involved in dealing with persons drowned or apparently drowned. The Northumberland coast was always an intensely dangerous place for shipping. The graveyards at Bamburgh and Holy Island have dozens and dozens of memorials to ship-wrecked mariners. One famous ship's captain on the Tyne recalled that the first time he sailed into the river he counted 25 sunken wrecks on the rocks off the coast of Tynemouth.

Some families, the Haggerstons for example, gained part of their wealth from the salvage they were able to claim from shipwrecks as lords of the manor. John Sharp tackled this problem in a characteristic way – with a whole mass of initiatives. First of all he provided temporary accommodation in the castle for rescued sailors, while injured sailors were admitted to the infirmary and the bodies of the drowned rescued were brought to the castle as well … which brings me back to the bellows.

The bellows provided by the Royal Humane Society had an unexpected use; they were used to blow tobacco smoke up the rectums of men who had drowned in the hope that the smoke would help them recover. It never did of course, because they were already dead, but doctors kept on believing in them for decades.

Simpler, kinder and probably more effective solutions were applied as well fortunately. Efforts were made to contact the families of those who died, or failing that the companies which owned the ships, but if that turned out to be impossible, then the bodies were provided with proper burials, their graves marked by gravestones paid for by the Trust.

In other measures to help with safety at sea there are huge chains in the basement of the Castle Keep that were used to haul ships to shore, and there were pumps to clear the ships and help with the rescue. They devised a system using different flags displayed on the roof of the keep to send signals to other parts of the coast when ships in difficulty had been spotted.

In 1786, a London boat builder called Lionel Lukin was commissioned to design what turned out to be the earliest attempt at a lifeboat ever made. It was a converted coble and was meant to by unturnoverable (I'm sure there's a better word than that, but you know what I mean). I think it was less successful than the one designed a few years later at South Shields but it was clear evidence of how far the Trust (and Dr Sharp) were prepared to go to help people in need.

The initiatives went on and on. They allowed petitions from individuals who needed money for some project – they were a grant awarding trust, in fact, long before such things existed

All of these contributions that they made were recognised as being extraordinary at the time. This is what William Hutchinson wrote about John Sharp in 1776: *'He resides many months in each year in the Castle of Bamburgh, superintending the works of charity and has his eye upon every new channel by which he may give relief or consolation to his suffering fellow-sufferers. The shipwrecked and the diseased are comforted by his visitations and the calamities of life are alleviated by his care …'*

Eventually, almost a hundred years after John

Sharp's death, many of the voluntary concerns of the charity had become the responsibility of others, of the government and local corporations or of specialist organisations like the RNLI, so the extraordinary life of Bamburgh Castle drew to a close and it was sold to the industrialist and inventor, Lord Armstrong and the Lord Crewe Trust withdrew back to the original purposes for which it was set up, but its presence can still be felt around Bamburgh. 50-plus years ago I myself spent the whole two days of my honeymoon in the Lord Crewe Arms at Bamburgh, a business that is still owned by the trust. It was a lovely time and I had one experience during that short stay that I had never had before. My goodness, it was exciting. I had two eggs for breakfast. That's what honeymoons are all about.

Windmill at Bamburgh Castle built by John Sharp in the 1760s to grind corn that was given free to the poor.

Clockwise from top, cottages at Blawearie, Etal, Tarset and Akeld.

13. ORDINARY BUILDINGS

There have been quite a lot of posh people's houses in this book so far and there will be more, but there hasn't been a lot of information about how poor people lived and that, in my opinion, is because on the whole, until, at the earliest the middle of the 1700s, their houses were too mean to have survived. As far as I can think there are hardly any surviving houses in Northumberland from before that time that were the homes of really poor people. I could be bolder and say that there are none. If I'm wrong somebody will tell me and my knowledge will be enriched.

The bastle houses that I was describing in the chapter on the 16th century look like pretty basic accommodation to us nowadays – just a ladder up to a single room on the first floor with the animals living downstairs in the basement, but bastles were so massive in construction that they must have been expensive and hugely labour-intensive to build, so there must have been a whole substrata of even simpler houses lived in by people who didn't qualify for bastles.

We don't know exactly what they were like, though there are occasional and fleeting glances of them from time to time. When William Camden came to look at the Roman Wall in 1599, you might recall, he described how the locals spent the summer in little huts in the hills; and there have been a few excavations high in the hills and across the county line in Cumberland that have exposed at least the foundations of some very simple little rough dwellings. Some of them seem to have had low stone footings to the walls, just resting simply on the ground and to have been built of turf higher up. In others the walls were entirely stone.

Even a hundred years later, in 1699, the traveller Celia Fiennes saw people living in houses like this. She wrote about *'little huts made up of drye walles only stones piled together'*. As it happens Celia Fiennes and William Camden were both writing specifically about sheilings up in the hills, but other writers and travellers described houses in more accessible parts of the county that seem to have been almost as simple.

William Hutchinson, who wrote about his travels in the north of the county as late as the 1770s, sounded really shocked by the standard of ordinary people's houses. He described them as *'deplorable'*. He said that they were made with timber uprights joined together by wattle and daub panels; *'wattled and plaistered with mud'* was how he put it. The roofs were either thatched or covered with turfs and the walls had a single small pane of glass to admit *'the beams of day'*. Inside there was no fireplace, just a hearthstone that held the turf and peat fire. The furniture was pitiful – *'a wretched couch'* and a few *'wooden utensils ... that scarce retain the name of convenience'*. The single room was divided in two with one half being for *'the domestic beast'* – no, not the teenage son – apparently he meant the family cow *'that stalls with its master'*.

The problem with this description isn't that it is technically inaccurate, the picture is borne out by a number of other writers and there is a reconstructed house of similar type at the Yorkshire Folk Museum at Hutton le Hole near Pickering. The problem is that he makes it sounds so revolting. The house is *'deplorable'*, the couch *'wretched'*. In the roof timbers above the room there are not just poultry but *'<u>disconsolate</u> poultry that <u>mourn</u> in the rafters'*.

Everything is ghastly. The people are *'of abject countenance'* and *'miserably clothed'*. When they are at work he describes them as *'indolent herdsmen lying prostrate on the ground'* instead of watching over their flocks or guarding the corn. It's such a miserable picture that you have to wonder whether even the smoke from the miserable fire had the energy to go upwards.

Hutchinson and other writers and historians from about the same time seem to have been convinced that there was something almost subnormal about the lowest classes in rural Northumberland. Most of the very poor had never been inside a church, they said, and spent their Sundays in whisky houses (pubs to you and me – one of them in Upper Coquetdale was called The Slyme Foot!) where they gave themselves over to hard drinking and gambling – *'lost in a whirl of dissipation to all care and recollection'* (it sounds great. I could do with a couple of nights down the old Slyme).

Another writer who cast a pretty jaundiced eye on the lower classes was the first Duke of Northumberland (of whom you've just been reading). As you know, he and his wife settled in Alnwick in the 1750s and set about restoring the castle along with the rest of the old Percy estates, which had been much ignored for a long time; among the things he did which I haven't mentioned so far was to build a hunting lodge called Kielder Castle near the head of the North Tyne Valley. He wasn't from Northumberland and was surprised by what he saw among the tenants on this part of his estate. He described them as *'quite wild'*. There were *'half naked women chanting a wild measure'* which apparently went

'Ourina, ourina, ourina', while the men *'brandishing dirks, danced a war dance'*. He said the men were savage and could *'hardly be persuaded to rise from the heath'*. His biographer, writing in 1848, said that the Duke had found the area round Kielder to be inhabited by a race which "*was scarcely less savage that the Indians of California*".

Obviously my researches in the hills have required me to keep an eye out for those half naked women but my experience is that they're few and far between nowadays (there are just too many midges) while the men, on the whole, have abandoned dirks in favour of laptops and mobile phones. But you never know, there may be still the odd dirk-brandisher and scantily-clad maiden lurking among the heather. One can but dream.

The problem with all of these writers is that they were upper class or middle-class urban dwellers with no understanding of working-class life in the countryside. The Duke doesn't seem to have had any knowledge of sword dances or the gentle melancholy of the Northumbrian pipes, so what he saw seemed like savagery. Hutchinson was the same. He was less posh but lived in an extremely nice Georgian house in Barnard Castle and he saw poverty as moral decay. It was a common attitude; it has always been common, it still is common for the comfortably-off to blame the poor for their own poverty. There's an inscription over the door of a medieval tower in Whittingham near Alnwick that reads

By the munificence and Piety of
LADY RAVENSWORTH
This ancient tower which was formerly
Used by the village as a place of refuge
In time of rapine and insecurity
Was repaired and otherwise embellished
For the use and benefit of the deserving Poor
A.D. 1845

You'll notice that it's only the "deserving" poor who get to use the new facility. The implication is that the undeserving ones, the ones who can't be bothered to rise

Joe the Quilter's Cottage at Beamish.

from the heath or who get lost in a whirl of dissipation in the Slyme House have only got themselves to blame.

Well I'm not convinced by these early writers on the rural poor and I don't trust their judgements about the houses people lived in. For example, I have visited the reconstructed house at the Yorkshire Folk Museum, the one in which the space was shared between the people and the family beast and while it clearly wasn't up to modern IKEA standards it was neither deplorable nor wretched and there's no evidence that the animals were especially disconsolate. It was … interesting … it was airy and even agreeable but most of all it was the way that poor people lived all over the country, all over the world in fact.

That's not to say it was right that people should be forced to live in such basic conditions and as the 1700s and the first half of the 1800s progressed, the situation in the Northumberland countryside very gradually began to change and better-built and slightly roomier cottages began to appear.

If you want to see what was possible for a working class person in those days once the improvements were under way, you could do worse than to leave Northumberland altogether and venture nervously south into County Durham, to Beamish Museum in fact, to see the reproduction they have built of Joe the Quilter's Cottage.

Joseph Hedley was a quilter who lived in a small, heather-thatched cottage on one of the quiet lanes in Warden, just west of Hexham on the banks of the Tyne. He made quilts and finished off quilts for ladies from the farms round about. He lived alone after his wife died and on the evening of 3 January 1826 he was brutally murdered. Earlier that day he had gone shopping to one of the local farms and bought some sugar, some milk and (as you do) a sheep's head. At about 6 o'clock a chum had called in for a chat and about 7 o'clock a pedlar called Mrs Biggs called to ask the way to a neighbouring village. Sometime after that he was murdered quite horribly. The body wasn't found for a couple of days but there was blood everywhere – on a quilt, on the floor and on the snow on the road outside. His throat and face were slashed and there were multiple stab wounds to his body. The evidence pointed to there being two murderers and the assumption was that they were after Joe's fabled but non-existent riches.

The story was a national cause celebre. The King himself offered a reward of a hundred guineas but the murderers were never found and the case remained unsolved. The cottage was demolished later in the 19th century but its footings survived beneath the soil and its appearance and a plan of its interior and contents were made as part of the inquest. On top of that, quite a precise drawing of the cottage appeared in the local paper, so Beamish carefully excavated the site and, with their characteristic skill, reconstructed an exact copy of the house.

There must have been hundreds of cottages like Joe's in Northumberland and now there are virtually none. There used to be hundreds of heather-thatched roofs but now there are just three or four so the Beamish cottage doesn't just illustrate a small local tragedy, it also provides something that is rarer than churches or mansions – it gives a vivid picture of how ordinary people lived in a place like Warden in Georgian times.

From the outside the cottage looks small and simple, its walls rough, its windows tiny, its extraordinary roof of heather thatch wild and shaggy. The crack in the wall beside the door is an exact copy of one shown clearly on the 1826 drawing. But the inside comes as a surprise. There is no ceiling, just the great high sweep of the roof timbers and the thatch above it. It makes for an unexpectedly generous-feeling space. There's a fireplace, and last time I was there one of the ladies from the museum was sitting beside it in her gown and pinny and mob-cap, sewing a bit and looking after the fire. We sat together and talked about the cottage, the beauty of the flames and the smell of burning wood. The furniture that the museum has chosen to illustrate the room is quite surprising because it includes a couple of rather smart pieces, family heirlooms that Joe would have held onto jealously.

It's a nice house in fact, not spacious or smart but liveable in. I don't know for certain when it would have been built but I suspect that, despite its rough simplicity,

it was probably built as late as the 1770s or 1780s. I don't really know who would have built it or paid for it either, but I think that even a house as simple as this would have been beyond the scope of the poor to build for themselves so that it must have been provided by a landowner as part of the improvements being made to an estate and a man like Joe would have been a tenant, renting it from the landlord.

All over the county, in the 1700s and the first half of the 1800s, Northumberland's landlords, the owners of the big estates that still dominated the landscape transformed the housing of working people.

———————————————

At the end of the Border wars, Northumberland was a very poor place, less densely populated than it had been hundreds of years earlier and much less well developed than most other parts of the country. Most of England is full of medieval and post medieval farmhouses and cottages belonging to relatively independent yeoman farmers and the poorer labourers who worked for them. In places like Kent and Suffolk the landscape is dotted with medieval houses; in other places the rebuilding of houses occurred later but still much earlier than in Northumberland. Even in the wild fastnesses of the Lake District there are splendid farmhouses that date from the 1660s onwards but Northumberland has nothing like that and even by the end of the 1600s there were very, very few small and ordinary houses being built.

To a greater extent than almost anywhere else, the land was still owned by the same great families who had held it throughout the wars and after 1700 they began, first of all to rebuild their own houses in more modern styles and then gradually, from the middle of the century onwards, over the following hundred-odd years, they increasingly turned their attention to the improvement of their estates.

It was a process driven by the desire to make money. They wanted their estates to become economically productive so they built hundreds of farms. On the marginal lands high up on the moors or the upper reaches of the valleys, they built small individual

farmsteads, often just a cottage attached in a single row to a line of outbuildings – but on the more productive land they built extraordinary farms. They range from big farms to giant farms that are among the wonders of the county (I remember I described them as "Northumberland Super-farms" in another book). You could go further and describe them as among the agricultural wonders of the country as a whole. You see them everywhere in the valley bottoms along the Tyne valley and on the coastal plain. They are so extensive and so well-built that it is obvious that the finance to create them could only have come from a major concern like a great estate. Their farmhouses are as vast and splendid as manor houses and were lived in then (as now) by well-to-do tenant farmers.

But it is the farm buildings that are the most impressive. Not for Northumberland the picturesque muddle of farms in so many other parts of the country. Time after time our farms are laid out with a formal splendour. The main building is usually U-shaped or even E-shaped. The long range at the back is almost always made up of an elegant row of low segmental arches that open on to the fold yard in front. These arches provided shelter sheds for the animals and they are architecturally splendid – among the greatest architectural delights of Northumberland.

Quite often the centre point in the rows of segmental arches is emphasised by a dovecote-tower, often made even grander by a tall pyramid roof. The side arms of the buildings have byres on one side for the cattle. Byres can be recognised because they have ventilation slits but no windows, evidently cows prefer to be kept in the dark (though whether anybody has actually asked them I'm not sure). Horses prefer light, so the stables have windows. The stables form the third side of the U.

As well as this basic (and elegant) arrangement there are a whole host of specialist buildings. There is usually a *calving room* and at the back of the farm, a respectable distance away from the cows, is the bull house. What a nightmare for the bulls – all those cows but no way to get at them. There were pigsties of course and hen houses but in Northumberland they have often been combined into two-storey *poultiggeries* with hen houses built upstairs so the warmth from the pigs below would help in the production of eggs. Each farm has its *tack room* and a **smithy** of its own. There were very few barns because Northumberland was too cold to be a major corn growing area but animals need to be fed, of course, and increasingly, as time went by, each farm was built to take control of all the processes of production so the cereal that was needed for animal feed was ground on site and stored in long low rooms above the animal shelters. Often there were holes or chutes in the floor of these granaries that allowed feed to be poured directly down into the feeding troughs for the cattle below. At first, in many places, the corn was ground using horse power and many of the farms have circular buildings called horse-engine sheds (if you were being posh) or **gingangs** (if you weren't) where the horses, attached to a rotary beam, trudged endlessly round and round to drive the grinding mill, We call it going to work nowadays. Later farms had windmills to grind the corn and later still, from the early 1800s, they were fitted with coal-powered steam engines, which you can recognise because they have high chimneys like factory chimneys in northern industrial towns.

Some farms have all of these things. Chollerton Farm has a tall windmill tower in the middle of its buildings and a later steam-powered engine house to one side. The farm at Ingram had a steam engine too, but could switch to water power using the water wheel attached to the rear of the buildings if the River Breamish, which runs past the farm, was providing enough water.

Sometimes there are other specialised buildings. In the Tyne Valley, where the climate is drier and warm enough to allow wheat to grow, many of the farms have Dutch barns.

In the north-east of the county, near Berwick, as well as a dovecote many farms have big hen-houses (by which I mean big houses for hens, of course and not houses for big hens. That would be scary – though I did once visit a farm near Hexham that specialised in rearing huge capons so you could buy 16-pound chickens). But the hen houses near Berwick were big because there was a trade in the export of eggs to London. The eggs were preserved in isinglass, apparently, stored in jars and transported from Berwick. It's easy to tell the difference

between a dovecote and hen-house because the nesting boxes built into the walls need to be much bigger for hens

The Berwick area was innovative in a number of other ways. The farms there were experimenting with burnt lime as a fertiliser as early as the 1500s and in the 1730s turnips were first introduced (by farmer John Procter from Rock near Bamburgh) as a way of feeding animals through the winter.

Glendale near Wooler had some of the most impressive farms in the county. Improvements were introduced initially by two brothers called, George and Matthew Culley, who settled there from south Durham in the 1760s. They were later joined by their younger brother James and they worked alongside another agricultural reformer called John Bailey, who was the Land Agent for the Earls of Tankerville at Chillingham Castle. Together (and alongside dozens of neighbouring famers) they experimented with all sorts of adventurous new practices to do with stock breeding, irrigation and turnip growing to the extent that Northumberland became one of the most advanced agricultural regions in the country – quite a change you might think from biffing the neighbours and stealing their cattle.

And of course, these remarkable farms needed workers and workers needed somewhere to live and so the landscape became dotted with neat new cottages for the working man and his wife and large family.

In the 1820s the Tyneside historian Aeneas Mackenzie recorded the process. Writing about the hamlet of Holburn, north-east of Wooler, he first of all described the houses that had been there a few years previously. They were made of bits of trees, he said, resting on the ground and leaning against each other to form a sort of roof – little rough cruck houses is what I am imagining – hovels. But now, he wrote, *'these rude log houses are replaced with neat well-built cottages'*. When he visited areas where such improvements hadn't yet taken place he was shocked and said *'in many parts of the county the landlords still appear shockingly ignorant of the advantages that result from increasing the comfort of the labourers. It is shocking,'* he says, *'that a man, his wife and half a dozen children should be obliged to live huddled together in one miserable hovel."*

Elsewhere in his book he praised those who made a difference. He was particularly impressed with the second Duke of Northumberland. His name, incidentally, was Hugh and he had replaced his father Hugh, the first Duke, in 1786. On his death in 1817 he passed the title to his son (Hugh).

What Mackenzie liked about Hugh (the second) was that he had worked so hard to build efficient new farms and had introduced long-term tenancies (initially 10 years but rising to 20) at reasonable rates, which allowed his tenants to commit themselves to their land; and he liked the number of cottages he had built for the labourers, again on extended tenancies.

Each of the cottages had a third of an acre of land to allow families to be more self-sufficient and a yearly pig was included in their tenancy agreement to ensure a steady supply of bacon sandwiches – without which, as all right-minded people know, life becomes a bleaker and less colourful place.

Occasionally you get a chance to know the precise moments when landlords realised the need to do more to house the working classes. I wrote in the previous chapter how, after the Earl of Derwentwater had been executed for taking part in the 1715 Jacobite Rebellion, his huge estates in Tynedale and in the north east of the county were given to Greenwich Hospital to support its charitable concerns, The Trustees of the charity did little with their Northumberland possessions for almost a century until 1807, when they came north to examine their north-eastern holdings. They were shocked with what they found and almost immediately began a process of redressing the balance; they rebuilt farms all over the county including some splendid examples like Thornborough Barns near Corbridge and Inlandpasture at Scremerston near Berwick.

But my personal favourite example of their farms is East Farm at Cheswick, south of Berwick, where they built a gorgeous farmhouse, splendid farm buildings and a beautiful row of cottages on a hillside by the road. They are single-story cottages (virtually all the labourers' cottages in the north of the county are influenced by the proximity of Scotland and are single storey) and not very big.

Originally the revolution created after 1807 was to build two-roomed cottages instead of one-roomed! Generous to a fault. These cottages are still in use, but nowadays to match modern expectations, two cottages have been joined into one and additional kitchen and bathroom extensions have been added to the back. It was a start though.

East Farm, Cheswick, one of John's favourites.

All of the estates and the families that have emerged in these pages so far, and many that haven't, built splendid farms. The Blacketts (and their descendants the Trevelyans) created wonderful farms at unexpected places like Greenleighton, a few miles north of Wallington and right on the edge of country that had been wild, uncultivated land for centuries. Another of their beautiful farmsteads is called Gallows Hill – a suggestive reminder of the change from violence and indiscipline to proper land management.

In the early 1800s the Middletons of Belsay rebuilt every single structure on their estate and added many, including neat well-made farms as part of a complete transformation of the landscape. The Lord Crewe Trustees rebuilt the farms around Bamburgh including the splendid Friary Farm just north of the village. The Ridleys, owners of the Blagdon Estate just north of Newcastle, built New Horton Grange, one of the finest of them all. The improvements sprang up all over the county. After being a virtual wilderness for centuries, the county took on a new and productive form.

I love these farms and their cottages. When I started being a listed building man 40 years ago. I thought I knew lots about the buildings of Northumberland but I knew nothing about the farms. I can't believe it now. I must have been driving around with my eyes closed, so when I first came into contact with them I didn't understand what I was looking at.

I've written before how it was on my first active day as a Listed Building Fieldworker. I had driven north from Newcastle amassing a minor fortune in mileage claims, called in to Wooler Police Station (Sgt John Renton, bus driver from chapter one) and set off to visit my first buildings. I had plumped (if that's the word I'm looking for) plumped for what I thought was the village of Horton just north of Wooler, except that when I got there I discovered it wasn't a village at all, though it looked like one on the map. It turned out to be two huge farms that faced each other across the road. Both had a big and impressive farmhouse; both had extensive farm buildings of the sort that I have described here, and both had several rows of single-storey cottages – for all the world like a village, but not.

White House Farm, Lowick, before and after being redeveloped.

But villages or not, these vast and extensive steadings must have been lively communities. I met a farmer once at a super-farm on the coast; the day was cold and he was on his tractor, protected from the wind by the cab that tractors have nowadays. We talked about what I was doing, my interest in the history of his farm and others like it, and he talked wistfully about what it had been like when he was young. He had been born on this farm, his father and grandfather at least had farmed it before him. He said that as he grew up it was teeming with life; more than fifty people lived and worked on it and that didn't include the children who lived there; and look at it now, he said, now there's just me, I can do the

Extremely picturesque former miner's cottage at Blanchland.

lot on my own with all the machinery I have and do you know what, he said, sitting in his cosy little cab? I can't even feel the wind any more.

The cottages built for all those farm labourers have all sorts of uses now and the farm buildings have as well. They are all so well built that they remain utterly in demand. Some are still the homes of country families; others are second homes or have become the houses of the well to do. Dozens, possibly hundreds of the steadings have been converted to domestic use, and utterly beautiful they have become. It has been one of the extraordinary changes to Northumberland to have occurred in recent times.

In the early 1980s, when I was working in the area, only one set of farm buildings had been converted into cottages. It was at Brandon Farm near Wooler. Another farm at Glanton was converted in the middle of the 80s and that was it – but look at them now. The farm work has migrated into modern and more adaptable sheds; the old buildings have been brilliantly and imaginatively made into housing, holiday accommodation, industrial units, office centres, craft workshops, cheese shops – an extraordinary burgeoning of rural creativity married to architectural sensitivity. It has all been very exciting.

As well as the agricultural revolution that transformed the Northumberland landscape in the 18th and 19th centuries, there was another way that the great estates were providing houses for ordinary people … they were building estate villages.

Among the earliest was one on the Wallington estate. Sir Walter Blackett inherited the estate in 1727 and a bit after that (probably about 1745) he started to rebuild. He remodelled the big house and built some very nice and quite substantial houses for estate workers around the courtyard behind it, but a mile to the north, gorgeously placed on a ridge looking south over the valley of the Wansbeck, he built a proper village at Cambo – two terraces of single-storey cottages. He didn't quite start from scratch – there was already a church and an old defensible tower.

Interestingly he built simpler houses in Cambo than the two-storey houses he made for servants in the Wallington courtyard. Cambo, after all, is not right on the doorstep of the big house and part of the approach to it so it didn't need to make a statement or show off. Cambo was built for more practical reasons – it doesn't look like our modern preconceptions of one now, but what he built was a mining village. Cambo has been massively prettied up by later owners of Wallington, but at the start there was coal on the estate so he built plain single-storey cottages to house his miners.

Terraces of rather plain single-storey cottages are very common in the estate villages of Northumberland. Near Cambo is Capheaton where a simple village of single-storey cottages was built by the Swinburnes, probably about 1790, at the same time as they were extending their splendid Capheaton Hall.

The Capheaton cottages look terrific now. There's just a single row of them, facing south. They are solid, plain and dignified, but they hide a sneaky and interesting secret. Inside they have, or had, domed ceilings, like the underside of a bridge. They were vaulted like this, according to the historian John Hodgson who was vicar at nearby Kirkwhelpington, because originally they were built with arched roofs made of concrete! In 1790! Alas, the concrete wasn't sufficiently effective and has been replaced by more conventional pitched roofs now.

Lots of our estate villages from the first half of the 19th century are still dominated by long rows of simple one- and two-storey cottages, not unlike their forebears at Capheaton. Longhirst, Chatton and Denwick are three that spring to mind but there are many more. Acklington, Howick, Bilton and Rock are even more that spring to mind. They are all over the place, but this is not meant to be a criticism. I love them. We all love them. They're as popular now as when they were first built. The builders of these villages (architects like John Dobson, David Stephenson and John and Benjamin Green) continued, well into the 19th century to create strong and typical Northumbrian villages – not fancy but splendidly built in solid Northumbrian stone.

However, there are a few sets of estate buildings that break the mould and are less plain and more picturesque than the Northumbrian norm.

Right from the earliest days of North-Eastern cottage building , in the middle of the 1700s, the Lord Crewe Estate, which owned Blanchland as well as Bamburgh, converted the medieval buildings round the former outer court of the Abbey into an irregular L-shaped square (if that isn't too much of a contradiction in terms) of extremely picturesque cottages. They are like a dream nowadays, strong and simple but with a marvellous patina of age and inside they contain all sorts of ancient bits and pieces, fragments of their monastic past. They look entirely desirable but (like the buildings at Cambo) they were miners' cottages, for workers at the estate's lead mines.

Belsay is the other outlier in terms of style

There used to be an old village at Belsay. It was up near where the hall is now. Only one fragment of it still stands – Its medieval village cross survives though rather hidden behind some trees at the edge of the field in front of the castle. The rest has gone. Its eighteen houses were

alongside a road that used to pass in front of the castle. Its chapel now lies beneath the beautiful grassy knoll between the hall and the stable block. So old Belsay was a relatively substantial village.

It was also in the way.

Sir Charles Monck had come back from his 17-month honeymoon in 1807, full of plans to build himself a house and estate worthy of the stuff he'd seen in Germany and Italy and Greece and those plans clearly didn't include having eighteen neighbours spoiling the view so he rebuilt the village somewhere else – out of sight. To be fair he rebuilt everything else on his estate as well – every farm, boundary wall and outlying cottage ... but alongside all of this he created one of Northumberland's estate villages.

It's a good one. You all know that. It's built of the same glorious stone as the rest of the estate and it comprises one long row of two-storey cottages with a few outliers including a school (replaced by the very pretty present school in the 1870s) and an inn (a private house now). Single rows of cottages facing onto a road or a stream were a traditional layout for old Northumberland villages.

Lots of vanished medieval villages follow this pattern and it can still be seen in perfection at old places like Colwell on the A68, or nearby Great Bavington. But the Belsay row that Sir Charles built isn't traditional. It's modelled on the villages he had seen in southern Europe on his honeymoon. Arcades of splendidly irregular arches (as if they have grown up and been altered time and time again over the centuries) line the ground floor. Their function in Belsay is not clear. In their place of origin they protect the villagers from the pitiless heat of the noon-day sun but this is rarely a pressing need in Northumberland.

The function of the cottages themselves is a little complicated. They left Sir Charles free to clear the area round the hall, of course. They were an investment; better cottages meant better rent. They were somewhere to house the increasing numbers of workers and servants that a large 19th century estate needed. They were probably also a way to massage Sir Charles's philanthropic soul - improving the living standards of

Belsay village - still looking nice and, below, the estate village of Capheaton in 1955.

the workers was a common and laudable concern of the wealthy. All of these are reasons why Sir Charles built himself an estate village, but there was another reason - at least as important and probably more so. The real function of the new Belsay was to look nice - to satisfy the taste of their owner and provide an interesting talking point at the entrance to his estate.

I realise that I have provided an awfully hasty survey of the houses provided for the poor and the poor-ish in the 1700s and early 1800s and especially between about 1750 and 1830. The process was going to continue throughout the rest of the 19th century with a whole host of estate buildings in the prettiest of Arts-and-Crafts styles at one extreme and at the other the solidly workaday pit villages of south-west Northumberland, but those earlier houses, that period of 70 or 80 years after 1750 were a time of revolution in Northumberland, a revolution in social housing that improved the plight of the poorer inhabitants and enhanced the architectural character of the county as well.

I4. INDUSTRIAL AGE

My wife and I were in Santa Fe in New Mexico a few years ago as part of a trip around the Western states of America and we went into an art gallery which sold textiles because that is a subject dear to Mrs Grundy's heart. We bought a little piece of quilting and as we were paying, it dawned on the gallery owner that we had foreign accents so we admitted that we had come from England. He told us that he had recently had a three-week holiday in England, staying with an acquaintance who had invited him over.

"I don't know that you'd know it," he said, "It was near a town called Newcastle. Have you come across that town?"

We acknowledged that we knew it quite well.

"Well," he said, "it was near there. It was such a nice little place and I had such a good time."

"What was it called?" we said.

"Widdrington Station," he replied and we were amazed.

We were amazed because Widdrington Station isn't the sort of place that people normally enthuse about when they are describing Northumberland. It's a pleasant but fairly ordinary former pit village with a collection of quite attractive 20th century houses around a small station on the East Coast Main Line about half way between Morpeth and Warkworth. It lies in the SE quadrant of the county, towards the northern edge of the area that (before the pits all closed down) used to be the Great Northern Coalfield. It's an area that tends to get ignored by tourists and when people are writing about the beauties of the county; if you've been paying attention while reading this book you will have noticed that the whole of this area has also tended to get ignored by me so far; I've mentioned Tynemouth from time to time and Wallsend way back in the Roman past; Seaton Delaval and Seaton Sluice were briefly featured in the chapter on the 18th century but I think that's about all.

South of Alnwick and Warkworth a substantial triangular tract of the county between the sea and the A1 have been passed over, not only by this historian (if I have the temerity to call myself that) but by the vast majority of writers about the county ... and yet it was, and in many places remains full of the sort of beauties that we normally associate with Northumberland.

Widdrington Station and its near neighbour Stobswood are set in quiet but pleasant pastoral countryside on the Northumberland coastal plain. They are only a couple of miles from the sea, from Druridge Bay in fact, which is just as exciting as the more celebrated coastline further north – and a good deal quieter. The great sweep of Druridge Bay with its high dramatic dunes and the similar vista between Blyth and Seaton Sluice are magnificent coastal landscapes and inland there are plenty of things to admire. Widdrington,

Left, Woodhorn Pit, which is still standing, splendid and entire as a museum to the north of Ashington.

just north of Widdrington Station, has a fine 14th century church surrounded by old trees, while the church at Woodhorn, a few miles further south is even older, with all sorts of Anglo-Saxon bits and pieces built into it and lying about it.

Longhirst, near Morpeth, was once a pit village but it is also an excellent example of a typical Northumbrian estate village, built from the 1830s and 40s by the Lawson family whose home, Longhirst Hall, is probably the finest design of the great Tyneside architect, John Dobson. Nearby Bothal is another tremendous place with a splendid and complicated parish church, a fine 14th century castle, a satisfying group of estate houses and cottages and to cap it all, a beautiful location on the tree-lined banks of the River Wansbeck.

The Wansbeck, as it flows towards the sea between Stakeford and Ashington, is a good example of the surviving beauties of this overlooked area. Below Morpeth the river is tree-lined and unspoilt almost the whole way to the sea. After Bothal it passes the village of Sheepwash, which was described by the historian Aeneas Mackenzie in the early 19th century as being '*in a delightful situation on the Wansbeck surrounded by scenes as various as beautiful*'. That description still feels appropriate today and the river continues to be a joy as it passes the next village downstream, which Mackenzie described as '*a pleasant small village … it contains one good farmhouse and a few cottages*'.

Well, Ashington (because that's the place old Aeneas was talking about), is no longer *'a pleasant small village'*. It has turned into a solidly unpicturesque (but very characterful) town of about 28,000 people and you will know, I am sure, that the change was brought about by coal. The 58 people who lived there in 1841 were boosted by workers imported (many of them from Ireland) to work in the first pit opened close to the village in 1846 by the Duke of Portland, the lord of the manor. That first Ashington pit had an interesting name, perhaps descriptive, perhaps ironic, perhaps prophetic. It was called The Fell-em-Down Pit. The "em" that got felled were, of course, the trees and the natural beauty of the landscape, which became harder to spot as pit followed pit and spoil heaps proliferated.

Ashington alone got four new pits over the next few years, all run by the Ashington Coal Company, which, on its own, was responsible by the end of the century for an annual output of two and a half million tons of coal a year and by that time south east Northumberland had at least 61 pits and this area, this triangle forming the south east section of the county, was rapidly overlain by a totally new world – a world of coal.

Actually coal had been a feature of south east Northumberland for many centuries. The Romans had dug it, and coal stores have been identified in a number of the forts on the Wall. In the Middle Ages there were pits along the banks of the Tyne and all around Newcastle and by the 13th and 14th centuries the coal was being exported from Newcastle to places all up and down the east coast and beyond. Deliveries of Newcastle coal were recorded at Corfe Castle in Dorset; it was carried across the sea to the Low Countries and into the Baltic, but principally, and increasingly, it went to London where it was known as 'sea coal', probably because it was delivered to the city by boat. By the middle of the 1300s north-east coal was being exported to France as well but all of that was just the start …

… because, from the end of the Middle Ages, over the next 300 years, coal got more and more important. Timber, which was the only other stuff you could put on the fire, was getting rarer and more expensive as the forests were cut down and the countryside was increasingly turned over to farming, so the demand for coal grew and you know what happens when demand grows – businessmen emerge out of the woodwork to satisfy that demand.

In our case it was the businessmen of Newcastle who stepped into the breach (and made themselves fortunes at the same time). From Elizabethan times onwards, Newcastle's 'Hostmen', as they were called, created an environment in which they were the only people who were allowed to own the pits … or the collier boats that exported the coal … or the keelboats that delivered the coal to the larger sea-going boats; they

The underrated beauty of North Seaton Bridge, over the River Wansbeck near Ashington, and scenes from the beach at Blyth.

231

were the only people who were allowed to sell it or to make deals with merchants from outside of Tyneside who wanted to buy it. They controlled the whole caboodle in fact and over the centuries developed an insatiable desire to mine more and more of the stuff so they could sell more and more to make bigger and bigger profits …

… but there was a problem; it was getting harder to get the coal from the pit head to the market.

As the easily exploited coal along the coast and the river banks ran out, new seams were found further away from the water and it was hard, slow and expensive to move such heavy and bulky goods with horses and carts on the rubbish roads that they had in those days, so the industry was crying out for some more efficient way to improve the situation. Not to put too fine a point on it, what they needed (though they didn't yet know it) were railways.

Enter (stage left) Huntingdon Beaumont, an entrepreneur from Leicestershire who seems to have invented the idea of them. In 1603 he built a two-mile waggonway with wooden rails to transport coal from a mine at Wollaton near Nottingham down to the River Trent. This was probably the world's first railway. The second (and third) appeared three years later at Bedlington, our very own Bedlington, when the same man acquired mining rights on land near the river Blyth.

I have a friend who used to be a digger driver for an open-cast mining concern in South East Northumberland and he told me about removing the topsoil to uncover coal seams on land near Bedlington and coming across shallow workings, hundreds of years old; they had been bell pits he said, and you could clearly see where they had dug out the coal while leaving columns of coal every few metres to support the roof. These, he surmised, had included the coal workings acquired in 1606 by Huntingdon Beaumont and from which he built the waggonways to the river; the coal was transported downstream on boats to Blyth (or Cowpen) from where it was exported.

Huntingdon B had invented a system that would transform mining and ultimately the world … but not immediately because, sadly, he got the ideas right but

the business economics wrong and he went bust. His endeavours in Notts and in Northumberland both failed, leaving him with unmanageable debts. He died in a debtors' prison and nobody seems to be sure whether his Bedlington waggonways survived the crash or how long it was before others caught on, but they did eventually and by the early 1700s there were waggonways all over the coalfield, dozens and dozens of them.

The most famous have tended to be far away, in foreign lands – or County Durham as we call it, including the Tanfield Waggonway, which featured the magnificent Causey Arch, completed in 1727 and supposedly the widest single-arched bridge in the world when it was built. But Northumberland had many waggonways too, carrying waggons from deeply rural collieries to the rivers Blyth and Wansbeck and especially, of course, to the Tyne and Newcastle, which became the premier coal port in the kingdom and therefore in the world.

Visitors were astounded (and repelled) by it. They called it *'a world of coal'*, the '*Peru of the north*' because of the fabulous mineral wealth pouring out of it. They described the people with their '*carbonated physiognomies*' and their impenetrable accents. One posh ~~prat~~ visitor wrote that '*They speak very broad up here so that as one walks among the common people one would think oneself in a foreign country'*.

The waggonways became known as '*Newcastle Roads*'. On the flat the horses, assisted by the smoothness of the wooden rails, could haul far heavier loads than on traditional roads. On the many steep hills down into the river valleys, the horses were abandoned to trot along behind the trains while the waggons descended by gravity, each with a driver who stood on a great wooden brake to keep the enormous weight under control. As time went by, the heavy descending trucks were increasingly attached by ropes to empty trucks at the bottom, which they hauled back up the hill – the weight of the empty trucks acting as a counterbalance to the hurtling full ones.

From the 1780s, and perhaps earlier, some, at least, of the wooden rails were strengthened by cast-iron strips

Illustration from John Gibson's 'Plan of the Collieries on the Rivers Tyne and Wear' shows the waggonways taking the coal to the staiths.

fastened to the top, which not only helped them to last longer but made them smoother and more efficient to use. It was an increasingly sophisticated operation and as the 1700s turned into the 1800s a new and massively significant element was added to the mix – the world of coal was to be transformed by the introduction of steam power.

The early stages, the big initial inventions to do with steam, weren't made by North-Easterners.

Thomas Newcomen from Cornwall was the original pioneer. He was concerned with the problem of flooding in Cornish tin mines and, in 1712, came up with the world's first steam engine to pump the water out. His invention was big, hugely expensive to build and run, and relatively inefficient – but it worked far better than any other system that had been previously tried and eventually hundreds of them were built at mines all over the world.

Later in the 18th century the Scottish engineer James Watt improved Newcomen's design and towards the end of the century another Cornishman called Richard Trevithick was the first to attach a steam engine to a set of wheels and create a locomotive. Actually, he made a sort of car first of all and sent it up a hill all on its own and when it reached the top, to the wild applause of the spectators, it caught fire and exploded. But a couple of

year later he put his invention on a waggonway for a bet and it was able to pull 10 tons of iron and 70 passengers for 10 miles, the first recorded example of a working steam locomotive. He went on to design two or three more; one of them was built in Gateshead in 1806 and was intended to work at Wylam Colliery but there seems to be some confusion as to whether it ever went there, or if it did whether it ever worked and after that Richard Trevithick disappeared from the scene. He spiralled off into foreign parts, to South and Central America and was seen no more on these shores … which made space for our local chaps to pick up the baton and take the steam engine racing faster and ever faster down the line.

Old waggonways like this one at Wylam now provide attractive walking routes.

Local Chaps

There are many local chaps who should get a mention and some who will.

The first is Matthew Murray, who was born in Newcastle in 1765 and, like almost all of the other key players in the steamy game, had no formal education and no formal training as an engineer. He, like all the others, just found himself doing the job and got better and better at it under his own volition. He worked in textile mills in Newcastle and Darlington until he was driven by a recession to move to Leeds, where he worked for a famous flax spinner called John Marshall before setting up a company of his own as an engineer. In 1812 he designed a steam locomotive in the Trevithick mode (but better) to run on a waggonway at Middleton Colliery near Leeds. It worked, and is seen as the world's first commercially successful steam locomotive. It may well have been called the *Salamanca*.

Middleton Colliery deserves a special mention in this book because it was owned by John Charles Brandling, the latest head of an ancient family of Newcastle merchants who had been making fortunes from coal in the North East and beyond for hundreds of years. Their principal mansion was Gosforth House, built in the 1760s and still standing today as the basis of

A sketch of Gosforth Colliery by T.H.Hair.

the Newcastle Race Course grandstand. So, as a North East family it is no surprise that they employed local men to run and improve their businesses, and their man on the ground at Middleton was another self-taught Tynesider; he was called John Blenkinsop and he was from Felling (which is where the Brandling family originally came from) and he played an active part in the development of the Middleton railway.

Matthew Murray, following the lead provided by Richard Trevithick, was convinced that a locomotive with smooth wheels would get sufficient traction on metal rails to run efficiently, but John Blenkinsop was equally sure it wouldn't so he invented and patented a new system called a rack and pinion. It's the system still used on mountain railways like the line that goes up Snowdon and on lots of Alpine railways. It uses a cogged wheel (the pinion), which engages with a special toothed rail (called the rack) to drive the engine onwards. Blenkinsop was convinced that it would be much more efficient than the smooth rails and his patent was added to Murray's design.

Now, to bring the Northumbrian connection nearer to home (well at least, nearer to my home), one of John Charles Brandling's other pits happens to have been round the corner from my house in Gosforth. The Kenton and Coxlodge Colliery had two pits. One of them was at Kenton and the other, you will be surprised to hear, was at Coxlodge. The one nearest my house was called the Regent pit and the site where it stood is now the Regent Centre along with Gosforth Library and Gosforth Baths and so on. From it a waggonway ran down towards the Ouseburn and ultimately the Tyne via South Gosforth and in 1813 it was converted by Mr Brandling and his viewer, John Blenkinsop, into a steam-driven waggonway using one of Matthew Murray's engines, which had been modified by Blenkinsop's rack and pinion system. It opened on 2 September 1813, the North East's first successful venture into commercial steam transport. Among the crowd present at the opening was George Stephenson, of whom more later.

I don't know who else was there, but I strongly suspect that among the spectators was another mine owner called Christopher Blackett.

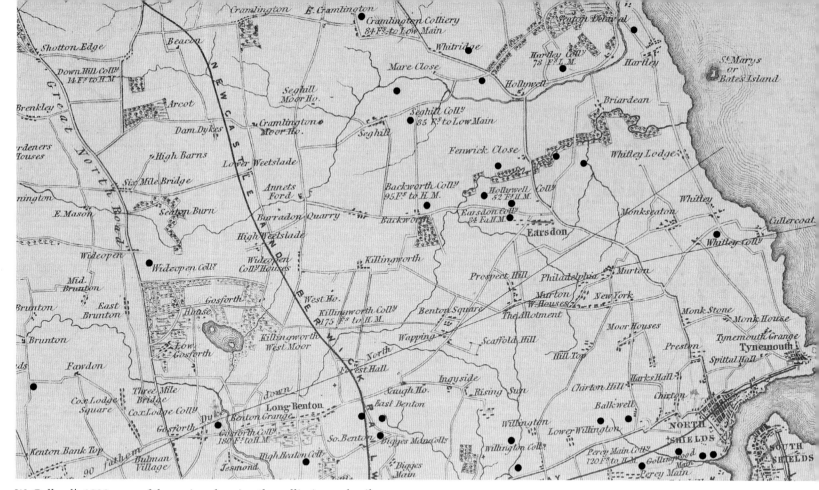

W. Collard's 1838 map of the region showing the collieries and railways.

Christopher Blackett was the owner of Wylam Colliery and a scion of another ancient family of Tyneside Merchants. If you were to use your fingers and toes to keep a record of how many times Blacketts had been Mayors of Newcastle you would have run out of digits before the end. He was a relative of Sir Walter Blackett who featured so heavily in an earlier chapter at 18th century Wallington.

Round about 1806, when such things were still distant gleams in the eyes of most mine owners, he had taken the bold step to buy a locomotive off Richard Trevithick and when that move failed to pay off, for whatever reason, he didn't give up but encouraged his workmen to develop ideas of their own.

The employees included two of the key names in the development of steam, two key names in the whole history of the Industrial Revolution. William Hedley was his viewer, his colliery engineer, and Timothy Hackworth

his colliery blacksmith and together (along with a few of the chaps of course) they designed and built what are now the oldest and second oldest surviving steam locomotives in the world.

The oldest is also probably the most famous. It is affectionately known as Puffing Billy and it is now on display at the Science Museum in London. It was completed and in use by 1813 so must have been in active preparation at the same time as Matthew Murray's engines were appearing at Middleton and Gosforth and the reason I guessed that Christopher Blackett might have been at the launch in Gosforth in September 1813 is that he is known to have been keenly interested in the question of whether the rack and pinion method of propulsion was necessary.

His house in Wylam is called Wylam Hall and it stands just above the colliery site. A short but steepish drive leads up to it from the road through the village and

the story is that an experimental section of track made of cast iron was laid on the drive to test whether the new Wylam locomotive could manage the gradient with its smooth wheels. It obviously could because that was what it got and all the subsequent locomotives made in the North East (and the rest of the world) in the years after 1813 were made with smooth wheels on smooth rails. John Blenkinsop's patent has continued to be used in places (like mountains) with extreme gradients but for all other places smooth wheels on smooth rails gave sufficient traction.

Before I move on, there are a couple of other things about Puffing Billy I would like to say. The first is that it puffed. Now you will say, wearily, that all steam engines puffed but there's more to it than that. Beamish Museum acquired the complete drawings of the engine a few years ago and built a replica of it exactly to the specifications of the original and blow me, when they fired it up it didn't steam, it puffed in a quite distinctive way. So there.

The other thing about this engine (and Wylam Dilly, which followed it, and the engines built in the next couple of years by George Stephenson at Killingworth) is that they were all built on site, by untrained colliery workers, blacksmiths and enginewrights in rough and ordinary sheds in the colliery yard.

When I was listing the buildings of Wylam in the 1980s the colliery's blacksmith's shop was still standing in its original form, being used as a car repair shop by men in oily overalls. It still had the greasy and untidy look that it must have had in 1813. People who repair cars are like gods to me, casual users of mysteries so far beyond my level of technical skill, but the idea of designing, building and modifying a complex engine in a shed behind the cottages, in a world that, up to that moment, had been dominated by horses and carts, fills me with even more stunned admiration. They were amazing; they were like today's teenagers mastering their mobile phones and you can't say fairer than that. And they were just doing their job. They were just trying to get Wylam's coal to the ships a bit quicker and a bit cheaper; they just wanted to make their colliery economically viable. Such clever men.

So, by the early decades of the 19th century, at least one of the problems that confronted the mining industry had been effectively tackled; the improved transport links brought about by waggonways and later by steam engines and locomotives meant that coal found almost anywhere in the area could be got to the ships at a reasonable cost …

… which brings me back to those 61 pits and the transformation of the south-east corner of Northumberland.

Some of them had existed since the 18th century or even earlier. There was clearly coal being dug at Bedlington when Huntingdon Beaumont laid his early waggonways in 1605, the original Wylam waggonway was laid in 1748, for example, and the pit was in existence long before that improvement was made; but the growth of the waggonway network allowed more and more to join them during the 18th century and many others were sunk in a period of adventurous expansion in the first quarter of the 19th century. Coxlodge and the other pits near my house in Gosforth fell into that category including the one I haven't mentioned yet, the South Gosforth Colliery, which was sunk in a pretty part of the Ouseburn Valley in 1825.

The coal at South Gosforth turned out to be quite easy to reach because it wasn't far below ground level but very soon after they started digging, it became clear that

North Warbottle Colliery.

there were going to be major difficulties because they were faced with ***The Main Dike***, a fault line in the underlying geology of south-east Northumberland where the coal seam was broken in two by a massive crack or slip so the coal disappeared and was only to be found hundreds of feet deeper down. It took four years to overcome this problem so the pit was unproductive until 1829 when engineers finally managed to sink shafts down to the deeper seam.

The owners (the Brandlings inevitably) were well pleased when they made the breakthrough and on 31 January that year they held an underground party 1,100 feet below the ground in an L-shaped ballroom, 15 feet wide and lit by lamps and candles. Ladies and Gentlemen and pitmen and their wives were lowered down the shaft in baskets and at 9.30 in the morning the event kicked off. There was a feast with cold punch and plentiful drafts of malt liquor and at 3.00 they started dancing to music provided by the Coxlodge Brass Band before everyone hewed themselves a commemorative lump of coal and they were hauled back up in the baskets. An inscribed stone in the parish church graveyard marks the site of the main dike and records this event (the rave in the grave, perhaps).

That story reveals a sort of Klondike-like enthusiasm for the expansion of the coalfield and the names of some other pits reveal a similar excitement. The "Fell-em-Down" pit at Ashington is just one of the new pits given 'up-and-at-em' names. 'Wideopen' is another. Like South Gosforth its shaft was also sunk in 1825 with the first coal being won in 1827. Nobody (that I can find) has recorded where the name came from, but it has an ironic tone that suggests endless possibilities.

There's a farm in the county from about the same time called Makemerich and a small colliery settlement near Beamish called No Place. Wideopen, as a name, has a similar feel and a slightly tongue-in-cheek tone. The name suggests that anything could happen there. At other places the names are remorselessly prosaic. Holywell had three pits and they were called A pit, B pit and C pit. Others were more personalised and took on the family name of the owners (the Brandling Pit at Coxlodge, for example) or were named after family members (South Gosforth had a Mary Pit and a Fanny Pit).

Occasionally the names reveal when they were opened. Walbottle Colliery had two new pits opened in 1815, the year after the Battle of Waterloo. One (predictably) was called the Wellington Pit; the other was named the Blucher Pit to commemorate the Prussian military leader whose forced march and timely arrival at the battle with 45,000 troops saved Wellington's day and made him a hero in England.

Bomarsund Pit (and village) between Bedlington and Ashington commemorates a different date and a different war. It recalls a battle in the Crimean War, but not, I was totally surprised to discover, not in the Crimea but in the Baltic where a Russian Fort was taken by a combined Anglo/French force in 1854 – the date that the colliery was sunk. Who knew that the Crimean War had spread out to other areas of Europe? Not me.

But whatever their names, the pits have all gone now – apart from one. They still exist in the virtual world, of course, in hundreds of thousands of splendid old photographs and in the wonderful drawings done by Thomas Hair in the first half of the 1800s but the only actual complete survivor is the Ashington Coal Company's Woodhorn Pit, which is still standing, splendid and entire as a museum to the north of Ashington.

It was the last one built; it was begun in 1895 and is perfectly preserved with two shafts, complete with their winding gear and a bewildering range of ancillary buildings. If it was *my* museum I would personally make it a bit grubbier as would befit its grimy industrial origins, but it is still a marvellously complete vision of what these places looked like in their heyday. Elsewhere in the area there are a few fragments of collieries, ruined early modernist baths and offices at Cambois and some bits and pieces of Weetslade Colliery near Wideopen.

There are probably others but not much because when the pits closed, the urgent need seems to have been to clear all vestiges of the coalfield away, to sweep it out of view. Some of the sites still exist, often reused as modern industrial estates and sometimes cleared and re-purposed as country parks or as new housing estates.

They have become useful to us in myriad new ways, cleaner than they used to be but still valuable to us, but back then they were there in all their untidy bulk, increasingly ubiquitous in the landscape, vast, dirty and noisy, belching out smoke…

And beside each of them there were brand new villages. By definition they were Northumbrian villages – but not as we know them (Scotty). There was nothing pretty or picturesque about the new villages of the 19th century coalfield – no Tudor frills or carefully worked local stone like I was describing in that earlier chapter about ordinary people's housing in more rural parts of the county. None of the new colliery villages are carefully or tastefully placed to take advantage of the landscape. They are all (I think this is true) made up of rows and rows of completely plain brick terraces, often two storeys high at the front with long sloping roofs so that they are just a single storey at the back. There's very little variation other than the number and length of the rows. They range from Ashington, (the biggest pit village in the world as they used to say) which has innumerable, immensely long rows, to the three tiny little streets on the edge of the sea at North Blyth. The size of the settlements change but the style and layout don't.

All of the surviving houses in all of the pit villages were built or rebuilt from the 1850s, or more commonly the 1870s onwards. They were built (usually as cheaply as possible) by the colliery owners and it's very difficult to find out what miners' settlements had been like before the rebuilding took place. A few examples might suggest that the arrangement was quite different.

George Stephenson was born into a poor mining family who lived in an isolated cottage by the side of Wylam waggonway; the Blackett family of Wallington (as we saw in a previous chapter) built a row of single-storey cottages for miners at the village of Cambo; lead miners in the hills above Alston lived in isolated farmsteads and walked to work or lived in communal "shops" at the mines during the week; at North Seaton colliery, where the shaft was sunk in 1859, the first houses were described as being "two rows of wooden houses with outside staircases". I can't imagine what those looked like.

Northumberland miners and their families. Life lived in close proximity to the pit was often difficult and the housing conditions were poor, however this could often foster a strong community spirit.

So there aren't many clues as to what had gone before, and the new pattern just seems to have descended everywhere in its completed form – and that form, even today when we are used to such things, looks rigid and alien when seen in maps and later aerial photographs. The short, sharp, hard-edged profiles of the villages clearly contrasted (and still do) with the older landscape all around and people (especially outsiders) didn't like what was on offer. Reports in the local papers about Dudley and Holywell in the 1870s reveal the disapproval. One article stresses first of all that Holywell is built in '*a lovely dene with a noisy stream dashing over its rocky bed*' but the new village itself is '*by no means a clean place*'. It has '*a want of drainage and a deficiency of sanitary arrangements*'. '*There are no privies or ashpits*'. the writer says rather worryingly '*so behind the houses there are rather more than usual of those sights and smells so injurious alike to social morality and public health.*'

Rather grudgingly, the journalist writing about Dudley in 1874 acknowledges that it looks nicer in summer than it had done earlier in the year but still contrasts the beauty of the surrounding fields with '*the greyness of a pit village*'. His disapproval goes further and includes the houses themselves and the facilities on offer. He stresses how small they were. They only had two rooms each, a large kitchen on the ground floor and '*a cold dismal garret above*'.

Descriptions of the houses in lots of places mention the dangers involved in using the upstairs garret because it could only be reached by a ladder and a hole in the floor through which people fell, fairly regularly it seems. The Dudley report says that the houses are '*too small for men with large or moderate families, for the day has now gone when two small rooms are enough for a mixed family to bring up their sons and daughters*'.

At Coxlodge one man recalls his granny sleeping in a bed under the stairs and even in the relatively luxurious accommodation of the pit cottages rebuilt in Beamish, which each had two rooms on the ground floor, there is often a double bed in the living room. Younger children tended to sleep upstairs while the older ones bedded down in the kitchen. People were probably used to it but it can't have been nice.

I can recall having to sleep head to toe when I shared beds with my older cousins when I was little and they were lovely big boys and I was relatively tiny but I can't imagine what it would have been like to do that through my teenage years. People worried about the morality of it too if there were boys and girls. At least one of the workhouses in the county was established because the local vicar was concerned about brothers and sisters sharing the same space and even the same bed.

And then there were the baths, of course, the tin (or zinc) baths in front of the fire, filled with water heated on the range. You'll have seen that famous (restaged) photo from the Beamish collection of the miner scrunched up in his little black underpants while his missus tops up the bath with a jug of water and his modesty is preserved by the clouds of steam. Well, everybody in the family had to bathe like that because there were no bathrooms and no running water. I was told a story by a retired miner from Blyth. He had dated a girl from Cambois on the north side of the harbour and on the first date he went back to meet her family. He was chatting to her dad and it had gone really well until she started to get out the bath and fill it with water, clearly intending to use it herself. He got uneasy and was eager to leave but her father said,

"What's troubling you son?"

"Well she's going to have a bath".

"Diven't fash yerself, lad," her father said, "she'll niver wet you".

So, the evidence is that they were quite harsh places. And yet … there's one photograph that I've seen that shows the back lane of a street called Doctor Row, which was one of the streets attached to the Doctor Pit in Bedlington; It was built in 1874 and I think it was demolished in about 1988 after the pit was closed. To be honest, it's a beautiful picture in a strange sort of way.

The back of the houses are single-storey and each one has a big water barrel attached to the down pipe from the roof, to collect water that could be used for washing, The toilets (the netties) are on the opposite side of the lane and at the end of the row there was a cess pool where the contents were emptied periodically.

There was no drinking water, not at first, though piped water was brought into the street (but not into the houses) a few years later. Initially somebody had to be sent down to a tap at the pit at the end of the street to bring back drinking water. The lane itself is unmade up and reportedly became a quagmire in bad weather.

Another picture that I saw on the internet showed the 'front' of the row. I put the word 'front' in inverted commas because it looks as if the front was rarely, if ever, used. It looks so bleak and unloved, but the back lane, by contrast, is full of life, despite the squalor. People are chatting at their back doors, children are playing, a little girl has a toy pram. It looks ancient, this picture, but there are telegraph poles along the side of the lane. There seems to be a standpipe halfway along the row and there's a delivery van in the distance so the picture must have been taken in the 20th century and provides evidence of how long it took for living conditions to really change …

… but above all, it provides evidence that the communities who lived in these inadequate environments were able to rise above them with energy and creativity in ways that … well, in ways that can seem romanticised if you're cynical about them but don't seem like that to me. The photograph reveals the rich street life and the vibrant sense of community that existed even in the back lanes. I've got a back lane behind my house and nowadays it has been reduced to a place to put out the bins on a Tuesday night and somewhere for workmen in so many neighbouring houses to park their white vans and the skips for their rubbish, but in Doctor Row and all the other back lanes it wasn't like that at all. There was washing to hang out and cricket to play, back walls to climb. One elderly lady told me a few years ago that she blamed the social evils of the modern world on the changes in the back lanes and in particular to the way that coal sheds and netties had been demolished…

"The problem is, Mr Grundy," she said, "the bairns have got nowt to dee nowadays. In the past they could gan netty lowping."

The sense of pit village community wasn't only to be found in the back lane, of course, it showed itself clearly in all sorts of other ways. It was present in the new schools that began to appear from the late 1830s onwards. It was to be found in the welcoming pubs on the street corners and in the chapels that were dotted all around the villages. Often the miners raised the money for the chapels themselves and they often provided the labour to build them as well. Because they aren't usually

Allotments in Ashington.

surrounded by large grounds like C of E churches and because they don't have to point east and can be built as part of rows of other buildings, and above all because they tend to be quite simple and ordinary buildings, the nonconformist chapels in industrial villages don't tend to get noticed but they are (or were) all over the place.

Fifty years later, I was brought up in a world of chapels like you find in Northumbrian pit villages. My mother used to give Mother's Union talks and I would go with her after my father died so I became an aficionado of simple little chapels, each with a cast iron stove at the rear, a high central pulpit and simple varnished pews filled with people gazing up at the speaker. I used to eat the pews. I acquired a taste for the softened varnish and the wood beneath it and I left my teeth marks in chapels all over the place.

My Auntie Bessie used to play the harmonium energetically in such places, pumping vigorously on the pedals until her dress hem rode up and revealed her underwear, a most unwelcome sight. My uncle George and my uncle Norman were both chapel enthusiasts and their loud "Amens" punctuated all the prayers in a way that was torture to the little Grundy. All of my experience of such places happened in Cumberland, but I am entirely satisfied that is was part of the life of the Northumberland coalfield as well.

Photographs of Doctor Row and lots of other places reveal that behind the netties there were long gardens in which extraordinary veg could be grown. I remember filming such a garden once and there were leeks like tree trunks and onions like cannonballs, I said to the man, "Are you going to take them to the show?" but he said, "No, those are the ones that weren't good enough". There seems to me to be something deeply meaningful in the way that miners and those who spent their working lives deep in the darkness below ground could show such passion for the outdoors, for gardens and river banks. They kept whippets and took them for walks and set them racing against other dogs; they spent long hours trapping eels in the Blyth and the Wansbeck. They kept pigeons and watched them fly.

Leek clubs, bowls clubs, allotments, chapels and pubs and later on the extraordinary riches of the Miners' Welfares, which provided sporting possibilities in everything from football to golf: these were the things carved out by the coalfield communities and they shouldn't be underestimated. There was also a richness in the language they used, the "pitmatic" dialect that characterised the coalfield and which left those from outside floundering to keep up. My friend Normie, who comes from Ellington, told me the one about the man who had been injured and off work. He met a friend, who said,

"Are you ready to go back to work?"

"Work", he said, "I can hardly waak".

'Work' in that sentence rhymes with 'fork' while 'waak' rhymes with 'park. You should try it out loud (when you've checked to see that nobody's listening) and if you're still puzzled you should know that, as Normie put it, "Work is what ye dee; waak is where you gan". I hope that helps.

———————

You'll have noticed that in the stuff that I've written above about the life of the pit villages I've oscillated like a tennis ball between opposite points of view. Sometimes I seem to be saying it was hard going; sometimes I have been praising its energy and community spirit. Does the man not know which it was, you must be asking. No, is the answer and wherever you look you get different points of view and you always have.

One early commentator and visitor to the coalfield was William Cobbett, who came on a tour up North in 1832 and was impressed. He was from Surrey where, at that time, an agricultural worker was likely to be earning 7 or 8 shillings a week. This is what he wrote about the North East: '*The pitmen have 24s a week; they live rent free, their fuel costs them nothing, and their doctor costs them nothing. Their work is terrible to be sure and perhaps they do not have what they ought to have; but at any rate they live well, their houses are good and their furniture good; and though they live not in a beautiful scene, they are in the scene where they were born and their lives seem to be as good as that of the working part of mankind can reasonably expect.*'

Hm! Sounds good … but was it true? Some writers nowadays cast doubt on the comparatively high wages described by William Cobbett. They claim that mining families were only better off than other labourers if they sent the children to work in the mine as well as the adults.

As it happens, in that very year, in 1832, the pitmen of Northumberland (and Durham) were on strike, just like they had been the previous year and just like they were going to be quite regularly for the rest of the century. They had won the strike the previous year and among the concessions they had wrung out of the owners was that they should be paid in cash and not in tokens, which they were forced to exchange for food at the company shop. Another change was that boys working underground could only work for 12 hours a day instead of the 17 or 18 hours they were currently required to do.

But in 1832 the miners lost and when the strike was over the owners were in control and they refused to re-employ active supporters of the union and over the next few years they systematically reduced the miners' wages

The next strike after 1832 was one of the really biggies. It occurred in 1844 and it was brought on because the miners wanted a list of quite specific changes to their working conditions:
- They wanted the Government to examine the safety of mines because they had "by sad and manifold experience been subject to frequent disastrous explosions of gas".
- They wanted Inspectors of Mines just like the Factory Inspectors there were now.
- They wanted a ban on iron ropes for lowering men in and out of the pit.
- They wanted accurate weighing machines so a man could be paid properly for what he had done.
- They wanted weekly wages.

These all seemed reasonable requests (and they were submitted to the owners in a very polite and reasonable tone) but they were ignored and the strike became a bitter catastrophe. There were mass evictions all over the coalfield. The police arrived with a ragtag army of unemployed men to forcibly remove people from their houses. They were called "candymen" and they were hated. During one of the later strikes in County Durham, songwriter Tommy Armstrong wrote, with immense bitterness: '*The miners of south Medomsley they're going to make some stew. They're going to boil fat Postick and his dirty candy crew.*'

The pregnant, the blind, the aged, families of small children, everybody was cast out into the street and their possessions too. There were far too many of them for alternative lodgings to be found so they lived by the roadside all around the villages for weeks and weeks. Meanwhile, blacklegs were brought in. They were recruited in Cornwall and Ireland and wherever there were unemployed men; they too were hated passionately. There were riots between evicted men and the blacklegs all over the place – at Delaval, Dudley, Holywell, Seghill and Stannington for example and awful retributions took place. Here's a song about what happened

The Blackleg Miner

'Tis in the evening after dark
When the blackleg miner creeps to work
With his moleskin pants and his dirty short
There goes the blackleg miner

O Delaval is a terrible place
They rub wet clay in a blackleg's face
And round the heaps they run a race
To catch the blackleg miner

And divvent go near the Seghill mine
Across the way they stretch a line
To catch the throat and break the spine
Of the dirty blackleg miner

They grab his duds and his picks as well
And they hoy them doon the pit of hell
Down you go and fare you well
You dirty blackleg miner

So join the union while you may
Don't wait until your dying day
For that may not be far away
You dirty Blackleg miner

So life in the colliery districts was a strange melange of vibrant community and bitter strife and however much the community's spirit brought to coal-mining world, it was still a hard life; it was still a dark, dirty, frightening and dangerous life.

The danger was ever-present.

Early in this period, before steam-driven cages had been invented to get men into the mine, you could die before you even got to work. The only way down the shaft to the coalface was to hang from a rope, the same rope that hauled the baskets of hewn coal to the surface. You just had to hang on to the rope and hope you didn't let go or that you wouldn't be knocked off by a basket coming in the opposite direction.

But if you survived that constant danger there were plenty of other ways to die in the mine itself and all of them worked with grim efficiency and regularity. You could be drowned by a sudden influx of water like the 40 men and 30 boys who drowned when the pit in Heaton flooded in 1815. You could be crushed by a pony or a runaway wagon, buried by an unexpected roof fall, miss your footing and fall down the shaft or reach for the rope and misjudge the distance. You could get off the cage too early or you could be crushed beneath it at the foot of the shaft.

Each of these unexpected but effective accidents happened quite often; all of them were recorded at the Seghill pit, for example, where 107 men and boys aged from 12 to 70 died in the course of the 19th century; but it was the same in almost all the other pits as well. The problem was that the work environment and all the things you worked with were dangerous so there were always new and unexpectedly hideous ways to die – like 15-year old John Ternent, from Delaval pit, who stole a stick of dynamite, hid it in a piece of lead piping which he shoved down his trousers where it was ignited by a spark from his own safety lamp!

Seghill was also one of the many pits in which whole groups of men were killed in an explosion. It wasn't one of the worst disasters. It occurred in 1864 and left seven dead, which was relatively few by coalfield standards, but I don't suppose that was any comfort to the families of those who died.

Just a few of the other pits that experienced multiple deaths in explosions included:

Killingworth where in 1806 and 1809 a total of 18 men died
Wallsend, 1821 (52 died)
Willington, 1841 (32 died)
Burradon, 1846 (76 died)

The problem in all of these places was gas.

They knew all about gas in north east mines and had learnt to recognise all sorts of different ones. (For some reason they were all called "damps" from the German word "dampf", which meant a vapour). There was methane or **firedamp,** which was explosive and could kill you that way. **Blackdamp** was carbon dioxide, which didn't explode but killed you by suffocation. **Stinkdamp** was hydrogen sulphide, which smelt of

Monument celebrating George Stephenson in Newcastle.

rotten eggs so at least you knew it was coming unlike **whitedamp** (or carbon monoxide) which kills almost instantly but has no smell at all (which is why they carried canaries in mines, because if the hypersensitive canary died or showed signs of distress it was a warning to the miners to get quickly out of the way).

The gasses were trapped in fissures in the rock and could seep out and fill cavities in the galleries, waiting for an accident to happen, or they could be released suddenly and catastrophically in the course of digging away the coal and exposing trapped pockets of gas behind it.

There were a number of things they did to try to avoid gas explosions in the first half of the 1800s. One of them was to deliberately set fire to small escapes of gas before they had a chance to build up to more dangerous levels. This was the responsibility of the Firemen in the pit, who did a job that you and I would definitely not want to do. I can say that with absolute confidence. Being a colliery fireman could be classified as one of the least desirable job of all time. When firedamp had been detected, the fireman's job was to approach the source of the gas with a candle on the end of a stick and deliberately set fire to it. The fireman would lie down as he did this in the hope that the subsequent flash would pass over his head. Then he would stand up as quickly as possible and make a run for it because it was known that suffocating blackdamp would rush in and fill the ensuing vacuum!

George Stephenson's dad was a fireman at Wylam Pit. Remember that for a minute or two.

George Stephenson was born in Wylam. He was born in 1781 in a cottage that fronted onto the Wylam wagonway, which was to become so important in the pursuit of steam. His childhood home is usually described as "a humble cottage" but to be honest it seems pretty nice to me. I suspect that there are awful lot of working-class families nowadays who would still see it as a very desirable property (and lots of middle-class ones who would snap it up as a second home). But the Stephensons weren't a well-off family. Dad's dangerous but fairly lowly position at Wylam Colliery meant they couldn't afford for George to go to school, which should have been a disadvantage to him but in terms of the life he was going to lead, it's probable that the lessons he needed to learn were passing day and night in front of his garden; from the beginning, his life must have been dominated by coal and railways, by his father's job and the constant traffic along the waggonway in front of his garden, and by the experiments that were going on in the village along the line.

When he was 17, he started work in a pit, still illiterate but determined to improve himself. He went to night school, moved jobs two or three times, got married, became a father and then (tragically early) a widower. He got a job as a brakeman at Killingworth Colliery in about 1804 then moved to Scotland for a few months before coming back to Killingworth, where he was working when the two gas explosions occurred in 1806 and 1809. He was still there in 1811 when the pit was having a bit of bother with its Newcomen pumping engine – and that's when it all changed for George.

He volunteered to work on the engine and give it a bit of a seeing to and did such a good job that he was promoted to the key position of enginewright for the colliery. It was a big step up and over the next few years he did some pretty sensational things with the job. He surveyed and laid out a new waggonway from Killingworth down to Whitehill Point on the Tyne and he designed a whole heap of new locomotives of his own.

These were all extraordinary achievements for an uneducated and self-taught man, but if his subsequent reputation had depended entirely on the work he did at Killingworth he wouldn't have ended up as the household name he became; he would have just been one of the lads. Lots of other people had created waggonways and there were lots of other engine designers and, if I am to believe people who understand these things better than me (which is almost everybody to be honest), there was nothing startlingly advanced about his designs. He was a good solid and reliable engineer at a time when the North East was thronging with such men … but little Geordie from Wylam had only just begun.

His next achievement seemed to come out of

absolutely nowhere.

In the wake of the Felling pit disaster he designed a miners' safety lamp.

The Felling Pit Disaster of 1812 killed 92 men and boys in a particularly horrifying explosion. Of course all pit disasters are horrifying and devastating for the local community but the impact of the Felling disaster was amplified by the local vicar at Heworth Church, who was the same John Hodgson who has featured heavily in this book as one of Northumberland's greatest historians. His presence in the aftermath of the explosion made it a matter of national concern and principally among the things that happened was that there was a competition to create a lamp that would be safe for miners to use in the pit. There was a substantial reward on offer for a successful design.

By 1815 there were three contenders for the prize. One was designed by a Sunderland surgeon called Doctor Glanny but it didn't really work (though he was to go on and create much more successful versions in the years to come); the others were by George Stephenson, ordinary, uneducated little local chap from Killingworth on the one hand, and on the other, famous, internationally renowned chemist and member of the Royal Society, Humphrey Davy. Both of their lamps worked in similar ways though both had flaws as well. Both were to go on and become widely used in real pits for the next century and more. So, go on, have a guess whose design won the Rumford Medal awarded for an *'outstandingly important recent discovery in the field of thermal matter … by a scientist working in Europe'*. Who got a prize of £1000 from the Royal Society and a further £2000 from the colliery owners of Great Britain? And which designer was offered a relatively measly 100 guineas by way of a consolation prize?

Clue: the winner didn't live in Killingworth.

Despite being the winner, Humphrey Davy remained dissatisfied and convinced that George had somehow stolen his design and throughout the rest of his life he remained adamant that it was impossible for an untutored mechanic with a Geordie accent to have mastered the complexities and the chemistry needed to produce the goods on his own. That was an attitude that

The Felling Pit Disaster is remembered at St Mary's, Heworth.

Stephenson was going to have to face almost for the rest of his career. In later years, when he was summoned to Parliament to answer questions on his plan for the Manchester and Liverpool Railway, the story is that they needed to send for a translator so they could understand him.

And, of course, the prejudice went deeper than mockery of his dialect; there was also, as happened with Humphry Davy, an assumption that because he had a local accent he was thick. Barristers and even fellow engineers who were part of the establishment, but who lacked his vision and self-confidence, men like Francis Giles and John Rennie, mocked him unmercifully. When he suggested that it was possible to provide a safe route for the railway over a bog called Chat Moss, he was described as *'stupid and incredulous'* and *'possessing ignorance almost inconceivable'*. He was dismissed and replaced as engineer to the company, but they had to bring him back and he was proved right; his scheme worked as so many of his other schemes did too.

The week I'm writing this (in October 2020) there has been a series of stories in the press about the difficulties experienced by local students with regional accents at illustrious universities. Durham University was one where only about 8% of the student population was from the North East and fewer still from working-class backgrounds and with local voices. Those students were complaining of the almost relentless prejudice they suffered from other students and tutors …

… but I have leapt onto my hobby horse and I am getting ahead of myself. George Stephenson's career as a creator of railways and the butt of national mockery was still in the future, but in 1815 the doubts about his ability and the prejudice about his humble origins meant that he didn't win the prize. However, there is lots of evidence that Humphrey Davy was wrong and that Stephenson *was* capable of coming up with the design himself:

– He had already demonstrated his lamp to an audience at the Newcastle Lit and Phil before Davy's lamp was finished.

– There's clear evidence that he showed extraordinary courage in personally testing his design on real escaping gas in a real mine.

– His father was a fireman at Wylam pit. When your dad's done stuff like that you are likely to understand the principles involved.

– He had direct experience of explosions. He was at Killingworth in 1806 and 1809 when that pit suffered two explosions that killed a total of 18 men.

- He was an engineer and knew about making stuff.

He knew what leaked and what didn't. He knew about the movement and the control of gases because otherwise his engines would never have worked.

It is, in fact, absurd to suggest he couldn't have done it. He had probably been thinking about it for half his life. I assume he turned up at the original meeting because he knew he was the man to solve the problem.

The single slightly nice thing about this story is that

though he was rejected for the prize by the national scientific and mining community, his contribution was recognised locally and the mine owners of the North East made a special award of 1000 guineas. Actually 1000 guineas was worth more than a bob or two in those days so it wasn't a "slightly" nice thing but a life changing accolade and it was to the credit of our community that they recognised his worth.

––––––––––––

Anyway, with a new safety lamp increasingly available in the years after 1815, you might have hoped that the danger of explosion would have faded away, but there are two reasons why that didn't happen.

Firstly neither lamp was perfect; both had weaknesses and both could still give rise to disasters.

Secondly the existence of a safety lamp gave some mine owners the excuse to ignore other safety measures, and in particular some neglected to provide a second shaft for their pits.

For years it had been known that the main protection from gas was to keep the pits well ventilated and the way to do that was to have two shafts in each pit with one of them being a ventilation shaft. A fire would be kept burning at the bottom of that shaft or suspended in a metal basket towards the bottom so that, on the principal that hot air rises, the shaft would act like a chimney, expelling hot air and drawing fresh clean air down the other shaft. It was a clever idea and usually worked – providing the mine wasn't owned by an employer who omitted to provide the second shaft.

In 1862, New Hartley Colliery only had one shaft but it was divided in two by a timber and iron screen called a brattice so that one half of the shaft acted as the ventilation shaft, with the other half providing the fresh air. It was still a common arrangement in North-East pits, though after the disaster at Burradon in 1846 there had been calls for the practice to be changed but nothing had happened.

What happened at New Hartley on 16 January was that the pumping engine beam at the top of the shaft snapped, sending vast amounts of debris crashing

Memorial Garden at the former Hester Pit of New Hartley Colliery.

down, initially onto the cage, which was ascending at the time with eight men in it; five died instantly and three were eventually rescued. These were the only men to be rescued because the fall blocked the single shaft completely and the 199 men still below all died, despite desperate and frequently heroic attempts to reach them.

For a couple of days, because there had been no explosion, there were hopes that there might be survivors below the blocked shaft, but when the rescuers finally broke through they were met with foul and noxious vapours. As I've just said, pits contained rich concoctions of gases and a terribly varied number of ways to kill, so with no second shaft to dissipate the gas, the miners in New Hartley gradually suffocated as poisonous levels of blackdamp built up. Even when the rescuers broke through is was still far too dangerous to

enter and it was several days before the full horror was exposed. They found men cradling the bodies of their sons and brothers huddled together in death; a note scribbled on a crumpled sheet of newspaper recorded a last prayer meeting but everywhere the ugliness of death was made even worse because the bodies had lain for days in the heat of the mine. It doesn't bear thinking about.

On the surface the effect was as dreadful as you can imagine; grief and anger were mingled and interchangeable. To protect families from the grotesqueness of death in such circumstances, wherever possible the bodies were identified by surface workers who knew them and were put in coffins without being seen by their loved ones.

But the coffins were then taken home and the local paper recorded how in every cottage in the village you could see coffins through the windows and open doors. Sometimes they were resting on the bed; sometimes the bed wasn't enough and there were other coffins on the chairs beside it and, in at least one cottage, coffins were piled as high as the ceiling. All 204 bodies were buried in a mass funeral at Earsdon church with the graves dug by the colliers from the neighbouring Delaval Colliery. They included the bodies of four 10-year olds, five who were 11, six boys of 12 and, at the other end of the scale, one

71-year old man. A monument, paid for by public subscription, recorded the names of all who had died and following the inquest and a public enquiry it became law that all pits had to have two shafts so that there always had to be two ways to escape.

I started this chapter recording my surprise that an American visitor could take pleasure in the village of Widdrington Station and the ignored south west of the county, a relatively forgotten landscape of ex-mining villages, new towns and industrial estates all connected by a confusing network of old and new roads. The names that cover the map, places like Cramlington and Killingworth, Blyth, Ashington, Camperdown, Seaton Burn, don't feature in the pages of travel books as often as the more obviously beautiful places in the north and west of the county. At the beginning of the chapter I acknowledged the survival of a few historical and natural beauties but implied that the rest was now blighted by the extraordinary industrial world that had spread across it in the last two or three hundred years. That wasn't fair; it wasn't right and I'll tell you why.

In the summer I went for a walk, part of an organised route called the Tyne and Wear Heritage Way that threads its way past several of those unromantic-sounding towns and villages until I came to a Country Park on the edge of Wideopen.

I'll tell you what; it was lovely – there were broad swelling acres of pale grassland with beautiful purple thistles, rosebay willow herb and great clouds of creamy cow parsley. There were dog roses and ragged hedges of elder trees and hawthorn. The path that led into it was flanked by rich meadows and fine banks of woodland to the south and to the north fields of pale green wheat (or possibly barley) stretched out to a typically Northumbrian farmstead with a big solid 19th century farmhouse and ranges of impressive farmbuildings and workers' cottages all around.

It was, in fact, a beautiful rural scene – except for the fact that the whole park was on the site of the former Weetslade Colliery, which had closed down in 1967 and lain derelict for a couple of decades before The Northumberland Wildlife Trust and other agencies had set to work to re-green the landscape at the end of the last century. This re-worked industrial history gives such a piquant extra dimension to the scene. The pretty hills, which the paths wind up, used to be slag heaps; the richly rural path I walked along to reach the park passes over the East Coast main railway line and under the hideously busy A189 Spine Road but before it did either of those things it was a waggonway where first of all horses and later steam locomotives hauled coal waggons to the staithes at Blyth or near Willington on the Tyne.

The thing I like most about this landscape is that it tells no lies. It doesn't pretend that everything's perfect or drag you blinkered past the ordinary places. It doesn't pretend that the north east is all extraordinary and beautiful and made up exclusively of cathedrals and castles. Instead it shows you what you can find if you walk down to the end of the housing estate and behind the shops

What I saw at Weetslade, and what I would have seen almost everywhere in the old industrial parts of the county, is a vision of Northumberland that reflects its landscape, its history, its social history and its particular character. There is natural beauty everywhere - deep natural denes and valleys, dramatic coastal outcrops, broad views of fields and woods, but there's tough human stuff as well – hard jobs and the equally hard sense of loss when the jobs dried up.

Pictured: The former Weetslade Colliery site.

15.

THE TYNE

In the last chapter I quoted the writer William Cobbett's rather upbeat description of the cottages and home lives of North East miners. On that same visit in 1832 (on October 2 1832 to be precise) he followed the bank of the Tyne from Newcastle to North Shields and this is what he said about it: '*These sides of the Tyne are very fine: corn-fields, woods, pastures, villages; a church every four miles, or thereabouts; cows and sheep beautiful; oak-trees, though none very large; and, in short, a fertile and beautiful country.*'

The pastoral beauty that impressed William Cobbett had always existed alongside a river busy with traffic, especially the fleets of colliers on their way to London and elsewhere, but the character of that traffic, along with the river and its banks was already beginning to change when he walked the shore (or possibly rode it … or pogosticked it; I realise I know nothing of his mode of transport).

It was changing in a whole variety of ways. There was steam on the river as early as 1814, when a paddle steamer called *The Tyne Steam Packet* was launched at Gateshead to carry passengers from Newcastle to Shields. There's another thing I don't know; I don't know whether it was to North Shields or South – but it doesn't matter because it failed to attract custom and was withdrawn, remodelled and re-launched as a tug – the

first steam tug on the Tyne and not far from being the first fully effective steam tug anywhere. It was called *The Perseverance* and it towed its first ship in July 1818. It was a massively successful first run. Even though the tide and the wind were against them, *The Perseverance* and its charge made the 13 miles to the bar in 2 hours and 10 minutes, which seemed miraculous at the time. It was a game changer. By freeing the collier boats from the vagaries of tide and wind they made the trade much more profitable. A collier boat was able to increase the number of journeys it made to London from 8 to 13 a season, and in no time at all the tugs proliferated and were soon joined by sea-going steamships.

The first was called *The Rapid*. It was a 24-ton paddle steamer that promised to transport people to London with stops at Whitby, Scarborough and Great Yarmouth. It claimed to be fitted with "*every accommodation for passengers*" and set off for its maiden trip on 11 August 1823 into the teeth of a howling gale, which caused it to spring a leak and limp into Whitby harbour … not a good start, but it was back again the following year after repairs and it made London in a spanking 54 hours after '*a delightful passage*'.

From then onwards, improvements were as rapid as the boat's name. In 1827 a new ship called *The Hylton*

Left: From the mouth of the Tyne to its old industrial centre, the river today is still a hive of activity.

Jolliffe carried 50 passengers to London in 40 hours and everybody was well chuffed by the '*comfort and accommodation*'. In 1830 the same ship was delayed for three days by a storm but still managed to arrive in London several hours before the stagecoach that had left Newcastle on the same day as the ship had set sail.

The interesting thing is that passenger ships to London continued to be popular even when the railways could do the journey in a fraction of the time. (In fact, and very surprisingly, the sea-born transport continued until 1934 and was only finally defeated by the arrival of buses). The ships changed, of course, and improved. *The John Bowes,* launched in 1853, was the first propeller-powered ship and very shortly after that, screw-driven colliers and fishing boats became common. By the 1880s boats began to appear with electric light. One ship, *The Royal Dane* advertised dinners for 2/6d (12.5p), a cup of Bovril for 3d and a pint of champagne for 4/-. There was a grand piano on board and concerts performed by the crew after dinner.

The ships might be improving but the dangers of the sea weren't disappearing. Further north, on the Farne Islands it was a steamship called *Forfarshire* that ran aground on the Big Harcar island in 1838 and led to Grace Darling and her father heroically rowing to the rescue of the survivors clinging desperately on the rocks; while on the Tyne, one of the most notable steamship captains, a man called John Cracknell, who apparently made 2500 journeys between the Tyne and London, recorded that when he sailed into the river on his first command, there were 35 wrecked boats on the Black Midden Rocks off Tynemouth. 35. Not 3, not 5 but 35! That is a lot of wrecks.

As far back as 1789 a wreck on the Herd Sands on the south side of the river had caused the people of South Shields, who had watched helpless from the shore as the boat broke up before them, to set up a competition to design what became the world's first lifeboat.

The residents of

The John Bowes.

By the start of the 20th Century the Tyne was an extremely busy river, having been key to the growth of many of the region's industries.

Tynemouth had a similar experience of powerlessness on October 24 1864, when they had to watch two ships break up simultaneously on the Black Middens. What they did about it was to found the world's first Volunteer Life Brigade (the second was at Cullercoats) and a few years later to build themselves a watch house that stands on the headland above the rocks and remains to this day one of the most remarkable and atmospheric buildings in England.

It is beautiful on the outside – timber clad and brightly painted, the absolute quintessence of a seaside building; while inside it is stuffed to the gunnels with memories of disaster and rescue. Stirringly big-bosomed figureheads from shipwrecks jostle with rockets and breeches boys. Hanging from the ceiling there's a barrel to which a Dutch sea captain strapped his five-year old daughter in a desperate attempt to save her from drowning. As his ship sank, he threw her overboard; he drowned but she was rescued.

The Volunteer Life Brigade movement was (and remains) a community-based charitable organisation, important but limited in scope, but in 1850 a third, hugely important change took place at an official Governmental level that was going to have a profound and long-term effect on the river. Newcastle finally lost its control of the river. For centuries, since the 12th century at least, the river had been tightly clasped in the iron hand of Newcastle. The town and its corporation had fought savagely to maintain that control, including burning down anywhere that looked like challenging its hegemony. Some things were allowed to happen that weren't controlled by Newcastle if they weren't perceived as a threat; South Shields was allowed to develop its salt pans, for example, and North Shields was allowed to become a fishing port but as soon as the Toon sensed a threat in any community down river … Oh! They didn't like that.

This happened, for example, in the 1820s when the Duke of Northumberland, the Lord of the Manor at Tynemouth, decided to build a New Quay at North Shields in an attempt to capture some of the trade that came into the river. The surviving buildings reveal that

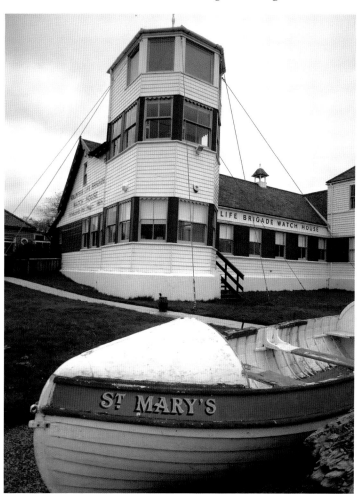

The Luna, wrecked at Whitley Bay in 1897 and, right, the Tynemouth Volunteer Life Brigade Museum.

it was intended to be posh, an ambitious development, but 'twas not to be. The power of Newcastle stopped it in its tracks. Throughout the 18th and early 19th centuries it became clear to everybody (except the people of Newcastle) that Newcastle was willing and eager to make as much money as possible out of the river and its increasing trade, but very unwilling to spend any of it making the river more suitable for the job it had to do.

They neglected the channel, making it slow, dangerous and erratic to sail up. Ships were often stuck in the river for weeks on end because the bar at the mouth of the river was never dredged; there are stories of market traders being able to wade across the river from North to South Shields at low tide; the channel became choked with wrecks, there were no lights and too few buoys marking the route, so in 1850, by Act of Parliament the Tyne was finally wrenched away from Newcastle and placed under the control of a new organisation called The Port of Tyne. What a difference that made, and in the following few decades the river was transformed, docks and riverside wharfs were built and the channel was dredged and maintained and properly marked …

… and the piers were built. They were begun in 1854, massive monuments to the power and ingenuity of our Victorian forefathers. They took 50 years to build. So savage were the conditions in which the builders had to work that the north pier was actually knocked down by a storm shortly after it was completed and had to be reconstructed. They are astonishing achievements – the north pier in its brutal simplicity, the south pier almost elegant as it ambles out to sea in a series of serpentine curves. What they did though, these piers, was to turn the mouth of the river from a place of danger into a harbour of refuge.

So … in contrast to William Cobbett's gently rural experience of 1832, I found a picture, a print giving a bird's-eye view of the river 50 years later, sometime in the 1880s. The viewpoint is from high above North Shields, looking up-river towards Jarrow and Wallsend with Walker Shore in the far distance. In the foreground is Albert Edward Dock (now called Royal Quays Marina), which was opened in 1882 by the Prince of Wales, who had come down the river in a steamboat from Newcastle to perform the deed and had got sloshed on champagne on the way, so that when they arrived at the dock gates he said, "What lovely dock gates; but where is the dock?"

This view differs from Cobbett's description in every possible way. It could not be more different. It is harshly but vibrantly industrial. There is steam and smoke, and chimneys everywhere. Dozens of small smoky boats are on the river. In the middle background Is Whitehill Point, the staithes and terminus of the Killingworth Waggonway, built 70 years earlier by George Stephenson. Behind it is Jarrow, a vast industrial complex, billowing smoke. The writer Augustus Hare, who was very fond of the beauties of rural Northumberland and wrote very, very extensively about them, was appalled by Jarrow at that time: '*…a teeming population of blackened, foul-mouthed rogues, living in rows of dismal houses, in a country where every vestige of vegetation is killed by noxious chemical vapours on the edge of a slimy swamp…inky sky…* [blah… blah… blah] *… furnesses vomiting forth volumes of blackened smoke …* [blah…blah] *… nature seems parched and blackened under the pollution …* [blah…blah].

I have another picture of about the same time, a photograph that dates from just after 1876; it shows a vast ship passing through the open Swing Bridge on the Quayside at Newcastle with the High Level Bridge looming in the background. It is a dark and gloomy picture with the sky and ship swathed in smoke, but it is exciting too; it clearly records an event, the ship is swarming with crew members lining the side of the ship facing Newcastle and in the background the lower deck of the High Level is lined with onlookers.

The story is that this picture was taken as the largest ship in the world was passing through the largest movable bridge in the world on the way from the largest factory in the world where it had been to pick up the largest gun in the world, which was being exported to Bari in Italy where it would be unloaded by the largest dockside crane in the world. And all of those things had been made in Newcastle – indeed they were all the work of one man, the Tyneside inventor and entrepreneur, William Armstrong.

Above: A harsh and vibrant industrial Tyne in the 1880s and, below, another picture from the same time showing a huge ship passing through the open Swing Bridge.

William Armstrong was born in 1810 in Shieldfield on the outskirts of Newcastle. He became a lawyer and went into partnership with a friend of his dad, a man called Armorer Donkin, but from his youth his natural bent was towards science and once, when he was on holiday in the Pennines, he was impressed by the power of a waterwheel, but at the same time aware of how much of the potential power the wheel spilled and wasted, so he came home and (as you do) became an expert in hydraulics.

He invented a hydraulic crane that was powered by surplus water in the Newcastle system and persuaded the Town Council to build it on the quayside where it was a notable success, revolutionising the business of loading and unloading ships. The authorities went on to build three more of his cranes and (as I've said elsewhere) Robert became his uncle. He made a fortune out of hydraulic machinery. He opened a factory to build the stuff by the river at Elswick in the west end of Newcastle, which was eventually so successful that by the late 1860s he was able to persuade the council to allow him to demolish the stone bridge on the Quayside and replace it with a new one of his own design, which opened using his own hydraulic motors and allowed ships decent access to his factory.

In the meantime, he became an expert in loads of other things. Shocked by reports of the inefficiency of British Army artillery in the Crimean War, he developed a new field gun with a rifled barrel. It was breach-loaded and fired shells instead of cannon balls and was massively more accurate and easier to use than earlier guns. In an act of patriotism (or a cunning wheeze) he gave the patent for his new gun to the government to do with as they chose, and among the things they chose was to buy lots and lots of armaments from the vast (and getting vaster) armaments factory that he built beside his existing factory in Elswick, where he eventually employed 25,000 men.

But … you've probably recognised his dilemma … what's the point, he must have said to himself, of making great big guns if you don't also build the battleships to put them on? And what's the point of making great big cranes (and stuff) if you have to ask someone else to take

Armstrong's Ship Yard, Newcastle.

Lord Armstrong and his Elswick empire.

them away for you. So he made himself into a ship builder on a massive scale as well and he became an industrialist and an entrepreneur on a massive and complex scale. He wasn't the only such man on the river. Charles Palmer, at Jarrow, owned coalmines and iron mines and he had an ironworks powered by his own coal and a shipyard where he could build ships made of his own iron; he too had an integrated industrial empire.

There were several such empires on the Tyne, but Armstrong's was the biggest and the most successful. He sold his guns and his warships to the Russians and the Japanese and a whole mass of other countries. His cranes and hydraulic engines and other inventions went all over the word. Kings and Czars and Emperors visited his works (and his home) in their droves. He was knighted for his services to science and industry, the first man to be so, and he was later made a Baronet.

His extraordinary success attracted others to the river too, men like Charles Mitchell, who came down from Aberdeen and started the other greatest shipyard on the river, and men like Charles Parsons, the son of an earl who had just graduated top of his class from Oxford

and who came to Tyneside, initially to become an apprentice at Armstrong's works because he wanted to learn at the feet of the master, but went on to invent the steam turbine, which revolutionised the world of marine travel. In 1897 his ship, *Turbinia*, arrived at the Spithead Review of the British Navy and ran rings around all the other ships there, at a stroke conveying older engines to the dust of history.

All sorts of marine firsts happened on our river around that time – the first iron-hulled collier boat was built and the first screw-driven fishing boat; the first icebreaker and the world's first oil tanker were designed and built at Mitchell's yard on the Tyne at Low Walker

And the Tyne's massive expansion of invention and creativity wasn't confined to the water; there was an inventive crackle of electricity along the river in those days as well. Joseph Swan (born in Sunderland and living in Gateshead) invented the electric light bulb and first demonstrated it in The Newcastle Lit and Phil, which became the first public room in the world to be lit be electricity. John Henry Holmes was present at Swan's historic Lit and Phil lecture and he did something really clever as well – if Swan had shown the world how to turn on the lights, Holmes showed it how to switch them off again – he invented the electric-light switch. Charles Parsons turned to electricity as well; he developed his turbines to generate electricity and built the world's first proper power station, making Newcastle in effect, the birthplace of modern electric power.

So the 19th century saw an extraordinary change on the lower reaches of the Tyne and in my mind there is one surviving monument that best represents the changes that took place.

Towering above Armstrong's Swing Bridge in the photograph I mentioned a little while ago is the High Level Bridge designed by Robert Stephenson, George Stephenson's son, opened in 1849. It is a stupendous structure designed by a stupendous engineer.

Robert Stephenson was born at Killingworth in 1801. His mother died giving birth to him and so he was brought up by his father. Given that George himself was born into relative poverty and was illiterate and uneducated until his late teens, it seems to me that one of the most remarkable things that he achieved in an almost entirely remarkable life was the way he brought up his son in a single-parent family, educated him brilliantly and turned him into something like a genius.

That success alone could make him one of the greatest single-family dads in history. I can't think of one more impressive.

Because Robert was seriously talented. In 1820, when he was only 19, he became the Managing Director of Robert Stephenson and Co, the Locomotive works opened by Robert with his father. When I was 19, I had only recently abandoned my first paper round and was still wearing short pants, so I am impressed by Robert. The works was the first locomotive factory in the world and it had hugely impressive credentials. The two oldest locomotives in America were made there and so were *Locomotive No1*, which powered the first trains to run on the Stockton and Darlington Railway, and *The Rocket,* which won the Rainhill Trials in 1829 and was the poster train of the first proper passenger railway, the Manchester and Liverpool Railway, which opened in 1830.

It was Robert who designed *The Rocket*; he did it when he was in his early 20s so he had huge potential as a steam engineer but instead he went on to become internationally renowned and rather fabulously successful as a bridge designer. I may be biased … allow me to re-phrase that – I know I am biased but to me he seems to have been a pretty admirable man. He married

J. W. Carmichael's 1849 painting of the High Level Bridge, designed by Robert Stephenson (pictured).

but had no children; like his mother, his wife died young; those aren't the admirable bits but he never remarried after her death, which perhaps suggests a strength of feeling and loyalty. He was offered a knighthood but turned it down.

When he died, his funeral cortege was given permission by Queen Victoria to go through Hyde Park, which was an honour normally reserved for royalty. He was buried in Westminster Abbey, one of a remarkably small number of Northumbrians to be granted that honour. The others are all posh. Elizabeth Percy, the 1st Duchess of Northumberland, who featured in one of the earlier chapters in this book, has a rather splendid monument erected in 1776 and she and most of the more significant members of the family since were buried there; I can't think of anyone else; except Robert Stephenson who, despite being from a humble background, has not one but two memorials in the Abbey. His gravestone was designed by the great architect, Gilbert Scott, and beside the grave is a memorial window designed by William Wailes of Gateshead. It is a mass of little pictures of great bridges through the ages, starting in Ancient Egypt and ending

The Tyne at Newcastle, pictured in the late 19th century during its industrial peak, and below the modern riverside photographed by Steve Ellwood.

inevitably on our own (our very own) High Level Bridge in Newcastle. Robert left his mark elsewhere in his home county. His Royal Border Bridge over the Tweed at Berwick, built at exactly the same time as The High Level, is a more conventional bridge in stone and brick but still visually thrilling and there are a series of other similar, but smaller, railway bridges on the route from Berwick towards Kelso, but the High Level is the one that came out of the top drawer. It is massive, innovative and thrilling and in those revolutionary railway days it connected Northumberland to the rest of England the moment it was opened.

———————

If you pass under the High Level and keep going, noting with interest the site of Armstrong's factories, and on both sides of the river from time to time the rows of terraces and Tyneside flats climbing the steep banks, and noting more obviously the changes wrought in the townscapes by the 20th century, you find yourself, after three or four miles, in a very different place indeed; beyond Newburn on the north bank and Blaydon on the south, the Tyne morphs into a rural river, just like the river that William Cobbett walked along in 1832, beautiful and tree-lined, occasionally opening out to meadows, from time to time passing old and traditional villages and towns, and it remains like this from the western edge of Newcastle to its source – or to be more accurate, to its sources because just after Hexham there is a bifurcation (I have always wanted to use that word but though I have spoken it in an ironic and suggestive tone, I have never written it down before. It's good to realise one's dreams).

The bifurcation at the village of Warden sends one branch of the river north into the wildness of the Border Hills and the other, the South Tyne, into the wildness of the North Pennines. Upstream from Tyneside the river is all about rural beauty and increasing levels of isolation and wildness; at first glance, and for quite a lot of glances afterwards, it seems as if the Industrial Revolution never happened.

Not much breaks that pattern. There's a brief interlude of industry at Low Prudhoe just below the castle, and for a few miles the profile of Hexham with its medieval highlights is marred by the ghastliness of the woodchip factory on the river bank, but apart from that the mood feels relatively timeless and questions might be asked about the extent that the river and its valley were affected by the sort of changes that occurred in the 19th century.

Well, quite a lot is the answer. The vast majority of the villages and virtually all of the farms in the valley were built or rebuilt in the 1800s and though there are older buildings, lots of splendid older buildings (and especially a magnificent collection of older churches), they are comparatively few and far between and need to be sought out rather than dominating the view. So the valley, though traditional in feel, is more 19th century than you might think and it does have at least one large and complex 19th century structure of international significance and tremendous local interest.

The Newcastle and Carlisle Railway was first proposed as early as 1824 and its construction was sanctioned in 1828, gaining its Royal Assent in 1829, third only to the Stockton and Darlington and the Liverpool to Manchester Railways in terms of antiquity. By 1832, when my chum William Cobbett was here on his travels, the construction was well underway, he saw the men at work building it. The whole line was completed and formally opened in 1838. It was 61 miles long, by far the longest railway in the country (and the world) at the time and the only one to cross the country from side to side. It was also (and here you see the Grundy bias at its most obvious) by far the prettiest. I have been riding on it for the last 65 years so I should know.

The reasons for its existence aren't quite as obvious as they were for the two other railways that preceded it. There was no obvious product like the coal of south Durham that needed to be carried to the waiting ships, or no major cities like Liverpool and Manchester that needed to be connected. I suppose Carlisle, which was a reasonably important cotton-manufacturing town but

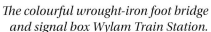

The colourful wrought-iron foot bridge and signal box Wylam Train Station.

lacking a port to export it from, would be expected to benefit from the connection, but there was very little stuff that needed to be carried in the opposite direction because the North East had ports of its own and north Cumberland would never have been a major market for north-eastern goods.

There was lead mining in the hills south of Hexham, of course, and for a while coal and iron mining in the North Tyne Valley round Bellingham, but those commercial needs, though significant, weren't enough to justify the line, so from the start it was designed to carry people as well as stuff and for that reason it was the first line in the world that was provided with stations at intermediate stops between the two termini. Liverpool had a station of course and so did Manchester but there were no stops in between – clearly in 1830 nobody had thought they were necessary, but here, in the Tyne Valley, a few short years later there were stations built at every town and village down the line.

They are lovely stations. I was an avid trainspotter in my youth, so even when I was a boy I found them

irresistibly attractive and many of them have lost none of their appeal in the intervening ~~centuries~~ decades. The line opened in sections between 1835 and 1838 and the first bit to come on line was the bit between Gateshead (where the original terminus was) and Hexham. The stations in that bit were officially opened on 10 March 1835. They include Hexham and Corbridge, Riding Mill, Stocksfield and Wylam and they have a good claim to be the oldest stations in the world or at least, given the surviving buildings at Manchester, the oldest stations still in passenger use.

They haven't changed massively since they were first built. They all had a station master's house and a waiting room. It's clear in quite a lot of places that the original platforms weren't raised like they always are today but were level with the track like they still are in America or India and places in Europe. At Wylam, for example, you need to step down into the stationmaster's house from the present conveniently high platform and in many places sections of the original lower platform can still be seen at the ends of the stations.

The things that have been added since the earliest days are those endearingly railway-ish items specifically designed to stir that hearts of little railway enthusiasts. Wylam (again as an example) has a splendid signal box and a brightly painted and highly characteristic wrought-iron foot bridge. Haltwhistle (opened in 1838) has the same but with the addition of a satisfyingly massive water tower, festooned with cast-iron plates giving dates and makers' names. At one end of almost all of the stations is a road that could be cut off by sturdy, white-painted level-crossing gates when trains were approaching,

These stations are all built of local stone in a gentle, traditional and rather comforting Tudor style; it's a style which feels comfortingly traditional today – but it felt that way in the 1830s and 40s as well. It was popular because it reminded people of "olde England" and choosing it as the face of a revolutionary new mode of transport was a clever way to make it more acceptable.

People were frightened enough of the roaring engines without the stations unsettling them as well. Nothing like them had ever been known before. There were no bus stops or stations on the routes of stagecoach travel so an appropriate form had to be invented for the new stations and oddly, given their newness and revolutionary purpose no one seems to know for certain who came up with the idea.

The people who built the line and the engineering structures associated with it are reasonably well known. The first chief engineer, for example, was that Francis Giles who had been insulting about George Stephenson at the enquiry into the Liverpool and Manchester Railway. He didn't last very long actually and was replaced in 1833, but not before he had built some terrific bridges at the Cumbrian end of the line; his Wetheral Viaduct over the River Eden is one of the most beautiful railway sights in the country. He was replaced by a local man called John Blackmore who designed most of the bridges at our end of the line and interestingly (and here I am tapping the side of my nose in a knowing and meaningful way) interestingly he became a partner in the Newcastle architectural firm of John and Benjamin Green.

That fact made me tap my nose in a significant way because, for a long time, people have suggested that J and B Green could well have been the architects of the stations. I first came across that suggestion in a book (*North Country Lore and Legends*) published in the 1890s. The Greens went on to build similar, equally pretty but more elaborate stations a few years later, on the line from Newcastle to Berwick and they were innovative and creative architects as well. They designed Newcastle's Theatre Royal, for example, and they invented, or at least introduced, the use of laminated timber in Britain, which they used, towards the end of the 1830s, to built at least two large and impressive timber viaducts at Byker in Newcastle and Willington near Wallsend, but whether they also invented railway stations or not, it remains true that the stations were one of the great innovations that this line introduced to the world.

There were other things as well, though. It was the first line to use Standard Gauge track (4ft 8 inches and a bit) for the whole of its length – a practice that was first used by George Stephenson and has since spread almost everywhere in the world. Pre-printed tickets were invented on the line as well. They were invented in 1837 by Thomas Edmondson, the stationmaster at Brampton in Cumberland, and used on the Newcastle and Carlisle from the start. Edmondson made a fortune out of his invention, which has also been in use all over the world ever since.

So the line, as well as being exceedingly pretty, was pretty damned revolutionary as well. The whole thing opened officially on 18 June 1838 with a riotously mismanaged special event for which 3500 tickets were sold and 13 trains took everybody to Carlisle in driving rain. The last train arrived in Carlisle at 6.00 in the evening and there was a massive stampeded for refreshments because nobody had eaten all day. The trains set off back to Newcastle from about 10.30 and the last passengers arrived home at 6.30 the following morning. The papers published amusing accounts of the trains having to stop in the countryside to allow chaps in need to leap off into the bushes in the rain, and of impatient train drivers blowing their whistles causing the same men to rush back from the bushes with their

clothing still awry …

… but from these rustic beginnings the railway soon settled down to a pattern that revealed how much it was needed.

Nowadays there is an average of about 40 trains a day between the two cities and the journey takes about an hour and 32 minutes. It wasn't as fast as that nor as busy back in the day but its achievements weren't insignificant either. Within a year there were four trains a day in both directions and the journey took about three hours. Heavily loaded freight trains were much slower, but passenger trains reached regular speeds of about 39 mph and in 1837 one of the locomotives, an engine called *Eden*, went from Brampton to Carlisle at a speed of 60 mph.

It seems obvious to me that these changes opened up new possibilities to people. Some of the possibilities were to do with business – people could travel quickly to set up deals and search out new markets; a speedy modern postal service could develop; new networks, commercial networks and private ones could develop; as I've written once before in this book, people were liberated from the places they were born, or at least had more chances to get away. A few years before this line opened, the great print maker and engraver Thomas Bewick set off from his home near Prudhoe to visit relatives in the Eden Valley. He walked it, with money stitched into the lining of his trousers. Once the railway

had arrived, he would have been able to pop over for tea with his auntie and be back home again at Prudhoe station in time for EastEnders. That's what progress can do for you.

Over the next couple of decades after the opening of the Newcastle and Carlisle the great railway mania took hold in Britain and the network exploded with a riot of new lines. In the North East the Newcastle to Berwick line (with a whole heap of splendid stations at Morpeth, Acklington, Chathill and Belford, for example) completed the route through the whole of England. The line was extended to the west from Berwick to Kelso. There were routes from Alnwick to Coldstream; west from Morpeth there was a line over the beautiful Wannies Hills to Bellingham - and from the Tyne valley two new railways were introduced to extend travel north and south.

Knowing the Northern countryside as you do, you won't be surprised to hear that neither of them was very successful from a commercial point of view.

The first to be built was the line that went from Haltwhistle to Alston. It was opened in 1852 specifically to carry lead ore from the north Pennines but sadly, before too long, the bottom fell out of the lead market and there was far too small a population to support the line so it limped on until it was finally withdrawn in the middle of the 20th century.

This route was (and still is) extraordinarily beautiful

and built through such uppy-downy country that moments of extreme engineering brilliance were needed to make it work. There are at least two entirely memorable bridges for example: the first is a splendid stone viaduct that crosses the South Tyne just after the line leaves Haltwhistle. It crosses the river at an angle and its arches are elaborately skewed, which means that the two sides of the arch aren't directly opposite each other; they're offset. That made it extremely complicated to build so it's an amazing construction, all skew-arch bridges are; each individual stone has a distinct shape to fit into the jigsaw. Nowadays you'd get a computer to design the shapes and tell the robotic cutter how to slice up the stone but in 1852 it was obviously done by hand, brilliantly designed and executed with everything twisted at an angle as if the stones had been stretched to fit.

The other bridge on this line is even more impressive. It's called the Lambley Viaduct and it's an extraordinary tour de force, also from 1852. It is still there though the trains have long gone, still immensely high, still long and graceful on a line to nowhere (though you can still walk over it).

The Border Counties Railway was the other line, the one that went north. It opened in bits from 1858 to1862 and ran from Hexham up the North Tyne Valley to Redesmouth near Bellingham, where it joined the Wannies Line from Morpeth and continued on past Kielder to Riccarton Junction in Scotland and places north.

The premise behind it was that it might provide an alternative main line from Scotland down into England and that it would be paid for by transporting newly discovered sources of coal from Plashetts (which now lies under Kielder Reservoir). In the event both sources of income failed. The Scottish connection made better routes through Berwick and Carlisle and the Plashetts coal reserves turned out to be less than expected so the line never really made a profit. There was a tiny local population (I'm not referring to their height you will realise) so passenger numbers were intensely disappointing and the line struggled on into the 1950s when it finally gave up its ghost. It was beautiful, though;

virtually every inch of the way was beautiful and after it had gone the local population was so tiny (remember: numbers not height) that there was no pressure to find new uses for the route so much of it can still be seen. Any trip near it provides moving and stimulating experiences – beside Chollerford Bridge, for example, the former station was converted many decades ago into a beautiful house that generations of subsequent travellers have lusted after; just beyond that building there's another skew-arched bridge, much smaller than the Haltwhistle viaduct but on such an extreme bend that the arch is

Anglers share the Tyne at Wylam with the heron.

twisted in a quite extraordinary way. It must have been so difficult to design and make. Where there is no engineering brilliance the line keeps its interest because it is has the melancholy appeal that all great abandoned structures have – you might pass little groups of cows standing slightly forlornly on the arch of an abandoned bridge as if daring a ghostly train to chase them away, or a mournful family of sheep peering over the parapet of an accommodation arch.

Another of the former stations, Thorneyburn, between Tarset and Falstone, has disappeared almost entirely; the route of the railway, minus its rails, passes in front of a single-storey railwayman's cottage surrounded by wilderness. There isn't another house in sight; you can't imagine that there could ever have been enough passengers to use it in such a deserted landscape. Beside the cottage there's a perfectly preserved but totally unnecessary pair of level-crossing gates and a tiny lineman's shed, made of wood with a cast-iron stovepipe chimney, looking for all the world like something you would find in the Klondike. At the Heritage Centre in Bellingham there are all sorts of artefacts from the railway; my favourite is the sliding door of a train shed covered with generations of graffiti in pencil, the work of naughty boys, no doubt, who grew up to be pillars of the community. And way north of

Bellingham, partly flooded at the head of the Kielder Reservoir is the Kielder Viaduct, yet another ambitious skew-arched construction made even more memorable by having battlements for its parapet.

I seem to have mentioned quite a lot of bridges in this chapter but as it happens these are just some among quite a lot of splendid 19th century bridges that cross the Tyne(s). The river famously flooded in 1771 and only the bridge at Corbridge survived the devastation so there are a number of late 18th century bridges that were built after that flood; Hexham has one, Haydon Bridge another and Chollerford a third, but many of the bridges over the river are 19th century and together they make a fascinating bunch. Some are traditional stone structures including Bywell Bridge built, among a wonderful collection of older buildings, by an architect called George Basevi in 1838. I don't know what George Basevi was doing up here; he was a major southern architect, the designer of buildings as significant as the Fitzwilliam Museum in Cambridge and Belgrave Square in poshest London, but Bywell Bridge is worthy of its designer. It's an elegant but muscular bridge and, in a matter of absolutely no significance I would like to tell you that one of my former neighbours, who had been brought up in Stocksfield near the southern end of the bridge, once cycled along its parapet for a dare. This is a thing I myself

Left: Corbridge Bridge, survivor of the 1771 flood, and right, West Wylam Bridge, possibly the first such bridge in the world to carry a railway.

wouldn't have done for a king's ransom, even if it had meant falling off one of the finest bridges into the very beautiful River Tyne.

But most of the 19th century bridges on the river are not stone and in no way traditional. Haltwhistle has a second bridge alongside its skew-arched viaduct; it has a pretty and decorative wrought-iron superstructure on stone and brick piers. Wylam has got two bridges over the river. What is the road bridge now was built in 1836 to carry both a road and a rail link that led from the station to the colliery and a brand-new ironworks on the north side of the river. It was given a new steel superstructure later in the century and a pretty late-Victorian toll-house at the north end but underneath these alterations there is a row of powerful, utterly plain stone piers, loads of them forcing their way across the river. They are actually remarkable plain for their date with no references at all to earlier bridges or earlier architectural styles, and they look terrific. It is worth climbing down to see the bridge from below.

Wylam's other bridge, West Wylam Bridge, is just as remarkable. It's a parabolic arched bridge like the Tyne Bridge or the Sydney Harbour Bridge but much earlier. It was built in 1876 and is probably only the second such bridge in the world and the first to carry a railway.

And finally there is the bridge between Prudhoe and Ovingham, which is single track, very narrow and a trifle unnerving if you like the pristine paintwork of your car – but it is constructed, not of wrought iron but of steel, made by Dorman Long from Middlesbrough who did the Tyne Bridge (and the Sydney one too) but this one was done in 1883, which is really, really early for a steel bridge.

I could go on. You probably thought I was going to go on forever but even though there are many other bits and pieces from 19th century times that it pains me to ignore, I am going to stop and say something to sum up this river (62 miles long, according to the *Encyclopaedia Britannica*; 73 according to *Wikipedia*, not very long according to me). It is a place of extraordinary interest and variety. Its last 13-odd miles are both tidal and highly industrialised; the rest of it has been more lightly touched by industry and has retained a glorious and untrammelled beauty. Altogether it makes a place about which my father-in-law, when he had grown expansive after a good Sunday lunch, used to recite (to his wife's chagrin and his grandchildren's delight) the verse

The Tyne, the Tyne
The Queen of aal the rivers
Yer bugger.

Left: The decorative wrought-iron bridge at Haltwhistle and, right, the traditional stone structure of Bywell Bridge.

Cragside, emerges organically out of the landscape.

16. C19 Mansions & Churches

So, away from the queen of aal the rivers and away from the rampant industrialisation and engineering adventure of the SE quadrant of the county, how did the rest of the county fare in the 1800s?

I'm thinking of architecture in particular, and first of all …

Country Houses

In an earlier chapter I cast a rather cursory glance across the dwellings of ordinary people. This time I'm going to do the same with posher houses and in particular with the country houses built between 1800 and 1899 and I'm going to be radical first of all and start at the beginning.

Barmoor Castle, near Lowick in North Northumberland was built, or rebuilt, in 1801, right at the beginning of this chapter. It had a long history but eventually became a property of the Sitwell family from Derbyshire, who were to become a famously creative family in the 20th century.

The main branch of the family, the Derbyshire lot, was led at that time by a man called (rather imaginatively) Sitwell Sitwell, but it was his younger brother Francis who inherited Barmoor and brought in an excellent Scottish architect called John Paterson to build him a new house. Paterson came from Edinburgh and had been an employee and later an associate of the great Adam family of architects and he had become a renowned exponent of their gothic "Castle Style" – the style they chose for houses like Culzean in Ayrshire – and that was the style that Paterson provided for Francis Sitwell at Barmoor. It is a terrific example – tall and powerful with battlements and turrets and so on. It is also abandoned and partly roofless unfortunately, and has been for most of the last century; and it's surrounded by caravans; but despite these indignities it still looks terrific.

Francis Sitwell started well at Barmoor. He had his splendid new castle and a passion for agricultural improvements. He specialised in raising highland cattle and new breeds of sheep and he went all over the country to attend agricultural shows and confer with other pioneering agriculturists. He even took some of his sheep 300 miles to a show at Smithfield in London (heaven knows how he got them there; perhaps he rode them) and he organised shows of his own at Barmoor that attracted enthusiasts from all over the country. In the grounds of the castle there's a long, tall, battlemented stone wall, which is a surviving fragment of a pig show he put on in 1803.

But sadly I've just recently found out that the good times didn't last for Francis; I read an account by a historian called Hilary Matthews that revealed that he didn't like his wife (despite having 5 children) and hated

*Barmoor
Castle.*

from Bedlington. Cheese springs to mind, as opposed to chalk. That's how different Milbourne is to Barmoor. Where Barmoor is tall and craggy, Gothic and romantic, Milbourne is low and smooth, a beautifully plain Classical house but with a remarkable and unexpected characteristic – the simplicity of the exterior disguises a house in which virtually every room is an oval. Isn't that something? You really can't tell from outside. Joined to the back of the house is a stable and service block surrounding a courtyard which is also oval.

Years and years ago I went to a charity barbecue there. The cooking was done on braziers in the oval courtyard and as it got dark my friends and I were approached by the owner of the house whose name I no longer know. He was seeking our assistance to help bring out a paper balloon that he had made with his son. He led us through the house, across an oval hall enriched with delicate neo-classical plasterwork, curved doors and glazed cabinets. We went up the cantilevered staircase with its filigree of wrought-iron handrail.

Everything was beautiful but restrained and I have rarely loved a classical interior more. We ended up in the bedroom of a sleeping little boy and carefully carried out a large and brightly coloured tissue-paper balloon as delicate as the plasterwork. We took it outside and held it over one of the braziers until it began to fill with hot air and just as we let it go, at the very last second, it caught fire and billowed up into the darkness in a ball of flame.

Apart from these two house by John Paterson there are probably others by Scottish architects, especially near the border in the northern part of the county, where several look as if they could have been lifted bodily from Edinburgh, but overall the bulk of the county's early 19th century houses were designed by local chaps and the first of them, the greatest of them in fact, was Belsay Hall.

The Belsay estate, as you might recall from the chapter about the 17th century, had been the property of

his brother-in-law and that he became bankrupt and fled to escape both wife and creditors. He was also poorly and very aware of his approaching death; however he did have a lady called Harriet Manners with him to bring him comfort; it's not clear where she came from but she was his companion … partner, his something-or-other; she was much younger than him and he was deeply attached to her. While he was on the run, he wrote an extraordinary letter to his eldest son (also called Francis) with instructions that it wasn't to be opened until after he died. And that's what happened.

Francis the younger was only 16 when his father died in 1813 but the letter urged him to look after the house and Harriet. He did both. Five years later, when he was just turned 21 and had taken over possession of the estate, Francis junior married Harriet and they seemed to have lived happily ever after (until they died).

A year or two after designing Barmoor, Paterson was active again in Northumberland. He built Milbourne Hall, just north of Ponteland, for a man called Ralph Bates who was part of a wealthy coal-owning family the Middleton family for hundreds of years and in 1614 Thomas Middleton (and Elizabeth his wife) had extended their glorious romantic castle with the addition of a more conventional Jacobean house where the Middletons continued to live for another 300 years. It didn't change all that much until the arrival of Sir Charles Monck in 1795.

I call him Sir Charles Monck, you would have probably called him 'sonny boy' if you'd met him because he was only 16 when he inherited Belsay and he had only changed his name from Middleton to Monck so that he could inherit his grandfather's estate in Lincolnshire … but I shouldn't mock him because he comes across as an absolute good egg and where would we be without those.

Instead of living on his grandfather's estate he came north to claim his Northern inheritance. He married his cousin Louisa and in September 1804 the young couple set off on their honeymoon as you do – actually not as most of us do. For my honeymoon I set off from Newcastle for a sumptuous two nights in the Lord Crewe Arms in Bamburgh, where I experienced (for the first time in my life) two eggs for breakfast. Sir Charles was made of sterner stuff. His honeymoon lasted for almost two years, most of it spent in Greece. At Rugby School he had become passionately interested in ancient Greece so he and Louisa set off, not by EasyJet, which is the approved route nowadays, and not through France, where the English were still at war against Napoleon, but via Berlin, down the Rhine, across the Alps into Northern Italy and then straight over to Greece where he began seriously to study the surviving ruins.

I used to worry that he might have been so single-minded in his studies that the couple's married life could have been like the story of Dorothea in the novel *Middlemarch*. She went to the Mediterranean on her honeymoon with the ghastly Reverend Casaubon and was so ignored by him as he studied "the ancient mysteries" that all love was killed – but evidently that wasn't the case with the Moncks. They had a baby for a start. He was born in Athens in the summer of 1805 and they called him Atticus; two months after he was born the diaries describe Louisa climbing to the top of the pediment on the Parthenon. They went everywhere together, measured stuff and drew everything. It sounds fantastic and then they came home where he designed and started to build Belsay Hall, the Grecian home based on his studies and their experiences.

In 1807 when they started building, the Greek style was incredibly rare in English domestic architecture. It became a fashionable style later, in the 1820s and 30s, but Belsay was among the very first places to give it a try and it was absolutely the first in Britain to do so in such a full-blooded uncompromising way.

Some people don't like Belsay because its exterior is very severe but to me it seems so original, so beautifully built and so exquisite in its details. The only decorated bit of the exterior is the entrance, which is enriched with two full-height and brilliantly carved Greek Doric columns. They are a perfect copy, literally a perfect copy inch for inch, of the columns at the entrance of the Temple of Hephaestus in the Ancient Agora in Athens, and they lead into the entrance hall, which is a recreation of the inside of a Greek Temple.

It's amazing, not comfy but amazing; but the rooms that surround it *are* comfy. They don't look quite so comfy now because they are empty (it was a condition

Belsay, with it trailbrazing Greek style.

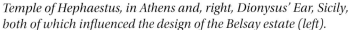
Temple of Hephaestus, in Athens and, right, Dionysus' Ear, Sicily, both of which influenced the design of the Belsay estate (left).

of English Heritage taking over the house from the Middletons that they would leave it unfurnished) but they are clearly comfy. They have huge, almost floor to ceiling windows so the light is beautiful and the main rooms have beautiful proportions as well; back in Sir Charles's day they were permanently warmed with fires in every room. He employed four men whose full-time job it was to provide the coal and the cut logs needed to keep them all going. That's what money does for you.

And then there's the garden that Sir Charles (and later his grandson) created. When the family were living in the old castle, they created a typically English landscape garden with swards of grass and clumps of trees, a picturesque folly farm, all in the Capability Brown style. Some of that garden is still there, around and especially behind the castle, but the horticultural world had moved on by the time Sir Charles created his new gardens in the picturesque style – a style that was designed to inspire emotions, and my goodness that's what they do. What he did was (and remains)

astonishing. Inspired by drawings of ancient quarries in Syracuse in Sicily, including perhaps the very remarkable cave known as Dionysius' Ear, he used the quarry from which the stone for his new house had been dug and turned it into his garden.

There is nothing like it anywhere else. It is magical and mysterious. It is an almost subterranean world of high sandstone cliffs divided into two by a narrow arch with a door that you always have to open, like a character in a children's story. Beside the door there is a palm tree and beyond it there are rhododendrons. I have been there on occasions when the rhodies were in flower and they and the palm tree were both laden with snow … it seemed like a suitable image for a northern garden inspired by the warm south.

By the time that the Moncks were living in their new house at least one professional northern architect had picked up the Grecian baton and set off running with it. His name was John Dobson and he was and remains the best known of all North Eastern architects.

He was born in 1787 in Chirton, just outside North Shields, where his dad had a large, popular and clearly impressive market garden to which fashionable people could resort, stroll along pleasant walks and have genteel picnics in arbours, all things I would love to do. If only I was fashionable. As he was growing up, Dobson learned to draw and fence and dance, the sort of accomplishments that would prepare him for working with the well-to-do and the country families. He went to London for a while to study as an artist and he took lessons in engineering and technical drawing, but then he came home and signed up as an apprentice with an architect called David Stephenson who had become the region's fashionable architect of choice in the years after 1800.

He stayed in that partnership for a few years before setting up for himself and developing a remarkable and varied body of work throughout his life. He did Newcastle's Grainger Market and substantial bits of Grey Street; perhaps most impressively he designed the wonderful Central Station, which was far and away the most impressive provincial station in the country (and the world) when it was opened in 1850; but he also became a country house architect of considerable stature. Like John Paterson he built in two different styles. On the whole his houses before 1830 were in the Grecian style while the ones in the 1830s and later tended to be Gothic and Tudor. They are all worthy of attention but the best of them are absolute belters (as we architectural critics say).

On the outside the Grecian ones are all quite simple and undecorated but utterly perfect. He himself claimed that the wonderful standard of stonework he was able to achieve on the walls of his houses came about because of the level of perfection demanded by Sir Charles Monck at Belsay. '*After Belsay*, Dobson wrote, '*a Northumbrian mason has been considered among the best that could be found in any part of the country*'. He exaggerated the elegant smoothness of his walls by burying the drainpipes in the thickness of the wall so you couldn't see them, which looks good but as you can imagine has led to moans from later owners when leaks and bursts have occurred and been difficult to get at.

They do look good though and most of the houses are also beautifully sited. Perhaps he was influenced by experience of his father's market garden, but he took great care about the setting and surroundings of all of his houses. He would go and camp on the site so that he could work out the precise behaviour of light and where the prevailing weather came from. Lots of the houses are on elevated shelves with beautiful views of the valley below but the entrances are rarely on the front façade; he placed the main doors on a more sheltered side wall, or occasionally even round the back, protected from the winds by banks of trees.

There are some wonderful details. The ground floor rooms on the south front of Nunnykirk Hall have full-height windows that can be opened completely; the frames slide into slots in the floor turning the room an open garden-room in nice weather; even the shutters fold back neatly into recesses in the reveals so that no light at all is lost when the day is bright.

But the masterpiece, inside and out, is Longhirst Hall just outside Morpeth, which was the home he built for a branch of the Lawson family who had the good fortune to find coal under their land. The entrance is dramatic and exciting – two beautifully carved full-height Corinthian columns under a pediment and behind it a magnificent stone hall and staircase.

But if Longhirst was built for a family with buried coal beneath their feet, the other houses were paid for in a variety of different ways. Nunnykirk was one of the traditional ones, built for a member of an old landed family. William Orde's family had been around from year dot and had fallen on good times by the 1800s. He kept a stable of racehorses including a mare called Beeswing, whose name lives on in a number of eponymous pubs and she was rightly famous. She took part in 63 races, finished 57 and won 51! She only came lower than second once in her career and was even (remember Francis Sitwell's sheep) taken down south once to win the Ascot Gold Cup in 1842.

(Beeswings's dad – I should have called him her sire since he was obviously a horse – also has pubs named after him, in Prudhoe for example. It's called The Doctor Syntax. He was described as having a broad nose with open nostrils and a high droopy rump – not unlike myself then, but unlike me, when he finished racing the good times started and he began his career as a stud before finally being – and I quote – euthenised at Newmarket in 1838).

Meldon Park, which is beautifully sited and has a magnificent full-height entrance hall with an imperial staircase, was built in 1832 for quite a different client.

Isaac Cookson was the third generation owner of a chemical works on Tyneside and he had enough money to buy the Meldon estate's 2000 acres for a whopping 57,000 guineas and then to pay John Dobson a further £7,185 for the mansion he built on it. There must have been money in them thar chemicals. His partner in the business was called William Cuthbert and a few years later, in 1836, he too employed Dobson to design him a splendid house called Beaufront Castle, high up on the north side of Tynedale near Hexham with a glorious view of the whole valley. It's not Classical at all, but Tudory-Gothic, a huge, free, completely asymmetrical and tremendously exciting design.

Longhirst Hall which, sadly, John doesn't own.

I've gone on about these houses (and I could and should have mentioned others) because they're a group, all built in a bit of a purple patch of about 10 to 15 years, all by the same man, a provincial architect who never (or very rarely) worked outside his homeland and yet all of superlative quality; and they all look as good today as they did when they were first built. One of them is a school now but the rest are all still in use as private houses (though hardly any in the hands of the families that built them). None of them, sadly, belongs to me.

In the 19th century, especially in the towns and cities, buildings changed. There were new sorts that had never existed before – stations and office blocks, warehouses, railway bridges, station hotels, much larger town halls to cope with the activities of expanded local corporations. Hospitals got bigger and bigger and there were insane asylums, police and fire stations, vast new prisons, pumping stations to deliver water to larger and larger towns, sewers and drainage systems to get rid of the waste. New schools were needed to satisfy the expanding reach of state education, and factories on a new and unimagined scale. Culture and leisure activities proliferated, including art galleries and public baths, the provision of public parks became a matter of pride.

Huge growth in the populations of towns meant that whole new ways of housing the working classes had to be devised including by-laws to encourage health and well-being. Victorian towns and cities experienced unprecedented growth and change and to cope with it there were vast changes in the technologies used.

Increasingly iron (and later steel) frames provided the skeleton of the new buildings. Cheaper and better plate glass made buildings lighter and shop windows possible, concrete, and eventually reinforced concrete, allowed for revolutionary new forms. And, of course, there were those fundamental, hidden but vital improvements as well, the sewers, the water supplies and the drainage systems that made vast improvements in public health possible.

It took time for these things to happen but after a slow start and over the course of the century the changes occurred. In Newcastle, for example, between 1800 and 1835 there was a 90% increase in the population but no changes were made at all in the provision of water supplies or waste disposal. Even by 1845 only one house in 12 was connected to a water supply. But change accelerated. In London, for example, in 1855 only 10% of houses were connected to a sewer but by 1870 the sewerage network was complete and in Newcastle, by 1900 most houses had a loo and a piped water supply. These were amazing transformations and people recognised it at the time. In 1870 the Prince of Wales recovered from Cholera and announced, "If I weren't a prince I would be a plumber".

Light and power were the other great innovations emerging in the 1800s and Tyneside played an active role in both. Newcastle was an early user of indoor and outdoor gas lighting but under the inspiration of Joseph Swan it was much more than that; it was an absolute world leader in the development of electrical power.

A time of massive change on Tyneside then, but in the countryside and even in the big posh country houses the speed of change was quite different.

Some older houses didn't seem to change at all and in others the speed of change was painstakingly slow. A previous owner of Chillingham Castle told me a revealing story once. The house had been abandoned in the 1930s though it remained whole and usable and in the 1960s his sister decided to hold her wedding there. Knowing it hadn't been used for so long they employed somebody from the village to come in for two weeks and keep two fires burning continually in the room they were to use. On the day of the wedding an elderly uncle, who had known the castle for many years, spoke to him. He said: '*I want to congratulate you my boy. I've been coming here for 70 years and I've never known the place so warm.*' The temperature turned out to be just under 50 degrees Fahrenheit.

Another medieval house I went to in the 1980s had just had central heating installed for the first time and the house was so unused to it that the heat made the panelling in the hall crack; I think it is quite likely that most, if not all of the county's medieval towers weren't plumbed in or wired for electricity until well into the 20th century. Even Wallington, which has no towers and no massively thick walls and is one of the greatest of all Northumbrian houses, wasn't wired for electricity until the second third of the 20th century.

At the very top of the social tree there were exceptions though. When Alnwick was remodelled in the 1850s by the fourth Duke he made enormous changes to the style and décor of the castle but there is enough evidence to suggest that he made more fundamental changes too. A new kitchen was built, a splendid reimagining of a medieval kitchen with a high, stone-vaulted ceiling, just perfect for a castle – except that it

John and film crew admiring Beaufront Castle in 1987.

was outside the castle walls, a good 60 metres from the dining room to which it was connected by a tiled tunnel under the castle lawns, along which the food was wheeled on trucks before being raised to the dining room in a lift.

I'm sure that there were loads of other improvements made at Alnwick where money was less an object than in most other places, but in general it was hard to make changes to solid, stony, complicated old houses. And anyway the underlying infrastructure wasn't there in the way it was in the towns; plumbed-in water-closets and running water were much harder to provide in isolated country spots where drains and pipes and sewers would have been phenomenally expensive to construct.

But the physical difficulties weren't the only thing holding back change; a natural conservatism was common among country house owners that made them stick to their old stone-built houses and held back the advance of new-fangled services and building methods.

And anyway, country-house owners had enough money to pay people to deal with the problem. There were armies of servant to keep the fires going and the rooms warm and flocks of chambermaids were available to carry jugs of hot water to the bedrooms and potties of oojah away to the midden so the pressure for change among the old houses wasn't so great.

But among newly built houses, even quite early in the century, there were a few new ideas that began to emerge, including a couple of new developments that we now take for granted but which were first introduced by John Dobson. He had watched an excavation at Haltonchesters Roman Fort in 1827 and seen how the Roman builders created a sort of cavity walling to conserve heat in the bath house by attaching hollow tiles to the inside of the walls. He adapted this idea and used it in his buildings after 1827, in the cellars at Beaufront Castle for example. He seems to have been the first architect to adopt the idea and he introduced damp-proof courses as well by protecting the footings of the exterior walls from the encroaching soil with a stone-lined trench.

So gradually other changes began to occur. It's quite hard to spot what happened where and when because visitors don't usually get shown the toilet arrangements or the water supplies, but from time to time you catch enough glimpses to suggest that improvements were beginning to filter through.

Longridge Tower near Berwick is one example. It was built in 1876 and had its own private gas plant. Highgreen Manor, in a gloriously isolated situation on wild moorland north of Bellingham, was even more advanced. It was built in the 1880s and extended in 1894 for the Morrison-Bell family and yet, despite its isolation, it had an electricity supply. I don't know how it was powered; there must have been a generator and a power house though I never saw it, but when I was there a few years ago I was shown a battery house at the back of the mansion – just a medium sized wooden shed filled with rows and rows of shelves bearing large glass batteries.

Among the examples I have spotted in Northumberland over the years were beautiful Victorian bathroom and toilet fittings in a number of places: Prudhoe Hall, built in 1878, was a private country house before it became the administrative building for Prudhoe hospital. It has a lovely original WC, all brass fittings and blue and white ceramic fixtures (which I was pleased to test); wrought-iron lamp standards on the stairs have now been converted for electricity but must

have been gas fitments when they were originally installed in 1878.

At Fenton House near Wooler, built in 1870 for the Lambton family, the only room I remember from my visits as a listed Building man was a bathroom on the first floor, which was clearly an original part of the building. It had superb fittings including a shower unit made with sheets of thick glass in a mahogany frame and with three taps marked (in beautiful Victorian lettering) – Hot, Cold and Rainwater.

The provision of a bathroom on the first floor implies that there was enough water pressure to make the shower and the toilet work – no mean feat in the countryside and especially in flat country or where there was no District Water Board to provide the force – so one of the clues that water technology was reaching country houses is when they have towers. Fenton has a tower; lots and lots of Victorian country houses were given towers; they can look good, of course and provide a platform to look at the view but they also provided a nice elevated place for the water tank, Not all the towers will have had this function but lots of them did and the most remarkable surviving example in Northumberland is the tower at Haggerston Castle, just south of Berwick.

For centuries Haggerston had been the property of the Haggerston family but it was bought and rebuilt in 1893 for a Liverpool industrialist called Thomas Leyland. Most of it was demolished in the 1930s and it is now turned into a caravan park, but a few bits remain that reveal that it used to be an absolutely gigantic house.

There is still a two-storey rotunda that was the entrance to the mansion. It's enormous; you could play golf in it, or hold yodelling competitions; and there is a tower, tall and thin – or to put it another way, thin and very tall. I climbed up it once and I might have become confused and got it wrong as I crawled pitifully up the last few flights, but I am pretty sure that I had to climb 12 storeys to get there. There is a sticky-outy room just below the top floor that provides startling views over the flat coastal plain towards the sea, but the main function of the whole thing was to house the water tank on the top floor, which was filled using a pumping engine at ground level and was high enough to send splendid

Niagara-like gushes flowing from the many taps and toilets in the house.

The architect of this gargantuan house (it had a private zoo as well incidentally, you can see the rhino houses and the antelope houses as you drive past it on the A1) the architect was the extremely famous and important architect Richard Norman Shaw and it is one of his other houses in the county that provides the clearest evidence of a changing attitude to country house technology ... not just in Northumberland but in the country as a whole.

Cragside was the home of the industrialist, entrepreneur and inventor, Lord Armstrong, who featured in the previous chapter. He had bought some land in the hills outside Rothbury in the 1860s and built a relatively modest little second home for himself (i.e. about 6 times bigger than my house), which he engaged Norman Shaw to extend for him in the 1870s and 80s.

The original house, the section built in the 1860s, had an interesting central heating system. It was a sort of plenum system by which air moves because of relatively small differences of air pressure. Prairie dogs use it in their colonies. They have entrances and exits at different heights – no more than a few feet but enough for the air pressure to be slightly lower at the higher end, which means that air flows from the lower to the upper entrances and creates ventilation.

A cunning wheeze you might think, and you would be right. Durham Gaol, built in 1815 uses the same system, ventilation at ground level and high chimneys to draw away the stale air. Armstrong's first Cragside building uses it too. There are ventilation grilles in the basement and a whole series of ducts through the walls, under the floors and in the ceiling spaces and hugely tall chimneys. The main difference from Durham Gaol was that behind the ducts in the basement there were a couple of rooms full of heated pipes to warm the air, which was then channelled into all the rooms.

From that start, the new, extended house hit the fast-forward pedal and became the Victorian Age's poster child of technological development. Here's a list of some of what was included:

A fully-grown central-heating system with a boiler

Early electric lamp and, right, bath at Cragside.

and radiators (in decorative wooden boxes). They were among the earliest radiators in use anywhere.

Electric lights. He started off with arc lights powered by hydro electric power – the first such lights in the world and the first use of hydro-electric power. In 1878 Armstrong had dammed the Debdon Burn that ran down through his garden in order to generate the power.

Electric lights (2). Armstrong was a great supporter of Joseph Swan and had been present at the Newcastle Lit and Phil when Swan first demonstrated his incandescent light bulbs in 1878. He bought 45 of them and converted existing fittings in Cragside to take them. It wasn't the first house in the world to be lit by electric light – Swan's own house in Gateshead was - but it was

Lord Armstrong's Cragside was at the heart of technological innovation.

among the first and he was delighted with it. He said it was the first artificial light source to be safe and free from smells and noises. He said it cast *'no ghastly hue upon the countenance'*. There were people who thought the light harsh. One lady wrote that there was '*nothing more unbecoming than the pitiless glare of electricity'* though I doubt whether we would think nowadays that 45 40-watt bulbs (because that's all they were) in a house the size of Cragside were capable of creating a pitiless glare.

There was a plunge pool in the basement, bathrooms and flushing toilets all over the house, provided with water from the huge water tank in a pretty little half-timbered cottage on the roof of a tower at the front of the building.

The same lakes that drove the generators provided hydraulic power for all sorts of treats. In the kitchen there was a hydraulic dumb waiter and rotisserie. There was a hydraulic lift, an electric gong to summon the household to the dining room, an extraordinarily early electric vacuum cleaner to get rid of the crumbs after the meal, a washing machine to remove the dinner medals on your waistcoat and an electric dishwasher to help get the dishes done. Beyond the house, in the estate, the sawmill was powered by electricity, the glass houses in the kitchen gardens were heated and the rows of plant pots had automatic watering systems and rotated gently in the sunlight, driven by hydraulic power.

I bet this remarkable list of technological innovations is far from complete, but the list is only one part of the significance of Lord Armstrong's house. Shaw's architecture also introduced new ideas. It's built in a new style for a start – a style that was radically new in the 1870s. It's known as the "Old English style" and is a picturesque and off-beat mixture of towers and gables, stonework and half timbering, as if it had grown up over the centuries. It doesn't look as if it has been imposed on the landscape willy nilly but that it had emerged organically out of it. It is intensely romantic, surrounded by rocks and trees (7 million of them, incidentally, which must have cost him a bob or two down the garden centre).

It's an Arts and Crafts House, an early example of the style, but a masterpiece, and as well as Shaw himself, lots and lots of the biggest names in the Arts and Crafts movement contributed to the house. Inside there is stained glass by Burne-Jones, Ford Madox Brown and Philip Webb. Some of William Morris's most beautiful wallpapers were hung there from the start. There are tiles and paintings by William de Morgan and a gigantic fireplace by William Lethaby.

These were all the most modern names in art when they did the work at Cragside and alongside Shaw's design they created beautiful rooms. The library is gorgeous, for example – not grand or splendid but gorgeous, comfy, warm, bathed in beautiful light; and the dining room is the same. It has a feature that was one of Shaw's signature features – an inglenook fireplace, a dream of cosy domesticity. Lord Armstrong had himself painted sitting in it, reading in the firelight. The mantelpiece is carved with the words: '*East West Hame's Best.*'

And that sums up the mood of the house, especially how the work done in the 1870s feels. It gets a bit grander and colder in the 1880s when the huge drawing-room was added with its gigantic marble fireplace – an object, I might say, that has more bosoms and bottoms and little boys' willies than you normally like to see when you're having a chat by the fireside – but the earlier rooms, the living rooms and the study and all the bedrooms are models of Victorian comfort and propriety – domestic bliss – but posh.

Posh enough for extremely significant people to be invited to stay. Bearing in mind that Armstrong had started off in a gently middle-class sort of way as a trainee solicitor in Newcastle, it is rather remarkable that the Czar of Russia, the King of Siam, two emperors of Japan and the Prince and Princess of Wales should all have come to stay, to be schmoozed most of the time,

Pictured: Detail of fireplace by W.R. Lethaby at Cragside.

into buying the ships and armaments from the Armstrong factories. He didn't do badly for a lad from Shieldfield and I think it's safe to say that his house is 19th century Northumberland's architectural masterpiece.

Cragside might be the high point of Victorian design in the county but there are two other houses that have to be recognised for different qualities. One of them is Wallington and the other is Ford Castle, both of which, as you know, had existed for centuries but underwent significant and delightful periods of change in the middle of the 1800s.

In the 1700s Ford had become a property of the Delaval family including, finally, Sir John Delaval who died in 1808 and left the castle to his granddaughter, who had married the 2nd Marquis of Waterford from Ireland. When she died, the property passed to her son Henry, the 3rd Marquis, who seems to have been, as a young man, a complete chip off the disreputable Delaval block. To put it mildly, he was a bit of a lad. Bertie Wooster and the Drones Club spring to mind, or possibly the Bullingdon Club and several of our recent Prime Ministers. One story will illustrate that claim.

In 1837 he was on his way to Melton Mowbray with some chums. They had all been to the races and were as

Ford Castle.

pickled as some cucumbers. They were travelling on a turnpike when they were confronted by a gatekeeper who tried to charge them to continue. Unfortunately the toll cottage and the gates were in the middle of being redecorated and there was a quantity of red paint lying about, which the 3rd Marquis stole, painted the toll-keeper red, nailed up his door and set off into Melton Mowbray where he and his friends set about painting the town red – literally. When a constable tried to stop them they painted him red. When they were refused entry into a hotel, they painted it red. Not unexpectedly the phrase we use today comes from a descendent of the wild Delavals and an owner of Ford Castle.

There were other similar stories about him but then, ask yourself, what does a wild, wealthy tearaway young man need? Answer: the calming influence of a good woman. In 1839 he met and married Louisa Stewart, the daughter of the British Ambassador in Paris, which made her the Marchioness of Waterford. They lived an evidently calm and happy life together in Ireland for 12 years, during which they came to Ford every summer for their hols and a bit of hunting. They both loved it and when he tragically died after falling from his horse in a hunting accident in 1859, she decided to move to Northumberland permanently. She lived in the castle until she died in 1891 at the age of 73.

She altered the place. She brought in a Scottish architect called David Bryce and they returned the entrance front back to its appearance in the 17th century. They built a new façade at the back of the house, which is excellent; it is restrained, castle-like and noble – Victorian design at its most worthy. She made millions of improvements around the estate and built a new model village beside the castle, which included a beautiful village school designed by Bryce and decorated over the following 20 years by Louisa herself …

… because on top of all her other virtues, she was an artist. She had trained under John Ruskin and was a friend of innumerable other prominent artistic figures of the time, including the painter and sculptor G.F. Watts, who was later to carve her beautiful gravestone in the churchyard, a stone's throw from her home. Well, for 20 years she worked to cover the walls of the school with

Painting by Lady Waterford in the village school.

man, earnest and brilliant, but kind and unselfish, always willing to help out his friends with their research and expecting nothing in return. She, on the other hand, comes across as enchanting. She certainly enchanted an extraordinary number of the country's most eminent painters, writers and thinkers. Ruskin (him again) said that '*Lady T kept us laughing all day long*' and he wrote about '*her wit and playfulness*'. She became friends with most of the Pre-Raphaelite painters, with Thomas Carlyle, the Brownings, Algernon Swinburne – all sorts of Victorian celebs with whom she communicated or who came to stay in the house.

The house the Trevelyans lived in was essentially the same Wallington that we see today except that in the middle, surrounded by four 18th century ranges, was a

biblical scenes using children from the school and people from the estate as her models. The paintings are wonderful. The school has become a gallery of her work and includes lots of other lovely paintings, drawings and sketches that she did, but the pictures on the school walls are the most memorable.

The only person ever to criticise them was Ruskin himself. He was disappointed with them and thought she could have done better – but he was quite capable of being a bit of a plank. The problem was that he was a pre-Raphaelite whereas Louisa's paintings are closer to the work of Raphael himself and they are one of the most heart-warming groups of mid-Victorian paintings to be found in the country.

And Louisa (Marchioness of Waterford) wasn't the only woman to have had a dramatic effect on the artistic life of the county. Another was Pauline Trevelyan, the wife of Sir Walter Calverley Trevelyan, the owner of Wallington. She was the daughter of a country vicar and only 17 when she met her aristocratic husband-to-be. He was 19 years older than her but they shared a passion for stones – for geology and palaeontology.

The marriage turned out to be childless and too short (she died in 1866 at the age of 50) but it seems to have been entirely satisfactory. He was a quite a solemn

Enclosed courtyard at Wallington featuring amazing artwork.

bleak, lifeless and entirely enclosed courtyard. It was neither use nor ornament and Ruskin is usually given the credit for suggesting that it be covered over and turned into a more useful part of the house.

 Pauline took control of this project. She called in our chum John Dobson, whose work in the centre of Newcastle she had admired when she first came north, and he became the architect. He did a terrific job and created a room that is both domestic and usable but impressively architectural at the same time.

It has two levels of arches on all four sides and on the ground floor. The columns between the arches are decorated with paintings of wild flowers. Some were done by Pauline herself, Millais did another and Ruskin contributed one too. Between them, set into the arches, there are eight remarkable paintings of scenes from Northumbrian History, which were the work a Pre-Raphaelite painter called William Bell Scott who was based in Newcastle.

They too are marvellous, vibrant, brilliantly coloured and immensely true to life. The scenes they portray start with the Romans and end, remarkably, and most impressively of all, with a magnificent painting of contemporary Newcastle. It's called "Iron and Coal" and it is stuffed to the gunnels with things from 19th century Northumberland. Robert Stephenson's High Level Bridge is in the background with a steam train crossing it. On the river there are sailing boats and steam boats; a coal-laden keel has just passed under the bridge. In the foreground, a little girl, patiently waiting to deliver her father's lunch, is sitting on the barrel of Lord Armstrong's revolutionary artillery piece and one of the shells from his factories lies by her side. In the middle, a powerful and heroic group of workmen wield hammers.

It is one of the greatest of all representations of the Industrial Revolution and of working-class labour and its place in one of the great traditional houses of Northumberland is a reminder that by the middle of the 19th century the county was no longer where it had been for so long, beyond the pale, on the edge of life as we know it, but firmly established as part of a modern Britain.

Our Glorious Churches

There are a few exceptions, but most of what I have written about in this book wouldn't appear in a more general history of England. Northumberland, as I've said before, is a long way from London, relatively poor and with a relatively small population so the stuff that has gone on here has rarely been deemed worthy of inclusion in national surveys. That is particularly true of our 19th century churches. I can say with reasonable confidence that none of the 19th century churches in Northumberland will have been given a second glance by those looking at the national picture …

… but I like them and it's my book. So there.

English Church architecture in the 1800s falls very roughly into three broad periods.

At the beginning of the century, between 1800 and about 1840, church architecture was at a bit of lowish ebb. It had been the same, more or less, throughout the previous century when the taste in places of worship had been more chapel-like with a liking for simpler spaces where the congregation went to listen to the preacher rather than to take part in elaborate ritual.

So churches built before about 1840 are often described, not altogether kindly, as "preaching boxes". They usually have some 'churchy' features, a simple tower perhaps and pointy windows, but they hardly ever look like real gothic buildings such as you would have found in the Middle Ages. There's no tracery in the windows and the interiors don't have arcades or aisles. They tend to be just big rectangular rooms, sometimes nicely proportioned, sometimes homely and comforting, but not convincingly 'old'.

Northumberland has dozens of churches built like that in those years, almost all nice but unspectacular.

One that I like is Cambo church, the home church for the Trevelyans at Wallington. It is a good example. It looks quite posh and churchy now because it had a fine prominent tower added in the 1880s and it stands on a splendidly prominent hilltop as well, but the body of the church is just a single, big, aisleless room with pointy windows like so many others. It was designed by John and Benjamin Green, who I suggested might have been responsible for the stations on the Newcastle to Carlisle Railway, and they gave the church one feature that is definitely worthy of notice – its roof is made of laminated timber – as far as I know, the only early surviving example of the technology that the Greens invented or introduced into Britain in the 1830s.

There are lots of others more or less like that but in Northumberland there is only one church from the early part of the century that rises above the others in terms of architecture. The church of St Thomas, on the Haymarket in Newcastle, was built in 1827 by John Dobson and it is a big, expensive and quite beautiful building inside and out. It's built in the Gothic style – but it still isn't a realistic copy of the proper Gothic. It has columns to create aisles – but they are made of cast iron. It has a vaulted ceiling – but it is made of plaster instead of stone. It has galleries round three sides so it's a "preaching box" – but a posh one. It is a terrific building, but not historically accurate.

But then, a few years later (in 1842) and three or four hundred yards away, the city (and the county) joined a revolution in church architecture. The Roman Catholic Cathedral was designed by Augustus Welby Pugin and it looks, for all the world, as if it had been built in the middle ages. As soon as you step inside you are carried

Big, expensive and beautiful - St Thomas' Church, Newcastle.

back to a dream of the Gothic past. There is a forest of pillars and arches and a rich atmosphere of ritual and mystery. The windows are filled with stained glass done as loving copies of the truly ancient glass in places like Chartres and York Minster, so the sunlight casts soft rainbow beams in the religious gloom of the building. All the strange ritual objects of the mediaeval world are there – richly carved fonts and altars, rows of elaborately carved stone sedilia for priests to sit on beside the altar just like priests used to do in Mediaeval times.

The explanation of the extraordinary changes that occurred round about 1840 was the arrival on the scene of a new and hugely influential religious movement called the Oxford Movement because, and I want you to follow this carefully, because it started in Oxford. It was started by academics from Oxford University who felt that the Church of England needed beefing up a bit, more ritual, more fancy bits, more kneeling down and standing up.

They were what we would call High Church nowadays, or even Anglo-Catholics. Some of them eventually went the whole hog and became Roman Catholics, in fact Newman ended up as a Cardinal in the Roman Catholic Church. When they looked back towards the Middle Ages they saw what they thought of as a more devout age and so they wanted buildings that reflected that time, buildings full of light and shade, religious symbolism, ancient craftsmanship, lots of beauty and atmosphere …

… and soon these chaps were joined by a generation of architects who were ready and eager to give them the sort of buildings they wanted, and the leader of the charge was Augustus Welby Pugin, who was a Catholic himself and a passionate devotee of historical accuracy and ritual exuberance. He exploded onto the scene at the very end of the 1830s and after that, for thirty-odd years, you were either there or you were square. For quite a few decades churches had to be true to the Gothic past and they needed to be stage-sets for ritual and religious mystery; that's the sort of churches that were being built all over the country …ish.

I say "ish" because in Northumberland, apart from in the expanding suburbs of Newcastle there weren't

The Norman-style Church of St James in Morpeth.

many completely new churches built in the middle years of the 19th century but there were a few, including several that I really like.

The first is the Church of St James in the middle of Morpeth, which was begun in 1843 and opened in 1846. Morpeth needed a new church because the town had begun to expand towards the north and the only other church, the parish church of St Mary, was inconveniently far away, up a hill, beside the castle on the opposite side of the river and the southern edge of the town.

The architect had no local connections. He was called Benjamin Ferrey and he had started his working life working for Pugin, and in Morpeth he did a spiffing job. It's a big, splendid, perfect-looking building in the Norman style, which was suddenly and unexpectedly a fashionable style in England at just that time. In fact, if you ever see a Norman-style building that looks too perfect to be real and ancient, it's a good trick to look wise, muse a bit and then say, "I would think 1842 or 43, possibly as late as 1845". You will be right and in a position to feel smug, though whether people will be impressed with your knowledge or think that you are a supercilious git is a moot point.

Ferrey's church is gorgeous inside as well as out. He

designed all the details and the furnishing as well, including tiled floors, the pulpit and the reading desk, the choir stalls and a splendid arcade of intersecting Norman arches round the apse. The only things that were added later were the wall paintings, which were done in the 1870s, and the rather beautiful screen, which was carved by a woodworking group from the congregation in Edwardian times.

Another new church that I really like from those days is a bit of a mystery. It's the church of St Maurice at Ellingham near Seahouses. It's on an ancient site, outside the village in a grove of old trees, but it was rebuilt entirely in 1862 by a vicar – the problem is that I am not sure which vicar. The last time I wrote about it was when I was involved in writing the second edition of Niklaus Pevsner's "Northumberland" volume in the Buildings of England series. Pevsner said the church was done using the designs of the Rev, J.F. Turner and I trustingly copied down what he had said but now I'm not so sure. I can't find out who the Reverend Turner was and the church's own history suggests that it was the Reverend Charles Thorp, the vicar at the time, who was responsible. Maybe they both did it. Maybe one of you will know and tell me all about it. Perhaps I'll find out the truth myself, but whoever it was I like what he came up with.

From outside it's obvious that it's a Victorian church, the stonework makes it clear that it isn't ancient, but the shape of the building fixes it firmly in the 'historically accurate' group. It's not a box. You can't tell from the outside of a box what's going on inside, how the interior is divided up, but St Maurice wears its heart on its sleeve; every bit of it reveals honestly from the outside what its purpose is.

The main thrust of the building is cross-shaped and high; there are lower lean-to roofs which are clearly aisles; a single-storey, sticky-outy bit is obviously a vestry, another is the porch; a small square projection up the corner of the tower seems to be shouting, "I am a staircase". There are battlements and gothic touches. The windows all have tracery in the late 13th century or early 14th century style, which was the almost obligatory go-to style in the 1850s and 60s, but they are all slightly

The mysterious Church of St Maurice at Ellingham with it magnificent windows (below).

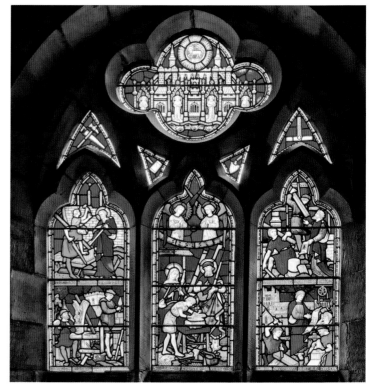

different as if they were carved at different times; and they are all different sizes; big windows light the important bits of the building, small ones the minor bits. It's all very honest and clever.

Inside the atmosphere is dark, moody and rich. It is still lit by candlelight and there are elaborate brass candleholders, a wonderful brass lectern with branching candelabra and all sorts of gleaming decorative and carved bits and pieces. It is intensely satisfying and the glass … well the glass is terrific and tells a series of different stories.

First of all there's the east window, which is clearly different from anything else in the church. It shows Christ in Majesty flanked by a couple of saints and it's beautifully drawn and richly coloured and I happen to know that it is not Victorian at all but 16th century Flemish glass, which came here from Durham Cathedral where it was being replaced in a restoration. It was 'liberated' from Durham by the Rev Charles Thorp – no not our Rev Charles Thorp … I'm sorry to confuse you (he lied) but it was his dad who got them. His dad was also called Rev Charles Thorp. He was an Archdeacon at

The moody interior of the Church of St Maurice in Ellingham.

bank' to encourage the poor to save and have access to loans.

He was a passionate anti-slavery campaigner and after the end of slavery he helped to set up a university in Sierra Leone so that freed slaves could have access to learning. I could go on but none of that is relevant to this chapter except that he was born in Newcastle and went to the Royal Grammar School and his son was the vicar of St Maurice where I was telling you about the glass because there are at least two other stained glass windows in the church that stick in the memory.

In the north transept is a brilliant window made in 1862. It's a "Creation" window. It has God, looking splendid at the top and surrounded by angels and underneath 12 panels tell the whole story of the creation. We see the world being made in a welter of volcanoes and apocalyptic storms. We see the fishes and then the birds and then all the creatures of the land. There are fossils and beautiful plant forms and finally all human life is there to see, some of it sensibly praising God and being well behaved while others sadly end up, in the bottom right-hand panel, tormented by the flames of hell.

Durham but he was also the vicar of Ryton Church near Gateshead and he filled that church with Flemish glass too, and **his** dad (our Charles Thorp's grandpa, do try to keep up) had also been a vicar and an Archdeacon in Northumberland and Charles the elder clearly had a soft spot for some of his dad's churches too, so he gave Flemish glass to Bamburgh church and furnishings from Durham to St Cuthbert's Chapel on the Farne Islands (which he owned, incidentally, they were worth a bob or two the Thorps) and to Norham church as well. He spread his Durham gleanings widely and to cap it all his son's vicarage in Ellingham got a fantastic 17th century oak staircase from Durham.

I do him an injustice, Charles Thorp the elder, implying that he went around Durham nicking stuff, because he was a remarkable man. He bought the Farnes and employed a warden to look after the wild life – possibly the first ever such environmental appointment in the country. He was one of the founders of Durham University and its first Warden. He established free education in his parish at Ryton and opened the country's first 'penny

The other window is my favourite, though. It's in the south wall of the nave. It is all about architecture and it starts at the top with Heaven, which looks nicely built as you would expect from the Holy City and underneath Heaven there is a series of panels. One shows Noah's Ark, which was made (you might be surprised to learn) in 2246 BC. Solomon's Temple in Jerusalem (1012 BC) is the next major building followed by Durham Cathedral (1093-1289 AD) and last of all, in the bottom right-hand corner, is Ellingham Church being rebuilt in 1862. Good company.

This window was made by William Wailes, who was born in Newcastle in 1808, started off as a grocer, developed an interest in stained glass when he was still a boy, built a kiln in his back yard, went to Germany in his teens to study the craft and came back to found his

17th Century glass donated by Charles Thorp.

own stained-glass studio in Newcastle. It was very successful, he was one of only eleven glass designers who were invited to exhibit at the Great Exhibition in 1851, and eventually he employed 76 people including a number who went on to set up their own studios. His work is to be found all over the country but there's masses of it in Northumberland, often signed and quite easily recognisable; his figures are lively and animated and the colours bright and fresh and beautiful, like the 13th century windows that had inspired him. Among my favourites is a window in St Andrew's Church in Newcastle, which commemorates his own son, John, who died when he was only 9 years old. John was deaf, or possibly deaf and dumb, and the windows are filled with tender figures using hand signs that demonstrate love and sadness. Wailes remained committed to philanthropic work with deaf and dumb children all his life and left money to the cause in his will after he died in 1881.

In Northumberland there aren't many brand new churches in these middle years of the century because there weren't many people. What there was instead was a lot of churches which got restored, either because they were in bad nick or because they weren't pretty enough to suit modern tastes.

Actually that was more or less true for the whole of England. By the late 1850s more than a quarter of the country's old churches had been done up; that sounds OK because you wouldn't have wanted them to fall down would you? But it all depended on what sort of restoration took place and at the time there were three different approaches to the job: -:

The commonest by far was **the destructive approach.** (That's what they called it at the time). This was the approach used by people who thought that churches, whatever they were like to start with, should be made as Gothic as possible and always in the typically English Decorated Gothic style of the late 13th and early 14th centuries. And anything that didn't fit had to be got rid of. Between the 1840s and the 1870s, thousands of churches were dragged kicking and screaming into this modern style

A remarkable example of this approach in Northumberland is the church of St Bartholomew at Whittingham between Alnwick and Rothbury.

When a new vicar, the Reverend Goodenough, arrived at Whittingham in the 1840s he decided his church wasn't … wasn't good enough. He clearly thought it was a disappointing muddle of periods and styles. It had an Anglo-Saxon tower, a 13th century south aisle with pointed gothic arches, a 12th century North aisle with rounded Norman arches, and an 18th century Chancel. Too messy! Oh! Good grief that was no good, so his architect (J. Green again) demolished the North Aisle and built a new one in imitation of the South aisle. He had demolished the upper part of the Saxon tower and stuffed the lower part with gunpowder in readiness for blowing it up when the congregation, in an interestingly early example of conservationism, stepped in and stopped him. That's just enough, Goodenough, I believe they said, and the remaining Saxon bits survived – but not the 18th century chancel, that was an affront too great for the High Victorian mind and so in 1871 it was replaced with something a bit more up to date by an architect who played a big part in the story of Northumberland's Victorian churches.

He was called F.R. Wilson. He came from Cottingham near Hull and worked on the Houses of Parliament before coming to Northumberland in 1854 to be the site architect for the restoration and rebuilding of Alnwick Castle. He must have been a man of taste and discrimination because he never left the county until he died here in the 1890s. He made his mark with all sorts of buildings including at least one large and delightful country house (Cheswick Hall), lots of vicarages and a couple of brand new churches, but he is especially remembered for the restorations he carried out. In particular he remodelled or rebuilt the east end (the chancels) of lots of churches and he invariably made them much more gothic, fancier and richer than they had been before.

The idea among all the mid-Victorian architects was that churches should get more intense the closer you got to the heart of the mystery, to the altar and where the communion took place, and a really good example is the chancel of Holy Trinity Church in Embleton, which F.R. rebuilt in 1867.

The rest of the church is typically Northumbrian, strong, plain and simple with local stone, mainly built in the 13th century but Wilson rebuilt the east end in a style you would describe as typically High Victorian. It's multi-coloured with alternating bands of pink and buff coloured stone and the roof timbers are elaborately carved in a rather spiky style. His work is much fancier than the rest of the church and I didn't like it when I was younger, I didn't like *him* actually; I thought he was a bit rough and ready and too High Victorian by half, but I like him now. I recognise that he was a product of that Oxford Movement that Pugin introduce into Newcastle in 1842 but that he had an instantly recognisable style all of his own.

It helps that he had a lovely touch with windows – sometimes (at Whittingham for example) they are brilliantly and intensely coloured; at other times (Ponteland and Elsdon for example) he filled the windows with elaborately patterned clear glass with leaded panes that are among the prettiest thing to be found in any of Northumberland's 19th century churches.

So that's the first two of the broad periods of 19th century church buildings and by the end of the 1860s the mood was beginning to change and the third period was peeping its sneaky head above the parapet. As the century progressed, architects began to show a bit more freedom to design what they wanted. They began to be more … liberated, more eclectic and personal in their designs. They began to find their inspiration in different places. Cullercoats, for example, is French in style and so is Milbourne Church near Belsay.

Different periods became fashionable too as it became less necessary to stick to the 13th and 14th centuries, so there are quite a lot of churches in the perpendicular Gothic style, the style of the 15th century, and some of these have high and splendid towers, big windows and plenty of space inside.

Apart from Cullercoats, which is by the nationally-known J.L. Pearson, almost all the late 19th century churches were designed by locals, and especially by a chap called R.J. Johnson, who actually came from Stokesley in North Yorkshire but settled on Tyneside and never left it. In fact, when he died in 1892, *The Builder*, the magazine of the architectural profession, said this about him: '*Mr Johnson was one of the very few men standing quite in the front rank of his profession, who continued to work in the country instead of being sucked into the great vortex of London.*'

I love his buildings. I admire his restorations too because there is no hint of the "destructive" approach adopted by lots of others. Brinkburn Abbey is the great example, a ruin that was effectively reconstructed with so light a touch that it feels convincingly original; you could imagine Augustinian Canons being totally at home there; but his newly-built churches are beautiful too.

Wylam is a favourite of mine and Stannington, but I reserve my highest approval for All Saints church in Gosforth on the northern edge of Newcastle. Several of my offspring were choirpersons there and so I had plenty of opportunity (during the sermons) to dream and study the beauty of the building and its fittings, and especially the rood screen that separates the chancel from the rest of the church. Johnson designed it and it was carved by a local Newcastle artist and craftsman called Ralph Hedley, whose work seems miraculous to me. It is lacy, a filigree of delicate but complex patterns. The Rev Brindley, the vicar of the church when it was first built and when the screen was carved, said, '*it is so beautiful that it has haunted me ever since I first saw it … I literally could not sleep for thinking of it*'.

The qualities I have just been talking about – work of the highest calibre by local chaps – reached its climax at another suburban Newcastle church – St George's Church on Osborne Road in Jesmond, which was paid for by Charles Mitchell, the wealthy shipbuilder who featured in the previous chapter. He lived in a very large and highly desirable house called Jesmond Towers on the edge of Jesmond Dene and in 1888 he provided a new church for Jesmond. His architect was a chap called T.R.Spence who was secretary of the Newcastle Arts Association but had no clear record as a designer of churches. What he built is magnificent however, part English, part Italian with a tall and splendid Italianate tower that you can see from so many other parts of the city.

Inside, the decoration is gorgeous. It is all in Arts and Crafts style, with really strong touches of Art Nouveau as well. It is rich and imaginative, brilliant in colour, design and execution. There is wonderful stained glass by a man called John Brown, who was born and trained in Newcastle but had moved to London. There are mosaics, metalwork, carved stone including extraordinarily intricate carved marble around the altar. Ralph Hedley carved the pulpit and Mitchell's son, W.G.Mitchell who was a pre-Raphaelite painter and a friend of William Morris and his chums, provided many of the designs.

Everything about the interior is all remarkably modern and forward thinking for 1888; but the most telling thing of all is that every one of the designers and practically all of the manufacturers and craftsmen were from Newcastle or were North-East based. The church is a brilliant showcase of local talent.

But my final choice to illustrate what happened to church architecture in 19th century Northumberland is very different to St George's. It's just a little building, didn't cost very much and was designed, furnished and decorated by a man on his own with virtually no connection to the county at all.

It's the church of St Christopher at Gunnerton, a couple of miles from Chollerford in North Tynedale, and it was built in 1899 by a young architect from London called John Cyril Hawes, though you can call him, if you choose…Reverend John Cyril Hawes or…

Fr John Cyril Hawes or…

Monsignor John Cyril Hawes or…

Fra Jerome…

…because he became all of those things.

St Christopher's Church at Gunnerton.

This is what happened. He was working as a new young architect and had just completed his first commission, some quite nice houses that are still standing in Bognor Regis. He was also attending night classes where he met and was being influenced by some of the most forward thinking architects in the country, men like William Lethaby and C.A.Voysey but then, in 1898, while walking up Regent Street in London, he popped into the church of St Thomas where he suffered a massive conversion like St Paul on the road to Damascus, and decided there and then to give up architecture for the church.

This is a scary story to me. I'm decidedly fond of my imperfect existence and ever since hearing about J.C., I have been nervy and unsettled on Regent Street lest it should happen to me; but for John Cyril it really couldn't have gone better. He had already designed a church and made a model of it to enter into a competition and, as it happened, his uncle William … Bishop William Bird Hornby, the former Bishop of Nyasaland, to give him the full works, had become the vicar of Chollerton. He was conscious that his parish, like many rural parishes in

Inside St Christopher's at Gunnerton with its Arts and Crafts features.

screen, designed and possibly made the striking candle holders by the altar, chose the vibrant colour scheme. I don't know what the congregation thought about it but I love it, he loved it. Despite what happened in the rest of his life he continued to show tremendous affection for his first church.

I say "his first church" because he went on design dozens of others, maybe more than dozens, including at least one cathedral.

In 1903 he became a vicar, the Reverend John Cyril Hawes.

In 1907 he went to the Bahamas where his Uncle had now become Bishop of Nassau and was in need of assistance because a hurricane had destroyed or damaged almost all the churches on the islands. He stayed there repairing and rebuilding the devastated churches until …

1911 when he had a second conversion. This is what happens when you let your guard down. You keep on going. This time he became a Roman Catholic so he had to leave his parish. He went to Canada and became a labourer on the Canadian Pacific Railway and then …

In 1913 he became Father Hawes, a Roman Catholic priest. At a conference in Rome he met the archbishop of Western Australia who persuaded him to come and build a new Cathedral at Geraldton, which he did, along with at least 11 other churches scattered among the mining settlements in the deserts of Western Australia. All of them, if you see them on the Australian websites I've been looking at, were enthralling buildings so it's no wonder that he got promoted and became …

Monsignor Hawes.

He stayed in Western Australia until 1939, when he retired back to the Bahamas and changed his name to Fr Jerome and built himself a hermitage on top of a mountain on Cat Island and that really is a remarkable building. It's like an early Christian settlement. It has a round tower, like an ancient Irish tower, and a low, stone-roofed church where he lived until he died in 1956 and was buried in a cave he had dug underneath his hermitage.

Quite a life! So let's raise a glass to Fr Jerome and to Gunnerton Church where it all started.

Northumberland, was a far-flung place and that some of his congregation lived a long way from the parish church and had no alternative place of worship closer to home. Gunnerton was the place he had in mind and he persuaded his nephew to build an actual church based on the model he had made and that's what happened.

I would have to tell you that it's a remarkable building. You can tell it's a church but the details are so different from churches earlier in the century. There are no windows in the east end and the side windows are round-headed and more like domestic windows, hardly churchy at all. It's an Arts and Crafts building in all its detail, the only such church in the county and one of the most radical buildings of its date in the whole country.

Inside he painted the frescoes, designed the furniture, possibly carved the beautiful Arts and Crafts

17. KEEPING THE COUNTY NICE

Obviously Northumberland has been affected by almost all of the earth-shattering changes that have taken place all over the country (and the rest of the world) since 1900. I'm going to list some of them, and your job, should you choose to accept it, is to decide whether they were changes for the better or the worse.

Some of the answers seem pretty clear; there were two world wars, for example, and a whole heap of nasty littler wars and conflicts ever since. The lives of women have changed a lot – not enough of course, but in quite a lot of ways, and just to give a couple of examples, in 1913 Emily Wilding Davison of Morpeth was fighting for the rights of women to get the vote when she was trampled to death beneath the hooves of the King's horse during the Derby at Epsom Racecourse.

In 1965 Judith Macgregor of Jesmond got married to me and decided to buy a washing machine on the never-never, but despite having the vote and holding down a full-time job she was refused permission to do so and had to return with her (rather pitiful) husband in order to sign the documents. In 2021, after all the improvements in the lives of women since the death of Emily Davison, Mrs Grundy still does all of the cooking and most of the housework in our house.

Moving swiftly on … there are cars now, you've probably noticed them all over the place, substantially more than there were before 1900. Did I read the other day that 97% of the country is within 270 yards of a road? In 1900 planes had not been invented and neither had radios, televisions, computers, mobile phones, electric tooth brushes, battery-operated cork removers, digitally-enhanced toenail clippers, CCTV systems, car alarms, sirens, vehicle reversing signals …

… but then on the other hand neither had arterial stents, titanium replacement hip joints, hearing aids, radio-active implants, or any of the multitude of life-saving or life-enhancing drugs and hardware that have kept me going (so far) for more than 30 years longer than my father survived the trials of this world.

Since 1900 the world has changed to an extraordinary extent and of course Northumberland has more or less kept pace with other places in the adoption of the new ways of living, so there's no point in me rattling on about the universal stuff, my job in telling the latest bits of the county's story is to focus on those changes that are a bit more particular to us, either because they reflect the sort of people we are or because they have influenced, or maintained or undermined the special character of the county.

Not to beat about the bush, I'm concerned in this final chapter to explore the various changes, people and organisations that have kept Northumberland nice despite everything that the last century and a bit has been able to throw at it.

Left: Beach at Bamburgh with its famous castle in the background.

If there is one common theme that has run through this book since the beginning it is that Northumberland's beauty and the character of its history is of a distinctive and unusual nature. I'm talking about wildness. Wildness and comparative emptiness have been recurring themes, a source of endless hardship for those living here in the past but a source of intense pride for those who live here now.

The pride isn't just a 20th century invention of course. This book started with the assertion that prehistoric residents seem to have loved the same things about the Northumberland landscape that we do today. In the 18th century the first duchess of Northumberland felt drawn to the harshness of history and it drew her back to the homelands of her "braw" ancestors; Walter Scott felt it in 1791 when he came for his hols to that farmhouse deep in the Cheviot Hills so that he could be as close to as many camps and castles and fields of battle as possible. He expressed the pride perfectly in words my Scottish father-in-law used to intone regularly;

Breathes there the man, with heart so dead
That never to himself hath said
This is my own, my native land

John Hodgson was another who knew all about it too as he wrote his *History of Northumberland* in the 1820s. He was a founder member of The Newcastle Society of Antiquaries in 1813 and this is what he wrote in the first volume of their journal, *Archaeologia Aeliana*, in 1822: ' *... there exists in human nature a propensity in ... all classes of people ... to be acquainted with the history of the place where they were born. The antiquity of a man's family, of his house or his village is narrated with a desire which seems to increase as the history of the object grows older.'*

Apart from being a vicar, the leader of the committee to discover a miners' safety lamp, an antiquarian, and the author of one of the great county histories, John Hodgson also found time to become an archaeologist; he became one of the first people anywhere to attempt a proper systematic excavation when he started digging at Housesteads in 1822 and it was men like him and other members of the Society of Antiquaries who effectively discovered the Roman Wall.

Before they came along the Wall was known to its neighbours mainly as a quarry from which they could carry off stone to construct new buildings; to people who didn't live right beside it, it was barely known; there were no trains or buses or cars, no guide books or signposts to tell people where to go; people didn't pop off there for picnics or days out so it was largely unknown, and early paintings of it, especially ones done by a the artist Henry Burdon Richardson in the 1840s, show no people in sight and barely a building; his pictures are the very essence of wildness but amazingly enough they also reveal to us, almost 200 years later, that the landscape, especially the landscape of the central section of the wall has barely changed since those days. Northumberland was wild and empty then, but it's wild and empty still.

There are more Roman stones visible nowadays since all the years of excavation have allowed them to peep out of the ground, but not much else has changed and that is because those 19th century antiquarians saved it all for us. Some of them, like Hodgson, were hard working and passionate. Others, especially the schoolteacher John Collingwood Bruce, were passionate communicators and brought the Wall to a wider audience, and some were wealthy.

John Clayton was the wealthiest of all. His dad, Nathaniel Clayton, had been the Town Clerk in Newcastle and John succeeded him in the post. There seems to have been a bob or two available to Town Clerks in those days because the family were very rich. John became a key supporter of Richard Grainger's redevelopment of central Newcastle in the 1830s but his home in the country was Chesters by the Tyne at Chollerford and in his garden were humps and bumps of a Roman fort that he excavated for 50 years from the 1840s onwards.

Being well off, a passionate Antiquarian and a great lover of Northumberland's landscape and history, he bought lots and lots of surviving bits of the Wall. He bought Housesteads in 1838 and four farms to the east and west of it so that he could examine and preserve that iconic central section. Over the rest of his life (he didn't die until 1890 when he was 98) he kept on buying until he owned five of the forts and most of the land in between them. He had a small team of excavators permanently on the go throughout that time and his son (another John) kept the work going into the 20th century.

The thing is that if men like the Claytons hadn't stepped in there's no guarantee that anything would have survived. Other bits of the wall that were beyond the reach of John Clayton, the stretch between Newcastle and Wallsend for example, all got covered over at that time and most of the first few miles west of Newcastle disappeared under suburban development in the 1920s and 30s and the same could have happened out in the county. It could all have gone, buried under the ruthless expansion of the modern world. That's what happened to so much of our ancient heritage.

My own personal fort, the one whose corner I accidently exposed in my garden in Carlisle, had been discovered, glanced at and ruthlessly covered beneath an ordinary late Victorian terraced street and the same thing was happening everywhere, not just to Roman remains but to churches and castles, all sorts of old houses and prehistoric earthworks … but gradually people began to waken up to the dangers.

I mentioned an early example of the fight back against the brutalisation of ancient buildings in the 1840s at Whittingham Church where the Rev Goodenough and his architect were prevented by the village from blowing up the Saxon tower; I showed how men like R.J. Johnson fought back against the "Destructive" style of restoration that was the fashion in the middle of the century.

It was the fashion everywhere, of course, not just in Northumberland and in 1877 William Morris and his chum Philip Webb, shocked by the threat of a destructive restoration at Tewkesbury Abbey, founded the Society for the Protection of Ancient Buildings (SPAB), the first formally organised group to try to protect our heritage.

At about the same time as SPAB was formed, the Government made the first tentative steps towards taking responsibility for the protection of the country's heritage. Britain was almost the last country in Europe to provide Government protection to its old buildings

Chesters, formerly the home of Antiquarian John Clayton.

but in 1873, shocked by a threat to build a railway across Salisbury Plain and through Stonehenge, they introduced the idea of an Ancient Monuments Protection Act. Initially there was too much opposition from country landowners who loathed the idea that anyone could restrict their freedom to do what they wanted with their own property so the Act wasn't actually passed until 1882.

At first only a couple of dozen of the most important prehistoric sites in the country made it onto the schedule, the sort of places that you can't imagine anybody wanting to destroy, but it became increasingly clear that the scope of protection needed to be extended.

Landowners were still knocking down anything that

Remains of the The Roman Wall, east of Housesteads, which were acquired by John Clayton.

got in their way; enormously significant buildings continued to be at risk; the one that gets mentioned was a threat to demolish one of the greatest tower houses in the country, Tattershall Castle in Lincolnshire, and that brought extensions to the range of buildings covered by the legislation.

There were new Acts in 1901 and 1910 and especially in 1913, by which time cathedrals and medieval monastic ruins were under protection and so were major castles, so up here that meant that Warkworth Castle and Dunstanburgh, Tynemouth Priory and Castle, those really major ruined monuments came under the care of the Ministry, but lesser buildings, or those that were still lived in, or more complicated ones were still outside the meaning of the Act.

The Wall (The Waal) was a particularly good example. The more obvious stuff, the big forts that had been at least partly excavated, were protected by the Act, but the littler bits, the surviving fragments of wall between the great set pieces weren't, and weren't going to be protected for ages and that made our beloved Wall vulnerable to exploitation.

The crags on which the whole central section is built are made of whinstone, which is an especially hard and useful source of roadstone, and there were plenty of quarrying companies that wanted to get their hands on it. Cawfields Quarry, north of Haltwhistle, continued to gnaw away at a marvellous bit of the wall until it finally closed down in 1952 and though it has become a splendidly atmospheric site since then, a great deal of Roman stuff was lost and more would have been if the quarry had kept going.

Even more dangerously, in the late 20s and early 30s, a threat to start quarrying in the absolutely critical area immediately west of Housesteads made the Government strengthen the Ancient Monuments Act in 1931, so by that time there was a reasonable level of protection for some of the more important of our ancient monuments, which was a very good thing especially as the Act continued to be stretched to include other sites throughout the rest of the century …

… but as you know by now, you will expect me to have a but and it's always a big one and that is that the wildness and the particular beauty of Northumberland may be enhanced by the major buildings but its essence is to be found throughout the county, in places far beyond the influence of the tip top stuff and the protection of all the rest of our terrific landscape and its history required a whole different tranche of things to happen …

… starting with the *Town and Country Planning Act of 1932.*

Before the 1932 Act people who wanted to build something could do so if they owned the land or if the landowner had given them permission; they could build more or less what they liked. There were some rules of course; as I've just been saying some very important sites had the protection of the Ancient Monument Act and there were already some other conditions that affected developers' freedoms of action.

Various 19th century governments had passed laws about sanitation and ventilation and the provision of drainage and so on, and local authorities had passed by-laws setting minimum standards. They defined what size a space had to be to constitute a room and whether you had to have a corridor to reach a bedroom; they established the width of houses, the size of back yards and the width of the back lanes. In my street for example, which was laid out by a developer in 1898, the by-laws specifically ban certain activities. I can't brew beer in the back yard, for example, or keep pigs and I'm not allowed to have an erection more than 30 feet in height. Major restrictions.

But beyond these minimum legal standards, developers could do more or less what they wanted if they had the land and in particular there were no rules which required people to ask, "is this a suitable thing to do on this bit of land? Will the development you are undertaking spoil anything that is already here? Will it make the place less beautiful?" Those are important questions, we take them for granted nowadays but until 1932 nobody was forced to answer them.

Of course, a lot of what they did in the early years of the 20th century was super and there are beautiful Edwardian suburbs built in lots of places without planning controls, where now we would be trying to

maintain the rural landscape – on the edge of Corbridge, for example and along the banks of the Tweed west of Berwick. Bamburgh has a host of fine Edwardian and 1920s houses and so does Alnmouth and so do lots of other places that we have, on the whole, found exciting and desirable. And, by the 1920s, council houses were being built in many places, which seemed a highly desirable innovation at the time and still would if we were allowed to build them anymore. The earliest ones tended to be built of brick in a friendly garden-villagy sort of way.

I don't know what's happening to me here, but I'm beginning to sound like an old softy. It's true that in the most rural parts of the county, and apart from in Newcastle and the most built-up areas of Tyneside, I find it hard to think of many examples from the early part of the 20th century that should or would not have been allowed after the Act was passed, and, even among the ones that almost certainly wouldn't have been allowed after 1932, there are developments that have an interest and a charm that, in my opinion, makes it impossible to regret that they were built.

My favourite examples in this category are two groups of unplanned and uncontrolled shacks in the Tyne Valley near Ovingham and on the coast, among the sand dunes south of Low Newton.

Round about the villages of Ovingham and Ovington, just west of Newcastle, there are a number of groups of little shacks. Some of them are on a path through the fields and woods of Whittle Dene to the north of Ovingham church; others are visible in fields on the south side of the A69 near Ovington.

There's even a small village of them among woods on the banks of the Tyne south of Ovington. There are rows of them, all around the edges of the fields, linked together by soft grassy paths. Every shack is different. Most of them seem to be of wood but there's hardboard too and probably mysterious materials I don't know about. They're painted all different colours – usually quite nice colours though there's the odd rather virulent purple or yellow one. They're almost all single-storey but there is one in a field between the two villages with a tiny little upstairs window that I assume lights an equally tiny

sleeping loft, possibly for a little tiny child to sleep in a little tiny bed. To be honest, they have the sort of fairy story look that makes you talk in that tiny little way. They almost all have little gardens and a lot of them have verandas in front. There are flowers everywhere – in old kettles and plastic pots, in white painted car tyres and any sort of container you can imagine.

None of them are sophisticated designs though a few, which seem to belong to people with natural and alternative lifestyle interests, have woven willow arches and picturesque touches of that sort. One at least that I know has an elaborate Heath Robinson-ish arrangement for catching the rainwater for re-use and I suspect that many of them are cunningly using car batteries to provide electric light – which is sufficiently sophisticated and scientific for me.

Inside they're tiny, well the ones I've been in are tiny and often very richly decorated, tended with loving care and lots of small and unnecessary ornaments. One was heated by an iron-stove and was just so cosy I could have stayed … well I did. I had a nice cup of tea.

The desire to have a little place of your own by the seaside or in the countryside – not a permanent home but a weekend place, something to escape to, really began in the 1890s on the south coast of England, I think Shoreham in Sussex has a claim to have had the first, but by the turn of the century they were appearing all over. There was even a magazine called *The Bungalow*, which described itself as being for people who "have a sneaking fondness for an easy, natural mode of life."

This is why the verandas were really important. They allowed things to happen outside, which in more formal houses only happened inside – like eating, sleeping, family life. They allowed for sunshine. The early 20th century was the time when the world began to discover the joys of sunshine. It became fashionable to be sun-tanned instead of pale and interesting.

The bungalow movement had started off as a pretty middle-class affair but by the middle of the 1920s more ordinary people began to jump on the bandwagon. Everybody wanted to get back to the land, to find a place in the sun and there were a number of factors that helped them get it.

1. By the 20s virtually everybody had weekends free – even annual holidays were becoming commoner for ordinary people. People suddenly had time and often a bit more ready money than had been the case in the past.

2. Then there was an agricultural recession and farmers were often quite eager to sell off little plots of land. You could often get a bit of land for as little as a fiver and it was easy to build a bit shack for no more than £50. It wasn't silly money. It was feasible.

3. And finally there was access. Bikes, motorbikes and vastly improved public transport meant that ordinary people could get out of town much more easily than before.

That's exactly what happened round Ovingham. In the 1920s, working class Tynesiders came out of town at weekends and built quite charming things. Some of the oldest just started with an old caravan. In some of them you can still see the skylight of the original horse-drawn 20s caravan peeping out of the roof ... and then gradually people would add extra rooms on to it. That's the great advantage of a bungalow. There's nobody on top of you. You're not joined onto the house next door so you can expand outwards if you want to.

On the coast at Low Newton there's a more well-known, but equally interesting, set of bungalows. They are in the dunes, some nestling in hollows, others bravely breasting the tops and facing everything the sea can throw at them. There are 40 of them in all, I think, though they are extraordinarily difficult to count since their arrangement is higgledy piggledy and difficult for a bear of very little brain to grasp. The layout is one of the nicest things about them. They are built wherever the landscape allows them to be built and so they have an almost accidental relationship to each other – some

O! You who drink my cooling waters clear
Forget not the far hills from whence they flow,
Where over fell and moor and year by year
Spring summer autumn winter come and go
With showering sun and rain and storm and snow,
Where over the green bents forever blow
The four free winds of heaven; where time falls
In solitary places calm and slow
Where pipes the curlew and the plover calls,
Beneath an open sky my waters spring
Beneath the clear sky welling fair and sweet
A draught of coolness for your throat to bring,
A sound of coolness in the busy street.

By Wilfrid Gibson

Blawearie.

The Bathing House at Howick.

Acknowledgements

Special mention has to be made to my friend Tim Watkinson whose splendid photographs have made such a difference to this book. His pictures are recognisable by their brilliance and lyrical beauty. I wish I could have taken ones as good.

Photo Credits

Vindolanda Photos courtesy of the Vindolanda Trust.
Prehistory artifacts photos courtesy of Great North Museum: Hancock. From the collection of the Society of Antiquaries of Newcastle upon Tyne.
Photo of Modern Newcastle Quayside courtesy of Steve Ellwood.
All other modern photographs © John Grundy and Tim Watkinson.
Historic images © Newcastle Libraries unless otherwise stated.

FURTHER READING

Life in the English Country House by Mark Girouard
The English Terraced House by Stefan Muthesius
Northumberland (Buildings of England Series) by Niklaus Pevsner, John Grundy et al
Landscapes of Faith by Michael Sadgrove
Durham Cathedral: Light of the North by John Field
John Dobson: Architect of the North East by Tom Faulkner and Andrew Gregg
The Illustrated Bede by John Marsden
England's Landscapes (Volume 7) North East by Fred Aalen (ed)
Upper North Tynedale by Beryl Charlton
Archaeology in Northumberland National Park by Paul Frodsham (ed)
Towers and Bastles by Peter Ryder
Hadrian's Wall: English Heritage
Lindisfarne Priory: English Heritage
Cragside: National Trust
Wallington: National Trust
Alnwick Castle Guide
Battlefield Walks by Rupert Matthews
The Golden Age of Northumbria by Jane Hawkes
Northumberland Panorama by Tome Faulkner (ed)
The North of England by Frank Musgrave
Blood of the Vikings by Julian Richards
Blood of the Isles by Bryan Sykes

INDEX